Theodore Olson is associate professor in the Division of Social Science at York University.

The basis of this book is the provocative thesis that the idea of progress results from the uneasy eighteenth-century union of elements of millennial and utopian thought. Professor Olson traces changes in the major elements of millennialism since the days of Hebrew exile in Babylon, of utopianism since Plato's reflections on the ideal republic, and of progress since the unlikely merger of these very different world-views in eighteenth-century Europe.

Forced to re-examine the history of their people's relationship with God, the exiled Hebrews produced various interpretations of their past and probable future. The notions of a saving élite, of history as a dynamic and periodized drama, and of an end-time at which history would be fulfilled all emerged in this period of crisis. Apocalyptic writings, the literary form of millennialism, came later in the book of Daniel. Olson views Jesus and his followers as millennialists and apocalyptic expression as a characteristic Christian response to crisis.

Plato's reflections on the decline of justice were taken up by Thomas More in his *Utopia*, a society outside history valuing objective truth and justice, where the arbitrary rule of the Tudors and the collapse of the Christian commonwealth could be avoided. In the seventeenth century a number of other 'rationalist' utopias emerged.

From these two world-views, one historical and dynamic, the other rationalist and ahistorical, the idea of progress was forged – history becomes blind necessity willing the betterment of mankind. This dominion over nature, which has seemed both realizable and desirable to many in the twentieth century, appears the ultimate end of progress – yet it would eliminate human will. Olson argues that our only hope for dealing with the problems created by the doctrine of progress lies in understanding its problematic origins in order to begin a constructive critique.

THEODORE OLSON

Millennialism, utopianism, and progress

UNIVERSITY OF TORONTO PRESS
Toronto Buffalo London

© University of Toronto Press 1982
Toronto Buffalo London
Printed in Canada

ISBN 0-8020-5506-0

Hm
1∅1
.O55
1982

Canadian Cataloguing in Publication Data

Olson, Theodore, 1932-
  Millennialism, utopianism, and progress
  Includes index.
  ISBN 0-8020-5506-0
  1. Progress. 2. Millennialism. 3. Utopias.
  I. Title.
  HM101.047   303.4   C81-094684-X

This book has been published with the help of grants from the Social Science Federation of Canada, using funds provided by the Social Sciences and Humanities Research Council of Canada, and the Publications Fund of University of Toronto Press.

Contents

Preface

Whatever claims to originality this book has rest upon the incisive and faithful scholarship of many people in several fields, especially in biblical studies and social thought. Throughout the period of preparation of this book, beginning in 1974, I have been encouraged by the independent and simultaneous formation of groups to study late classical Judaism and early Christianity as movements rather than as the background of texts. Similarly, as Whig history fades, it has become increasingly possible for many to see our medieval and early modern forebears as something other than precursors of what we favour or fear.

But Whig history is reborn in our time in the briskly utilitarian convictions by which scientific and technological enterprises justify their claims on the public purse. And only inattention to what people actually say could have convinced anyone that the notion of progress – of infinite, inevitable, qualitative improvement as the motif of history – is dead. Historical pessimism is not the antidote to this undemonstrable but tenaciously held thesis. As I shall try to demonstrate, optimism and pessimism are irrelevant to the issue of whether or not there is progress. But I owe much even to those whose views I shall treat harshly. And to those who have addressed part of my problem – and their success is perhaps due to having been more realistically modest than I – I owe more than can be acknowledged in footnotes.

My own preoccupation with Joachim of Fiore, first roused by Will Herberg many years ago, has been given direction and substance by Marjorie Reeves and her collaborators. Frank Manuel has not only illuminated the thought of key progressivists but also provided a model of urbane writing that I cannot hope to equal. Let these two stand representative of many others. I owe something also to several patient generations of students who have had to wrestle with the thesis of this book. Mrs Roanne Leneck, first one of these students, later prepared the typescript of a work rather larger than now confronts the reader.

A manuscript that attempts a good deal has many ways to go wrong. But an editor who both makes the project his own and retains the skills of a sensitive editor is a powerful aid against digression and a complacent amplitude. John Parry, of University of Toronto Press, is such an editor and has sought to reconcile the demands of the argument and those of the Press itself.

Manila, October 1981

MILLENNIALISM, UTOPIANISM, AND PROGRESS

Introduction

Where does the idea of progress come from? Why has it been so discredited in our time? Why, despite this criticism, do so many people still hold to it as an explanation of the world or as a justification of their own hopes for the future of society? What is at stake in the doctrine of historical progress, of self-executing improvement in successive eras of human history?

This last question animates the present study. I believe that the answers are not to be sought directly in the eighteenth century, when the doctrine of progress achieved the form it has maintained ever since,[1] but in two other great folk-ideas about the shape of human existence: millennialism and utopianism.

The study of social and political ideas as they appear in the writings of great thinkers has obscured the importance of ideas that influenced them. Folk philosophies such as millennialism, utopianism, and progress are powerful; despite the scant attention great thinkers may pay to them, these traditions maintain themselves with remarkably consistent content over many generations. They work in

---

1 In part II of the present study I shall maintain, contrary to the views set forth by R. Nisbet, L. Edelstein, and, less directly, J. Passmore, that there is no ancient or pre-modern doctrine of progress properly so called.

Nisbet, in *History of the Idea of Progress* (New York 1980), makes a strong case for an ancient idea of progress and for its constant presence in Western history ever since. He does this by defining progress in a rather wider fashion than I have done. Evidence of a theory of social development or entelechy thus becomes evidence for an idea of progress. He specifically allows for catastrophism within his notion of progress, so long as it takes place within an encompassing account of past and future development. Nisbet's procedure brings together a good deal that I have kept separate, and much else as well. What is obscured in this treatment is much of the novelty of the modern doctrine and what I regard as the integrity of the separate utopian and millennialist traditions. And it is just this integrity of each that produces, in my view, the problematic of progress and that provides us with the possibility of radical analyses of the notion of progress.

a pervasive way at the popular level, even conditioning the reception of the ideas of the great men. They work because they answer the ultimate questions of social life: What is the point of it all? Where are we going? What can be achieved? How should we organize human effort to realize our goals?

These folk-traditions are powerful because they are pervasive; they can be appealed to as 'what everybody knows'; they can mobilize people, demand sacrifices, and provide coherence to the apparently conflicting demands faced by ordinary people. Leaders can lead because, often, they are able to tap these sources of power. The work of the great men can of course be used by small élites. But even when leaders appeal to the mass of men on behalf of ideas from Bodin, Descartes, Locke, Hegel, or Mill, what is often heard and acted upon is the call to achieve the kingdom of God, the full and harmonious development of human potential, or the inevitable unfolding of a better life as the fulfilment of all past history.

There has been little attention given to the particular shape of these enduring traditions. J.B. Bury's vast prestige allowed him to inaugurate the modern study of the notion of progress in 1906 with his *The Idea of Progress*, an exceptional book in an otherwise orthodox career. Dean Inge, similarly, gave the same title to his 1924 study, a passing glance in a career directed to many other concerns. Here we have a mighty doctrine, which has animated vast public endeavours for many generations. Whether it is true is a matter of some consequence. Because it emerged so recently, in the eighteenth century, its origins ought to be a matter of absorbing interest. In this book I will argue that it emerged only in the eighteenth century. Its truth seemed so incontestable that almost no one questioned it; yet it is a comparatively new concept. Few people have seen these facts as problematic. Thus the paradoxes of progress emerge: merely popular but pervasive and determinative, incoherent but incontestable, the master unity of all human history but reserved for modern man to discover.

The issues are sometimes evaded today by assertions that 'no one believes in progress any more.' The problem can thus be only of historical interest. Though men today seldom speak of progress in the utterly confident tones of a Condorcet, for whom it was the grand motif of the human and even the cosmic story, it is regularly employed, often in unacknowledged ways. The spread of Western technology over the globe and the increasing role of technology in Western life, extending even to the biological foundations of human life, are either actively justified or passively accepted as a sort of fate, because of a supposed (and unanalysed) inevitability. Indeed, so deeply ingrained is the notion of progress that some of its opponents can think of no alternative to it except *re*gress to some earlier period or appeal to some counter-inevitability.

Where does the notion of progress come from? The great thinkers at the time of its emergence virtually ignored it. So where did it originate? What are its sources?

I have looked for help to the other two great folk-philosophies of millennialism and utopianism. Both antedate the rise of progress. Both have been persistent and pervasive. Is it possible that in some way progress has been built up from elements in each of these? Here we find a feasible hypothesis. Nothing is more marked in discussions of millennialism and utopianism than confusion between these two quite different traditions.[2] One could fill a chapter with citations in

2 See F. Manuel ed *Utopias and Utopian Thought* (Boston 1967). In his introduction, Manuel attempts a series of dichotomies: 'the soft and hard, the static and the dynamic, the sensate and the spiritual, the aristocratic and the plebeian, the utopia of escape and the utopia of realization, the collectivist and individualist utopias' (viii). None of these distinctions penetrates very far, but they all indicate that something dichotomous exists 'in the inchoate body of utopias.'

But so long as no particular weight is given to the radically different origins of utopia and the millennium, all such attempted typologies break down as soon as they are applied. The Anabaptist incident at Münster in 1534–5 is described by Manuel as utopian, despite its clear intention to assimilate itself quite literally to millennialism (xiii). Northrop Frye confuses the millennium with 'the conventional idea of the utopia' (34). Crane Brinton labels the Shakers as religious utopians, despite the Shakers' own explicit self-identification as a millennial church (55). Manuel calls attention to nineteenth-century 'open-ended utopias' and discounts the presence of millennial elements in these ventures as being evidence of their static character. Such elements are literary echoes, not fundamental (80).

Both Manuel and his critics here accept a static notion of millennialism which, as we shall see, cannot be sustained. Judith Shklar appears to agree (110) with Manuel, even though earlier (104–5) she has accurately identified millennialism as historically concerned and utopia as timeless. Mircea Eliade accepts Peter Worsley's notion that Melanesian cargo cults can be properly described as millennial. Fred Polak tells us, against Shklar, that 'utopian thought always relates to the future' (282); and Paul Tillich is quite prepared to identify Judaism as utopian (298). Similar confusions could be cited from among the contributors to S. Thrupp ed *Millennial Dreams in Action* (The Hague 1962) and from other writers.

Studies of communitarian groups have habitually used the word 'utopian' in their descriptions, whether the impetus for the group was a vision of the perfect society put forward as a pattern for emulation or a gathered group anticipating or realizing the second coming of Jesus. For a recent example of this, see Rosabeth Moss Kanter *Commitment and Community: Communes and Utopias in Sociological Perspective* (Cambridge, Mass, 1972), 1–18; also Mark Holloway's 'Introduction' to the republished *History of American Socialisms* by John Humphrey Noyes (New York 1966, from the 1870 original). Noyes avoided the term utopia, which occurs only in connection with Josiah Warren's experiment which itself used the word. Noyes was aware of the different bases upon which community could be erected.

Nevertheless modern scholars continue to conflate the radically different; Glenn Negley and J.M. Patrick, the editors of *The Quest for Utopia* (New York 1952) (hereinafter *Quest*), tell us that 'amongst the ancient Hebrews, Amos, Hosea, Jeremiah, and Ezekiel show incipient utopianism' (256). Negley's student, P.E. Richter, in the 'Introduction' to his edited *Utopias: Social*

which all pictures of a better world or a better time are bundled together and called utopianism. The name of millennialism is fastened on revolutionary ventures of all sorts. 'Utopian' is used as a pejorative label, while millennialism is arbitrarily separated from its setting in main-line Hebrew and Christian thought, the better to distance these religions today from a tradition seen as belonging to wild-eyed visionaries and fanatics.

Given this loose usage, it is not surprising that scholars enquiring into the origins or background of progress have failed to find stable, coherent traditions that could have contributed major components to it. What ought to be an embarrassing mystery – our inability to account for the origin and content of progress – is rendered less embarrassing by being largely ignored. Some studies have quarried the past, in a somewhat desultory fashion, for 'anticipations' of the doctrine. But progress has few if any advocates prior to the eighteenth century – and yet within a century it had become axiomatic in Western society. As recently as 1968, Sidney Pollard, in his conscientious and thorough *The Idea of Progress: History and Society*, suggested that progress is not an idea with an origin and a history but a fact gradually discovered and identified as an important social truth.

The specialization of scholarship has left few enquirers able to understand both millennialism and utopianism. The first subject has become the province of biblical scholars and the few who work on the 'inter-testamental' period (ca 350 BC to 50 AD) when millennialism achieved its characteristic form; the second is an area for those who read More, Bacon, and the French utopians in connection with early modern political theory. The two groups are isolated from each other. But if we are to address the problem of progress we shall need to bring the results of both fields together.

How can we accurately distinguish millennialism and utopianism? Is the apparent confusion between them a reflection of reality? How can we know that the internal coherence of each is real?

Ideals and Communal Experiments (Boston 1971), tells us 'Some of the most influential movements in history – Judaism, Christianity, Confucianism, Islam, communism, democratic socialism – have developed from a utopian vision' (1).

In their newly published study, *Utopian Thought in the Western World* (Cambridge, Mass, 1979), Frank and Fritzi Manuel employ the term utopia to cover all melioristic social visions. They treat millennialism as a precursor and a source of continuously resonating images within the utopian enterprise. And the genre approach rather precludes a clear differentiation between utopia and progressivism. I am trying to look at the logical parents of progressivism, to delineate each as accurately as possible, and then to see how they came together, each with its distinct contribution, in progressivism. They are the real historical as well as the logical parents of that problematical child, progressivism. The questions I bring to the body of material I share in part with the Manuels are thus different and lead often to rather different answers or characterizations. And on millennialism, which is not their principal concern, we differ quite materially.

I did not begin my study of these matters with the doctrine of progress and then seek its origins. I began from consideration of each tradition. Detailed historical studies convinced me that there is a stable and consistent body of convictions, with a distinct and common origin, and a continuous history, to which the name millennialism is usefully restricted. Similarly utopianism is a set of interdependent propositions; it arose on different soil from millennialism.

The principal intent of this study is to show, as closely as the facts known to me permit, and as cogently as argument can support, that progress, as it crystallized in the eighteenth century, is crucially and almost entirely dependent on contributions from millennialism and utopianism. Millennialism and utopianism, while almost antithetical in character, are combined in the notion of progress. The resulting problem of coherence affects what we are offered as progress.

If we are to understand what progress is we shall have first to understand millennialism and utopianism. The problematic nature of progress cannot be felt adequately until we see the antithetical quality of the two traditions that make it up.

I shall describe the essential elements of millennialism and utopianism as they developed and their internal consistency through time. It will then be possible to use millennialism and utopianism as something like ideal types, developed on the basis of the historical evidence. Millennialism has been beset by a priori judgments and by consequent difficulties in establishing even the characteristics of its literary output.

In part I, I analyse millennialism as a product of Hebrew reflection, during the sixth century BC exile in Babylonia, on the Israelite past and on the conviction that the god of this people would, despite the exile, complete his historical work with his people. Three themes put forward then are later brought together in the crisis occasioned by the cultural genocide of Antiochus IV in the second century BC. At this time the book of Daniel presents millennialism and its literary form, 'apocalyptic.' Daniel – and not theosophical speculation using the format of Daniel – becomes almost exclusively the framework for Christian millennialism. In millennialism history is conceived of as 1) the locus of divine action and, accordingly, the only source of salvation or historical vindication; 2) a strongly periodized drama; and 3) as proceeding to its conclusion in a deeply dialectical fashion. The characteristic embodiment of millennialism is the social movement rather than the book. But its books, pre-eminently the Revelation, have provided Western history with both the concepts of millennialism and a stock of powerful, dynamic images. How millennialism worked, in Christian orthodoxy and in deviant social movements, is explored in chapters on the Revelation, on the Montanists, and on Joachim of Fiore. Joachim made it possible for his successors to identify their contemporaries as players in the enactment of the end-time of history.

Part II begins by ascribing to Plato the positions held, with remarkable consistency, by later utopians. Despite this early formulation, the literary genre of utopia – and it is primarily a literary form – did not develop until More produced his *Utopia*, the foundation piece of the genre. Campanella's *City of the Sun* is examined as an example of how a utopian can work in response to the different problems of his period. Attention is given to the claim that the magical-theosophical groups of the late sixteenth and early seventeenth centuries are utopian. Part II concludes with a look at the classical 'rationalist' utopias.

The premises of utopianism are that man's proper focus is on transcendent truth derived from a higher realm in a hierarchical universe. History is not a source, or the source, of value or truth in the task of embodying what is necessarily and eternally true. (The many 'utopian communities' of the nineteenth century are the creation of progressivism.)

Part III tries to establish how both utopian and millennial motifs were brought together to create progressivism. The active God was made immanent and depersonalized, from God to Providence[3] to Nature. Similarly, fervid English Civil War millennialism declined into the Cambridge Platonist conception of the world as a teaching process. The deist underground in France, fuelled at first by the influences of English deism, Shaftesbury, and Bolingbroke, provided the ground on which utopianism and the English millennialism could come together. From these advanced milieux came the first progressivism; and from the latter emerged Turgot, Mercier, and Condorcet, who formulated the credo of the doctrine. Part III concludes with a detailed review of the relation of utopianism and millennialism to the notion of progress.

But what is the importance of the doctrine of progress? How has it mattered in the past and how does it shape human activities today? In Part IV, I outline three areas – public life, emotional and interpersonal life, and the national community – in which it had a powerful influence. Saint-Simon was the first serious thinker to deal with the industrial system as the basis of productive, progressive civilization; Fourier founded his notion of progress on the unblocked passions; and Bellamy brought together the industrial system, the passions (in their Victorian guise of sentiment), and the distinctive new democratic nationalism of self-transcending community. I seek to identify the utopian and millennialist ele-

---

3 Nisbet, in *History of the Idea of Progress*, has seen clearly that some version of Providence is required to make a progress doctrine work. He differs from my treatment of this issue by finding a continuing notion of Providence through Western history since pre-Christian antiquity.

ments in each, as well as their contribution to the progressivist doctrine being advocated.

In this way the foundations are laid for an examination in part V of the distinctive problems encountered within the doctrine of progress in the twentieth century. The reader will perhaps have noticed that I have not yet offered a definition of progress. One of the oddities of the doctrine is that it is so seldom set forth clearly by its advocates. Once precipitate its complex of beliefs into a definition and the problems in it become apparent. The doctrine of progress proposes that *there is a blind force in history, a force uncontaminated by historical contingency, yet dedicated to the continued improvement of man.*

Thus, in our time, technology and views of human will and of the purposes of community are brought together under progressivist assumptions. We focus first on Francis Bacon, who linked technology to man's unfettered domination of nature. Only in the present century could his vision be acted upon. But what happens when the human is encountered as itself a limit to completion of this project? This challenge is taken up by B.F. Skinner. But first I review the general will tradition to see how corporate will can aspire to transcend not only politics but even the limits of time and space. Skinner then emerges as the ultimate general will theorist: the community of humans is turned into the universal adaptive environment in which at last consciousness itself is the final enemy to be overcome. The three strands – Bacon, general will, and Skinner – seem to come together in the willed end of the possibility of willing.

I conclude, in part VI, by allowing utopianism and millennialism to address themselves to the paradox of progress: how a blind force (and it must be blind to be inevitable and irreversible by man) is set on the improvement of man. I believe that the response from each of the two older traditions – as different as they are – can help establish a starting point for constructive social theory that avoids the terrible dilemmas into which progressivism has led us as a culture.

One feature of the notion of progress obscures our enquiry from the start and makes it difficult even to identify what is entailed in the doctrine. The progress doctrine must present itself as having always been the principle of human history. It must disguise its parentage; it must have been parthenogenetically born from the womb of Nature or sprung full-armed from the brow of History. Even when it is seen that the notion of progress arose rather late in time, one aspect of it remains accepted: our society is seen as so different from both utopianism and millennialism that their similarities to each other are far greater than the likeness of either to our own beliefs. But to accept this conclusion renders us unable to analyse radically some deep questions: What may we hope for in history? Is human nature given? What is the foundation of human community? What is the relation of what we make to what we are? Is freedom an absolute? How do we recognize the presence or absence of freedom?

Thus, to disentangle what is bundled together in the notion of progress is to regain the possibility of thinking more clearly. The human will and its roles in social existence are handled in utopianism differently from the way they are treated in millennialism. As we shall see, God (and his will) are variously smuggled in and out of the progress doctrine; and it is crucial for the effectiveness of the result that we forget having made these moves. In millennialism and utopianism, the role of a god (if any) is there to be inspected and dealt with consciously. It is no matter of mere taxonomy to distinguish utopianism and millennialism or to trace their origins and development. This procedure enables us to understand the origins of the doctrine of progress, its contents, and the role of the elements it absorbs from the two earlier traditions. Beginning with utopianism and millennialism provides us also with two different and useful bases for asking radical questions about progress and for continuing to ask radical questions about the human condition and the prospects for mankind.

PART ONE

Millennialism

1

Millennialism as a type

We begin first with millennialism for several reasons: 1) It is more difficult of access to modern people than is utopianism, despite the persistence in our time of powerful, disguised versions of millennialism. 2) It has a certain temporal priority, at least in its origins. 3) It has a continuous history and can be used to that extent to frame the quite different development of utopianism. 4) It is more problematic and controversial than utopianism; thus the clarification of terms and concepts will expose more of the issues at state in this study.

Part I offers first, in this chapter, an outline of millennialism as a type. The succeeding chapters, 2 to 6, focus on the key moments and groups in Hebrew history through which, by the second century BC, the millennialist group, its genre, and its central convictions came into history. But, as important as millennialism became in Jewish life, it did not remain centrally important in that community; it brought about successive disasters that resulted in its being consciously subordinated to other emphases in the Judaism that survived into later Western history.

It was the earliest followers of Jesus, faced with the necessity of explaining his strange career (chapter 7), who found in millennialism the crucial means of interpreting what they came to believe was his significance to his own people and to all men. When this small but growing group, now no longer solely a Jewish movement, encountered the full force of Roman opposition to Christianity as an illicit superstition, it responded (chapter 8) by reappropriating the analysis of the book of Daniel, the defining set-piece of Jewish apocalyptic writing. In doing so it turned that analysis into a thoroughly Christianized interpretation of how God will bring about his will in the imminent, catastrophic climax of history. It was through the powerful organization of this picture and its accompanying highly charged symbols that Jewish millennialism was transmitted into later Western history.

When later Christianity moved away from this orientation it provoked a powerful and sustained reaction on the part of the Montanist movement (chapter 10), which set the pattern for the Christian underground of the Middle Ages associated with the name of Joachim of Fiore (chapter 11), a movement that applied to the dominant institutions of Christian civilization the categories of interpretation formerly reserved for the opponents of God. At the same time the Joachite movement offered a new millennialist scheme of interpretation capable of being employed by common men everywhere to cast their contemporaries in all the roles contained in the drama of the imminent end-time (chapter 12).

It was this notion, and the suppression of the Joachites, that turned millennialism into a flexible and radical criticism of constituted authority and a means to identify the new élite who were the true carriers of the meaning of history. It was in this double capacity that medieval millennialism came into early modern history: as 1) the conserver of the comprehensive and dynamic interpretation of the whole of history central to Jewish and early Christian millennialism; and 2) the carrier of the newer and more problematic notion of the elite with a mandate to change history.

Millennialism is that activity arising from anticipation of the end-time. This end-time. It is a part of history, its climax and fulfilment, and not the abandon-meaning of which has already been disclosed in the events described and attested to in Hebrew and Christian scriptures. These lived events have shaped the historic existence of Jews and Christians; they are normative events in which God is seen as having acted directly as the author of the drama of human existence.[1] They are not isolated events – epiphanies – fundamentally different from other events; history is one story. But they disclose what is at stake in the present moment, as the drama moves towards its climax. The role of Jesus apart, Jewish millennialism and Christian millennialism do not differ in their conception of the end-time. It is a part of history, its climax and fulfilment, and not the abandonment of historical life for some other sort.[2] The great events of the end-time are

---

1 It is not helpful to read all this as 'religious' language and to attribute to millennialism one's own notion of what religion 'really' is. By many definitions of religion, millennialism is non-religious or even anti-religious. And, as we shall see, the structure of millennialism can be retained even when the direct connection with Jewish and Christian 'content' is abandoned or repudiated.

2 The common notion that history lapses back into 'eternity' at this point cannot be supported from the most influential documents by millennialists. The arguments of O. Cullman, which purport to demonstrate this from linguistic usage, cannot be sustained, as J. Barr shows at length, *Biblical Words for Time* 2nd rev edn (London 1969) 67–85. The whole point of millennialism is the vindication of history, or God's self-vindication in history, not its annulment. This is expanded upon at length below.

themselves a preparation for a transformed historical existence, the 'new heavens and a new earth.'

Millennialism arose in particular periods of crisis in which new events seemed to cast doubt on the adequacy of past formulations of the meaning of Jewish history. Millennialism undertook to show that these new events, rather than imperilling that past interpretation of history, actually confirm it and deepen our understanding of it. These new events are the birth pangs of the end-time. The first followers of Jesus, as a result of their experience of his career, execution, and resurrection, announced Jesus as the principal figure of the imminent end-time – his return in power will inaugurate the end-time. As the wait lengthened, various purposes were assigned to this interval. The same process occurred among Jews as the age before the arrival of the messiah prolonged itself.

Millennialism thus exhibits three principal characteristics:

1 It is an interpretation of history as one story, concentrating on events in a particular history, which are seen as significant for all mankind and all history.

2 It establishes periods in history, periods of development (not progressive, improving periods), from a beginning to a climactic end state. History is a drama.

3 The drama is propelled by conflict among contending forces in a dialectical fashion. History is not melioristic in character; the period of the birth pangs exhibits the conflict at its most intense pitch and on the widest possible scale. The outcome is not in doubt, however, because prior history, rightly understood, discloses to us unmistakably the victor – the author of this drama – his character, and his intentions towards us.

Millennialism's characteristic form is as an organized force within its society, a movement rather than a literary effort undertaken by individuals. In possession of the vital clues to the shape of history, it is a practice, not a proposition.

Apocalyptic is the literary genre of millennialism,[3] from *apokalyptein*, to unveil. Despite the fact that millennialism has always been investigated through

---

3 *Apocalyptic* is sometimes used as a covering term equivalent to millennialism. *Messianism* is often used in the same way but refers to the agent of the end-time, a usage to which I shall keep. Not all millennialism has such an agent, and he is often quite differently conceived. Some see *millenarism* and *millenarianism* as useful distinctions; the field is sufficiently confused that I will avoid subtleties of this sort. *Chiliasm* is the original Greek work for millennialism. Finally *eschatology* is sometimes used for millennialism. It is a blanket word for the study of 'last things' and is too inert to convey the startling dynamic of millennialism, which is a social activity and ferment, not an 'ology.' *Millennialism* stresses the thousand-year kindgom of the redeemed over an unreconstructed world, prior to the final and complete renovation of the cosmos. As a word it has fewer faults than some others and is sanctified by long usage. Its emphasis on the role of the redeemed has the virtue of stressing the this-worldly orientation of millennialism and its concern with historical vindication.

examination of such documents, it is crucial to keep to the correct order. Millennialism is the product of historical communities. It arises within and at the end of a historical process. Among the Jewish people some of the experiences which helped to form it reach back to the mysterious events when 'Israel' was saved out of Egypt in the thirteenth century BC. Apocalyptic, in the sense of documents, begins to circulate only in the great crisis of the second century BC.

Despite its religious associations, millennialism must not be read as having to do with the transcendent or with 'heaven.' It has to do with the present world and with the choices for action made by living communities. Moderate millennial movements adopt a mode of life appropriate for the period of transition before the end-time. Approaches can range from the withdrawn quietism of first-century sectarians in the Judean desert to the ambitious plans of the Fifth Monarchy men to lead a purified England on a conquest of the Continent. A more extreme form of millennialism simply makes a more extreme judgment about the end-time: that it is here and that men are entitled, or obliged, to live now according to the norms of the new age. The Bohemian Adamites of the Hussite wars horrified even their militant neighbours by moving boldly into the new age as they understood it and living communally, nakedly, and promiscuously.[4] In the Münster episode, the city was declared to be the New Jerusalem and its leader the messiah.[5]

The view of time, history, and the cosmos assumed in the classical millennialism of 200 BC to 400 AD is Hebrew in origin. The tendency to overstress the uniqueness of Hebrew historical thinking arose in recent scholarship as a reaction to earlier attempts to seek the origins of Hebrew thought and institutions in surrounding cultures. A more balanced approach[6] now accepts the existence of non-Hebrew historical thinking in the Middle East and sees Hebrew thought as a reaction against the cultural pull of these other societies. It achieved its remarkable self-consciousness and coherence in this struggle for survival as a culture and a people. Yet the origins of this struggle must themselves be traced back, as we shall see below, to an earlier consciousness that Israel was a people created in time by a deliberate act of God's will in history. Israel is not, in its own documents, a primal people, self-evident or given in nature. Indeed, Canaanite and cultural Hebrew nature-cycle festivals were historicized in the Hebrew scriptures and

---

4 Here a cyclic understanding of time foreign to original millennialism has allowed this group to assimilate the new age to the notion of Eden made innocent again; here the end-time must re-present and resanctify what was taken to be mankind's original state.

5 See N. Cohn *Pursuit of the Millennium* (London 1957). Cohn's conception of millennialism is dealt with critically at the end of chapter 10.

6 See R.C. Dentan ed *The Idea of History in the Ancient Near East* (New Haven 1955).

brought within the one story of a willed beginning, of covenant peoplehood, and of a still open and linear future. Only within this normative history could there arise millennialism. This sense of a normative history was transmitted to later Western thought through Christianity, itself originally a millennial movement.

2

The Exile and Hebrew history

Why begin with a historical survey of the development of millennialism? First, although what I shall say is almost commonplace to scholars of the Hebrew Bible, it has had little impact on discussions of progress. Second, misleading stereotypes of millennialism are propounded in intrareligious controversies which influence public discussions of millennialism. Third, millennialism has been defined by merely adding up characteristics from documents whose claim to be apocalyptic is precisely the issue. Millennialism cannot be defined by working ahistorically from genre studies.

We shall focus immediately on the circumstances of the exiles of 597 and 587: Israelite[1] élites in honourable captivity in Babylonia.[2] Here are people subject to many pressures, not the least of which is the attractiveness of a sophisticated world culture. Those who wished to resist assimilation were compelled to produce a more reflective interpretation of the meaning of their history than had yet been undertaken.

1 The term Israel refers to the Hebrew people as a tribal confederacy and a nation (two nations after ca 922 BC) from ca 1200 to 587. The name of the surviving fragment (after destruction of the larger part, ca 721), Judah, gave its name to the people, the Jews, who persisted as a single people despite the temporary loss of their homeland. From ca 538, some returned to Judah; but perhaps never thereafter was the majority of Jews resident in Judah/Jehud/Judaea, as it was called variously over time. Palestine includes more territory than was every occupied or ruled, except briefly, by Israelites or Jews.

2 Two general surveys covering the period of exile and its aftermath, and providing brief remarks about its literature, are P.B. Ackroyd *Israel under Babylon and Persia* (London 1970), hereafter *IBP*; and D.S. Russell *The Jews from Alexander to Herod* (London 1967) (*JAH*). More detailed scholarship and discussion of controverted points are contained in Ackroyd's *Exile and Restoration* (London 1968) (*ER*) and Russell's *Method and Meaning of Jewish Apocalyptic* (London 1964) (*MMJA*), which contains an extensive bibliography. The biblical apocalyptic is identified and discussed extensively by Ackroyd and Russell. See chronology below, 34 n42.

The various groups in exile produced programs for the future based on different interpretations of the Israelite past as a history of interaction with their God. This people could only understand itself historically. An inspection of the Hebrew scriptures discloses that this people understands itself as constituted by its own history and that it can only see a restored future on the basis of motifs from this past. These convictions contrasted directly and programmatically with those of Babylonia.

In the Babylonian world-view,[3] the cosmos itself is the totality of what is. It is, in effect, divine. The gods or divine forces are both localized and suffused throughout the cosmos, its objects, persons, and processes. The lower world is representative of and derived from the divine life of the gods. The changes we see, whether in natural life or in human affairs, reflect changes in the life of the gods. The cosmos is thus suffused with meaning, hierarchically arranged. The gods are not the origin of the sacred; the cosmos itself, of which they are the highest parts, is sacred. Thus no question of *why* the cosmos is can be pressed. Instead it is both self-evident and inexplicable. Its ordered rhythms answer most questions and preclude even the asking of others.

The Hebrew community was formed in conscious reaction to this world-view, long the common possession of Middle Eastern peoples. The earliest Hebrew reflections show us a distinctive interpretation of time, cosmos, and god. The act of one god in saving the Hebrew people at the Red Sea unified these reflections; and the crisis of exile forced the reworking, into almost their present form, of the earlier narratives of the Hebrews' involvement with their god. The great narratives[4] of clan life with this god – of his having made them a nation in order to

---

3 Its greater accessibility to modern scholarship than the ideas of other Middle Eastern peoples must not lead us to suppose that it was universally dominant. The equally important Egyptian conceptions are more complex and less unified. But the Babylonian conceptions must be presumed to be more salient as 'influences.' For a vivid presentation of Middle Eastern sacral kingship based on current scholarship, see A.T. van Leeuwen *Christianity in World History* (New York 1961).

4 Notably outlined by M. Noth in *History of Pentateuchal Traditions* (Englewood Cliffs, NJ, 1972) and in *Exodus* (London 1962). Modern scholarship since the early nineteenth century has established the composite character of much of the Hebrew scriptures. The first five 'books' were built up from oral and liturgical formulae, other recitations, and documentary notes, into coherent literary traditions and subsequently combined into our present documents, often at a very late date. Both the archaic character and clear evidence of later work are preserved in the works.

The established scheme is used in this present work. Oral and literary traditions developed into strands: 1) J and E, parallel (except for J's primeval history) historic and theological works perhaps from the southern and northern kingdoms respectively; 2) P, the 'priestly' strand, an interpretation of the meaning of cult, fixed in a comprehensive and highly reflective historical schema; and 3) D, including the present Deuteronomy, much material in the historical books (and in their editing), and some interpretive material in the rest of the Pentateuch.

achieve his own ends in history, and of their oscillation between covenanted peoplehood and assimilation to the general ontocratic pattern of the Middle East – are all reworked in the Exile.

MOTIFS

What motifs of pre-exilic experience and conviction are drawn upon in the exiles' programs for the future, in which this god will complete his project with this people?

1 God is unique.[5] He is dependent on nothing. He discloses himself as and to whom he will. He establishes enduring relationships by his actions in times of peril, promise, and threat. He is awesome, unpredictable, and uncontrollable.

2 The clans were brought into close relation to one another by the Exodus and by the gradual occupation of most of Palestine.[6] This process consolidated them in one roughly defined cultic community distinct from the 'nature religion' and culture of their victims and neighbours.

---

5 The Hebrew scriptures show little interest in monotheism. This theme is taken up in the famous statement of Deuteronomy 6, 'Hear, O Israel, the Lord our God is one God' and stressed in the Deutero-Isaiah of the Exile (see ch 40–5). The great bulk of the Hebrew scriptures simply does not argue for the existence of just one god. Theories of the evolution of monotheism, and of the importance of a single god, have been slow to adjust to the testimony of the Hebrew scriptures.

6 The actual location of the Exodus has not been established. The text does not require a crossing of the open Red Sea or even of the Red Sea as we know it at all. The text, however, does not permit us to rationalize the event or to assimilate it to a class of similar events. The saving, however one analyses the text, is unique and is the action of Yahweh. We are not dealing here with the pious attribution to Yahweh of the escapers' finding of a way across at a moment of crisis, for no such conventional understanding of the event can acount for its power to attract to itself all the other traditions now found in the book of Exodus. One may choose to believe that the escapees were mistaken; but one may not choose simply to assimilate their testimony to one's own judgment of what is likely or possible.

The second element in the testimony ('and made us a people') is not the same as the saving at the sea. To the degree that 'made us a people' is to be linked to the covenant tradition, it is unclear whether we must follow the present narrative (in joining that covenant-making to the vicinity of the saving) or whether a post-conquest Palestinian event is being read back into the pre-conquest period.

See Joshua 9 for the occupation. On the general problem of the so-called conquest, see M. Weippert *Settlement of the Israelite Tribes in Palestine* (London 1971) and J.M. Miller 'The Israelite Occupation of Canaan' in J.H. Hayes and J.M. Miller ed *Israelite and Judaean History* (Philadelphia 1977) 213–84.

3 This god made them a historic people.[7] Babylonia saw itself as the eternal locus of divine connection with the world of men; the Hebrews acknowledge that they came into existence contingently, at a particular time. They have been created a people to fulfil a purpose not their own, the full dimensions of which remain obscure until exilic reflection enlarges upon it.

4 Hebrew kingship exhibits a paradox from its very origins. It is a betrayal of the true (divine) king; yet God is said to have provided Israel with a king. Later, God is said to have made an unconditional promise of continuance to the house of David. Kingship is suspect as an assimilation to the Babylonian pattern; at the same time, the dynasty of David will be the means through which God will achieve his (still-unclear) will.

5 The prophetic enterprise, originally a shamanistic guild of ecstatics which continues until the Exile (I Kings 22:1–23; Jer 23:9–22), corrects the tendency of kings and people alike to treat the cult, the dynasty, the nation, and the cosmos as objects of veneration (Jer 7:1–8:3; 15:4, 44:17–23). The prophets stand as self-authenticating witnesses to the desire of this god to *use* this people, to remind it of its contingency, and to resist other ways of life.

In the reflections of exile this enterprise is seen to have failed. The failure of the people to respond to it is the chief reason for God's sentence of exile and national dissolution. He is not to be mocked; his purposes, his project, are paramount. The late canonical author, the Chronicler, summarizes the matter: 'Yahweh, the god of their fathers, sent persistently to them by his messengers, because he had compassion on his people and on his dwelling place; but they kept on mocking the messengers of God, despising his words, and scoffing at his prophets, till the wrath of God rose against his people, till there was no remedy.' (II Chron 36:15–16).

STRANDS OF INTERPRETATION

There were many strands of interpretation of Israelite history during the period *before* the Exile; three should be emphasized. 1) The 'priestly tradition, visible in the later Pentateuch, held that the cult (the objectified requirements of the sacrificial system and law codes) constituted the matrix of right relation between Israel and Yahweh. 2) The Zion tradition focused on the achievements of the

---

7 The motif 'and made us a people' is linked to the rescue at the Red Sea and consequent upon it. The covenant-making traditions, the epiphany at the mountain, and a large amount of cultic material are brought into contact with the Red Sea event. The conviction that these accounts all concerned encounters with this deity made it possible to group them together in the Pentateuch close to the Red Sea event.

house of David and the unique status of Jerusalem ('Zion' is its cultic name) as the locus of the divine-human interaction. 3) The Deuteronomists were heirs of the covenant-in-the-wilderness, anti-monarchical, prophetic tradition. That tradition had held that faithfulness to Yahweh – as in this tradition's idealized picture of the post-Exodus holy community and the holy war of the conquest period – would result in Yahweh's fighting beside his people to bring them victory, no matter what the odds.

These traditions are the focus of intense reflection *during* the period of exile. Among those who held that Yahweh would yet fulfil what he began, these traditions were expanded and radicalized into programs for the anticipated 'restoration' of Israel. In 'superheated' conditions, these élites, no longer responsible for an actual people, use the traditions of their people in a new way as visions of the glorious, vindicated future.

In this period the characteristic emphases of millennialism are formulated. But a priori reasoning continues today to play an unwarranted role in our interpretations of the Exile and its reflections. These judgments need to be examined before we look at the programs themselves.

1 Millennialism is often judged to be dualistic, deterministic, dangerous, and given to ungovernable flights of fancy – on the basis of late documents. Its origin is then placed not in the reflection of exile, but later, in Persian and Hellenistic times. It is seen as a foreign growth, regrettable but understandable in a hard-pressed people under strong foreign influence. This millennialism is contrasted unfavourably with 'biblical eschatology' – a more controlled development of later periods, when millennialism has been shunted aside.[8]

2 If millennialism is responsible for the prediction of Jesus' return in power at an early date, and if this event did not happen, and if Christianity survived this failure quite well, then early Christianity could not have been predominantly millennialist, else it could not so successfully have surmounted the non-occurrence of Jesus' return. Since the Christian interpretation of Jesus was dependent on that of main-line post-exilic Judaism, it would follow that the (falsified) millennialist emphases must have been exotica, not centrally related to exilic or post-exilic Judaism – much less to the main elements of Israelite history prior to the Exile.

3 The principal determinant of the a priori view that millennialism is an exotic, post-Exile growth is the somewhat simple-minded notion that what actually took

---

8 After the destruction of the second Temple in 70 AD, many wished to portray what later became normative rabbinic Judaism as having always been the central structure of post-national Jewish life. This position ultimately became dominant after the disastrous uprising of non-Palestinian Jews in 115 and the final failed Palestinian revolt of 132–5. In order to become dominant, this position had to relegate to peripheral status not only millennialism but also other tendencies of the Exile and later growths.

place in the period after the Exile must necessarily have been the fulfilment of what had been intended by exilic thinkers and planners. There is no reason to suppose this to have been the case and every reason to suppose the contrary.

An inspection of the programs of the exiles provides the best refutation of this reasoning. We shall examine the Deuteronomists, the P or 'priestly' scheme, Ezekiel, Deutero-Isaiah (ch 40–55), Trito-Isaiah (ch 56–66), and finally the 'remnant' tradition. From these emerge the principal elements that thereafter constitute the movement of millennialism. Some of these groups or themes originated before the Exile. Some were precipitated by it. All reflect on the earlier period, characterize the present, and, on the basis of the historic themes of Israelite life, both anticipate and prescribe the shape of the future with their god. And not only their own life: gradually there developed a sense of the future of the world.

The Deuteronomists

The Deuteronomists had perhaps the most difficult task. Perhaps originating as popular Yahwistic revivalists in the old northern kingdom, in the south they had proposed the utter suppression not only of other cults but of Yahwistic cult centres, however old, in favour of the single sanctuary in Jerusalem. All prior history of the national period was read as a falling away from the purity of the honeymoon period of Israel in the wilderness when, according to Deuteronomy, the one holy people had gathered around the ark of the covenant in its tent. In Deuteronomy, kings were judged almost solely by the extent to which they attempted to curb the dispersion of cultic activity, so vulnerable, when scattered and uncontrolled, to pagan influence and to unforgivable apostasy. Its thesis was that centralization, once carried out fully, would ensure the integrity of the nation; Yahweh would then fight off the nations for them.[9]

The young king Josiah (ca 640–609), prompted by the discovery of a supposedly ancient document (an Ur-Deuteronomy) or supported by it in a campaign already begun, embarked with great success on a Deuteronomic program in the waning period of Assyrian suzerainty (after ca 640), even carrying it into the somewhat paganized north. The ancient Yahwistic cult places, as well as pagan shrines, were closed and the sites defiled so that they could never again be used. Josiah and the militia of Judah attempted to impede an Egyptian army marching north to intervene in the last struggles of the Assyrian empire. The Israelites were crushed, Josiah was killed, and an Egyptian nominee from the royal family was placed on the throne. The Deuteronomic movement was discredited by events.

9 See G. von Rad *Studies in Deuteronomy* (London 1953) 45 ff; also his *Deuteronomy* (London 1966).

Though in eclipse in the remaining few years of nationhood, the movement could later claim that Josiah's reforms had come too late to avert the destruction,[10] but that its scheme had to be the foundation of any program for dealing with the situation confronting the returnees.[11] Such a vision suggested that the polluted, wasted land pictured by the exiles was no more polluted than in the days of their heedless fathers.

The plan in Deuteronomy was based on a personal and corporate identification with Yahweh's benefits (of peoplehood and land), conferred through no merits of the people but out of sheer grace.[12] The great rituals of Deuteronomy, and its sense of the Law as a living 'way' of response, are designed to evoke just such an identification. Deuteronomy brought forward a practicable scheme for a restored Israel.[13] But it reflected little of the experience of exile. The Exile is passive confirmation of the judgment announced for failure to carry through creation of the holy community. The particular character of the Exile appears to count for very little, though it may be equated with the wilderness period as a beginning, full of promise.

The P schema

This 'priestly' tradition is not to be construed as concerned with 'mere' cult and ceremonial matters. Its historical schema is strong and comprehensive and is the

10 II Kings 23:25–7 argues that though Josiah had been a king uniquely true to all that Yahweh had ordained, the sins of his grandfather, Manasseh, had so polluted the land that doom had already been pronounced on Judah before Josiah came to the throne.
11 'Though it came too late to avert the final disaster, this was at least delayed. What had so nearly succeeded once could be seen to be a source of restoration subsequently' (ER 68). See also Ackroyd's comment (ER 71) on Jer 36:3 as being concordant with the D program. Yet Jeremiah is strangely silent about the reform of Josiah.
12 The Deuteronomistic preface to the Sinai chapters in Exodus makes this free grace the very substance of the covenant-making, which is here logically and structurally independent of the Ten Commandments. 'And Moses went up to God and Yahweh called to him out of the mountain, saying, "Thus shall you say to the house of Jacob and tell the people of Israel: 'You have seen what I did to the Egyptians, and how I bore you on eagles' wings, and brought you to myself. Now, therefore, if you will obey my voice and keep my covenant, you shall be my own possession among all peoples; for all the earth is mine; and you shall be to me a kingdom of priests and a holy nation.' These are the words you shall speak to the children of Israel." Moses came and called the elders of the people and set before them all the words which Yahweh had commanded him. And the people answered together and said, "All that Yahweh has spoken we will do,"' (Ex 19:3–8a). I have followed Noth's identification of this section as D, a procedure disputed by others.
13 For the development of the Deuteronomic movement, see B.W. Anderson *The Living World of the Old Testament* 2nd edn (London 1967); von Rad *Studies in Deuteronomy* and *Deuteronomy*; and E.W. Nicholson *Deuteronomy and Tradition* (Oxford 1967).

basis for the structure of the Pentateuch. This historical view casts Yahweh as the Creator God, lord of the cosmos and history, shaping both to his own ends. The seductions of the Babylonian gods of nature and cosmic processes are resisted. The polemic against idolatry inserted in Deutero-Isaiah (Is 44:9–20) is shallow by comparison, suggesting that gentiles quite simply identify their images as their gods. The P material offers a world-view to oppose to the Babylonian world-view.

P does not render sacred either human history or the natural world.[14] Their meaning is not self-evident; their meaning is declared by Yahweh. Israel is not simply substituted for Babylon as the centre of the world. Israel is indeed central to the world's history, and P reflects on this; but it is central only because called into being for a purpose. The ancient 'table of the nations' preserved in Genesis 10 surveys the entire political geography of the then-known world, but has no mention of Israel. Israel is not read back into history as its eternal meaning; Israel is a particular creation of Yahweh for a historic purpose. Israel in 587 has lost its status as a nation-state, previously taken for granted. Much prophetic activity before the Exile was directed against this assumption; now reflection was unavoidable.

P re-accents Hebrew history. It has long been noticed that P has no central place for the covenant at Sinai. P's supposed fixation on ritual and cult replaced covenant as the central interest. But P's interest is rather history, and we find covenants in profusion in P. There are two primeval covenants with all men, through Adam and Noah – these are unique to P. P makes the covenant with Abraham normative for all of God's dealings with Israel. Here P has moved back the decisive moment of covenant from Sinai; the prophetic curses have been so radical, and now so radically fulfilled, that they cancel the Sinai covenant[15] – it can no longer function, in P's scheme, for a restored Israel.

P, like the Deuteronomists, emphasizes God's free grace; the cultic provisions are predicated upon it. P's adaptations of ancient ritual emphasize that God has provided thus and so for our benefit; there is no attempt to rationalize these actions. They are mainly a remedy for sins. P's austere history provides no privileged period, no wilderness honeymoon, by which to judge other periods. P

---

14 We must beware importing later or alien categories familiar to us into the Hebrew context. There is no Hebrew word for our modern 'nature.' The non human world is historicized, inseparable from human events, and subject to the will of Yahweh in all its particulars, just as man is. Later work from the Hellenistic period such as Job and Ecclesiastes begins to treat 'nature' as something to reflect upon. The psalms speak of natural phenomena in both fashions: the floods clap their hands for joy and the hills sing for joy at the coming of Yahweh (Ps 98:8); but Psalm 104 is a sustained argument that nature's reliability shows Yahweh's unfailing concern for us.

15 See ER 95.

equates wilderness with exile; both generations must die, for the sake of that better time to follow. P looks ahead for the consummation of history. The 'genealogies' which mark the divisions of the work provide a time frame which extends no further than the 'last two or three centuries B.C.'[16] The last days are imminent.

Ezekiel

Not everything in the biblical materials[17] of the Exile and return fits in with the Deuteronomists and P – most notably Ezekiel and the additions to Isaiah (ch 44–66 and parts of ch 1–39).

Ezekiel marks a new style of prophecy and establishes one of the conventions of apocalyptic writing. Ezekiel's visions[18] of restoration include a detailed representation of a new Temple and describe the boundaries of the 12 (!) tribes in a physically changed Palestine. These and other more bizarre visions tend to obscure his anchoring in the community in exile, where he must respond to shock, dislocation, and temptation to despair and to assimilation.

If D and P have elements of theodicy, this theodicy is rooted in traditional formulations. Ezekiel's formulations seem to have originated in the crisis of exile. The ways of Yahweh are explicated; the immediate needs of men prompt his work but are not its organizing centre. The condemnation of the history of the two kingdoms is put with a sustained intensity[19] that is unmatched elsewhere. And the judgment is read back into the period of the Exodus. Restoration is nonetheless promised by Yahweh, for his own sake, rather than that of his people. Their merits are too frail.[20]

This restoration follows a battle of 'Gog of Magog' against Israel. Gog gathers a host, representing the gentile world, against a returned Israel (Ezek 39:1–9). Yahweh overthrows the host of Gog; and the burial of that army requires seven months' labour on the part of Israel. Both the Exile and the overthrow of Gog are

---

16 ER 91. The Samaritan Pentateuch provides 300 additional years and the Septuagint, translated at the end of the Hebrew text's allotted time, 780 more years.

17 Biblical material is all that has survived from this period of Hebrew and Aramaic Jewish writing.

18 Or those of his successors. The work of almost all the prophets has been added to by disciples or people who regarded themselves as such. This is most widely accepted in the case of the large body of materials Isaiah 40–66. The work of a 'school' has been assumed. Ezekiel has prompted similar suppositions, but no consensus has been reached.

19 See, for example, ch 20–3.

20 'The declaration "I am Yahweh" ... – characteristic of Ezekiel and H and also found in Deutero-Isaiah – is the absolute ground of all events, and so the only source of hope. But Ezekiel thereby strips himself and his people of all pretensions' (ER 106).

owing solely to Yahweh's self-vindication and his desire to display himself clearly before all men: 'I will set my glory among the nations; and all the nations shall see my judgment which I have executed and my hand which I have laid upon them' (Ezek 39:21).

Then the true restoration begins – a transformation of land, people, and cult. A 'new and spiritualized geography,' a 'land which has become ideally regular' (ER 114), replaces the mountains on which the armies of Gog had come to grief. The lovingly detailed description of the new Temple and its ritual, and of the arrangement of a new Israel about it, completes the conception of a holy place and holy people. Israel becomes a purified centre for a world whose hostility has been broken forever by Yahweh himself. The restoration and completion of Yahweh's intention with Israel are not connected to any event of the Exile itself, as happened in later work during the Exile.

It is widely accepted that Ezekiel is a source for later apocalyptic. Often, however, this judgment accords too great an importance to form in both Ezekiel and in apocalyptic writing – to the vision mode and the strange colouration of future events.

Deutero-Isaiah

The corpus of Isaiah is almost always divided between Palestinian materials associated with the historic Isaiah of the eighth and seventh centuries, and the rest, written in Babylonia.[21] The early arguments for the 'spirituality' of the later prophets focused on ch 40–66. But the material resists this thesis. Though the David and Zion traditions are handled in an exalted fashion, much in this text is particular and material, leading to the judgment that there is real 'difficulty of finding an entirely satisfactory method of analyzing their main contents. It is not that the main themes cannot be readily discerned, in spite of the uncertainties ... It is that any attempt at producing a logical exposition is frustrated by the complexity of the thought' (ER 120).

One bold solution of these problems has been to transfer the provenance of 40–66, or parts of it, to Palestine.[22] This thesis, though not completely sustained, frees the material from a completely Babylonian context and brings some of the 'complexity of thought' into contact with post-Exile controversies. The bulk of 40–66, after all, looks forward. There are clearer indications of a continuing

---

21 See the discussion in ER 118–19. The usual divisions are 1–39 for the historic Isaiah, 40–55 for Deutero-Isaiah, and 56–66 for the rest, sometimes referred to as Trito-Isaiah. But there are sections in 1–39 which must be regarded as late; and many different arrangements and assignments have been proposed within 40–66.

22 See J.D. Smart *History and Theology in Second Isaiah* (Philadelphia 1965).

School of Isaiah than of any other prophetic body.[23] The traditions from which it worked, however, are those most shaken by the Destruction and Exile. The Zion and David traditions were tied to the worldly success of the dynasty and the holy city where Yahweh was pleased to make himself known.

In Isaiah 40–55, however, it is not Israel which is to be vindicated, but God (43:25; 48:6–8). It is for his own sake and for his vindication before the nations that Yahweh is about the work of *a new saving history* culminating in a new Zion, the centre of the world. Israel is the almost passive beneficiary of the new creation and the new exodus. Egypt is spoken of as the place of captivity, as well as Babylonia, in order to stress the analogy with the first exodus; and the former exodus is linked to the creation. In the new account, Israel is said to have crossed 'the deep' in the Exodus – the words of Gen 1:2 which echo the old Babylonian story of Marduk's struggle with Tiamat the dragon. Deutero-Isaiah refers to God's cutting of 'Rahab' in pieces, his piercing of the dragon, as part of his action in the Exodus (51:9–11; 43:15–21).[24] Israel's passivity is emphasized in order to stress the irresistible activity of Yahweh (43:11–13). He who subdued all the gods and forces will not be deterred by the gods of Babylon.

The notion of the first Isaiah that the Assyrians were being used by Yahweh as his unconscious servants (10:5–12) had been echoed in Jeremiah's remarkable reference (25:9) to Nebuchadnezzar as God's servant. This idea is taken up by Deutero-Isaiah and applied to Cyrus (ch 45).[25] Neither Babylon nor Persia can withstand the purposes of God, but will be used, knowingly or not, as his instruments (45:4–5). Israel is also Yahweh's servant and is addressed and described as such in a number of passages (later combed by Christians for 'messianic' references to Jesus).[26] Israel is to be a conscious servant, purified by its suffering; the commercial and quasi-legal language[27] emphasizes that the suffering has a limit

23 See Is 8:16 and the strong internal evidence of the different hands, some of whom may come very late. See Russell *JAH* 213 ff, where ch 24–7 may be as late as the third century. See also Ackroyd *IBP*: 'There is a unity of tradition in the book of Isaiah, in spite of the fact that more than 200 years probably separate its earliest from its latest section (i.e., *c*. 740 B.C.–*c*. 500 B.C.); some parts of it may have to be assigned to a much later date' (233–4). Though Ackroyd refers to ch 24–7 as being possibly the latest portion, his conclusion is not disturbed if applied to 56–66 or to bits within 40–55. On these sections, see below.

24 For more general references to Egypt and the Exodus, see 41:17–18; 43:2; 50:2.

25 The so-called 'Cyrus cylinder,' perhaps contemporaneous with the events it describes, portrays Cyrus as the tool of Marduk, affronted by the religious reforms of Nabonidus. See J.B. Pritchard ed *Ancient New Eastern Texts* (hereafter *ANET*) 2nd edn (London 1955) 315 ff.

26 These passages begin at 42:1 and conclude at 53:12, but are not continuous. The focus on an individual servant is much argued about; the principal problem arises in the section beginning at 52:13. The attention given to these sections in isolation is commented upon by Ackroyd *IBP* 137–41.

27 40:2; 41:1, 11–12, 21–4; 42:9 ff; 45:20–1

set by the damages actually caused by Israel. Israel too will be a servant, willing or not, as a cautionary example or as the purified community of the new Exodus.

The new Zion is Yahweh's self-vindication (52:1–10). It is inhabited by those whom the nations have rejected and degraded. The returned exiles live in a transformed Zion, the centre of a world deeply impressed by God's dealings with Israel.[28] Yahweh is vindicated publicly, but Israel moves centre-stage as the wondering objects[29] of Yahweh's enactments: 'I will give you as a light to the nations, that my salvation may reach to the end of the earth' (49:6b). These nations send treasure to Jerusalem and make reverence to Israel 'because of Yahweh, your God, and of the Holy One of Israel, for he has glorified you' (55:5). The prophet removes from the exiles all ground for self-vindication (43:25–8; 48:7–8), yet promises them a historic vindication (including the original covenant). The present world-order cannot support such a change; in the new Jerusalem, not only will the political arrangements be altered, but also 'instead of the thorn shall come up the cypress; instead of the brier shall come up the myrtle' (55:13a).

Trito-Isaiah

Isaiah 56–66, the so-called Trito-Isaiah, is thematically close to Deutero-Isaiah, but there is a radicalization of the themes of 40–55.[30] Trito-Isaiah does not constitute a single, connected work. The notion of Deutero-Isaiah, that nations and kings shall honour Israel, and humble themselves before Israel, is here stretched to the limit: 'You shall suck the breast of kings' (60:16a). Foreigners are given a new role – not only will they come in homage, but also they are to be taken into the holy community, to be Yahweh's servants, and to minister to him in his 'house of prayer for all peoples' (56:7b). The text of 66:18–21 contemplates the reception of gentiles as priests and Levites.[31] Chapters 56–66 stress also the Zion tradition and speak of the Temple as central. But in sections where one would expect a mention of the Temple (eg ch 58) the text offers no mention of it.[32] In

---

28 Taking 52:13–15 as a proper continuation of the rest of the chapter, as a typical humiliation – exaltation contrast

29 There are short passages in Deutero-Isaiah in which the nations are directly abased before the restored Israel: 45:14; 49:22–3, and 52:1. But these are in a context in which Israel's role as mediator or example is emphasized. 52:1 does not necessarily exclude all but the exiles, given the apparent openness of the invitation to return (49:8–13) and the picture of the gentile pilgrimage to Zion, the centre of the world (55:5).

30 See here the valuable work of P. Hanson *The Dawn of Apocalyptic* (Philadelphia 1975).

31 Correspondingly, the role of Israel as mediator between God and his (new) people is stressed (61:5).

32 Hanson calls attention to violent anti-Temple polemic in Trito-Isaiah and identifies this with the work of elements opposed to the party then in power (*Dawn of Apocalyptic* 161–81).

others the exaltation of Zion reaches a new pitch of fervour: God replaces the sun as source of illumination (60:19).

Smart posits a Palestinian orientation for 40–66 and a post-Exile setting for Trito-Isaiah. Response to his proposals for Trito-Isaiah has focused on the speculative character of much of his reconstruction of events in the period. Smart has forced us to consider the important questions of 1) why, when we know little of either Babylonia or Palestine during the Exile, interpreters should prefer to locate 40–66 in Babylonia and 2) why we know so little of Palestine after the Exile. The second point will be dealt with in the next chapter, on problems of the 'restoration.'

The 'remnant' tradition

One element of exilic reflection not exclusively identified with any single documentary tradition is that of 'the remnant.' This interpretation of Israel's past and future provides a standard by which to discern an inner and an outer reality to history, a true Israel and an apparent one. As early as the latter days of the northern kingdom, Hosea or his successors tell us that the entire period of conquest and confederacy was a falling away from the honeymoon period of Israel with Yahweh in the wilderness. Similarly, the later Deuteronomists posit entry into Palestine as that time when Israel had the possibility of following Yahweh with all its heart.[33] But the Deuteronomists do not judge all subsequent Israelite history by one absolute standard. Reconstruction depends on the labours of the populace; it will not do to suggest that no good thing has happened in 600 years.

In later thought we see the notion that at any given time in Israel a remnant has been faithful, or will be the faithful instruments of Yahweh's will. Isaiah, in the days of the fall of the northern kingdom, suggests that a remnant is preserved by God for his own purposes (10:20–3). It participates in the destruction, but is returned to carry out God's will. It is not that he needs worshippers – the dynamic and terrifying God of the first Isaiah needs nothing – but his purposes remain firm. The reason for the destruction is the reason for the promised restoration of

33 The account we are given in Numbers 13–14 is that, after the lengthy stay at Sinai (over a year), the new people proceeded to the borders of Palestine, reconnoitred the land, and then quailed at the prospect of having to overcome so many mighty peoples. Yahweh cursed them to a life of further wandering in the desert. Only their children would inherit the promised land. Reconsidering, the people then attempt to frustrate this sentence by invading Palestine after all, only to suffer defeat. Thereafter they complete their sentence, with only Joshua and Caleb, who had trusted Yahweh to deliver the land to Israel, surviving into the actual conquest after the forty years of wandering.

the remnant of the ten tribes of the north: to carry out his own purposes. The Deutero-Isaiah will say that none of his words is ever void: 'It shall not return to me empty; but it shall accomplish that which I purpose' (55:11). Whatever Israel's purpose among the nations may be, it was destroyed for rebelling against that purpose and will be restored, if only in a remnant, in order to complete it.

Jeremiah, in the last days of the southern kingdom, saw Judah's doom as irrevocable. Since no remnant had yet returned to reconstitute the lost north, and since the south had not really profited by the lesson of the north, the new destruction would be radical. Yet a remnant would return from both earlier and later destructions to serve Yahweh (23:1–8). His faithfulness to his own purposes guarantees this result: 'I have loved you with an everlasting love,' he says in the midst of a passage on judgment and return, 'therefore I have continued my faithfulness to you' (31:3b). In Jeremiah, a new beginning is made – a new covenant in the latter days (31:31–4).

It is common to conflate with this notion of the remnant the idea of the righteous minority. No doubt the prophets called vainly in Yahweh's name on a heedless people and on obdurate kings; and there is evidence for successors to Isaiah and Jeremiah.[34] But, more importantly, Isaiah says that if the southern kingdom – already a remnant – only trusts Yahweh completely, it will be delivered by his action.[35] It is not always possible to disentangle the two separate ideas in the reflection of the Exile. There is the *righteous* remnant, whose faithfulness is rewarded; and there is the remnant *purified* through suffering, who will be the foundation for God's acts of self-vindication.

In the Exile the first line of analysis – identifying oneself with the rejected prophets as a righteous remnant – leads to radical assertions about the meaning of suffering by the righteous. The sinful suffer justly on their own behalf. But why does the righteous remnant suffer? In the later years of the Exile, when it may be assumed that even the sinful have made full expiation and that the land has paid the full penalty, why does exile continue?[36] The exiles suffer for others. Thus, in Deutero-Isaiah's 'servant songs,' the sufferings of an Israel now made righteous are undergone not for the past or for itself but for the nations. The nations' realization and acceptance of Israel's role on their behalf lead them to abase themselves before Yahweh in the restored Jerusalem. It is possible to hold simultaneously to this interpretation and to the drawing of rigid lines between Jews and

34 See Is 8:16–18 and the prominence of Baruch in Jeremiah.

35 Is 30–1; 10:20–6; 14:1–2; and the passages – 2:1–5; 4:2–6; 24:21–3; and 25:6–9 – usually assigned to the later Exile or the restoration.

36 The historical basis for this reasoning might be the worsening of conditions in the later years of the Babylonian empire, perhaps as a consequence of the religious reforms of Nabonidus.

gentiles, as we see it in the community of returnees after 538. But it is also possible to regard this vicarious function of Israel as one which breaks down such barriers so that Yahwists of all kinds are to be included in the holy community: 'My house shall be called a house of prayer for all peoples' (Is 56:7b).

The other line of analysis accepts its people's continuity with the historic burden of sin. In the Chronicler's judgment (II Chron 36:15–21) God sent 'messengers' out of his compassion; but these were persistently rejected 'until there was no remedy' except the destruction of the nation. The Exile is not expiatory and vicarious suffering; it corresponds to the omitted sabbath years only. The Chronicler accepts the remnant framework, but shows little trace of a new Israel wider in principle than before.[37] The innovation of elaborate Levitical orders of Temple functionaries he reads back into the foundation of the Temple by David and Solomon; and elaborate genealogies are provided for the returned Levites.

CONCLUSION: EXILIC THOUGHT AND MILLENNIALISM

All parties or groups in the Exile are concerned with Israel's or Yahweh's vindication. All parties take as normative Yahweh's dealings with the nation over the long centuries. And, in different ways, they are concerned to relate that history to human history as a whole. The questions and plans of the Exile are radical in character; yet all rely on the past for themes which will validate these radical programs. In the remarkable construction of the Pentateuch, especially in the Exodus narratives, each of the traditions is allowed a place in these founding events and no voices are suppressed, even when they stand in tension with one another. The result is a densely woven narrative. The Pentateuch is crowned by the Deuteronomists' attempt to make Israel of the Exile present in those early events and to make those events normative in the anticipated community of returnees from exile. However radical any exilic program might be, its charter had to be located in the context of God's founding actions and the prophetic word.

The creation of the Pentateuch – in a people with no notion of 'scripture' – and the rich variety of exilic plans demonstrated the Jews' understanding that *God is seen in human history and in specific encounter or not at all*. Human history is not self-evident or beyond question, but precisely the place to which questions must be addressed and from which answers will come. The proposed solutions to Israel's crisis are not conceptual or existential, but historical. There must be a

---

37 A somewhat different view of this matter is taken by Ackroyd; this will be reviewed in connection with the reforms of Nehemiah and Ezra, below (35–8).

holy community visible in the real world, or else Yahweh has indeed cast off his people forever. The alternative, defectors' solution is that Yahweh has been defeated by superior power and we must all make our way elsewhere as best we can.

Earlier history had its high points and humiliations. And it contained the trauma of the loss of the north. But it exhibited no discontinuities sufficiently marked as to create *the sense of periodization* present in the accounts we now have. The experience of the Exile accounts for the origin of this vivid sense of periodization.

The exiles were upheld from the beginning by the prophetic word of return, restoration, and glorification. The Exile itself must be explained as a part of the drama of Yahweh's dealings with Israel. Reflection on the contrast between Exile and kingdom period leads to reflection also on Deuteronomic and prophetic contrasts between kingdom and the preceding confederacy and wilderness periods. The P material may already have contained its universal scheme of periods at this time.[38] The past took shape as a set of periods, of various significance, welded together in a narrative leading from primeval times to the present. If for P the high point of the past is the establishment in Sinai of the full cult apparatus, for the David and Zion traditions it is the David-Solomon period, and for Hosea and the Deuteronomists the wilderness. But all had to be interpreted in light of the Exile. The Isaiah tradition saw the crux of Israelite history as the failure of Judah, under Assyrian threat, to trust wholly Yahweh for deliverance. The reforms of Hezekiah only delayed the falling of judgment.[39] II Kings 21 and Jeremiah 15 make decisive the reign of Manasseh, on account of which an irrevocable doom is pronounced.[40] These different periods and turning points organized the entire past in light of the judgment that had now fallen and been accepted.

38 O. Plöger *Theocracy and Eschatology* (Oxford 1968; from 2nd German edn 1962) 36–7 argues that this comprehensive scheme is only formal: that P really narrows to Israel what remains true for all men. He depends heavily on the assertion that P's historical work stops prior to the Israelite entry into Palestine. Plöger is concerned to contrast a later 'theocracy' in the restoration period with a dynamic eschatology derived from other sources. But this construction presupposes too easily the monolithic character of the restoration, as well as identity between earlier program and post-exilic reality. I shall argue that neither of these views can be held.

39 The text of II Kings 20, in which this is spelled out, is reproduced in the present Isaiah 38–9.

40 The Chronicler alone offers evidence of a repentance of Manasseh, induced by an otherwise unknown Babylonian captivity undergone by this most evil of all kings. See II Chron 33:10–17. Perhaps the Chronicler seeks to account in this way for the prolongation of the kingdom for 100 years after the pollutions introduced by this monarch, as well as for his long reign among a people for whom 'length of days' was a sign of divine favour.

But the Exile in turn was seen – as break, expiation, or preparation – to open the way to the climax of the drama, which will follow the Exile.[41] History has now been organized, on the basis of this periodization, into a single dramatic whole. Jerusalem will be the centre of mankind's attention; Yahweh will be acknowledged everywhere. This new age will not annul the past: the ten lost tribes are to be restored in some fashion. And those most concerned to set Yahweh's action and thus Israel's significance on the widest stage could contemplate opening the holy community to gentiles. The last age thus answers finally the fall of all men recounted in Genesis, where no solution is found. God will now vindicate all his actions throughout the course of the drama.

If this characterization of the emphases of the period[42] is valid, we have no need to seek the fundamental elements of millennialism in 'foreign influences' or resort to labels such as 'syncretism.' Millennialism's concerns are precisely these emphases first ordered into coherence in the Exile. *The thought and anticipations of the Exile are fundamental to millennialism*. Yet the thought of the Exile does not, by itself, give rise to millennialism. In the events of the 'restoration' we will find the conditions that result in millennial movements and create the apocalyptic form which became their literary vehicle.

---

41 The self-vindication of God in a public manner certainly can be seen as opposed to the desire for communal vindication: 'O daughter of Babylon, you devastator! Happy shall be he who requites you with what you have done to us! Happy shall be he who takes your little ones and dashes them against the rock!' (Ps 137:8–9), a wish which may use Babylon and the Exile as a coded reference to some later situation. But this desire for communal vindication need not be seen as opposed to Yahweh's self-vindication. If this latter is to be truly historical, how is it to be exhibited except in requitals of the sort history normally affords? Such passages as that in Psalm 137 are often explained away as understandable but unfortunate lapses from the level of ethical understanding in the 'high prophetic faith.' But if the people of Yahweh look for *his* self-vindication, should they not rejoice when it occurs? We should not neglect, of course, to see here a mixture of motives. The simple desire for revenge happily coincides with satisfaction at the prospect of requital in larger redemptive-historical terms. A contrary view is found in Ps 115:1–2: 'Not to us, O Yahweh, not to us, but to your name give glory, for the sake of your steadfast love and your faithfulness. Why should the nations say, "Where is their God?"'

42 A brief chronology of the period of the Exile:

609   Death of Josiah
597   First deportation of Judah's élites
587   Destruction of Jerusalem; second deportation
582   Third deportation, supplemented by refugees from Egypt
587–538 Nebuchadnezzar's rule in Bablyon, followed by that of Nabonidus, a religious innovator
538   Persians under Cyrus conquer Babylon. Sheshbazzar, under Persian patronage, leads a Jewish party to Jerusalem.
522   Zerubbabel leads second party, begins to build Second Temple.
445?   Nehemiah establishes Jerusalem area as Persian administrative unit.

3

The crisis of return

It is essential to our understanding of millennialism to realize that none of the exilic programs was achieved. What took place had its own dynamic and was not the filling in of any one blue-print or any group of them. It is highly misleading to speak of a Hebrew 'restoration' in Palestine at all. Even the word 'return' is misleading, for only certain groups of Jews returned, in 538, in 522, and later with Nehemiah and Ezra. Our sources for the period are strangely episodic and selective, in contrast to what had been preserved through the catastrophe of the Exile. They imply that all the real Jews had been deported to Babylon. The vast bulk of the population, which remained in Palestine, is dismissively ignored or treated as if it had perished in the period of exile, to be replaced by ill-defined groups of non-Jews.[1]

1 We do not know what happened to the Jewish population of Palestine after the deportations. The numbers given in Jer 52:28–30 for all 3 deportations total less than 5,000. The Jewish group that fled to Egypt in fear of reprisal, after the assassination of the post-destruction governor Gedaliah, must have been substantial; its members lived in three places and were the subject of extended and detailed prophecies of doom (Jer 42–5). Curses were also laid on those surrounding peoples who sought to take advantage of Judah's weakened condition after the Babylonian devastations. But it is not at all clear how much these events reduced the Jewish population of Judah. In the initial phase, after the destruction of Jerusalem (uninhabited, along with the 'cities of Judah,' according to Jer 44:2), there was a consolidation of presumably refugee Jews who had waited out the destruction in adjacent lands. These – or their chief people – are said to have gone into Egypt, however, in the post-Gedaliah migration.

 What happened to all the Jewish Palestinians – peasants and serfs, perhaps – who were not exiled? It is hard to believe that disease, emigration, and defection could have wiped out Yahwistic peoples from the area. And none of the exilic sources suggests this. They know enough of Palestinian affairs to denounce encroachment by opportunistic neighbours. Surely, had the remaining Yahwistic peoples gone over to pagan or syncretistic practices, these sources would have known it and denounced it vigorously. And we have the remarkable evidence, from the beginning of the period, of the Yahwistic pilgrims from the north. So far from such

The post-Exile canonical documents offer a triumphalist picture of the true Jews, led by a prince of the house of David, returning in triumph in 538 with a Persian subsidy and with the Temple furnishings. Then these returnees are ignored. The returnees of 522, led by the Davidic Zerubbabel, rebuild the Temple. They reject the overtures of 'the people of the land,' who are treated as superficially Judaized heathen descended from the gentile populations imported to Palestine by Assyrian kings of the eighth and seventh centuries. Zerubbabel, the object of exalted promises from the new prophets, disappears from history. The promises are transferred to the high priest, Joshua. One version reports the new Temple as being completed by an anonymous group of 'the elders of Israel.'

Then we have a great gap, extending at least to 445. The chronology of Ezra and Nehemiah is a vexed problem. In 445 either Nehemiah or Nehemiah and Ezra begin their efforts to rescue the returnee group from oppression by the assertedly non-Jewish surrounding culture.[2] Mass divorce of returnee descendants from non-returnees was enforced by the threat of being excluded. Associated with Ezra's return, ca 398, is the reception of a document called variously the book of the law, the book of Moses, or the book of the law of Moses.

The very idea of holy community propounded in the Exile has exacerbated the conflicts. The exiles could not have foreseen rival groups each claiming to be the authentic community, or part of it. A community is united, holding the same values, deferring to the same authorities, even though there may be strains and tensions – rival conceptions of what constitutes community and competing notions of where the boundaries lie cannot be admitted. Parties or sects can exist in a community only if there is an understanding of pluralistic community. Pluralism is most likely to occur and to be accepted in a long-established community and is

people being opportunists (the implication of the late Ezra 4:1–4), their very existence and their appearance at this time are a powerful testimony to the persistence of Yahwism under adversity; for apart from the brief revival under Josiah the north had been under alien occupation for 140 years.

2 What are these perils? Nehemiah, the Jewish royal official at the Persian court, asks 'concerning the Jews who survived, who had escaped exile, and concerning Jerusalem.' He receives the response that 'the survivors there in the province who escaped exile are in great trouble and shame. The wall of Jerusalem is broken down and its gates destroyed by fire.' Were we not so firmly anchored, by Nehemiah 1 and 2, in the middle of the long reign of Artaxerxes I, we should think we were in 587, more than 140 years earlier. The Chronicler would omit no detail of hostile action by the assertedly non-Jewish 'opponents.' But this presumably new catastrophe of ca 445 is not attributed to them. Was it in fact some Jewish involvement, voluntary or not, in the general uprising in the west against the empire ca 450? See Ackroyd *IBP* 173–5, 250–2. The late prophecy, Zechariah 12, speaks of famine, heavy taxes, and enslaving of children that would fit the circumstances of the period. But these burdens do not appear to have been imposed by Palestinian opponents. The habit of conducting biblical scholarship by commentaries on individual books has long retarded the raising of such questions.

most unlikely when survival depends on common definitions and unreserved commitments, when it is *holy* community that is at stake.

What emerges from the Chronicler's curious narrative – and his silences – is that the first returnee group, of 538, is treated as if it had disappeared without a trace. The indigenous population is assimilated to the ancient groups consigned, in Deuteronomy, to extermination at the hands of the conquering Israelites. Only blood-descent from returnees identifies true Jews. Others can join this group only by agreeing that their own heritage is heathen. Ritual and cultic purity now determine Jewishness. An enormous effort has been made to avoid those 'pollutions' viewed by the Chronicler and the Deuteronomists as responsible for the Exile. The events of the return resulted in a new version of community and in the attempt to impose it on a complex reality.

A number of exilic programs were achieved in truncated form at best. The Chronicler's loving detail about the Temple ritual provides us a glimpse of one program deeply satisfying to its practitioners. But this success had been achieved within a small community. Not even the 12 tribes of Ezekiel's vision, much less the nations, grouped themselves around Jerusalem and its Temple. So far from its very geography being transformed, Zion was a beleaguered provincial city in a land rent by intrigue and faction. No new exodus had taken place. A great many Jews in Babylon were content to wait, to observe, and to carry on a life of their own. In another hundred years, many from Judah would go to Alexandria, thrive, and remain.[3] Above all, the conviction that after the Exile God would bring about the triumphant conclusion of redemptive history remained unfulfilled. The Temple was not a house of prayer for all peoples, a light lifted up for the nations, but lay behind walls and institutions designed to protect it from people who may themselves have been Jews.

The sense of dramatic structure in history was imperilled by the ambiguity of these developments. But a new appreciation of dialectical development in history may also have come about. God has not lied; he has kept faith with us. Out of our previous defection he has brought new works, and he will continue to do so, out of weakness and ignominy. What he has promised he will bring about. Doubtless this sense was not prominent among those who supported the reforms of Ezra or among those for whom the great rituals formed an enveloping and self-justifying world. But few among the proponents of other schemes would have been satisfied. And, at least for some, the impossibility of truncated Judah fulfilling her role

3 The very existence of the Diaspora or Dispersion communities, both early and late, may have provided a degree of protection for dissident communities in Palestine, perhaps including conventicles in Jerusalem and Judah. So long as one large community existed outside Palestine which could never be controlled from Palestine, there could never be a universal triumph of those in power in Jerusalem.

meant that God himself would act directly in human affairs in an unprecedented fashion to bring about the climax and dénouement of human history. In the later crisis of the second century, those who so believed would take the initiative from the Ezraic authorities.

Elements from each of the major schemes played some role. But none was achieved in anything like its fullness. And in the so-called 'Samaritan separation,'[4] in perhaps the mid-fourth century BC, we can see considerable strains within the purified returnee community. The Samaritan Pentateuch, dating from this time, is substantially identical to the canonical Pentateuch. But there are evidences that the prophetic canon underwent an attempted closure at this time.[5] A number of late oracles now attached as tail-pieces to various canonical prophetic books testify both to the attempt at closure and to the difficulty of carrying it through. But why was it attempted? The Samaritan separation, so far from dealing with people of 'mixed blood,' had more to do with the returnee community itself. A declaration that prophecy had ceased would prevent dissident returnee groups from uttering authentic oracles against the establishment. This experiment by the authorities perhaps led to a withdrawal of defeated groups from Jerusalem and their joining forces with non-returnee Jewish groups. This hypothesis reinforces the general picture of a dominant group prepared to incur very considerable costs in order to maintain Ezra and Nehemiah's 'restoration.'

4 Samaritans (ie members of the later 'schismatic' group) are not simply to be identified as the opponents of the returnees, centred (as the Chronicler asserts) on Samaria, the administrative province covering most of Palestine under the imperial régimes. The Chronicler assumes the heathenization of the whole of Palestine during the Exile. And for him the whole of the north – his Samaria – had been heathen, or at most syncretistically half-Jewish, for centuries. Josephus and I and II Maccabees follow this assertion and are responsive to later political and religious quarrels between the Samaritan and Judean communities. These authors equate the religious group the Samaritans with the alleged heathenism and syncretism of the north. But the Elephantine papyri show the early Jewish military colonists in Egypt recognizing the Jewish religious authority of the Samarian governor. See J.D. Purvis *The Samaritan Pentateuch and the Origin of the Samaritan Sect* (Cambridge, Mass, 1968); R.J. Coggins *Samaritans and Jews: The Origins of Samaritanism Reconsidered* (Oxford 1975); and M. Smith *Palestinian Parties and Politics that Shaped the Old Testament* (London 1971).

5 The very existence of the book of Moses/of the Law/of the law of Moses as an objective and normative authority in the returnee-descended community would itself operate to discourage new prophetic activity. What would happen if Yahweh's new word could not be reconciled with the fixed 'Law'? An authoritative book calls for an authoritative body of men to interpret it. Moses is priest, prophet, and civic authority. In the returnee community, 'religious' dissent can now be treated as subversion. The difficulties in lodging sole authority in this canon led to the later theory of the 70 books of *oral* law passed down from Moses to the present generations of sages. But in the fourth century the status of the prophetic materials posed a problem that could only be compounded if prophecy were allowed to continue. But how could so venerable and central an activity be ended?

After the collapse of the Persian empire in the late fourth century, the Jerusalem-centred group failed its own test. In the Macedonian-Egyptian empire of the Ptolemies for more than a century, the Jerusalem group became significantly Hellenized. Palestine changed hands in 198 BC[6] and became subject to the Macedonian-Syrian empire of the Seleucids. At first cultural autonomy was granted by Antiochus III, who wished well-disposed populations along his invasion route to Egypt. But under Antiochus IV, élite Jewish groups in Jerusalem co-operated in enforced Hellenization. In this crisis of internal and external Hellenization long-submerged exilic programs could be expected to resurface and make their claims. It is at this point that the book of Daniel appeared as the manifesto of what must hereafter be called millennialism.

6 A brief chronology of relevant events:

323	Alexander dies after establishing an empire over most of the known world.
323–300	His generals establish their rule over its portions.
323–285	Ptolemy (I) Soter rules in Egypt.
300	Palestine passes to Ptolemaic control; many Jews emigrate or are transported to Alexandria.
285–246	Ptolemy (II) Philadelphus. Cordial relations with Jerusalem leaders
246–203	Ptolemies III and IV. Origins of Septuagint, Greek-language version of Hebrew scriptures; translation finished ca 150 in Alexandria
200–198	Palestine conquered by Seleucid Greeks of Syria (Antiochus III, 223–187)
198	First Roman intervention, defeating Seleucids at Magnesia
187–175	Seleucus IV. Ben Sira written
175–163	Antiochus IV Ephiphanes. Acute phase of Hellenization in Palestine
169–168	Antiochus, victor in Egypt, is baulked by Romans.
168–167	Degradation of Temple by Hellenizers and Seleucids, ending with its forcible desecration
168–164	Attempted suppression of Jewish cult and way of life
166	Beginning of revolt against Seleucids and Jewish Hellenizers. Judas leader 166–160
164	Temple rededicated. Book of Daniel published. Judas seeks alliance with Rome.
160–143	Jonathan leader, renews Roman alliance, seeks Spartan alliance.
142–134	Simon leader. Complete independence, renewal of Roman alliance. Supreme religious, military, and civil authority made hereditary in Hasmonean family.
134–104	John Hyrcanus. Extension of kingdom to Galilee and Idumaea, annexed by war, with inhabitants forcibly Judaized. Traditional period of the rise of parties in Judaism
104–103	Aristobulus I
103–76	Alexander Jannaeus, younger brother of Aristobulus I, marries his widow, Salome. Tension with Pharisees. Revolt against him, 94–86. Military defeats by Nabataeans in the south. Pharisees seek aid from Romans.
76–67	Salome reigns, assisted by leading Pharisees, who rule public life. Son Hyrcanus is high priest.
67	Hyrcanus, briefly king, is forced to cede office to his younger brother Aristobulus II.
67–63	Aristobulus II; civil war as Antipater and Nabataeans support Hyrcanus.
65	Both sides appeal to Romans, now occupying Syria. Pharisees want restoration of old pre-Hasmonean high priestly house.
63	Romans, after mediating for two years, occupy Jerusalem.

4

Daniel: the first apocalyptic

In order to identify millennialism as it takes its definitive form, we cannot interpret Daniel in light of the range of other documents later denominated as apocalyptic. How are the characteristics of that genre established in the first place? Unless one establishes its normative characteristics through observation of what it attempts to do over time, one must fall back on a pre-understanding of millennialism drawn from some dogmatic or extraneously derived principle. But Daniel stands at the start of the process, precipitating old themes and programs into a new framework for declaring the issues of the present and the imminent climax of the age. It is therefore important to ask what Daniel assumes, what it upholds, what it attacks, and what it asserts as new. It is in the answers to these questions that we shall find the elements characteristic of millennialism at the start of its public career as a movement and as an interpretation of history. Daniel is the one major piece of apocalyptic so well entrenched in the popular canon that it could not be dislodged when the formal canon was fixed at the end of the first century AD. It controls the content of Christian millennialism, including its major document, the Revelation. By examining Daniel we place ourselves in a position to identify the central emphases of millennialism both in the late classical period and in its later career in the West.

Antiochus IV attempted further to unify his peoples by enlisting élites and even larger populations in Greek local commonwealths, so that Greek cultural values would absorb all others. As a world culture, this Hellenism could legitimately claim to have superseded all merely superstitious, barbarous, or parochial cultures. In his Judean province, Antiochus wanted also to safeguard his land-bridge to an Egypt ready at last to fall to the Seleucids. Antiochus' final solution offered some Jews the opportunity, under governmental protection and sponsorship, to move fully into world culture. Other Jews saw this campaign as the ultimate and mortal threat to their existence. But the major institutions of their society, at the time of Daniel's composition, are in the hands of Hellenizers.[1] A military revolt is in progress, aided by some sections of a body known as 'the pious.'

Jewish response is conditioned by the renewed legitimacy of old programmes and by the possibility of new ones. Military revolt itself could carry a number of schemes, from mere restoration of the status quo, to a new sort of nationalism, to some new and more comprehensive piety. But not all programs required reliance on the guerrilla movement; and not all groups believed that God would long delay the end-time. In this period of crisis and fluidity, then, what does Daniel assume, uphold, attack, and assert?

Daniel assumes that Yahweh, the God of Israel, is potent in an alien and threatening environment. With Deutero-Isaiah, it takes him to be the god above all gods, the creator and governor of the world. It upholds the role of Israel as God's elect. With a lengthy tradition, it holds to the coming of the day of Yahweh. Like Deutero-Isaiah, it takes the average world empire as a phenomenon of nature: savage, uncontrollable, but not especially devilish for all that.[2] In its expression of horror at the defilement of the Temple, Daniel identifies itself, though hardly exclusively, with the Zion tradition and the P material.

The situation of 175–165 BC makes it imperative to consider the role of Israel among the nations, last dealt with extensively or with penetration in the Exile. Daniel adopts and expands upon the theme of Deutero- and Trito-Isaiah that the nations shall look to Israel for, at the very least, an intercessory role between themselves and God. This element is placed in the future in the prophetic material. But Daniel 1–6 shows it[3] at work in the relations between great monarchs

---

1 See Goldstein *I Maccabees* (Garden City, NY, 1976); his survey of the period presents a motivation for Antiochus' program that differs somewhat from mine.

2 See the visions of ch 2 and 7, in which the four world empires – Babylonian, 'Median,' Persian, and Greek – are first, in ch 2, components of an enormous idol and then, in ch 7, great predatory beasts. The desire of the empires for universal dominion is noted however (in ch 2): the great idol fills the earth.

3 The stories in ch 1–6 may have had histories of their own before being gathered together and put in their present context. The identification of the Daniel figure of these stories is controverted; but certainly no prominent Exile figure of that name is known in the contemporary sources or in the Chronicler's work. See the comments of Russell *MMJA* 48–50. These stories present the Babylonians, and to a lesser extent the Persians, as relatively benign: erratic, powerful barbarians, rather than dangerous seducers. The Babylonian astrological priesthood, seen here in terms of the later Persian magi, is not treated as an abomination. These attitudes argue for an early origin for the stories. But the compiler or author(s) had a quite inadequate grasp of the chronology of the period in which the stories are set – the earliest deportations of Nebuchadnezzar down to the reign of the third Persian king, Darius I (522–486). This might suggest a rather later origin.

and their Jewish captives. The book is silent on the subject of ethnic exclusiveness; but it upholds the practices which distinguish Jews from other peoples. That these practices had hardly existed in the Exile – the asserted setting of the book – does not prevent Daniel from reading back the dietary regulations, here standing for the whole complex, into the Exile.

What does Daniel assert in its own right? It distinguishes the latest of the world empires, that of the Macedonian Greeks, from its predecessors in a peculiar way. In a sense, all four empires[4] are one thing, as the vision of the great image or idol in chapter 2 makes clear. In chapter 7, however, the first three empire-beasts do only what one may expect of great predators. The fourth is of a different sort, its ferocity going beyond the requirements of predation or the bounds of nature. The changes that go on within it produce the 'little horn' with 'eyes like the eyes of a man' and a 'mouth speaking great things.'

Fundamental to Daniel's whole conception is the distinctive character of the *present* confrontation: 'He shall be different from the former ones' (7:24). The mouth speaking great things is Antiochus Epiphanes: God Manifest, whose coins portrayed Zeus with the features of Antiochus himself.[5] The campaign of Antiochus is seen as making plain the inner, specially anti-God reality of the Greek imperium.[6] The older empires had been content with imperium. This one requires acknowledgement that its values – across the full range of existence – are supreme; and it sought to conform all men to these values. So far from being an aberration ('Epimanes,' his detractors called him: the madman), Antiochus was indeed Hellenization made manifest.[7] Despite the differences between this and previous empires, all are nonetheless parts of the same idol (ch 2). The author connects that narrative – ending in the Babylonian king's humble gratitude to Daniel for his explanation – with the king's raising of a great image of gold, which all men are required to worship on pain of death. Both this juxtaposition and the explicit description of the first, 'of exceeding brightness,' draw the two images together. It is in the nature of worldly empire to assert itself against God; only now, in Antiochus, is the end of this process in view: a naked attempt to substitute pride and power for the service of God's redemptive history.[8]

4 Insistence on the existence of the 'Median' empire is peculiar and, as given, is unhistorical, though an independent Median power had existed before the fall of Babylonia.

5 For reproductions, see Russell *JAH* 64–5, or B.W. Anderson *The Living World of the Old Testament* 3rd edn (London 1967) 574.

6 The Ptolomies in Egypt, however, remain uncharacterized at all in Daniel, although Hellenization undoubtedly began in Palestine during their rule.

7 This point is taken up further below, 46–7.

8 It is this dynamic sense of history, then, which is exhibited by Daniel and not, as many assert without foundation, an abandonment of history. D.N. Freedman 'The Flowering of Apocalyptic' in R. Funk ed *Apocalypticism* (New York 1969) 169 argues that a determinism of history

Also differentiating the work of the little horn from the earlier empires is the seductiveness of Antiochus' campaign. The little horn is 'speaking great things' (7:8, 11, 20). Truth is cast down, and, in its place, 'the horn acted and prospered' (8:12). By his cunning he shall make deceit prosper under his hand (8:24). He makes covenant with many (8:27), seducing them with flattery (11:33). This flattery propagates itself, so that some of the seduced are able to worm their way into the ranks of the resistance, so that 'some of those who are wise shall fall' (11:34–5).[9] Here, too, the emphasis is on the ultimate nature of the test and, so, of God's answering action.

Daniel asserts that the outcome of this conflict is not in doubt (8:25, 11:45; 12:1). There had been and were Jews who denied this, or who defected to the winning side. But the writer of Daniel was only the latest in believing that Yahweh's rule was not to be overturned. His own contribution was his mode of putting it: the outcome of the struggle is already known and declared and may be written down now (in the Exile, as we are meant to believe), to be disclosed to doubters when the crisis is upon you, several hundred years from now. Nothing could be better calculated to state as strongly as possible the assured outcome of the great struggle of 175–165.[10] It makes vivid and clear the belief that, God being

here operates 'at the expense of human freedom.' But this is to exalt uncritically a notion of history as the realm of 'freedom,' without asking what freedom, in the biblical context, is for. If history is the arena of free action, then to be real history and not a mere name for indeterminacy, the consequences of historical action must be real. The actions both of God and of men in rebellion against him must be allowed to have real consequences, including the narrowing of the range of human choice, ultimately to the simple but fateful one of 'God or Antiochus.'

9 This winnowing of *individuals* in an ultimate test is answered also by the individual resurrection, to be dealt with below.

10 The issues in pseudonymity are complex. Some scholars ignore them as unimportant. Others are concerned with inspiration or authority of the Bible or with the moral authority of the pseudonymous document when its author apparently seeks to give his work the (false) authority of antiquity and authorship by a great man. It could be argued, of course, that the very reverence for ancient foundations so pronounced in the post-Exile community is itself the 'cause' of the attribution of new documents to men of antiquity. And we have the troubled state of all post-Pentateuch biblical revisions to remind us that heroic measures were often adopted to deal with the recalcitrance of reality. This explanation does not respond to the concerns of those who believe that the text cannot mislead its readers and still be as authoritative as they have supposed. (These people are not the same as those whose view of the Bible precludes its containing any inaccuracy whatever.)

Russell suggests that the real author adopted an ancient name 'not in an attempt to deceive, but rather as spokesman of a long line of tradition which he believes he has received from ancient times' (JAH 219–20). This answer does not quite meet the difficulty. Either the writer does mean to employ another's dignity or is content that his readers make the natural mistake. Russell (MMJA 127–9) takes up Wheeler Robinson's suggestion about a Hebrew notion of 'corporate personality,' in an effort to mitigate his own admission that in the main these writings do

who he is, a final and direct challenge to him (8:23–5) can have only one outcome: the fulfilment of his promises of self-vindication through his holy community. The scale of that divine action has been enlarged because the author of Daniel sees that the scale and comprehensiveness of the challenge to God have also been enlarged to encompass the world.

It follows that the chances of success of the holy community are not dependent on statecraft or might, but upon steadfastness. For a document published in the midst of a great popular uprising, Daniel is remarkably guarded in its statements about the revolutionary leadership. So far from being celebrated, it is deprecated, or admitted only grudgingly to have had a hand in God's deliverance of the people. This reticence is not merely an effect of the supposed prophecy of chapters 7–12 being cast in appropriately general terms. The 'king of the north' is described in detail as to both his actions and his character (11:21–45). But the new Jewish leadership is hardly mentioned at all; it is treated with the same reserve (11:32–5) as the pre-revolutionary leadership (11:22, 30).

The Balkan politics of the later period of Hellenization reproduced conditions similar to those experienced in Israel before the Exile, when the leadership of Judah attempted to play on its location between rival powers. This had always been denounced (Is 20:4–6; 30:1–5; Jer 37:5–10; 2:16–19, 36–7). There was apparently reason to link the intrigues of the high priestly clan with the exhilarations of military victory in the revolt. In both cases, human means of a worldly sort were being relied upon in a context where dependence on them by the people of God could only mislead people about the nature of the crisis. It is precisely when 'the shattering of the power of the holy people comes to an end' that the victory will be given by God's unprecedented direct action, not by the military expertise of God's people. Hence the euphoria of victory in the Maccabean revolt is dangerous because it obscures the unique character of these last events of the present world-order, and because it thus leaves men unprepared for its replacement by the final kingdom of God.

This concern of Daniel, wholly consistent with the rest of the book and with its prophetic antecedents, helps us to date the book. Because the 'prophecies' of

---

intend 'to be received as *bona fide* disclosures to an ancient seer.' H.H. Rowley reminds us, in his *Relevance of Apocalyptic* rev edn (London 1963), that the first part of Daniel is actually anonymous. It is the second part that attributes its visions to the central *figure* of the first part. Only when Danielic authorship of the whole was assumed did the question of pseudonymity arise, perhaps falsely. This perhaps awkward suggestion opens the way for pseudonymity to have arisen for one reason, or by mistake, and to have been continued or become a convention 'artificial only when it was woodenly copied by imitators' (Rowley *Relevance* 41). Rowley notes that the author of Daniel is not borrowing the name of an ancient worthy, since, outside this very text, no such sixth-century personage is known.

chapter 11 are given in such circumstantial detail, it is possible to see where they go wrong, at what year in the foretelling they become attempts at real prediction. This change occurs after the triumphant rededication of the Temple but before the death of Antiochus, whose last movements and death are given wrongly. Had Daniel been concerned simply to encourage the resistance, had his object been to raise war-time public morale, the book would have been better issued earlier. Had its object been a celebration of victory, it would not have taken the cautious line it did about the revolutionary leadership. Putting together the date and the reserve displayed toward the epic victory, we see that a distinctive program is staked out in the immediate post-victory period. As we know, the subsequent period was marked by Balkanization of Syrian-Palestinian relations and by a deterioration of relations between the new dynasty and the party of the pious.

What does Daniel attack? His special concerns are assimilation to the practices of the nations, the special characteristics of the Hellenistic imperium, the defection of many Jews, and the old notion that correct cultic behaviour will save the nation now. These elements are very closely related and lead directly to his distinctive doctrine of the selective and individual resurrection, taken up in the next section.

Daniel ignores the blood purity issue. We do not know how wide was his definition of Israel; but those who constitute Israel are to shun pagan practice. His anecdotal stories in chapters 1–6 provide a basis for militant resistance in the crisis of 175–165. The program of Ezra had already provided devices to fence off Judah from the surrounding cultures, but had failed to prevent Hellenism even in the classes longest habituated to Ezraic discipline; and these classes apparently had no capacity to mount a counter-attack against Antiochus' program.

The would-be divinity of Antiochus is contrasted to the figure of the 'son of man' introduced by Daniel, which stands for the holy ones who remain steadfast.[11] Despite their status as the new world rulers, the holy ones do not take this status as a warrant for claiming divinity. It is finally a manly task, as in the Genesis prologue, to exercise lordship of the world, under God.

The Hellenistic kingdoms have long been noted as marking a late resurgence of the ancient notion of sacral kingship. But these kingdoms are sudden, arbitrary, artificial creations, erected out of heterogeneous materials and peoples. That their originators succeeded in this task was taken as proof of their divinity: they had made something quite new. But their divinity was also necessary; it required an

11 This figure is personalized when he is introduced (7:13–14). But in the explanation of the vision (7:15–27) it is clear that this figure represents the rule of the holy ones who inherit world rule after the judgment is rendered against Antiochus (7:26).

immense exercise of power to produce and maintain these creations. Power on this scale could not be justified in terms drawn from previous communities or even from the older despotisms.

The Babylonian king may have been Marduk's son. But he was thereby circumscribed by the circumstances and the 'history' of Marduk. The Hellenistic god-king is a deity in his own right. The identification with Zeus or some other god is quite weak; Zeus was already a faded or denatured god in his homeland – how much more in Syria where he could only be a formal deity. Thus little check was provided to the unfettered exercise of deity by the god-king. His power was god-like, but driven to be so by the magnitude of the tasks he had set himself. However, he oversteps the bounds and comes up against Yahweh, whose particularity will not yield to Antiochus' universal imperium.

The gift of Greek culture apparently justifies the means adopted by Antiochus. But the universal claim of both Antiochus and of his culture can leave no place for Yahweh and for redemptive history. If Yahweh and his people are allowed exemption, then the claim of Antiochus' Hellenism to be a universal good refutes itself. But it cannot do this; for only the greatest universal good can justify the use of power on the scale it was exercised by the Hellenistic kings.[12]

Daniel does not expect all his Jewish contemporaries to resist. In the models for resistance in chapters 1–6, it is not stated that Jews as a body did resist. On the contrary, in the case of the golden statue, 'all the peoples, nations and languages fell down and worshipped' (3:7).[13] It is the three companions of Daniel who are singled out. In the food seduction only these among the Jewish recruits apparently resisted (1:8–19).

Nothing is said in these chapters about those who assimilate or comply with blasphemous requirements out of fear. In 8:11–12, a textually obscure section, it may be suggested, however, that Israel's transgressions are responsible for the little horn's desecration of the Temple. Daniel's prayer of intercession follows; formally set in the Exile and made on behalf of the sins that occasioned the ruin of the first Temple, this prayer, by its position in the book and by the whole strategy of the book, acknowledges Israel's sins as responsible for the desolations of Antiochus. In 11:14 we learn that, prior to the reign of the little horn, 'men of violence of your own people shall lift themselves up in order to fulfill the vision,'

12 This point builds upon but also expands the notion of dynamic history noted above (15, 32, 37 ff). Strongly implied here is a dialectical understanding of history. The inner logic of Antiochus' effort is grasped here, as well as the counterposed requirement of God's people to be most faithful precisely when a normal historical calculus would yield no reason for doing so. This dialectical understanding is worked out more openly in ch 13 of Revelation.

13 So in the related story of ch 6 it is not Jews as a body who resist the blasphemous ordinance of the Persian king, but Daniel only.

that is, as part of the general defection from Yahweh, 'but they shall fail.' When Antiochus returns from his second Egyptian venture, he gives 'heed to those who forsake the holy covenant' (11:30). 'He shall seduce with flattery those who violate the covenant' after the desecration; he offers inducements to abjure Yahwism completely (32). Defectors are given rulership over the now-divided land (39). He makes 'a strong covenant with many' (9:27). In the resurrection, however, some who awake do so to 'shame and everlasting contempt' (12:2).

Because of the specific character of Antiochus' program and of Israel's past sins ritual action will not guarantee immunity or safety. The first Isaiah had suggested that, even in extremity, faithful observance would lead God to defend Jerusalem himself. But Daniel sees a qualitative distinction between the old empires and the new phenomenon. Antiochus arises 'when the transgressions shall have reached their full measure' (8:23), when the issue is clear between the would-be deity and Yahweh. Antiochus dares even to 'rise up against the prince of princes' (8:25). His kingdom 'grew great, even up to the host of heaven; and some of the host of the stars it cast down to the ground, and trampled upon them' (8:10). A mere *deliverance* from this power, or its mere replacement by another empire, does not answer to the ultimate challenge posed by Antiochus' Hellenism. Daniel is therefore unable to countenance a mere escape by a righteous remnant from the little horn's ravages. The Seleucid challenge is so fundamental that it must be met by a unique act of God himself: 'By no human hand he shall be broken' (8:25).

This penetration by Daniel into what is at stake in the conflict leads to his other principal contribution to millennialism, the notion of personal or individual *resurrection* (12:1–3). A similar idea is found in Isaiah in a section (ch 24–7) often referred to as apocalyptic[14] and certainly not well lodged where it is now found. In 25:8, the reference is general: 'He will swallow up death forever.' But in 26:19 it appears to be more specific: 'Thy dead shall live, their bodies shall rise. O dwellers in the dust, awake and sing for joy.' It is not clear, however, that this awakening refers to a resurrection at the climax of God's self-vindication at the end of the present world order or a witnessing of some particular deliverance. And it is not clear that all parts of the complex of chapters 24–7 are to be received as a connected narrative. Yet, at the end of chapter 26, we are probably entitled to see at least the intention of 26:16–19 in the admonition for God's people to hide themselves till 'the wrath is past.' God is coming out of his place 'to punish the inhabi-

---

14 See the comment of Ackroyd (*ER* 221) on this passage where he remarks on the problem of labelling this section as apocalyptic and suggests that 'the problem of the literary definition of the term "apocalyptic" urgently needs attention.' But ch 24–7 are certainly very late – post-Ezra.

tants of the earth for their iniquity; and the earth will disclose the blood shed upon her, and will no more cover her slain' (26:20–1). What rises here is apparently the traditional 'shade,' the rather insubstantial remnant[15] which after death rests – heretofore forever – in Sheol, a place for such entities.

In Daniel's brief passage, however, the notion of shade is replaced by the expression 'those who sleep in the dust'; and it is clear that they are raised in their full humanity in order to receive what they deserve.[16] Though Daniel does not originate the notion of resurrection, we can see why it must be employed here and must take a new concreteness. The resurrection is individualized; it is selective; and it is disjunctive: judgment is inherent in the selection and in the fates of those so raised.[17] Here Daniel speaks in the context of party dispute, as well as in that of resistance to genocide. Now the unsung, persecuted individual, whose only witness is God, is to be vindicated personally and to share in God's self-vindication.[18]

Resurrection signals the transformation of the world-order. With the blasphemy of Antiochus, the present world order reaches its appointed climax. The rebellion of man as a whole, described in different ways in the Genesis prologue, has now unfolded its internal logic to the extreme. When it is ended by the decisive act of Yahweh, the world of history is not ended, however; it is not collapsed into some eternity. The resurrected are raised to historical life, in which they suffered before or were betrayed before, and where now they are to reign or be held in everlasting contempt. If God's self-vindication has anything to do with the resurrection, that self-vindication must take place where his justice was attacked and his redemptive history denied. The resurrection is a centre-piece of the evidence that the present world-order has done its worst and yet been over-

15 See Eccl 9:5.
16 For a full review of the ideas of survival of the person or shade and the resurrection, see Russell *MMJA* 353–79.
17 In neither the older nor Daniel's ideas is there the notion of the soul, or the concepts of eternity or a heavenly plane of existence more real or better than the historical world. Despite the presence of all these in later Judaism and Christianity, where they continue to be resisted, it is a gross and misleading anachronism to read them into Daniel. A soul, being an undying part of the eternal world, needs no resurrection. In the world in which soul, eternity, and heaven are at home, no biblical project of historical redemption makes much sense – hence the widespread charge against Jews and early Christians that they were atheists. They had no place for the whole complex of ideas which supported the classical world's concept of 'divinity.' Yahweh is not divine, one of a class of entities with thus-and-such characteristics; he is unique. Thus, too, there can be no soul to partake of the substance of the world of divinity. Resurrection is an act of grace. Immortality is inherent in the characteristics of the soul.
18 We do not know the extent to which the rise of the notion of individual resurrection, in its form in Daniel, is dependent upon the poisoning of the community by intrigue, persecution, and betrayal. In the pre-Exile documents it had been thought sufficient for a man to leave a 'name' in the ongoing community through his own deeds and through his progeny.

come. Its gods can kill. Yahweh can make alive. In the end, kingdoms which clothe themselves in divinity have been destroyed and have been replaced by the dominion of the saints whose 'kingdom shall be an everlasting kingdom' (7:27).[19]

This kingdom is not, in these fragments from Daniel 7 and 12, a redeemed and transformed world in the fashion of Revelation, chapters 21–2. In the world of Daniel 7 and 12 the holy ones of the most high enforce their rule over the areas formerly dominated by the empires, the beasts. Daniel does not say that all the dead are raised, only an indeterminate 'many who sleep.' And we should not necessarily read these as the same as those in 'Your people shall be delivered, every one whose name shall be found written in the book' (12:1). We appear to have a sequence: the intervention which ends the present world order of empires and the triumphant survival, through these rigours, of those whose names are in the book; and the subsequent resurrection of 'many' – some to join the saints of the most high in their rule, and some to suffer forever. Presumably both groups of those resurrected are Jews, rewarded for their roles in the great struggle of 175–165 and perhaps earlier as well. Since both groups are going to live forever, presumably the survivors, whose names are in the book,[20] are to live forever as well. God is acknowledged to be God; his saints rule irresistibly; the old order has done its worst and been vanquished. Daniel does not go beyond this to draw in the

19 We could see the universal dominion of the saints, or of God, as a fantasy of omnipotence, a 'compensatory' dream of the weak. However, not all Jews were subject to 'fantasies of omnipotence.' Millennialism is only one response to the threat of 175–165. The initial military resistance shows, in its tactics, a rational if desperate attempt to conduct effective guerrilla warfare. The account in Daniel takes an arms-length attitude toward all this. Submerged and disenfranchised groups, however their concerns emerge in the subsequent Hasmonean period, often had more urgent tasks to perform, prior to the crisis and during it, than to exercise their imaginations with 'fantasies of omnipotence.'

20 Properly the deeds recorded in the book, and so also the verdicts rendered upon their evidence, deal only with those alive at the time of the end of this world-order. It is not stated directly in Daniel that the testimony of this book is the basis of the rewards and punishments of the apparently selective resurrection. Certainly later Jews and Christians made such a connection, however. See the rabbinic saying in Pirke Aboth 2:1: 'Consider three things and you will not fall into the hands of transgression: know what is above – a seeing eye and a hearing ear and all your deeds written in a book,' and that of R. Akiba in Aboth 3:17 in which the activity of judgment is likened to the collection of debts based on a shopkeeper's account books. On the basis of this judgment, 'all is made ready for the banquet.' In the New Testament, Rev 20:12 shows us the judgment proceeding as the 'books were opened ... And the dead were judged according to what was written in the books.' In all these cases, from Daniel to the rabbis, the device of the book reinforces the idea of individual resurrection. Later millennialism developed the notion of the book in order to display the fixed character of history: it is all written down from of old. But Daniel's typology of Babylon-Antiochus, along with his clear sense of the reality of historical development – a conviction that fades later – prevents this kind of generalization.

characteristics of the new world order, perhaps because there already existed a good deal of descriptive material on the new Zion. Daniel's chosen task was to define issues in the present, not to issue a general exhortation about the future. The facts of the triumph and the resurrection provide adequate grounding for effort in the present. This restraint contrasts Daniel's interests with those of other documents that adopt the literary form of apocalyptic.

Considering what was available to him to draw upon, Daniel is cautious in his handling of angelic beings and numerological speculation, neither of which is necessary to his task. Here too he contrasts with many later works of apocalyptic. Relatively recent biblical materials, in the Isaiah prologue and in Ezekiel, offered visual renderings of 'powers' or servants of God.[21] Daniel does take the Isaiah prologue's God sitting on his throne; but Daniel's angels are workaday messengers of God. No words are spent on describing them; and in this Daniel follows the reticent policy of the archaic material.[22] His angelic explainers do seem, however, to follow the model of the angelic conductor of Ezekiel 40–8 who takes the seer through the landscape and architecture of the new holy land; and he makes use of the notion that particular angels have charge over specific nations.[23] The Babylonian number systems as keys to the cosmos have had a pervasive influence. And the P materials had been organized with some reference to mathematics. But in these writings, as in Daniel, the purpose is not to discern or argue for a historical determinism. Daniel's use of numbers is modest and is concentrated upon the scheme of day–year equivalences in the Maccabean period, except in 9:24–7, where post-Exile history is surveyed in the framework of 'weeks of years.' The later efflorescence of numerological interest for its own sake plays no role in Daniel.

21 The pallid or androgynous creatures of Western painting have very little to do with the terrible potency of these figures. Also see the testimony of Samson's mother, for whom the aspect of the angel was 'very terrible' (Judges 13:2–6).

22 See Gen 16:7–10; 18:1–2; 19:1–3; 28:12; and 32:24–30. The angelic messenger of Yahweh is well embedded in the tradition. No doubt its later formulation owed something to Persian angelology.

23 The Alexandrian Septuagint version of Deut 32:8 gives us this tradition. The 'watchers' who decree and then oversee the destruction of the great tree of Daniel 4 are only mentioned in Nebuchadnezzar's 'own words' in 4:13, 17. But in Daniel 10, we see the full picture of angelic princes of nations, who may apparently even contest with one another. We seem to have returned here to the Babylonian idea that events on earth reflect the politics of heaven. The princes of Daniel 10 may occasion the later notion of hierarchies of angels. The others remain unnamed, providing the heavenly court with its 'glory,' its music, and so forth. But in Daniel the named angels are princes of nations, not of angels. On Deut 32:8–9, see Russell *MMJA* 248 ff. Deut 4:19 may supply another relatively early instance of princes of nations, if the phrase 'host of heaven' refers to the heavenly court and if the word rendered 'allotted' has its root sense of 'divided among.' See Russell *MMJA* 236.

The doctrines of cosmic rebellion and of a cosmic opponent of God were also available to Daniel from Persian sources and perhaps from a closer background also drawn on by the authors of I Enoch. But Daniel is both very conservative and very radical here. He will not resort to a heavenly plane of conflict; his heavenly court is not really a place at all. It is the fact that Yahweh is directly challenged by the present organized order, through Antiochus, which makes the conflict all-embracing or 'cosmic.' The issues are settled where the challenge is made. Satan also remains unused by Daniel, although the word and the idea of a powerful 'accuser' before God were certainly well known by this period.[24] The later idea of Satan – as leader of a primordial revolt, adversary of God, prince of demons, and the malevolent active force behind historical opposition to God – is not to be read into Daniel at all, though by New Testament times it is common enough to be taken for granted.

The book of Daniel presents us with the characteristic central themes of Hebrew reflection, sharpened when the Ezraic program proved unable to repel the attractions of Hellenism. Daniel offers a comprehensive vision in which history is set on a new footing. Previous apocalyptic – anonymous or pseudonymous – had been appended to or inserted within the work of canonical prophets. Set in such a context it is difficult to analyse or to set in developmental order. But Daniel stands on its own,[25] clearly identifiable and set securely in a known historical context. It thus stands as the point of departure for subsequent millennialism. It can be used as a standard for later developments because it is the one piece of apocalyptic that achieved canonical status; further, it, rather than later developments of apocalyptic, is the principal inspiration for Christian apocalyptic. The great insights of Daniel – the ultimate nature of the challenge to God and the Jews by world empire, the necessity of God's direct intervention, the necessary victory of the saints, and the possibility of resurrection – inform the account of Jesus' life, death, and resurrection written by his followers.

24 For fixation of the accuser tradition, compare II Samuel 24 with I Chronicles 21. The II Samuel writer can accept that God incites David against Israel (for reasons not given) by leading him to conduct a census; this writer can accept as just David's choice (from among options offered by God) of pestilence on Israel as a suitable punishment for David's sin. The Chronicler, with his anachronistic picture of David as chief organizer of a holy community, must find another source for the sin of numbering the people: not David, not God, not a foreign power which would have no interest in this matter. For the Chronicler it is Satan who 'stood up against Israel and incited David to number Israel.' But he does so not as the prince of darkness but as the executor of God's *opera aliena*. For later developments, see below, ch 6.
25 Perhaps necessarily if, as is supposed, the text of the prophetic canon had been fixed by the time of Daniel's publication

5

Daniel and non-canonical apocalyptic

It remains now to examine non-canonical apocalyptic in light of the themes in Daniel, to see how it uses Daniel as a spring-board for other interests.

Using the book of Daniel as the point of reference, we can view briefly the character of non-canonical apocalyptic. The materials, and the critical problems arising from them, are varied and fascinating, but do not affect in a fundamental fashion my theses about millennialism.

The arguments are at a general level. W. Schmithals, for example, holds in *The Apocalyptic Movement* tr J.E. Steely (Nashville 1975) that neither Daniel nor the New Testament as a whole ought to be regarded as apocalyptic, because neither is like the documents that come between, which are seen as deterministic, dualistic, and so forth. Daniel is not even accorded status as a proto-apocalyptic. Rather 'he may very well have blunted some of the points of the apocalyptic understanding of reality and thus have approximated the traditional eschatological way of thinking' (190). 'Apocalyptic universalism is suppressed, and one must say the same of an apocalyptic dualism, which does not appear – at least not explicitly – in the book of Daniel' (190). Yet 'the contrast between the coming kingdom of God and kingdoms of the world is also conceived of in Daniel in radically apocalyptic terms' (190).

For early Christianity and the New Testament the same strategy is employed. 'In spite of all the historical connections that are undoubtedly present, it is not permissible to characterize early Christianity as "apocalyptic"' (206). 'One can easily extract from the New Testament a complete outline of history and on this basis unfold in all its dimensions, and document, the essence of apocalyptic piety.' (208). That is, the individual items 'can be lifted out of their context and fitted together into a comprehensive picture of apocalyptic thought and belief' (211). But 'in their Christian context, they are no longer a direct expression of an apocalyptic understanding of existence' (211). The book of Daniel and the preaching of Jesus both use the notion of the kingdom of God 'in a futuristic sense [denoting] the coming eon in which the dominion of evil will be broken and God alone will rule ... but otherwise it plays no role in the apocalyptic literature, even though it emerges in isolated instances' (211).

This procedure stands apocalyptic on its head. The non-canonical materials have become the basis for the definition of apocalyptic. But clearly Daniel is the foundation document of apocalyptic in both its concepts and its form. Daniel is the point of departure for the variations in concept and literary devices in much subsequent apocalyptic. These variations are considerable, but far from uniform; they do not exhibit a tendency to develop any given idea steadily in any one direction. And by Schmithals's own testimony, Christian canonical writings anchor themselves in the concepts advanced by Daniel. Why derive principles from the wide variety of documents of non-canonical apocalyptic or impose an artificial unity based on mere genre characteristics or upon an understanding not well-grounded in the actual history of the period?

It is sounder to build upon the relation between Daniel and the preoccupations of the Hebrew conception of what is at stake in the world, and then to notice the variations and departures from Daniel. Christian millennialism returns to the base laid down by Daniel and his predecessors, not to non-canonical apocalyptic. The exceptions to this have to do with the notions of messiah, Son of Man, and Satan, discussed in chapter 6.

We have no direct information about the circulation of any of the apocalyptic documents. Limited inferences can be drawn from the number of languages into which these writings were translated or in which they appeared. But this does not tell us the extent to which apocalyptic was read outside narrow circles. We gain better evidence of its effectiveness or popularity from the frequency with which Daniel's form was adopted by others. An ineffective or failed genre would not have been followed or imitated at all.

1 Enoch or Ethiopian Enoch is a useful document to consider, for several reasons. It makes use of a number of devices from Daniel. Its earliest strata originate in a period near the time of Daniel.[1] The document contains successive strata which

1 After Daniel, on grounds of the presumed imitation, though Charles was of a contrary view. This date has not been followed, or his organization of the original core. See W.O.E. Oesterley's comments, xiii–xv, in his introduction to The Book of Enoch tr R.H. Charles (London 1917). See also Russell MMJA 36 ff, 51 ff. Other materials extend down into the Herodian period. On the chronology of the period, see above, 39. A view of the book in its historical setting(s) is G. Widengren 'Iran and Israel in Parthian Times with Special Regard to the Ethiopic Book of Enoch' in B.A. Pearson ed Religious Syncretism in Antiquity (Missoula, Mont, 1975).

elaborate upon elements first appearing in Daniel. And these later strata use apocalyptic literary devices to frame new concerns that have little to do directly with Daniel's interests. These new concerns also show up in other documents of Jewish apocalyptic down to the fifth century AD. Thus *I Enoch* provides an entry into non-canonical apocalyptic.

I Enoch arises in the Maccabean[2] period and purports to be revelations from the antediluvian patriarch Enoch. Though Daniel is looked on as the father of apocalyptic pseudonymity, we should perhaps set the whole issue, here carried to an extreme, in a wider context. First Deuteronomy and later the whole Pentateuch had already been fathered on Moses. Prophecy after Ezra had been assigned places in earlier prophetic books. No Daniel is known. The enigmatic Enoch of Genesis 5:21–4 is rapt from this earth without death (and without further explanation for this remarkable act). Is it this singular[3] event, or his age at being taken, 365 (a point of entry into cosmological speculations), or his proximity to the Flood – so analogous to the imminent end-time – which accounts for the choice of Enoch? Given multiple authorship extending over a century or more and the differing interests and programs contained in the book, one cannot assign any single reason for the choice of Enoch.

The document displays, with varying fluency, many signs having to do with revelations of the origin of the cosmos as well as with the end of the present cosmic order. The earliest portions display a good deal of interest in the origins of sin and of more general evil. There are lengthy elaborations of the brief story in Genesis 6:1–4 of the 'sons of God' taking to wife the 'daughters of men.'[4] There is a heavenly rebellion of 'watchers' under the angels Azazel and Semjaza, a rebellion put down by other angels.[5] The book speaks of spirits and souls in a fashion foreign to the older Jewish writings and displays great interest in heaven and Sheol – here apparently definite places and not the mere figures they are in

2 I use 'Maccabean' for the revolutionary period and 'Hasmonean' for the period of autonomous government down to the Roman (or Herodian) period.
3 The book also notes and uses the carrying off of the aged Elijah to heaven in a chariot of fire and assimilates it to Enoch's experience. See 89:52.
4 The genealogies of Genesis 5 now separate this brief story from the Garden narrative and the account of the evil race of Cain and place the angels-women story close to the story of the Flood. This editorial arrangement occasioned, and was perhaps prompted by, the belief that the cohabitation of angelic figures and women was a prime source of the evil so condemned by God that he prepared the utter destruction of the Flood.
5 The elaborate angelic hierarchy of later apocalyptic is largely absent in *I Enoch*, though it mentions the names of a large number of leading angels, good and evil. More commonly it speaks, repeating Daniel's words, of 'a thousand thousands and ten thousand times ten thousand' angels (Dan 7:10; *I Enoch* 40:1; 60:1, etc). Ezekiel 9, as Russell notes (*MMJA* 259 n2), is the probable origin of the notion of archangels and the fixing of their number at seven.

Daniel. Sheol has become a place of present torment in the late chapter 103; and in chapter 39 the righteous dead are in the presence of God, enjoying the benefits of a 'heaven' and interceding for the righteous. In contrast, chapter 22, from an earlier stratum, knows only a separation, in the shadowy realm of the traditional Sheol, between the righteous dead and the wicked.

It is commonly assumed that apocalyptic anticipates a new Garden of Eden and so departs from an eschatology of the end-time. The earliest strata in *Enoch* do indicate the felicity of the final kingdom by describing different trees. In chapter 32 we see a 'garden of righteousness.' The link with Eden is made explicit when Enoch discovers that one highly attractive tree is that very 'tree of wisdom' whose fruit was eaten by Adam. But this chapter may have been so placed because of its reference to trees and plants. The writer may not intend to equate the end-time with Eden, which notion would undermine the strong sense we have seen, in late prophecy and in Daniel, of the reality of history.[6]

Despite Enoch's great concern with evil angels and his mention of satans (eg, 69:4 ff), the term satan remains generic in *I Enoch*, and not personal. The development of 'Satan' into the New Testament figure is a later development. And large sections of the book as it now stands are concerned with ethical exhortation of a general sort, which only uses the end-time as a sanction for high moral behaviour. The cosmological interest is employed in chapter 101 to teach that natural providence itself shows us the benefits of keeping within the bounds God has set. Chapter 94 is evidence for von Rad's attempt to derive apocalyptic from 'wisdom literature.'[7] It is formally apocalyptic but without any real anticipation of an end-time. Much of this strand of material can be summed up in the exhortation of 92:2 – 'Let not your spirit be troubled on account of the times, for the holy and great one has appointed days for all things.'

Later Jewish apocalyptic takes up the various paths marked out by *I Enoch*. *Jubilees* pursues the astronomical and calendar interest of chapters 72–82. The *Testaments of the Twelve Patriarchs*, a complex work of many hands and with a Christian overlay, follows the hortatory and ethical concerns of chapters 95–9. The *Life of Adam and Eve* takes up Enoch's interest in antediluvian history; and one section of *II (IV) Ezra* deals with the origin of evil. The *Assumption of Moses*

6 The Eden–final kingdom equivalence is taught in the later *II Enoch* and *Apocalypse of Abraham*. The garden-figure, with or without this equivalence, was used extensively, in conjunction with the non-Jewish idea of the primal man, in later Jewish mysticism and Kabbalistic speculation in the middle ages and early modern times. The garden appears less clearly in Irenaeus and in Joachim of Fiore, on whom see below, ch 11.

7 von Rad *Old Testament Theology* vol 2 (New York 1965) 306 ff. See also J.Z. Smith 'Wisdom and Apocalyptic' in Pearson ed *Religious Syncretism in Antiquity*.

brings the coded narrative of history down to the death of Herod the Great. The *Sibylline Oracles* characterizes the new age as one of peace and plenty, rather than one of the self-vindication of God. *II (IV) Ezra* introduces the Roman eagle as the last of the empire-beasts and is followed in this by *II Baruch*.

Treating the genre in this fashion, developing from Daniel, we see Daniel's devices employed in a variety of interests. Some of these, such as the concern with ethical behaviour, are of long standing and only hang their exhortations on formal apocalyptic pegs. An interest in the arrangements of the cosmos itself may owe its origins to Hellenistic speculation. But it may also be seen as an outgrowth, now almost autonomous, of concern with the disposition of the righteous and evil dead – itself an aspect of the mechanics of God's justice and self-vindication. The millennialist emphasis on periodization of history is spun out, perhaps under Hellenistic influence, into speculations that imply a pattern, an inherent teleology, or even an eternal cycle in the cosmos. Daniel's dynamic historical dialectic is broken down into good and evil principles, powers, or metaphysical entities or planes.

Many have observed these things being emphasized by writers who employed the devices and rhetoric of apocalyptic. But most analysts of apocalyptic have been so bemused by the devices themselves that they have failed to give due weight to the lack of common ground among the apocalyptic writers; each follows his own distinctive line of departure from Daniel. And because Daniel is concerned with the motifs of older Hebrew reflection, and because it is Daniel which is the foundation of Christian millennialism, it is Daniel which remains the normative piece of apocalyptic writing.

6

Three new figures:
Messiah, Son of Man, and Satan

David's covenant, in II Samuel 7, includes a formal and unqualified promise by Yahweh that 'your house and your kingdom shall be made sure forever before me; your throne shall be established forever.' The text of Jeremiah conveys God's confirmation of this promise for the future, despite the apparent prospects: 'In those days and at that time, I will cause a righteous branch to spring forth for David, and he shall execute justice and righteousness in the land ... David shall never lack a man to sit on the throne of the house of Israel. ... If you can break my covenant with the day and my covenant with the night, so that day and night will not come at their appointed time, then also my covenant with David my servant may be broken' (33:15, 17, 20).[1] Haggai, in the period of the early return, assigns to Zerubbabel the fulfilment of this promise. But Zechariah (3:8; 6:12) specifically refers to Joshua the high priest[2] (not of David's house) as 'the Branch.'

The term mashiah describes one anointed and refers to people consecrated for specific tasks. 'The messiah' is not a term employed in the canonical scriptures for the figure who is to fulfil David's covenant or deliver Israel in the end-time. Yet it is from the scriptural promise that the dominating feature of the later messiah arises: his role and his kingdom are part of the vindication of God's redemptive

---

1 This passage significantly expands and alters one in Jer 23:5–6: 'The days are coming, says Yahweh, when I will raise up for David a righteous branch *and he shall reign as king and deal wisely* and shall execute justice and righteousness in the land.' The clause in italics is missing in the version of ch 33, perhaps written when the impossibility of independence had become clear; or perhaps the revolt prior to Nehemiah's mission had caused such a phrase to be suppressed. Yet the fulfilment is the more strongly insisted on in the later passage. See Russell *MMJA* 306 n1, 310 n1.

2 And not Zerubbabel, as Russell says, *MMJA* 306 n1

history. The messiah tradition and that of the Son of Man remain separate until they are brought together firmly by Christian reflection on the resurrection of Jesus. The central role of the messiah figure for Christians and, at least formally, for later Jews should not be read back into the period of Hasmonean apocalyptic. In some documents, God's establishment of the final kingdom seems to require no human agency; at least, as in Daniel, none is mentioned. In others[3] where human agency is stated or implied, no messiah is mentioned. Though God's forces require a leader it is not found necessary to designate such a person as the fulfilment of the covenant, even though – as in Zechariah – these promises could be displaced from the house of David. The historical self-vindication of God is primary here: the means are secondary. But the way is opened to reclaim the promise of the kingdom given forever to David's line. Any final kingdom will be the completion of the promise to David – none of God's promises fails of fulfilment.

The Hasmonean independence, with its Levitical priest-kings, opened the way for a reaffirmation of the transfer, envisioned by Zechariah, of royal authority to a priestly line. But Zechariah's promise extended to the Zadokite priesthood, ancient in lineage and associated with the glories of Solomon's Temple and with such later exploits as ridding the kingdom of the usurping Athaliah, daughter of Ahab and Jezebel. It was this Zadokite line that had discredited itself in the crisis of 175–165 and been displaced ultimately by the Hasmoneans or Maccabees. The Hasmoneans, in turn, lost credit swiftly with the pious because the royal policy led the kings to quite ungodly shifts and twists. Perhaps the notion of a Levitical messiah grew up in part as Hasmonean propaganda and in part as a harking back to the stable theocracy[4] of Ezra. The references in the Testament of Levi, in the rest of the *Testaments of the Twelve Patriarchs*, and in *Jubilees* are capable of differing interpretations. The matter is complicated by Christian interference in the texts. The *Testaments* does, however, seem to offer us both a Levi and a Judah (Davidic) messiah. The Levitic messiah is to have precedence, though it is not clear whether Zadokite or Hasmonean reference is intended.[5] Each of the two messiahs has his own role.

The figure of the messiah can be differently assigned and quarrelled over. It is important in the Hasmonean and later Herodian (Roman) periods and emerges as a relatively fixed idea. In the *Psalms of Solomon*, from the early Roman period, the claim to a Levitical messiah is rejected and the Davidic character of the

---

3 See Russell *MMJA* 309 for a list.
4 It is apparently Josephus who so refers to the period and, indeed, coins the term for this purpose. See C.K. Barrett's note on Josephus' *Against Apion* ii 164 in *The New Testament Background: Selected Documents* (London 1956) 205.
5 The complex textual arguments are reviewed in Russell *MMJA* 310–17. See also A.J.B. Higgins 'The Priestly Messiah' *New Testament Studies* ns xiii (1966) 211–39.

messiah is insisted upon. Here too the label 'messiah' is firmly applied to the leader of the last days. Both his exemplary character and his military prowess are specified. The details – putting down the heathen, establishing Jewish hegemony, and so forth – are drawn together from earlier apocalyptic.

The reticence of the Jewish historian Josephus about military messianism makes it difficult to assign a messianic label to any of the military outbreaks of the Herodian period. The New Testament is more ready to speak of Zealotry as a messianic phenomenon. Josephus dodges the issue a number of times; but in his *Antiquities of the Jews* XVIII.1 he finally admits to a 'fourth philosophy,' along with Sadducees, Pharisees, and Essenes, among the Jews. It is identified as the creation of 'Judas the Galilean,' otherwise referred to as an adventurer and brigand. Here Josephus identifies the adherents of the fourth philosophy as absolutists for liberty, careless of death, ready to make any sacrifice, holding that 'God is their only ruler and lord ... nor can any fear ... make them call any man lord.' In the New Testament, the eminent Rabban Gamaliel is made to link Judas and his insurrections with Theudas, who announced that he was 'somebody' (Acts 5:34–7).[6] Josephus calls Theudas 'a certain impostor' (*Antiquities* XX 5.1), but shows him attempting a messianic act, repeating Joshua's opening of the Jordan's waters, itself a recollection of God's acts at the Red Sea in freeing Israel from oppression.

Military millennialism or messianism is an ambiguous phenomenon, however. In the turbulent Hasmonean and Herodian periods the borders of the Jewish state and of (enforced) Jewish status were extended, enclosing a number of areas traditionally the home of opportunist intrigues. Not everyone was prepared to 'await' the Coming One in order to secure redress. The Hasmoneans themselves both employed foreign mercenaries and farmed out Jewish mercenaries. The period of Hasmonean decay would not decrease the numbers of such opportunists, but encourage their formation into warlords. The rationale for such forces and their continuing resistance as guerrilla bands in the Roman period could only be messianic, whatever the real motives. Given the fate of previous insurrections, the raising of new forces could only be done on a messianic basis, as the episode of Theudas shows. This general background conditions the career of Jesus, determining in part what he can and cannot say and how he must define himself.

6 The chronology of Josephus, who puts Theudas in the régime of the procurator Cuspius Fadus (44–6 AD) is to be preferred to that put in Gamaliel's mouth, which dates Theudas back to a period prior to the uprising of Judas the Galilean. See also H.P. Kingdon 'Origins of the Zealots' *New Testament Studies* ns XIX (1972) 74–81; and B. Salomonsen 'Some Remarks on the Zealots with Special Reference to the Term "Qannaim" in Rabbinic Literature' ibid ns XII (1965) 164–76, which contains a review of literature on the zealots.

SON OF MAN

Jesus distanced himself from the title of messiah, with its expectation of military revolt, but not from the related but distinct 'Son of Man' concept. Some scholars have claimed that Jesus never applied the term Son of Man to himself. They distinguish between authentic sayings in which he speaks of the *coming* Son of Man (not himself) and other sayings in which later Christian piety has made him speak *of himself* as the Son of Man. This assignment of texts seems forced.

What is the background of this term? It occurs first in Daniel 7 where, as we have seen, it stands for 'the saints of the most high' – the pious resisters, whose humanity as Israel is placed here in sharp contrast to the bestiality of the empires and the would-be divinity of Antiochus. The collective Son of Man is given an unending kingdom and dominion.[7] *I Enoch* shows a clear development of the Son of Man notion in chapters 37–71, the Similitudes or Parables. The possibility of Christian interpolation is not to be discounted here; but to excise all mention of the Son of Man would leave intact his apparent equivalent, the Elect One, who appears with equal frequency in these chapters.[8] In this section of *I Enoch* the Son of Man is an individual. He is a man in appearance, yet no human ancestry is mentioned. He is at home in the heavenly court and, in that sense, not human. As the Chosen or Elect, he is the proxy of the holy ones, those to whom the final kingdom has been promised. In this capacity he has been chosen from of old, and in some fashion he will be the agent of their triumph. He will have his throne and play the role of judge of both men and angels.

II (IV) Ezra is the other major piece of Jewish apocalyptic to take up the Son of Man. Since it should be dated after the second destruction, of 70 AD, it can only give us inferential evidence for the earlier period. Here the Son of Man is a heavenly figure who performs great wonders and – like the kingly Jesus of Revelation – destroys the assembled enemies with a blast from his mouth. Russell

---

7 A possible reference to angels as 'the holy one' is discussed by Russell (*MMJA* 325 ff). I think this unlikely in Daniel, given his restraint on the matter of angels compared with *I Enoch*.

8 The identifiable Christian interpolations (see ch 10) are obvious, general, and clumsy; a clumsy interpolator of the Similitudes would have altered the Elect One passages also, had he been intent on 'proving' Jesus to be the Son of Man in this fashion. Further, his hand would be more obvious than it appears to be even in the 'altered' sections. Even if some Christian interference can be detected in the Similitudes, it is more likely that the interpolator was attracted by the Son of Man passages than that he invented them. See Russell *MMJA* 327: 'There is no indication here of any attempt to bring the teaching of the book concerning the Son of Man into line with that of the Gospels ... What we have here is an essentially Jewish book comprising a literary unity, at least where the Son of Man passages are concerned.'

argues[9] for a close identification in *II (IV) Ezra* between Son of Man and the messiah. This argument is better illustrated in *II Baruch*, of the same period, where the messiah takes on some of the characteristics of the Son of Man. The two figures generally fit awkwardly in the end-time. The messiah's kingdom must be temporary, so that the final kingdom may be everlasting. Thus *II (IV) Ezra* posits a messianic kingdom of 400 years. (*I Enoch*'s eighth 'week' of world history is another such limited period.) But in *II Baruch*, the close linking between Son of Man and messiah allows the prolongation of the messianic kingdom for as long as the earth lasts. The Jewish *Sibyllines*, of the second century AD, shows the same convergence of roles; the coming man is from heaven, is kingly, and exercises dominion over all.

The origin of these documents in the period after the second destruction provides a possible clue to this assimilation. The final overthrow of military messianism, coupled with the rejection by most Jews of Jesus as the messiah, could lead many to a more transcendent messianism. And after the disasters of 132–5 and the loss of Palestine, Son of Man speculation entered a new phase. It became theosophical and more closely identified with primal man theories.[10]

SATAN

In *I Enoch* the satans are plural and their offices appear to be varied. It may be that Azazel and his followers and also those angels who punish them are described as satans.[11] But the office, if that is what it is, is not personalized in this book.

9 *MMJA* 333, through a linking of the Eagle Vision (the reinterpreted fourth beast from Daniel 7, to fit the Romans) to the Son of Man passages. The lion of the eagle vision is a messianic figure; but the link between this vision and the Son of Man passages is not well established. Russell is correct to see a certain intercommunication of attributes between the two figures in these documents; but his point is better sustained in the interpretation which follows the vision of 'the Man from the Sea' in 13:1–13.

10 On this see *II* and *III Enoch*. For a review of scholarship which interprets the whole Son of Man tradition in these categories, see Russell *MMJA* 345–50, who nonetheless maintains that there was no conscious borrowing. When Jewish apocalyptists were aware of the background to ideas they were using, they used a symbolic vocabulary without taking with it the structure of thought originally found with these symbols. Such a judgment has to be modified in documents which, though apocalyptic in form, are primarily concerned with cosmology, the nether world, and other secret lore for its own sake.

11 So Russell *MMJA* 244 ff in the passages 62:11 and 63:1. See also 56:1. In 56:3–4 we are told that these angels of punishment go to 'their elect and beloved ones' (who are thus emphatically contrasted to the elect ones of God himself) to execute judgment on them, their fellow-rebels. Here angels of punishment (satans, if this identification is correct) are made the unwilling instruments of the torture and everlasting death of their minions and dupes. Is it likely that so

By the time of *II Enoch*, however, we see the kind of Satan doctrine that is implied in the gospels. The Satanail is instigator of a primordial revolt aimed at placing himself beside God. He leads the watchers, whose prince he is, to aid him in his plan. Some are imprisoned for this, awaiting the judgment. Some flee to earth, couple with women, and are similarly imprisoned. Satanail himself, while no longer admitted to heaven, is not imprisoned. Now known as Satan and the Devil, he contemplates making an alternate world to that of Adam but instead 'entered and deceived Eve' – reflecting here the notion, related elsewhere, of the physical seduction of Eve by the serpent-devil. In the *Life of Adam and Eve*, Satan's revolt is occasioned by his rivalry with Adam!

In the *Testaments*, Satan is called Beliar, the Belial of the canonical scriptures, where it is always used as an epithet of depravity and worthlessness: 'certain sons of Belial.' In the New Testament we have what appears to be the usage of the *Testaments*: 'What partnership have righteousness and iniquity? Or what fellowship has light with darkness? What accord has Christ with Belial?'[12] *Jubilees* (and perhaps the Dead Sea 'Zadokite document') speak of Mastema, 'the enemy.'

The Satan doctrine develops as it becomes impossible to locate the source of evil in surrounding nations or in the holy community. The idea of holy community makes it very difficult to admit that evil can arise from within. But the grave threat of Hellenization could not be ascribed to the Samaritans or to rigourist sectarians or desert conventicles. And its evils could not be fathered wholly on the Seleucid monarchs, one of whom (the father of Antiochus Epiphanes) had confirmed the liberties of the Judean community. The real threat arose from within; the defectors came from within the ranks of the Ezraic establishment, the very reason for which was vigilant purity. Such defectors represented not merely a loss to Israel but a leading of Israel into apostasy from Yahweh. And it cannot be

---

novel a notion would be so casually introduced? In ch 69, Charles's sub-heading identifies the functions of the five tempters and disturbers of verses 4–11 as those of satans. These functions are 1) leading astray the sons of God – presumably the other angels; 2) inducing them to couple with women; 3) providing weaponry to men and leading Eve astray; 4) providing men with wisdom of all sorts ('the bitter and the sweet') and with literacy; and 5) introducing men to invocation of evil spirits for human purposes. But the text of ch 69 is quite disjointed. The list follows without pause or introduction a detailed list of 21 names of the officer class among the 'watchers.' To erect a unified, personalized Satan doctrine on the foundation of this passage is to press the text too hard.

12 II Cor 6:14b–15a, where, in the English Revised Standard Version, the Greek *Beliar* has been conformed to the Authorized (King James) Version's *Belial* of the Old Testament. But the RSV Old Testament, published later than its New Testament, everywhere suppresses the literal 'sons of Belial' in favour of English constructions such as 'certain base fellows,' thus leaving its readers in the dark about the origin of 'Belial' (or 'Beliar') in II Corinthians.

accounted for, in this context of thought, except as part of a wider conspiracy against God himself.

The neutral if fearsome figure of the Accuser cannot be used here, for the Accuser accuses justly – *ex hypothesi* impossible here. The Tempter of David, to the extent that he is seen as doing God's business, cannot be utilized either, for a genocidal attack on Israel cannot be seen as God's work. Instead, some of the features of the Accuser and Tempter are joined to the malevolence of the anti-god of Persian myth[13] and of Middle Eastern spirit-belief generally.

The linkage of this new being with the dragon and serpent motifs is made explicit, as it is not in the canonical Hebrew scriptures, where dragon, serpent, leviathan, and behemoth remain allusions to subdued powers. The developed Satan attacks the holy community, from inside and out, precisely *because* it is so closely identified with God. The late section, *I Enoch* 91:5–10, tells us that 'violence must increase on the earth and a great chastizement be executed on the earth, and all unrighteousness come to an end' (91:5). It is of the structure of evil that the very struggles of Satan and his minions bring on the end and hasten the judgment against which they struggle.[14]

Thus we look originally for the development of the Satan theme in the circles of the establishment.[15] The writer of Daniel, who distances himself to a degree from the régime and from mere militancy, has no need of a Satan doctrine. He sees the history of the period developing its own inherent oppositions, arising out of the Ezraic settlement, its results, and the onset of Hellenization. His fourth beast, as 'devilish' as it is, is not said to be operating under satanic inspiration and direction. Rather, it is human pride and arrogance which wish to be god-like and so to depose God.

---

13 Though not his metaphysical equality with the 'good god'
14 We shall see this dialectic brought to great sophistication in Revelation.
15 And, of course, in anti-establishment circles, if these accepted the validity of the holy community idea and only differed about who were this community. But to look to the centre of the official community at all for the initial employment of the Satan notion is to call into question the dogmatic prejudice that Satan arose 'of course' among sectarians. This prejudice rests, in turn, on the supposition that the Jerusalem-Judean leadership had not itself adopted a sectarian strategy.

7

Jesus as a millennial figure

In the first century AD, with the arrival of Christianity and with the closing of the canon of the Jewish scriptures, it becomes necessary to consider millennialism in light of several distinctions: Jewish versus Christian, biblical versus speculative, accepted versus suppressed. These sets of distinctions do not coincide neatly; and in a comprehensive history of millennialism each would have to be taken up separately. Here we are concerned to establish whether Christianity may be considered an outgrowth of millennialist motifs (and the extent to which later, variant developments became central), or whether millennialism is a matter of superficial form in early Christianity, a form soon cast off in favour of more suitable garments.

Before considering the evidence on this highly controverted matter, I shall restate the contentions with respect to millennialism and Christianity that guide this study as a whole. 1) Christianity is more fundamentally millennialist than many investigators have been willing to consider or admit. 2) It is through Christianity's deeply millennialist self-understanding that basic millennialist motifs have entered the structure of later Western history. 3) Variations or speculative developments in later Western millennialism are often best explained as departures, conditioned by events, from this basic millennialism and not as part of a continuous tradition of speculative, non-Biblical millennialism surviving from the classical period. Each of these three points will be dealt with through an examination (in this chapter) of Jesus as a millennial figure, through a review of canonical apocalyptic (chapter 8), and through detailed scrutiny of the Montanist movement in early Christianity (chapter 10).

The central affirmation of the New Testament, the proclamation which occasions the writing of the new scriptures, is that Jesus of Nazareth is the messiah.[1] This

---

1 This statement should not be read as taking over all that was said in the first century AD about the messiah. The notion of the messiah receives new content from the Christian identification

bold claim at once marks those who make it as a millennial movement and as Jews, since the claim could not be made except by Jews. But it also marks off this new movement decisively from all previous and all subsequent Jewish millennialism, for it says that the messiah has come already. That the blasphemous felon Jesus is the messiah can be asserted because God raised him from the dead. They had seen him, they said, and spoken with him in the resurrected condition. His presence now with God identifies him as both messiah and Son of Man. The present period is given for men to change, to join with Jesus' followers, and to prepare themselves for the rigours of the coming period of convulsions culminating in Jesus' final appearance, as conquering messiah and Son, before the great final judgment. Thus everything hangs on God's validation of Jesus in the resurrection.[2]

It is necessary to stress the importance of the belief of Jesus' followers in his physical resurrection because of several alternative interpretations of the 'content' of Christianity. The nineteenth and early twentieth centuries saw a focus on the teachings or personality of Jesus and a view of 'miracles' (including the resurrection) as pious additions or naïve parallels to the stories of dying and rising gods in

---

of Jesus as the messiah. A second argument, that the deliverer of a Levantine people could not have been proclaimed intelligibly to the larger Roman world, overlooks the Christians' bold claim to be the completion of Israel or the new Israel, not confined by ethnic heritage but created by means of proclamation to all men, in anticipation of the end.

2 The 'passion stories' – the account of Jesus' last week – are tragedy at best apart from the resurrection. And the passion stories and resurrection account are the bulk and organizing centre of the gospels. The gospels are not biographies in any sense, but testimony or proclamation about the significance of his death and resurrection. The traditions of Jesus' earlier career circulated along with this central testimony and were only arranged in their present order when the gospels were composed or compiled from this material, which bears the marks of its earlier circulation.

In the order that we have the material, the following picture is presented. Jesus emerges from John the Baptist's movement of readiness for the coming kingdom. He too speaks of an imminent end. With this go healings and other wonders, and an unsettling attitude toward the Law. That he is the messiah becomes known to his followers, who are forbidden to noise it abroad, though others ascribe to him their own notions of what 'messiah' means. At length, after a career that may total only a year in length, he goes up to Jerusalem, performs actions associated with messianic claims, is arrested by the Jewish authorities, tried by them and by the Roman governor, and executed as a criminal pretender to messianic authority: blasphemy to Jews and sedition to Rome. The little movement is demoralized; but on the third day after the execution, the followers discover the tomb to be empty, are told by angelic messenger(s) that he has been raised, and see him for themselves in various settings in which he demonstrates both his corporeality and new physical powers. After a period of instruction, in which presumably his identity as messiah and Son of Man is confirmed, he 'ascends' with the promise of a return in power to complete the tasks of Son and messiah. The gospels differ at a number of points and are not readily harmonized without remainder.

other religions.[3] A second and more recent approach has been that we cannot know Jesus' consciousness and should dismiss his followers' millennialism as irrelevant. Instead one has to rely upon an existentialist analysis. The *fact* of Jesus constitutes God's call to decision, a decision for 'authenticity' or openness toward God or toward the future or toward the 'ground of being' or toward the new being that is possible.[4]

The status of early Christians as a millennial movement is undermined if their identification of Jesus as the central millennial figure is allowed to seem arbitrary or dispensible. These contemporary reworkings of the kerygma and of the likely historical account cannot be permitted to obscure what was the case in the first century. Their very success over the past two generations – to say nothing of the supposed findings of science – requires us to deal briefly with several issues.

The first issue is the origin of the millennialism of Jesus' followers, who proclaimed him, after the resurrection, in so uncompromisingly millennialist a fashion. If they did not get their millennialism from Jesus, then from whom? If Jesus is not a millennialist and they are, their very attachment to those popular traditions would almost preclude their identifying an executed felon as messiah and Son of Man. And there is not much incentive in their inventing a resurrection in order to carry out such a program. That merely exports their own problem to their hearers. The alternative is to invoke one or more of the bizarre plot theories which posit unknown religious geniuses, psychedelic cults, or conspiracies which lack any motivation likely in that period and place. It seems much less

3 This whole edifice was dismantled in the late nineteenth and early twentieth century by the work of J. Weiss *Jesus' Proclamation of the Kingdom of God* (London 1971, from the 1st German edn 1892); M. Kähler *The So-Called Historical Jesus and the Historic, Biblical Christ* (Philadelphia 1969, from the 2nd German edn 1896); and A. Schweitzer *The Quest of the Historical Jesus* (London 1910, from the German edn 1906). They showed that the 'apocalyptic element' in the Christian proclamation could not be skimmed off or regarded as an accretion. Rather, it was central and determinative; everything flowed from Jesus' messiahship. This conclusion was said to hold whether or not Jesus' claims or those of his followers were regarded as mistaken. Later scholars demonstrated more completely the growth of the early proclamation – the kerygma – from the asserted fact of the resurrection.

4 A third element standing in the way of assessing the proper weight of the resurrection tradition is the tendency of popular piety to focus on 'the Cross.' While this is perhaps a Protestant preoccupation, for Roman Catholics the centrality of the Eucharist as sacrifice functions as an equivalent. A glance at almost any Protestant hymnal will show many more entries dealing with 'the Cross' than hymns celebrating the resurrection of Jesus or that anticipated for his followers; and the Cross-hymns are sung regularly, while those on the resurrection tend to be reserved for Easter. The present study cannot address the question of a balance. One can be led seriously astray if one interprets the documents of the early church in light of recent trends in piety, however axiomatic they may seem. There is no single orthodox doctrine of the saving character of 'the Cross,' but the resurrection has a pivotal character.

forced, on merely historical grounds, to assume that Jesus was a millennialist, that he worked and behaved in a way that led to his execution, and that – whatever the reality or means of the subsequent resurrection – his followers were convinced of it and interpreted it in categories consonant with their master's convictions. Indeed, only a powerful certainty of the resurrection could account, short of plot theories, for their attempt to link Jesus' career to millennialism and to identify him as both messiah and Son of Man.

The existentialist version of Jesus' career[5] offers another sort of interruption, not only between Jesus and his immediate followers but also between them and their successors. And its implicit recourse to a subjective resurrection incurs other costs. We have already seen why a non-millennialist Jesus and a set of millennialist followers will not do justice to the likely facts. If we assume that Jesus *was* a millennialist, however, then for him to rise 'in their hearts' would hardly lead them to make the specific material claims about his resurrection and the coming kingdom that they did make. Why did they not say more plainly, more acceptably, that he had risen in their hearts? Their contemporaries would have understood so spiritual a notion. The immediate followers, however, would then have been the hidden geniuses of the plot theories *and have hidden the fact from their contemporaries*. If freed from the millennialist categories of the past, why did their esoteric teaching to their own disciples not at least approximate to their own convictions? In fact, there is no esoteric teaching.[6]

That Hellenistic categories of thought and expression were avoided by the earliest Christians is not a matter of chance. Their summons was couched in historical-redemptive terms: 'The God of our fathers raised Jesus whom you killed by hanging him on a tree. God exalted him at his right hand as Leader and Saviour to give repentence to Israel' (Acts 5:30–1). He is here presented as the fulfilment of promises and the resolver of all the tensions of Hebrew history. For the earliest Christians, 'the Resurrection of Jesus is not a circumlocution for the

---

5 This is associated with the names of Paul Tillich, J.A.T. Robinson, and, in its 'demythologizing' version, with Rudolf Bultmann. For access to the developments and debate see H.W. Bartsch ed *Kerygma and Myth: A Theological Debate* 2 vol (London 1953–62), which includes Bultmann's seminal 1941 paper, 'New Testament and Mythology,' from the German volume I of 1948. See also the survey of H. Zahrnt, *The Question of God: Protestant Theology in the Twentieth Century* (London 1969), which carries the issues a further generation of development. For recent confrontations see C.F. Evans *Resurrection and the New Testament* (London 1970) and C.F.D. Moule ed *Significance of the Message of the Resurrection for Faith in Jesus Christ* (London 1968); also see J.C. O'Neill 'On the Resurrection as a Historical Question' in S.W. Sykes and J.P. Clayton ed *Christ, Faith and History* (Cambridge 1972) 205–19.

6 There is, however, second-century gnostic teaching fathered on a variety of first-century worthies. The existentialist reconstruction of the first century requires the followers to have written an encoded proclamation that was only deciphered in our own century.

dawn of the new age, but its proof.'[7] 'The intention of the New Testament is not to proclaim faith, but to proclaim that something happened.'[8] 'The apostles are not aiming at something "authentic" in or behind the myth ... *There is nothing behind the myth*.'[9] These statements of G. Brøndsted, while directed by one theologian at others, seem to me to be the most appropriate way of reading the New Testament evidence. This evidence places early Christianity, for better or for worse, directly in the tradition of apocalyptic. It seems difficult to account for it at all unless Jesus had been conceived of – because of his bodily resurrection, whatever its mode – as having been made Son of Man and messiah. That is, the accounts show us followers, first totally demoralized by the unresisting death of Jesus, who are then driven, by what they believe to have happened in the resurrection, to use the categories of millennialism to explain what has happened and what it means. The parsimony of this reading of the evidence is in marked contrast to the ramification of suppositions entailed in the plot theories. And the simplest explanation of the origin of their proclamation is that they were, as *Jesus'* disciples, millennialists and that whatever the resurrection was, it was in keeping with, and a vindication of, the enterprise in which they had been followers.

As his resurrection disclosed to his followers his identity as Son and messiah, so it revealed new dimensions to his execution. He is also the obedient servant. He is now identified as the remnant, whose sufferings are undergone vicariously not to expiate any sins of his own, but those of others. Those who take him as leader of the new age also accept him as what Paul calls the last Adam (I Cor 15:45), the inaugurator and model of the humanity of that new age. As the first Adam opened history to what had not been but now was, through his historical choice – sin, so the second Adam in the same way, by historical action, has opened the way to the new manhood. In baptism men accept that God in Jesus acted for them. Paul insists to a mainly gentile audience that the man who 'dies' with Jesus in the dipping beneath the waters of immersion baptism, and who 'rises' with him out of these waters, is not rising to a magical plane of sinless existence.

The older apocalyptic idea of the righteous undergoes a deep change here, because of its new associations with the work of Jesus as servant who suffers. Now one is not recognized as righteous, but *made* righteous, and that not of one's own; it is the act of God in the suffering messiah. Jews and gentiles alike stand already condemned – gentiles as mere pagans, Jews as covenant-breakers. Jesus alone is the remnant, the servant who, for all of us, has suffered and brought us

---

7   Gustav Brøndsted 'Two World Concepts – Two Languages' in Bartsch ed *Kerygma and Myth* II 277
8   Ibid 281
9   Ibid 288

into the community of the kingdom and the presence of God. Attempts to assimilate the apostolic preaching to Near Eastern and Hellenistic dying and rising saviour gods simply fail to understand that the earliest Christians would not have existed at all had they not interpreted Jesus in millennial categories and then been driven to develop the meaning of his death in terms of the suffering servant and remnant. They were led to radical exploration of their own history rather than to borrowings from Hellenism in their attempts to explain or proclaim what God had done in Jesus.

God himself, in Jesus, we are told, has supplied the obedience required to inaugurate the end of the redemptive drama (II Cor 5:17–21). Thus the death of the innocent, who had no need to die for his own sins (II Cor 5:21); his resurrection is God's confirmation of his innocence. Death is an inappropriate penalty for one with no guilt; hence he is raised bodily, in time and space, as death occurs in time and space, as a historical event. Death has no more dominion over him (Rom 6:9) and is correspondingly broken as a universal power in history. The historical promises are fulfilled in Jesus. As new Adam or as pioneer (Heb 12:2) he exhibits what is to be true for those who abandon the quest for security through self-justification (Gal 3:6–14). Instead men are to accept the gift of right standing with God (Romans 5). Jesus is that gift; and by identifying with him, men show their acceptance of that gift. They gain power now and resurrection in the imminent end-time (I Cor 15:20–6), just as surely as that Jesus has already been raised (Eph 2:4–10).

The history of redemption is public history in space and time, not transcendental transactions or a flight from history. Yet it is hidden history as well. The events of Jesus' career, including his resurrection, are not such as to compel men to enter the made-holy community. And there are no inducements of a worldly sort in order to make possible a calculus of advantage. Those desiring success can draw no encouragement from the career of Jesus, nor can those who trust their own or their community's righteousness as the warrant for God's sending the messiah or the Son. Yet the present interval between Jesus' resurrection and his coming in power is given with gracious intent, so that before the judgment men may see him as fulfiller of Israel's history or as answer to the contradictions of pagan life. The interval of grace will end and public history will be the arena of God's direct action. Men will ask for signs, but till then none will be given; then it will be too late. Then men will be compelled to confess that Jesus is Lord (Rom 14: 10–12 and Phil 2:10, echoing Is 45:22–3). Finally will come the great judgment of the living and the dead and the new heavens and new earth.

Jesus had come proclaiming the imminence of the kingdom. He was apparently expected to return quite soon after his resurrection, to carry out the actions of the Son and messiah. If we may interpret the communism of the earliest Jerusalem community as a sign of waiting, he was expected 'soon.' The large amount of material in the gospels about the 'last days' pulls in two directions. On the one hand, they will be turbulent, a time of testing that will culminate in judgment and kingdom. On the other hand, Christians should not be led away by this or that. The end will come, but in God's way and time. It is fixed, but not by a timetable penetrable by man. The Jesus of the Acts reminds his followers that it is not for them 'to know the times or seasons which the Father has fixed by his own authority' (1:7). Paul argues that the interval is given so that the good news of Jesus may be given to all men. The tendency of Christians to leap into the life of the kingdom is rebuked.[10] But the reality of that future is to shape the present. Since his hearers are to judge angels, Paul argues, 'how much more matters pertaining to this life!' They should be ashamed to use secular courts to settle issues between Christians (I Cor 6:1–8). No doubt the short but very sharp persecution in Rome in 64 and the Jewish revolt in Palestine, culminating in the horrors of a protracted siege, were interpreted as signs of the imminent end.

That there was an agonized crisis over the 'delay of the Parousia,'[11] though often asserted, is quite undemonstrable. But the repetition of the warning that he would return unexpectedly gives ground for inference that the interval was proving longer than expected. For despite the prohibition to settle on dates, there was the peculiar word of Jesus that 'there are men standing here who will not taste death before they see the Son of Man coming into his kingdom' (Matt 16:28; cf Luke 9:27). Perhaps the words reported of Jesus, that neither the angels nor the Son know the precise hour of 'that day'[12] is given to mitigate the non-fulfilment of that apparently flat promise.

But there is little to indicate that the 'delay' occasioned any fundamental revision of the original proclamation. Further, any acute strain would be revealed by rationalization of the interval or by the development of a historical logic of the interval. Only the fragment in II Thessalonians even approaches such a task – and it is the earliest piece of Christian apocalyptic that we possess. Here Paul tells us that the 'man of lawlessness'[13] must be revealed, with his rebellion, before the

10 'Already you are filled! Already you have become rich!' is Paul's withering rebuke to the turbulent Corinthians (I Cor 4:8). And if II Thessalonians may be taken as a unit, the firm rule that all Christians must work is derived from the earlier discussion of the sequence of events which must befall the world before the judgment and kingdom.
11 Parousia is a term for the 'return' or 'second coming.'
12 Mark 13:32 = Matt 24:36.
13 He is not Satan, but his agent. The New Testament as a whole takes for granted Satan as the created and fallen adversary of God. Demons and powers were also granted a very effective reality, but it is clear that these are marshalled and directed by Satan, as part of his rebellion. Like other apocalyptic, the New Testament takes it that the direct persecution of the holy community by kings and peoples is directed by Satan. And it sees the end-time as marked by a

end. At present he is held back by him who (or that which) restrains (2:3–8). This 'restrainer' has not been convincingly identified,[14] though presumably Paul's readers understood the reference. The lawless one's rebellion is the occasion for the Parousia of the conquering Jesus. It is only in Revelation that we glimpse a historical logic which can account not only for the interval but also for its character as a period of increasing violence and contradiction. But Revelation does not seek to rationalize a delay; it asserts the imminence with renewed vigour. In Revelation, we shall see the historicity, the periodization, and the sense of the hidden working of the historical drama that we have seen as central to the Hebrew tradition as far back as the Exile.

cosmos-wide rebellion of kings and satanic powers. Note that Satan is not made responsible for *evil* and suffering, which are not a major theme for Hebrew reflection. *Sin* is at stake instead; it is not a historicized and dramatized version of *evil*; it is not metaphysical evil and finitude which are at issue, but unwillingness to give up a self-destructive autonomy and receive one's powers as a gift. Satan does not originate sin; he exemplifies it, with his agents. This 'man of lawlessness' is not to be assimilated simply to the later mythic figure of the 'Antichrist.'

14 See D.W.B. Robinson 'II Thess. 2:6: "That which restrains" or "That which holds sway"?' F.M. Cross ed *Studia Evangelica* II pt 1 (Berlin 1964) 635–8.

8

Revelation

The chief work of Christian apocalyptic, Revelation,[1] was produced only at the end of the first century. In this work the diffuse elements of Christian millennial thinking were drawn together into a remarkable whole which became determinative for all subsequent Christian anticipation of the end-time. This work takes for granted Jesus' status as Son and messiah as given in the gospels and other documents. It also displays a persistent tendency of Christian apocalyptic to base itself on older Hebrew themes, rather than on the speculative apocalyptic of the Herodian period. The book's fluency with the vocabulary of apocalyptic, taken together with its origin in western Asia Minor, suggests sophisticated scriptural understanding on the part of its mixed audience of former Jews and gentile Christians. But modern folklore and superstition about Revelation require that we look at it closely here.

Written by one John,[2] Revelation was produced at the end[3] of the first century in very special circumstances: the first large-scale, sustained, legal persecution

1 This, its Latin title, is a direct translation of *apocalypse*. As the pre-eminent apocalypse it is often titled 'The Apocalypse.'
2 This John is not the John of the fourth gospel and New Testament letters, although this false attribution was in part responsible for its inclusion in the New Testament canon. This supposed apostolic authorship – never claimed in the document itself – provided it a place even though, by the fourth century, millennialism was regarded with deep suspicion.
3 It has been argued that the present text was reworked at the end of the century from a document originating at the time of the local Roman persecution under Nero in 64 or in the period up to 80–5. See the citations in W. Kümmel *Introduction to the New Testament* (London 1966) 325; also M. Rissi *The Future of the World* (London 1972). But this solution to assorted difficulties perceived in the construction of the book is a minority position, unconvincing to many. See Kümmel: 'This approach to a solution of the literary problem of the Apocalypse is not successful' (325). The unity of the text is emphasized by A. Farrer *The Revelation of St John the Divine* (Oxford 1964). See also his earlier study on the composition of the book in *A Rebirth of Images: the Making of St John's Apocalypse* (London 1949).

of Christians. This campaign led to a large number of deaths, first apparently in the province of Asia, present-day western Anatolia, and later in other provinces.

The emperor Domitian had enlarged upon the *pro forma* divinization of emperors[4] and had apparently required recognition of himself as a god – perhaps in a civic oath designed to bind together the heterogeneous empire. All men, whatever their religion, could swear allegiance to one more god who would thus be the one deity held in common across the whole empire. Presumably Jews were exempt, on the basis of their special status, recognized since the days of Julius Caesar.[5] The imperial cult had already obtained a hold on Asia and perhaps went back into Hellenistic times. In 96, Domitian endowed a temple of the imperial cult in Ephesus, capital of the province. A rich province, Asia was also heavily settled with Jews[6] and, by internal evidence from Revelation, supported by the letters of Paul and the Acts, also had a substantial Christian population.

The zealous enforcement in Asia[7] of the requirement to sacrifice to the emperor (the apparent form of the 'oath') brought about a unique confrontation. The majority of Christians seem to have viewed the ceremony as idolatry and they discovered even deeper issues. The enforcement of oath-taking, in any case, provided Christians with a different problem than they faced when confronting other pagan practices. A world saturated with gods and minor deities – so that visiting the butcher or viewing a play committed one to recognition of some deity – made life difficult for Christians and led their leaders to forbid a variety of normal activities to Christian converts, in order to define and give effect to loyalty to Jesus. But these occasions could be avoided; none of them was compulsory, as

---

4 For a review of the background of this practice, see M.C. Charlesworth 'Some Observations on Ruler-Cult, Especially in Rome' *Harvard Theological Review* XXVIII (1935) 5–44. He distinguishes between demanded *latreia* and that spontaneously accorded the various emperors. Their practice was far from uniform. Yet the language of divinity, once adopted, tended to grow more extreme and less significant as it became routinized.

5 See the decrees quoted in extenso in Josephus *Antiquities of the Jews* XIV 10.

6 Ibid

7 There is no evidence as to how the measure was enforced elsewhere at this time. It may have been ignored as an irrelevant inconvenience or administered only to officials or to Roman citizens, at this period a minority in the provinces. In later times it was enforced more widely. For a third-century certificate of conformity, see H. Bettenson ed *Documents of the Christian Church* 2nd edn (London 1967) 13. This volume is hereinafter cited as *DOCC*. Here the requirement has been extended to village level. In the early second century, in nearby Bithynia, the younger Pliny, as governor, asked guidance from the emperor Trajan about the treatment of Christian nonconformists and describes capital punishment routinely meted out to the stubborn (3–4). Both Trajan and the later Hadrian cautioned their governors not to act on the basis of anonymous accusations (4, 7).

the oath-taking was. The imperial campaign would be frustrated if a large class of persons could claim exemption.[8] And – from the viewpoint of the officials or pagan populace of Asia – who would *want* to claim exemption from so simple a demonstration of civic unity? What could his motives be? It is out of this confrontation that Revelation emerged.

The book's title is often corrupted in popular speech to 'Revelations,' and it is accordingly regarded as a compendium of discrete and detailed oracles about the entire future of the world. Its use of numbers, combined with the similar practice in Daniel and Ezekiel, has provided an inexhaustible storehouse of combinations and permutations by which the secrets of the cosmos may be unlocked. But the book announces its own schema and keeps closely to it: 'the revelation of Jesus Christ which God gave to him to show to his servants what must soon take place' (1:1). What must soon take place – the Asian persecution being its sign – is the convulsions of the end-time, leading to the utter, complete, and final triumph of Christ over all his enemies and to the transformation of the cosmos itself into the new heavens and the new earth. It is the failure to take the book's announced program seriously that has led to fanciful interpretations.

John is in exile or detention on an offshore island when he encounters a voice and a vision on 'the Lord's day' – that is, Jesus' day of resurrection, Sunday. It is initially a vision of the risen Jesus. Here, and often subsequently, the mode of presentation is like cinema montage. The images succeed one another very rapidly, almost crowding past one another, some of them difficult to reconcile by formal logic, but together giving a strong impression, to the reader-viewer, of the great power and dynamism of the kingly Son of Man and of the events shown. The symbols are densely packed and, though direct quotation is avoided, are drawn from canonical and other apocalyptic and from existing Christian thought. The kingly Jesus begins by directing John to send seven letters, here dictated, to the seven churches of Asia.[9] These compact utterances, strictly parallel in form but cumulative and non-repetitive, lay out for the reader with great precision the issues at stake in the present struggle. They make both warnings and promises, with each promise the climax of an analysis rooted in the particulars of the local

---

8 Jewish exemption would not create this problem, for the Jews were a historic people, exempted from all pagan god-related activities. But Christians, as a heterogeneous folk, had no such claim. They formed no historic community, wore no distinctive garb, and had no land or language of their own. A distinctive advance on the relation of the parties and issues at this time is that of P. Keresztes 'The Jews, the Christians, and the Emperor Domitian' *Vigiliae Christianae* XVII (1973) 1–28.

9 The number *seven* is recurrent in Revelation and, despite efforts to show a greater significance, appears to mean no more than completeness related to divine action. The seven churches thus stand for the whole body of Christians in Asia.

group being addressed.[10] Together they provide the setting and the prologue for the vast visions that follow.

The organization of the great visions forming the bulk of the book is a matter of some dispute. The use of flashback and flash forward sequences has eluded some commentators and has misled others into arbitrary reconstructions. In what follows I shall be using the outline described below, which is my own. But the conclusions I reach about this book are not dependent on this particular organization, which does not differ importantly from that followed by others.[11]

I see, after the prologue and seven letters, two sets of visions substantially parallel, covering roughly the same period, from the first Christian generation to the Parousia and judgment.

In the first series (4–11) there are four large sections or movements. 1) There is a throne scene with the scroll of judgment and no one able to open its many seals until the messianic Lamb (Lion of Judah, root of David) appears – having been slain yet alive (4–5). 2) He opens six of the seven seals. Each time, a catastrophe leaps forth but (as we are told in 7:2) is not yet loosed on earth (ch 6). 3) A symbolic number of the faithful are marked with a visible sign on their foreheads to enable them to escape the impending disasters. This is followed by a vision of what is to be: a vast throng of those who have endured through what is now to take place (ch 7). 4) The last seal is broken and each disaster is loosed, each heralded by a trumpet blast. These disasters, instead of evoking repentance from men, are the occasion for fresh rebellions against God. Two witnesses appear in the earthly Jerusalem, are killed by the beast from the bottomless pit, and are resurrected. The last trumpet sounds and the inauguration of the kingdom is announced: 'The kingdom of the world has become the kingdom of our Lord and of his Christ, and he shall reign for ever and ever' (8–11).

10 What is required is faithfulness, steadfastness, vigour. What is promised is victory. Anti-Jewish polemic (2:9; 3:9) is perhaps occasioned by Jews distancing themselves from the Christians, as Christians had done toward the Jews in the Jewish revolt of 66–70. Here in the Revelation letters, Jews are denied the name Jew, which now belongs to the new Israel which sees in Jesus the fulfilment of the promises of Hebrew history and scripture. Acts 19 shows us hardened Jewish-Christian opposition in Asia from an earlier period.

11 My organization requires no moving about of texts. Some see the three series of sevens (seals, trumpets, bowls) as central to the organization. (So Farrer *The Revelation*, where this case is cogently presented, with a wealth of imaginative detail.) Others see ch 12–14 as both central and the effective beginning of a section parallel in content to the material of ch 4–11. I follow this latter. These differences by themselves do not produce marked divergences in interpretation of the book. Subsidiary problems, of minor significance in the present context, are: 1) the possibility of independent origin of different parts, and 2) the awkward explanatory material of ch 17 amplifying what we are given in 13:1–4. On this latter problem, see Rissi *The Future of the World*.

Here the second series begins, in which we go back to the origin of the church. 1) Failing in his attempt to destroy the newly born church, here identified with Jesus, the great dragon attacks the later Christians (12). 2) The dragon calls forth the beast from the sea, like himself but many-headed, crowned, and conquering. He deceives ordinary men, who worship his power, and he persecutes Christians. A little beast (like a lamb!) appears, makes a seemingly alive image of the beast from the sea, and requires people to worship it, on pain of death. To function in society one must now have on his forehead (!) the mark of the beast (13). 3) Seven angels empty seven successive bowls of wrath on earth, which only leads to further rebellion against God. All the powers gather together, led by the two beasts, to do battle with God at Armageddon (14–16). 4) The downfall of Rome is anticipated in detail (17–18). 5) Battle ensues, led by the kingly Jesus. The beast from the sea and the false prophet – the lamb-beast – are captured and thrown into the lake of fire. The rest are slain with the sword from Jesus' mouth. The dragon – Satan – is chained in the depths of the earth for a thousand years (19:1–20:3). 6) Christians slain by the beasts are resurrected and reign with the kingly Jesus for a thousand years over an unreconstructed world (20:4–6). 7) The dragon is loosed, rouses the unredeemed world, and surrounds the godly, intending battle. His forces are annihilated by a blast of heavenly fire and he is thrown into the lake of fire (20:7–10). 8) The general resurrection of all men comes, and the final judgment. The wicked are sent to the lake of fire, followed by death and Sheol – here Hades – the functions of which are forever terminated (20: 11–15). 9) A general picture of the new heavens and new earth is given (21:1–22:5). The whole book ends back on Patmos with John and with solemn assurances that all this will take place very soon; so the book is to be used now and not sealed.

The formal differences from earlier apocalyptic are the abandonment of pseudonymity and of the fiction of great antiquity. The time is imminent. It is not clear that apocalyptic in the gospels was intended to be pseudonymous. And none of the earlier New Testament apocalyptic was sealed or intended to deal with a remote future; there is no *remote* future to the New Testament writers: this era is coming quickly to its end. Kümmel in his *Introduction* recognizes Revelation as apocalyptic, but says the book is 'yet written according to a new Christian-prophetic point of view' (324) and describes it as 'prophetic-apocalyptic' (327). Such a contrast with earlier apocalyptic is unnecessary in the case of Christian apocalyptic and is overdrawn with respect to canonical Jewish apocalyptic.

It is true, however, that John is able to bring together into a coherent whole all the emphases scattered in previous Christian millennialism and to complete 'the total transformation of the Jewish into a Christian apocalyptic of history' (323).[12]

12 Christian apocalyptic rests in every respect upon Jewish. It is the Christian synthesis of elements kept separate in Jewish apocalyptic, and the bringing of the servant and remnant motifs

Jewish ideas, shorn of the speculative bent of some late apocalyptic, are transformed, by men who were themselves Jews and who regarded themselves, with their gentile fellow-Christians, as the new Israel. But John is so comprehensive that his title – the Apocalypse – now stands as the name for the whole genre.[13] Revelation was written in Asia Minor after several hundred years of Hellenistic pressure on Jewish culture. The population to which it was addressed was predominantly gentile.[14] But it is a remarkably Jewish document and stems directly from the Jewish apocalyptic writers. Let us examine its historical character, its periodization of history, and its sense of the hidden dynamic in worldly events.

Revelation is determinedly historical and this-worldly in orientation. The vivid throne scene of chapters 4 and 5 is not a scene of 'heaven' as a plane of life 'above this one,' to which men 'go' upon death when their 'souls' are 'freed.' The throne is the *presence* of God, and 'above' was the conventional metaphor for God's transcendence over the cosmos he had made. The whole point is God's redemption of his historical promises in a historical fashion: the battles are on earth. It is Israel – as John understands this term – that is redeemed. God's promises to it in history are made good. And in John's account the notion of history as a God-authored drama is given its definitive form.

The feeling of earlier apocalyptic for periodization is also sharply defined. The beasts of Daniel, representing successive eras of world domination, are all drawn together into the description of the beast from the sea.[15] Rome sums up the whole structure of world empire. In it the purpose of world empire is unmasked. Rome is Satan's final, climactic attempt to put himself in God's place. A second device, the thousand-year (ie millennial) rule of the holy ones, though mentioned here

into apocalyptic, which constitute the conceptual differences between Jewish and Christian apocalyptic. But these 'advances' are not the results of speculation or development, such as we are accustomed to in the history of thought. The followers of Jesus were driven to this 'transformation' by their experience of the risen Jesus. They believed themselves to be coping with a fact, not 'doing apocalyptic.' But they coped as Jews.

13 Other books with the word *apocalypse* as a title are, in fact, later than John's work.

14 We see in the New Testament letter to the Hebrews how thoroughly the church had taken over the Jewish scriptures as its own and how 'already in Galatians Paul expects ordinary Gentile Christians to understand difficult OT scriptural proofs' (Kümmel *Introduction* 280). Despite its title, which is not originally part of the book, there is no reason to suppose that Hebrews was written to Jews, and good reason to believe that a congregation of Jewish Christians would have found it unwelcome. So too here in Revelation the saturation in Jewish ideas and symbols is no reason to suppose an audience predominantly Jewish in background. Also, the long-standing Jewish–Christian tensions in Asia would militate against a large Jewish component among Asian Christians.

15 To Asia, the Roman empire was a sea-borne phenomenon. The descriptions of ch 18 amplify this identification.

only briefly (20:4–6), has had such an impact that the name has been used to describe the whole complex of apocalyptic and the movements giving rise to it or flowing from it. Earlier schemes had usually not prescribed a length for the final kingdom of the messiah or Son.[16] In Revelation, the thousand-year kingdom is not to be taken as a calendar millennium, given John's use of symbolic numbers.[17] It is not the all-but-limitless thousands of thousands of the attendants of God (5:11) or the twice ten thousand times ten thousand of the horde from the pit (9:16). It is, in contrast, a long but limited period followed by something else.

This millennium, it must be asserted against the later lore, is not the kingdom of the end. It is directly related to this age, as the vindication of God, and his made-holy ones, in a very worldly manner. It is this which makes it the chief image and conceptual mainspring of subsequent Christian millennialism. The millennium begins after the overthrow and destruction of the empire and its false prophet. And during the millennium, Satan is bound, powerless yet not destroyed. The kingly Jesus and his holy ones rule over an unredeemed world. These holy ones are not just those who have survived the terrible destruction of the trumpets and bowls. They include those who had been steadfast to death during the great persecution; these have been resurrected in a first resurrection.[18]

In an apparently quite worldly fashion, Jesus and these holy ones dominate and rule the earth which has heretofore been the prey of the great empires and of Satan. Men endure the rule of Jesus and the new Israel's saints because they must. It is not clear whether John intends to speak here of this period as one of

16 In *I Enoch*'s apocalypse of weeks, the phases of the end occupy the last three of ten weeks, after which the earthly kingdom does indeed disappear to be replaced by a heavenly one after the judgment. *II Enoch* offers a thousand-year realm followed by a new heaven. The dating of this book is late enough to make it difficult to suppose an influence on John. Two other documents, probably of the late first century AD, *II (IV) Ezra* and *II Baruch*, give us this same staging sequence. Whether John knows them or not, he does not follow their abandonment of earth in favour of another plane. A review of the various documents is in Russell *MMJA* 285–97, where his conclusions often diverge from mine.

17 *Thousand* here, like the Old Testament *forty*, is simply a round number of fullness. *Seven* always refers to the perfection of God and his actions. The *twelves* refer to Israel, old and new. The $12 \times 12 \times 1000$ of ch 7 is an intensification: the symbolic whole number of the saints of 'Israel.' The figure *four*, as in the heavenly powers, the cherubim, refers to their control of the whole cosmos, ie, the four points of the compass. The day–year equivalence is of course a venerable device first visible in Daniel and *I Enoch*.

18 The Testament of Benjamin, in *Testaments of the Twelve Patriarchs*, also has a double resurrection, first of a genuinely worthy élite, and later of all men. Because the date(s) of *Testaments* is a controverted matter, it is not possible to speak with certainty of the relation of this material to Revelation. Paul's resurrection of the saints and the Christian dead (I Thess 4:13–18) is compatible with what is given in Revelation. His discussion of the character of the resurrection body in I Cor 15 appears to fit better with the state of the final kingdom.

grace, of an opportunity for men, unhindered by the satanic and imperial structures of rebellion, to repent and join the saints. What is clear is that men and nations are required to acknowledge and live in light of the victory of God.[19] The very conception of redemptive history requires that some such visible, public righting of the balance be made.

Periodization is thus not an arbitrary import from Persia but something inherent in redemptive history. This particular period, the thousand-year reign, is vindication. It is not a break with the issues at stake in the present era; rather it is their proximate answer or solution. But it is not their final answer, for it does not deal with the particular judgment of all the dead, of the wicked, or of the good whose deeds have so often gone unrecognized or unrecompensed. Justice must be seen to be done. Only then is the way open for the new world. This new world, the age to follow the millennium and the judgment, is not a return to Eden. In its midst is the Lamb (22:1-5), the one who was slain and who lives, and whose name is written on the foreheads of the holy ones of all times. It is not Eden, as though redemptive history had not taken place. It is not a new earth – much less an abolition of earth – that cancels out the existence of the previous eras. The new world lies forward from the Fall, not in its cancellation.[20]

Revelation also pictorializes the sense of the hidden dynamic of history in the present era. Though this sense is analogous to that we have seen in Daniel, it develops out of reflection on the circumstances of the Asian persecution. The representations of this dynamic in Revelation have not yet been adequately dealt with. There is far more here than the pious hope that God would deliver his holy ones. We are shown why history must develop to a climax of absolute confrontation; based not on some alleged determinism inherent in apocalyptic but because of a historical logic of events.

We do not know precisely why the civic oath was imposed, or what it was intended to accomplish. If its intention was to assert Roman supremacy over the

---

19 This compulsion is no doubt a very unspiritual notion; and it is not surprising that most commentaries pass over this matter with little or no mention of it.

20 This in contrast to the Eden-like richness and bliss described in II (IV) Ezra and II Baruch. In other Jewish apocalyptic (II Enoch, Testament of Levi), it is not clear whether the Paradise is to be equated to Eden. In the apocryphal Christian apocalypses of Peter and Paul, this link is made explicitly. Irenaeus and his doctrine of 'recapitulation' are discussed below, 100. Medieval millennialists sometimes, as in the case of the mid-European Adamites, took the millennium (into which they had leaped) as a pre-moral Eden, and behaved in a manner conceived by them to be innocent and by their neighbours to be orgiastic and antinomian or lawless. But see R.E. Lerner The Heresy of the Free Spirit in the Later Middle Ages (Berkeley, Calif, 1972) for a rejoinder to the received view of the orgiastic tendencies of the free spirit, given by Cohn Pursuit of the Millennium (London 1957).

gods, and so over the god of the Christians, John's case is, from the Christian viewpoint, established. But if we assume something more benign, something more in accord with the known habits of bureaucracy, then the oath to the emperor was intended to confute nothing, only to bind together; and it was seen by its promoters only in terms of its modest benefits. Yet it contained an absolutization of the empire that remained latent until perceived by the Christians.[21] John draws a direct line from the official response through to the battle of Armageddon.

It became a matter of principle to enforce the oath; Christian resistance to a trivial civic form suddenly revealed what was at stake. The letters of the prologue show us the confusion of ordinary Christians confronted by the oath. The encoded nature of the document makes it difficult to see the specifics; but we can recognize here the same sorts of reactions that are known from later persecutions: temporizing; succumbing to the pressures and trying to remain in good standing in the church despite this; the purchase of certificates of *civisme* from corrupt or sympathetic officials; avoidance through flight; espousal of the official line that the oath was 'really' only a piece of administrative routine; and great strain between compliers and non-compliers.

Revelation is sure that the real character of the oath is revealed by the official response to non-compliance. For John and his hearers, following Jesus is no salvation society but the specific requirement of loyalty to the risen Christ as lord and messiah. Other New Testament writings show us Christians ready to obey the authorities, for these powers exercise on God's behalf his function of preserving order in a world prone to disorder.[22] To John, however, the state is now claiming to be a means of salvation. The oath, no doubt, was put in the framework of preserving the state; but the imposition of the death penalty for refusal showed that, under the cover of its godly office, this final world-state was the instrument of Satan. Hence refusal of the oath had become imperative for all who claimed to be the new Israel. What had been latent in the oath and in Christianity was called forth from each by the other.

21 The strange particularity with which great issues present themselves is made visible in Keresztes' assertion in 'The Jews, the Christians, and the Emperor Domitian' that Jews of the Roman period refused to use Greek epithets of imperial divinity but would use Latin ones. The latter had no resonance of the struggle against Hellenism. Perhaps the same tradition influenced the Christian response in Asia: clearly the relations between Jews and Christians are closely entangled in Asia and Phrygia, not only at this period but also later, during the rise of Montanism.

22 See, inter alia, Matt 22:15–22; Rom 13:1–7; I Peter 2:13–17. One element of the strategy of the Acts seems to be to show that Christians would never have been troubled by the Roman authorities had these authorities not been misled by the Jewish leadership; see Acts 21–8. For later Christian reaffirmations of loyalty to a proper régime, see I Clement 40–1 and Tertullian *Apology* (ca 197) 29–33.

This dialectic became the means of understanding the larger cosmic conflict. The mystery of evil is taken for granted in Revelation, but its workings here are displayed vividly as nowhere else, perhaps because John works on so large a canvas. Why Satan attacks the infant church is not discussed; but that he does is the occasion for God's special measures to protect it (Rev 12:5–6). Satan is baffled but – knowing that the work of Jesus and the church (here boldly identified in the same figure) are his own downfall – rouses the empire and uses it as the instrument to crush the church. Satan *must* act as he does now, in the face of God's initiative in Jesus. But the satanic mobilization of the world against the church brings the whole world into the struggle and makes it a *final* struggle. The Asian problem is a mere localization of the world convulsion, but it has required no more than the action of a few faithful men and women for the face of Satan to be revealed behind the masks of the beast and false lamb:[23] administrative routine and imperial reasons of state.

In both sets of visions – in the disasters that spring forth from the scroll and those poured from the bowls – there are elaborate staging and sequencing of these catastrophes. John can write economically when he wishes to; this elaboration is presumably presented for a reason. The sequence of these awful visitations is, I think, concerned with the possibility of repentance. After six judgments of the trumpets, John lists men's sins and their lack of repentance (9:20–1). The two witness-prophets of chapter 11 are sent so that men may once again have at least a declaration of the issues; but instead the world's leaders rejoice when the witnesses are killed (11:10). In the second series of disasters, after each of the first four, it is specifically noted that men did not change their ways. These disasters are seen by John as merited, both by general and by specific sin. But they should evoke in men a sense of the divine displeasure and, at the very least, a need to come to terms with God. This does not happen. At the end, instead, we have the battle of Armageddon. Satan, once opposed, shows and must increasingly disclose, at each new level of confrontation, his true face and true intention.

---

23 It is all too customary to lump together the historical opponents of God under the name 'Antichrist.' This term ought to be reserved for the one context in which it is actually used: the letters of John. Paul's 'man of lawlessness,' the (plural) false Christs of the synoptic apocalypse, Ezekiel's Gog of Magog, and of course Satan or the devil are not to be identified as the Antichrist. The Abaddon of Rev 9:11 is not Satan; the beast from the pit (11:7) is not Abaddon. The Dragon, the devil, and Satan are indeed the same (12:9 and 20:2), but the Dragon is to be distinguished from the beast from the sea and the false lamb (16:13) even though they are agents of Satan. In Revelation the 'Antichrist' occurs nowhere. I must insist, against Russell (*MMJA* 187, 277), H.H. Rowley (*The Relevance of Apocalyptic* rev edn, London 1963), and Rissi (*The Future of the World*), that to link these figures into an archetypal opponent is anachronistic. It is a hindrance to read the medieval Antichrist back into the New Testament materials. Ireneaus, however, does have a clear doctrine of the Antichrist, by name; *Adversus haereses* ANCL vol 5 (Edinburgh 1868) 25 ff.

The disproportion in his response also discloses that it is *his* response: all this force to crush the little bands of Christians; then the futile rebellions against God-sent 'natural' disasters. All are disproportionate actions; but Christians in Asia have experienced them and know that they are not disproportionate, for Satan knows himself to be at bay. It is important to note that in the end *it is Satan himself who creates the occasion of the battle of Armageddon*. Those who have found a determinism in apocalyptic are wrong to find it here. That Satan's rebellion is ultimately doomed is axiomatic in Jewish and Christian thinking. But to give the name of determinism to God's irresistible victory only illustrates the confusion brought to this biblical framework of reflection by the importation of alien philosophical categories.[24] Satan, it must be insisted, is free to rebel and to carry his rebellion to its conclusion, with whatever forces he can muster. Here, it is he who concentrates his forces and who risks all and who comes to ruin as a result of his own actions. It is the church's pacific but resolute behaviour which rouses in Satan and his multitudes the conviction that God can be defied and victory obtained. But this very course of action ensures his destruction. Though one of John's purposes is to warn Christians against the deceptiveness of Satan's campaign, it is the increasingly *open* character of Satanic opposition which occasions Revelation in the first place.[25]

What is the sign that the last days are at hand? For John, the decisive moment is signalled by the clarification of the issues: when all that is latent in the earlier stages of the historical dialectic stands openly revealed and when men have made their choices accordingly. In Daniel this occurs when the intention of cultural genocide is posed against God's intention to work a historical redemption through Israel. Where God has supplied the reason to resist and the means to resist, he will also supply the means of victory. In earlier New Testament documents and in writing contemporaneous with Revelation, it is Jesus' obedience that makes possible God's mighty acts through him.[26]

In Revelation, God acts to bring about the Parousia when the dialectic of faithful Christians and Satanic opposition has removed the ambiguity of history's cen-

---

24 The one example of apparent determinism in Revelation is the submission of the mass of men to the beast from the sea: 'Who is like the beast, and who can fight against it?' (13:4). But this is precisely a (false) fatalism, not determinism.

25 Satan even now is not destroyed but 'bound' for the thousand-year reign. Even Satan is not destroyed for 'mere' opposition. He is given one last opportunity to lay down his arms. It is only when he raises a final rebellion that God destroys him and inaugurates the final judgment on mankind.

26 See Romans 5; Hebrews 2; Phil 2:5–11; 1 Peter 2:21–4. Whether the Acts' speeches of Peter reflect early thinking or not, the obedience of Jesus is itself a gift of God. The new beginning in Jesus is the culmination of the whole history of Israel; it is foreordained; and it is the act of God himself working in and through Jesus (Acts 2:22–4).

tral issues. There is now nothing more to be *disclosed* in history, within the terms of the present era. The *movement* of history, with this qualification, has ended. All men, with as much freedom as history provides, are now marked with the sign of the beast or that of the Lamb. Once history has reached the state described at the end of the visions of the trumpets and bowls, nothing remains to hold back the complete fulfilment of God's judgments. For he must fulfil his promises. 'Great and wonderful are your deeds, O Lord God the Almighty!' sing those who have conquered the beast in the song of Moses and of the Lamb (15:3); 'Just and true are all your ways. Who shall not fear and glorify your name, O Lord? For you alone are holy' (15:4). Thus John leads us into the vision of the bowls 'which are the last, for with them the wrath of God is ended' (15:1). History must come to this end, not because of any determinism, but because God is God. The way is being cleared for fully redeemed history to begin.

Revelation is thus not at variance with much of the rest of the New Testament and it cannot be dismissed as the work of eccentrics or unstable enthusiasts. It takes the historical sense inherited from reflection on Hebrew history; and it takes the career of Jesus as interpreted in these categories. And it brings all this to bear on God's final self-vindication in the face of the extremity of human and satanic self-will.

9

Responses to Jesus' delayed return

The second coming of Jesus did not occur. While no systematic persecution of Christians was undertaken until the mid-third century,[1] Christians continued to be killed for a very long time. One must not underestimate the general insecurity produced among Christians even by quite distant persecutions. That insecurity may have operated to help sustain hope in the imminent Parousia.[2] But it also led to a desire for stability and for a level of accommodation with the authorities sufficient to allow the church to deal with problems other than its own survival. The demand for stability necessarily existed in tension with the militant response to insecurity. And the two tendencies – increasingly two groups, as we shall see – would find it increasingly difficult to understand or approve each other's motives and behaviour.

The various responses to the delayed Parousia are linked to the desire of all Christians to propagate their 'Way,' as Acts calls it, in a world very different from that of Palestinian Jews. We have, then, incompatible strategies for dealing with the world, but a common goal.

How was this tension dealt with? It is useful to focus on three phenomena. First, in late canonical apocalyptic we can see how the delay was handled by those

---

1 Even this was of relatively short duration. The great struggle of 303–13 will be considered separately below. One must also distinguish the enforcement of public policy from local outbreaks of anti-Christian enthusiasm. Christian accounts do not always discriminate in this way; and from their viewpoint there is little reason to make such distinctions.

2 It has been suggested that social deprivation gives rise to millennialism as a compensatory mechanism: the oppressed are better able to bear their lot or to mobilize against it because they are 'really' the elect. See N. Cohn *Pursuit of the Millennium* (London 1957) and V. Lanternari *Religions of the Oppressed* (Toronto 1965). This sort of psychosocial determination points to factors one must not overlook in reviewing social movements. But the growth and renewal of millennialism in both ancient and modern times is far too complex to be dealt with adequately at this simple level of causation.

who continued to hold solely to the millennialism portrayed in the synoptic gospels and Revelation. Second, we see in gnosticism an attractive alternative to the hazards of staking everything on the now long-delayed Parousia. Third, in the fourth gospel we see justice done to the Parousia doctrine, to the attractions of gnosticism, and to the need to recast the message in terms intelligible to the Hellenized Roman world. A short survey explains the pressures for modifications of millennialism and the basis for understanding Montanism, a movement of Christian millennialism under attack by other Christians and ultimately driven underground.

LATE CANONICAL APOCALYPTIC

It has been suggested that the delay of the Parousia determined the development of the early church.[3] Some scholars find the Parousia itself a bizarre notion or an encumbrance to Christianity today. Ernst Kinder's judgment is perhaps apt: 'It does not seem to be basically a question of a hermeneutic problem, as it is alleged, but a matter of a world view.'[4]

Yet the delay did constitute a problem. The Parousia did not occur in conjunction with the Jewish revolt of 66–70 and the destruction of Jerusalem. Despite the promise that 'this generation will not pass away before all these things take place' (Mark 13:30 and parallels), the generation of Jesus' hearers died without seeing 'the Son of Man coming in clouds with great power and glory' (Mark 13:26). The Asian persecutions did not bring the Parousia.

The author of the letter to the Hebrews pointedly refers to the fire and judgment when he advises his hearers to 'lift your drooping hands and strengthen your weak knees' (12:12). The writer of Jude alludes to 'the predictions of the apostles of our Lord Jesus Christ; they said to you, "In the last times there will be scoffers, following their own passions"' (Jude 17, 18). Here the existence of doubt about the Parousia is made to confirm its imminence; and doubt is equated with wilfulness.

II Peter, dependent on Jude, is more explicit as it deals with the question 'Where is the promise of his coming? For ever since the fathers fell asleep, all things have continued as they were from the beginning of creation' (3:4). The author responds that the cosmos is not self-evident; it exists by God's creative

---

3 See M. Werner *Formation of Christian Dogma* (London 1957). This line of interpretation may be said to have begun with A. Schweitzer. Its influence on the theology of Bultmann is dealt with in Werner's study and in P. Minear 'Rudolph Bultmann's Interpretation of New Testament Eschatology' in C.W. Kegley ed *Theology of Rudolf Bultmann* (London 1966) 65–82.

4 'Historical Criticism and Demythologizing' in C. Braaten and R. Harrisville ed *Kerygma and History* (Nashville, Tenn, 1962) 72.

word alone who erected it out of the primeval waters. It perished once in Noah's day when the sustaining word was withdrawn and the waters returned. Now, by that same word, the consuming fire is held back; for God 'is forebearing toward you, not wishing that any should perish, but that all should reach repentance' (3:9). Thus, for the author, no argument against the Parousia can be based on the supposed permanence of the natural world.[5]

GNOSTICISM

How did the Gnostics respond to the non-return of Jesus? Let us look again at II Peter. The author is not merely arguing against the discouraged or disillusioned who have been to the well of enthusiasm once too often. His attack on doubters is linked to his central concern: a polemic against what he calls cleverly devised myths, false teachers, and destructive heresies (1:16; 2:1). Here we meet a proto-gnosticism. The gnostics' argument is not from the fact of no-Parousia to the conclusion, based on a reading of history, that there will be no Parousia. Their argument is rather that the historical world is one of 'brute facts' only. At most these facts are representations of eternal truths, from the world of spirit.

With gnosticism (from the Greek gnosis, 'knowledge' of special mysteries), we have entered the world of Hellenism[6] and of the clear separation between matter and spirit. Gnosticism arose out of the combination of Greek views of the cosmos and the Hebrew picture of God, high and lifted up, yet intending the good of men. Salvation here is salvation from history, rather than in it and by means of it. The distance between the high god and the human is bridged by a series of divine principles or even entities. The first emanates from the pure, remote high God and in turn produces lower emanations, who in turn produce others until we reach the nearest deity who, by a fatal mistake, made the world we know and so became our creator-god. Jesus is accommodated within these systems as an ema-national revealer or as a special messenger from the true God, who comes down from the real world of spirit in the form of a man, reveals true knowledge of salvation, and returns unscathed to the world from which he came. This system

---

5 The final but not better argument in II Peter is that God does not count as we do: 'With the Lord, one day is as a thousand years, and a thousand years is as one day' (3:8). This statement also gave encouragement to later medieval enthusiasts for day–year equivalence in their schemes of Parousia calculus.

6 How much gnosticism is indebted to Jewish speculation and how much to Christianity are difficult questions, but not central for our purposes. The Hellenistic penetration of late Jewish apocalyptic suggests that less historically minded Jewish speculation would be even more susceptible. The gnostic mixture of Greek and Hebrew-Christian modes of thinking was apparently created by gifted and winsome teachers.

can accommodate the Hellenistic-Jewish speculation about the 'divine Wisdom' presented quasi-hypostatically in Proverbs 8 and more clearly in non-canonical work and in that of Philo, the first-century Alexandrian Jew. Gnosticism was congenial to speculation about angels and heavenly hierarchies, and provides a non-paradoxical framework for the Christian Trinity of Father, Son, and Spirit. The creator God, however, is to be contrasted sharply with the Christian Son.

The immortal soul, trapped in matter for the present, is the object of salvation; and this hitherto secret gnosis is the means of freedom from the world of contingency. The gnostic systems have significant differences; but in none can it be said that Jesus or 'the Son' has lived a genuine historical existence. Correspondingly, he did not die in the fashion of other men. He only seemed to die; or 'the Son' fled back to the higher realms, his mission of revelation accomplished, before the earthly shell underwent crucifixion. It follows that the resurrection was of quite a different character than is implied by a merely earthly reading of the accounts, which are ciphers for spiritual truths. Thus, too, the great calamities of the end-time are spiritual in character; and if not, they will at least not harm the truly incorruptible.[7]

Gnosticism offered the average man a way to interest himself in Jesus without having to commit himself to the absurdities, as it seemed, of Jewish history and its categories. It is important for a study of apocalyptic. Its popularity indicates the great resistance of the gentile world to Hebrew thought. Christianity appropriated

---

7 Gnostic systems were quite varied; and the dividing line between heretical gnosticism and Christian gnosis (see Clement of Alexandria and Origen) is not easy to establish. See R.M. Grant *Gnosticism and Early Christianity* (London 1959); R.M. Wilson *Gnosis and the New Testament* (Oxford 1968); J.H. Randall *Hellenistic Ways of Deliverance and the Making of the Christian Synthesis* (New York 1970); G. Scholem *Jewish Gnosticism, Merkabah Mysticism and the Talmudic Tradition* (New York 1960); W.H.C. Frend 'The Gnostic Sects and the Roman Empire' *Journal of Ecclesiastical History* v (1954) 25–37. Wilson surveys the development of research on gnosticism. Grant pursues a particular thesis about its Jewish origins. Scholem deals with Jewish gnosis from a different angle, connecting it to the later Kabbala and to its influence in modern times.

On the relation of gnosticism to the differentiation some make between Jewish and gentile Christianity, see I.H. Marshall 'Palestinian and Hellenistic Christianity' *New Testament Studies* ns xix (1972) 271–87. For Gnostic texts see R.M. Grant ed *Gnosticism: An Anthology* (London 1961), including a short section of pagan philosophical objections to gnosticism; also the reports of gnostic teaching recovered from the church fathers and presented in J. Stevenson ed *A New Eusebius* corrected edn (London 1968) 74–103.

The recent discoveries of gnostic texts bear out the picture given by its early opponents. For a particular piece of gnosticism that attempts determinedly to be Christian, see W.C. van Unnik 'Epistle to Rheginos "On the Resurrection," the Newly-Discovered Gnostic' *Journal of Ecclesiastical History* xv (1964) 141–67 and M.L. Peel *The Epistle to Rheginos: A Valentinian Letter on the Resurrection* (London 1969) especially ch 4.

gnostic terms and categories in the fourth gospel, and yet, through the fourth gospel, provided a major impetus for the redevelopment of the great millennial movement of the second and third centuries: Montanism.

The gospel according to John presents a complex programme. Our present concern is with its doctrine of the Paraclete – the advocate, counsellor, comforter, or helper, as various translations have it – the new thought about the Holy Spirit. The Jesus of the fourth gospel is a rather exalted figure, given to lengthy discourses; he knows his destiny in detail from the outset of his career and undertakes it freely; he and his Father are one in will. Yet he must also leave his followers not only because of his role as the lamb of God but, because if he does not, the Paraclete will not come (7:39; 16:7). Jesus, after all, is localized. The Paraclete will be with all his followers, teaching them 'all things,' giving them remembrance (14:26) of all that Jesus – the way, the truth, and the light – has said and bearing witness to him (15:26). The Paraclete is sent from the Father, but Jesus also sends him (16:7). He is explicitly identified as the Holy Spirit of other early Christian documents (14:26). In the world at large, his role is to convince the world of the reality of sin, righteousness, and judgment (16:8). What has not yet been revealed to any man (16:12–13) will be revealed through the Paraclete or Spirit of Truth (14:17; 16:13), whose authority is that of Father and Son and whose task it is to 'glorify' Jesus and give to the followers all that belongs to Jesus (16:13–15).

The fourth gospel does not do away with the end-time.[8] The wrath of God is coming (3:36). Jesus is the Son of Man (5:27), connected to the resurrection to life and the resurrection to judgment (5:29; 6:40–3). There will be a 'last day' (12:48). There will come a time when evil men will have their 'hour,' when persecution must be undergone by those who belong to Jesus (16:4; cf I John 5:19) as branches belonging to the vine. Jesus is the Christ or messiah (20:31). The epilogue to the fourth gospel, manifestly by another hand but definitely of the same tradition, has Jesus speak of 'until I come' in the fashion of the synoptic gospels' Parousia doctrine. The letter I John, somehow directly related to the fourth gospel, tells us 'the world,' in the sense of 'present world order,' is passing away (2:17). Here the

8 The Bultmann school of interpreters of the fourth gospel here consistently hold that a second hand has thus brought the document into conformity with the synoptic gospels' presentation of the events of the climax of history. But the readiness to identify the hand of an editor in precisely these spots appears to owe a good deal to the general strategy of making normative for both early and modern Christianity the fourth gospel (original version) and an 'existentialized' Paul.

notion of Antichrists is put forward: 'It is the last hour: and as you heard that antichrist is coming, so now many antichrists have come; therefore we know it is the last hour' (2:18; cf 4:3–4). But Christians may have confidence for the day of judgment (4:17).

Yet this material introduces a present dimension to the proclamation of the earlier Christians. Jesus' execution is assimilated to his resurrection as his 'glorification' (7:39; 12:23, 27–8; 13:31; 17:1–5). There is no need for the author to speak of an ascension; it has been swallowed up in the concept of glorification. Christians have 'eternal life' now: 'Martha said to him, "I know that he will rise again in the resurrection at the last day." Jesus said to her, "I am the resurrection and the life. He who believes in me, though he die, yet shall he live, and whoever lives and believes in me shall never die"' (11:24–6). Christians 'shall never perish' (10:27). The judgment in a very real sense is present already: 'He who believes in him is not condemned; he who does not believe is condemned already. ... This is the judgment: that the light has come into the world, and men loved darkness rather than light' (3:18–19). The judgment, as a term, tends to be reserved for the ordeal facing the lost; the followers of Jesus already have 'life.'[9] As Jesus' execution approaches, he says, 'Now is the judgement of the world, now shall the ruler of this world be cast out' (12:31). The work of the Paraclete is also judgment of 'the ruler of this world' (16:11), even though, in another sense, the world remains 'in the power of the evil one' (I John 5:19) until the last day.[10]

The dominant models of the fourth gospel are organic: the followers are part of him, as branches to the vine; he is in them as bread, giving life. Even the apocalyptic image of the Son of Man is adapted to this ruling motif, through a recasting of Jacob's vision in Genesis 28: 'You will see heaven opened and the angels of God ascending and descending on the Son of Man' (1:51). The power and the ubiquity of the Paraclete tend to rob the present of its character as interval before the Parousia. That event will come, though the author has no interest in its details or signs; but the glorified Jesus is effectively present now, through the Paraclete. The 'delay of the Parousia' has been solved at a bold stroke, though at some cost;

---

9 I John is compelled to grapple with the problem of sin committed by those who already have this eternal life. Hebrews also posits a strong present intercessory role for Jesus. Its teaching about post-baptismal sin is complex. 4.14 ff offers us 'a great high priest ... Jesus,' able to deal gently with our sins because he was tempted as we are, yet without sin: 'he learned obedience through what he suffered.' In 6:1–8, it is suggested, however, that Christians who fall away from their sonship will find it impossible to be restored. The ideas of present communion and organic relationship with the risen Christ are so strong that they nearly preclude regaining such a relation once it has been ruptured.

10 See R.E. Brown 'The Paraclete in the Fourth Gospel' *New Testament Studies* ns XIII (1966) 113–32.

for the fourth gospel, as authentic gnosis, now stands on its own as a revealed truth in scant need of the Parousia.

At the same time this Christian gnosis of salvation stands firmly against the emanational gnosis. Despite this writing's use of gnostic language, it insists that Jesus was fully a man, that he really died and was truly raised. He was 'flesh.' The fourth gospel's strictures against 'the world' are not against the world of history and matter, but against the world-order that prefers darkness to light. The theology of glorification and identification with Jesus, through the work of the Paraclete, is a theology of the sanctification of material existence and its transformation. This theology takes its place in the intense second-century struggle against emanational gnosticism and other speculation in Jesus' name, inside the church as well as beyond.

There is a new sense of 'the Church' in the organic models and in the abstraction of the kerygma from temporal sequence. The fourth gospel is well suited to a Christianity reaching out to new and more sophisticated constituencies and creating structures of authority to combat ungoverned gnosis in the church. Yet, as we shall see in the next chapter, the fourth gospel inspires and helps to provoke the new millennialism.

10

Montanism: the new millennialism

It was difficult for the church as an underground movement to establish internal controls; it did so at considerable cost. The problem of controlling and combating gnosticism could not be isolated from two other problems in the period leading up to the rise of Montanism. These problems are the influx of large numbers in both east and west,[1] and the effects of the persecutions. Montanism, the new millennialism, threatened the new infrastructure of the church – despite the consonance of Montanism's ideas, taken one by one, with the themes held by the rest of the church.

Jewish proselytization of gentiles, earlier a pronounced success in the somewhat demoralized world of late antiquity, was curbed after the disasters of 70, 115, and 135, when Judaism could be made to seem a danger to public order. Christianity, already a formidable competitor in some areas, began now to enrol large numbers, especially in the Syrian hinterland (where a kind of Christian culture was founded) and in the west. But there was no unifying language or culture for Christianity. These large numbers had to be assimilated on some other basis. As a proscribed sect, Christianity could count on at best informal tolerance, easily upset by local feeling or by the political needs of provincial administrations.[2] Even in areas of safety, the memory of past persecutions, the presence of refugees, and news of distant martyrdoms would combine to keep alive and vivid

---

1 By east was meant the richest and most populous area, from somewhere in present-day Yugoslavia through to Babylonia. This division was formalized in the late third century.

2 In 125, the emperor Hadrian felt obliged to remind one governor to allow anti-Christian proceedings only according to the law and to curb opportunities 'for plunder afforded by slanderous informers,' who ought themselves to be proceeded against with full vigour. This admonition applied only to normal, ongoing dealings with Christians, not to organized campaigns. See 'Rescript of Hadrian to Caius Minucius Fundatus, Proconsul of Asia' J. Stevenson ed *A New Eusebius* corr ed (London 1968) 16–17. This work is hereinafter cited as *NE*.

a sense of peril. Yet quite large numbers of people were enrolled under these conditions, perhaps often inspired by the steadfastness of those persecuted.

New means were required to lead the faithful, to minimize persecution, and to combat gnosticism. In the earlier church, there had been no uniform pattern of leadership or authority. First-century leaders had enjoyed plenary authority, yet even Paul was contradicted and defied freely. At Jerusalem the authority of James replaced that of the 'Twelve.' Local leadership was usually shared and was frequently claimed by itinerant evangelists and prophets as well as by resident ecstatics.[3] III John shows us the author's wrath at the attempt by local leaders to deny a place to itinerants. But the second-century *Didache* (or Teaching of the Twelve Apostles) provided means for testing their credentials, for the system of itinerant prophets was open to many abuses (ch 11–13). Over time that system was discouraged, and diffused leadership by groups was replaced by a *primus inter pares* or by a single figure. Later these leaders required the approval of neighbouring leaders, in order to prevent the infiltration of gnostics or other heretics.[4]

There was, if we may believe later complaints, a tendency to appoint to office not only men whose integrity would refute the common accusations against Christians (cannibalism, incest, and subversion) but also men whose connections could help ward off persecution. Such men might not be well grounded in Christianity: their talents were needed now; their theology could be dealt with later. In a centralized church, however, their decisions would quickly set the tone for others. The more urbane or politic these men, the more able they were to reach accommodation with officials, but the less likely to be able to appreciate militancy if that witness – *martyria* – further inflamed popular and official passions.

The influx of new recruits grew under adroit leadership. But when persecution came, large numbers of Christians conformed to the requirement to sacrifice to the imperial cult, turned in their copies of the scriptures to be burned, and informed on others.[5] After these campaigns, the church was faced with large numbers of lapsed persons who wished reinstatement. Here the leadership was confronted by an exceedingly complex problem. Astuteness or genuine concern for the weak would direct that no great obstacles be placed in their path.[6] But how

3 It is usual to date some of these phenomena rather later than the first half of the second century and to picture them, at least in part, as responses to Montanism. I believe they can be shown to be in place by the time of Montanism and to have been partly responsible for it.

4 Originally the word *heresy* refers to choice. It came to carry the connotation of wilfulness against the truth. Orthodoxy implies the right and the straight, but should not be applied to the period before the great councils which began in 325.

5 A late example of such behaviour under conditions of persecution is shown by an official memorandum and transcript from the period of Diocletian, given in *NE* 287–9.

6 If free readmission diluted Christian life, rigid exclusion seemed to run against the example of Jesus himself. And it could be charged that it risked the creation of a sectarian mentality of holiness achieved by one's own efforts instead of by God's grace.

explain that to the families and friends of those whose steadfastness had cost them property, exile, or even life itself under painful torture? 'Lax' leaders could be viewed as undermining the very possibility of that heroism which had been the means of the movement's expansion.

COURSE AND CONTENT

It was at this point, in the mid-second century,[7] that Montanism was born. Originated as the 'new prophecy' in Phrygia – adjacent to the centres of the Asian persecution – it spread as a movement dedicated to a renewal of the power and fervour of the earliest church. It, with its persecutors, proved in the end to be the means of releasing into Western society a free-floating millennialism capable of being infused with diverse contents.

Montanus and his associates claimed that the Paraclete had taken possession of them in direct fashion, and they proclaimed the imminent Parousia. They depended on the fourth gospel, despite their own insistence on the impending Parousia.

We can attempt to account for Montanism. Even in the fourth gospel's own terms, an interior, *religious* Christian movement is inadequate. If the Paraclete really has come, if he really links men to the glorified Jesus, then there is power now for us to live a new life. The Montanist gifts of prophecy and charismatic signs are the marks of the new life and of being destined for the millennial life to come. In this argument the fourth gospel is turned against those who would use it as a support of quietism. The vertical cosmic structure in the fourth gospel, and its possible concomitant, a vertical hierarchy in the church, are turned aside; Montanist use of the Paraclete aims at engagement with the world.

The advent of the Paraclete is taken to give a new constitution to the church, which is neither a memorial society nor merely one new religion among many. The coming of the Paraclete and the imminence of the Parousia tell us that we have moved into a new period of the redemptive history of the world. We are neither in the setting pictured at the close of the gospels nor in the millennium. The new outbreak of ecstatic behaviour inspired by the Paraclete is for the Montanists a forceful reminder that the radical early church period had not been a magic moment, never to be repeated, after which the church could settle into institutional domesticity. Paraclete-possession is to be accepted as usual; it is a rebuke to formalism and a sign for what lies close ahead.

Montanism was attacked, apparently from an early date, but there is a problem with the sources. Recent recoveries of gnostic documents show that the writers

---

7 See G.S.P. Freeman-Grenville 'Date of the Outbreak of Montanism' *Journal of Ecclesiastical History* v (1954) 7–15.

on gnostic and other heresies gave accurate representations of gnostic teaching. In their reports on the new prophecy, the words of its leaders do not appear heretical. The new prophets are attacked for their disorderly assemblies, for deceit, for timidity, for greed, and for the origin of the new prophecy in Phrygia, well known as the home of exotic religion. These charges are somehow erected into heresy, and by the fourth century, when legal enactments could be procured against the Montanists, they were placed among heretics to be suppressed.

Montanism, it appears, was a danger which led to *ad hominem* arguments being made. The danger must have seemed real but the heresy hard to demonstrate. The disorder of Montanist assemblies and the excitement they fostered were all too likely to revive or confirm the widespread suspicions about orgies and incest. The prominence of female prophets contravened Paul's directive to Corinth against active female leaders in worship.[8] The Montanist prophecy of the descent of the new Jerusalem at Pepuza in Phrygia could show excessive pride. But the Montanist critique of the hardening of church structures was bound to produce conflict with those anxious to prevent the church from evaporating into speculation or degenerating into a salvation cult. The anti-Montanist council that dealt with early Phrygian new prophecy is the earliest known church council.[9] The spread of Montanism thus strengthened the very tendencies which produced the new movement and now justified its further development.

It will be useful to examine the response of the 'official' church to Montanism and the reported utterances of the Montanist leaders before we proceed to a judgment on the movement and its role as the point of departure for the radical millennialism that emerged in the Middle Ages.

The earliest report on Montanism is the anonymous second-century source quoted by Eusebius, the fourth-century historian.[10] This source tells us that

8 This provision was apparently aimed at countering any impression of wantonness in assemblies made up in part, if Corinth is an example, of former prostitutes or exploited female slaves (I Cor 6:9–11). In I Cor 14:34 Paul speaks of this prohibition as common throughout the churches. It is clear in its setting that this refers to prophecy, in which the Spirit declared his will, and perhaps to office-bearing. That it did not extend to public prayer is plain from ch 11. Paul's letters commend female leadership in Christian propaganda and in the building up of new groups. The deutero-Pauline I Timothy is very sharp in its condemnation of female leadership as such; and proof-texts are brought to bear to show that their subordination is part of the God-given order of things in the fallen world; see I Tim 2:8–15.

9 The regularized leadership was probably also pastorally concerned with the instability of the Montanist movement, in which leadership was established and overthrown – and with it the faith of others – on the basis of possession or superior display of the Spirit's gifts of prophecy and other charismata. No doubt it was often suspected that forced growth and imposture were resorted to in order to advance personal ambition and to supplant existing leaders.

10 Eusebius *Ecclesiastical History* v.3, 16–18, quoted in *NE* 107–15

Montanus uttered ecstatic prophecy, 'that is to say, prophesying contrary to the manner which the Church had received from generation to generation from the beginning.' He argues that this is false prophecy, unknown in the early church, and cites Acts, but ignores Paul on Corinthian ecstatic prophecy (I Cor 12, 14) and Paul's own experiences as an ecstatic (II Cor 12). And the Anonymous recognizes the precedent of Acts for female prophecy. Though he dismisses Montanus's[11] utterances as 'spurious,' his principal weapon is innuendo. 'Some' of those present were angry 'as at one possessed and tormented by a devil' – a form of words which does not quite call Montanus demon-possessed. 'Others were puffed up, as at a prophetical gift of the Holy Spirit.' That is, their action could not be impugned except by calling it conceit. Their behaviour is 'frenzied, inopportune and un-natural.' The Anonymous recognized that this spirit also rebuked those who were possessed – this is dismissed as 'shrewd and plausible,' the better to deceive. The prophets are 'arrogant' and 'blaspheme the entire universal Church.'

This critique is all rather vague and argues only for the undoubted rigorism of the Montanists and for their denunciation of recent practice. We may well believe that Montanism occasioned the calling of some sort of council; but we are unprepared by this account for the conclusion that Montanism is 'heresy' and its adherents thus justly excommunicated. Both the Anonymous and Apollonius[12] assert that the early Phrygian Montanists produced no martyrs, their claims notwithstanding, and that they displayed an unseemly financial acumen. But this is far from heresy or from meriting the remarkable severity with which Montanism was treated by the Christian emperors.

Hippolytus, writing ca 220 in his *Refutation of All Heresies*,[13] after the usual invective, becomes more informative. Not only are Montanists heedless of 'those who are competent to decide,' but they also claim to have additional revelations 'than from law and prophets and the Gospels.' This claim places 'these wretched women' on a par with or superior to the apostles. 'Some of them presume to assert that there is something superior to Christ,' and 'some' are said to assert the Noetian heresy, the identity of Father and Son. These 'some' reflect the desire of Hippolytus to discredit the movement by the errors and excesses of a few.

The problem is clearly the Paraclete of John. If the Paraclete is indeed to operate as described in the fourth gospel, new knowledge of God's will is going to appear through the Paraclete's work among Christians. The fourth gospel emphasizes that the Paraclete is sent from both Father and Son; and presumably, there-

---

11 Even the label Montanism is pejorative; heresies were usually named after their originators, thus implying their notional character.

12 Also cited by Eusebius and quoted in *NE* 111 ff. W. Bauer *Orthodoxy and Heresy in the Earliest Church* (London 1972, from 2nd German edn) reviews critically the statements of the Anonymous and Apollonius, 132–46.

13 Bk VIII.19, quoted in *NE* 113–14

fore, new revelations will be consistent with God's past actions. Paul too reminds the Corinthians that no spirit speaking through an ecstatic can say 'Jesus is accursed' – not if it is the real Holy Spirit.

Yet new, authoritative utterance could only be seen by church officials as unsettling. When the official opposition to Montanism had hardened, one would expect Montanist oracles against the persecutors of the new prophecy. Yet the official church too claimed to be guided by the same Holy Spirit. What would happen when oracles were shown to be in contradiction – oracles of the one Holy Spirit?

In fact, the recovered 'sayings' of Montanist prophecy[14] do not provide us with any such discreditable oracles by Montanist prophets. W. Schneemelcher gives these sayings, as provided by anti-Montanist writers:

1. (Montanus says:) I am the Father and I am the Son and I am the Paraclete.
2. (Montanus speaks:) I the Lord, the Almighty God, remain among men.
3. (Montanus says:) Neither angel nor ambassador, but I, the Lord God the Father, am come.
4. (Montanus says:) Behold, man is like a lyre and I rush thereon like a plectrum. Man sleeps and I awake. Behold the Lord is he who arouses the hearts of men (throws them into ecstasy) and gives to men a new heart.
5. (Montanus says:) Why dost thou call the super-man (?) saved? For the righteous man, he says, will shine a hundred times more strongly than the sun, but the little ones who are saved among you will shine a hundred times stronger than the moon ...
11. (Quintilla or Priscilla says:) In the form of a woman, says she, arrayed in shining garments, came Christ to me and set wisdom upon me and revealed to me that this place (= Pepuza) is holy and that Jerusalem will come down hither from heaven.
12. (Maximilla says:) After me, she says, there will be no prophets, but (only) the consummation.
13. (Maximilla says:) Listen not to me, but listen to Christ.
14. (Maximilla says:) The Lord has sent me as an adherent, preacher and interpreter of this affliction and this covenant and this promise; he has compelled me, willingly or unwillingly, to learn the knowledge of God.

---

14 Epiphanius and Eusebius together provide seven: two by Montanus, four by Maximilla, and one by Priscilla. These are given in NE 113. Schneemelcher gives the same ones, often translated more fluently, and adds Tertullian's citations (five), one more from Epiphanius, and one from a third source. The literature discussing the authenticity of these and other sayings is cited by Schneemelcher, who takes these fifteen to be the ones 'whose authenticity seems to be secure' (685). E. Hennecke and W. Schneemelcher ed New Testament Apocrypha II English trn ed R.M. Wilson (hereinafter NTA II) 685–9

15. (The Spirit says through Maximilla:) I am chased like a wolf from (the flock of) sheep; I am not a wolf; I am word and spirit and power.[15]

As Schneemelcher observes, it is clear that these utterances are to be taken as those of the Spirit; as Maximilla says: Listen not to me but to Christ. The prophet is but a medium. Number 11, about the new Jerusalem, is cast as the prophet's report of a vision. Number 14, while presumably inspired, comments directly on the prophet's own role. It is difficult to find heresy here. And only the Spirit's complaint in number 15 can be taken as an utterance directly against the opponents of the new prophecy. The prophecy about the new Jerusalem descending upon Pepuza, if meant literally as a localization of the post-millennial events, is (so far as we know) quite mistaken. And in number 12 Maximilla is mistaken if she means that after herself prophecy will cease and give way to the Parousia. But presumptuousness is not the same thing as heresy.

The sayings omitted above are those of Tertullian, in his late career an adherent of Montanism (in its second, North African, phase at the end of the second century). Tertullian's role as apologist, originator of the orthodox formulation of the Trinity, and a zealous combatant against heresies assures his reputation. Yet he became a Montanist; and interpreters of his voluminous writings have exercised themselves to discover when his orthodoxy leaves off and his heretical Montanism begins. It would be inappropriate, it seems, to cite a writing from his 'Montanist period' to support an orthodox position.

Tertullian takes positions on church discipline that seem unlovely. His rhetorical strengths, which help gain approval for his statements on other matters, only highlight his narrow views on 'proper Christian conduct.' But he is no more eccentric here than other ancient doctors of the church on other matters. And his defense of the corporeal reality of the resurrection shows, along with much else, his penetration behind the Middle Platonism of third- and fourth-century Christian thinkers to an early Christian and Hebrew understanding of redemptive history.[16] I cannot think that this penetration and his Montanism are unrelated.

---

15 NTA II 686–7. Omitted sayings are those reported by Tertullian, who became a Montanist late in life.
16 See especially De spectaculis ch 30. Tertullian has been providing reasons for Christian non-participation in pagan shows and theatrical events. In ch 30 he turns the tables and discourses on the greatest spectacle of all: the Parousia, where Christians will indeed be spectators and participants (as they have been unwilling participants in the Christians-to-the-lions exhibitions) in the climax of the ages which brings judgment on the puny shows of Rome. In the Christian Sibylline oracles, a section of similar rhetorical construction on the same topic begins in bk VIII at line 43: 'Where then the Palladium' and ending at lines 122–30: 'Go on now building, ye cities, and adorn yourselves nobly / with temples and marketplaces and circuses ... Make yourselves beautiful, that ye may come to the bitter day ... Thou shalt be utterly ravaged, and done

Both run against the grain of the period; each reinforces the other, but neither appears to be heretical.

Montanism did, however, become schismatic, in both east and west. Phrygian Montanism was ejected, according to the Anonymous. In the west Montanism became schismatic after long wrangles. A remnant survived in Tertullian's native Carthage for a long time. Montanist-influenced Christians in North Africa probably became indistinguishable from many other Christians during the mid-third-century struggles over readmission of the lapsed after the exceedingly sharp and successful persecution under Decius. At this time, and later, in the fourth century Donatist schism in North Africa, vast numbers of Christians under orthodox bishops went over to a rigorist position. They were not given to enthusiasm over the Paraclete, and their schisms could be dealt with by accommodation or political repression. Montanism alone, among the rigorists, was labelled heretical.[17]

As soon as official Christianity could command public authority, in Constantine's time, an edict was issued against Montanists, bracketing them with gnostics and other heretics.[18] Montanists were deprived of their buildings and of their rights to meet at all. In 398 their clergy was outlawed. New and harsher enactments, including the death penalty, were made for those harbouring Montanist groups, and their writings were to be burned; those concealing such books were to be treated as sorcerers.[19] A series of later edicts testifies to the continuing difficulty of extirpating Montanism.[20]

by as thou hast done; / Lamenting thou shalt give in fear, until thou hast paid in full / Thou shalt be a triumph-spectacle for the world, and a reproach to all' (*NTA* II 727–9). This document, dated by A. Kurfess (ibid 701) at ca 180, may disclose a connection with Montanist activity. Or it may show, more probably, that millennialist activity was not confined to Montanist circles. The Sibyllines became a focus for later millennial speculation and were heavily interpolated and added to. On the setting for Tertullian's thought, see J. Pelikan 'The Eschatology of Tertullian' *Church History* XXI (1952) 108–22.

17 The council of Laodicea (ca 360) did not require rebaptism of those seeking readmission from the heretical Photinians, but did so require of Montanists, even though it noted their repute. (Other early authorities disagreed with Laodicea about Montanist baptism.) The shrines of Montanist martyrs were to be shunned.

18 In 322 or 332. The text is given in P.R. Coleman-Norton *Roman State and Christian Church: A Collection of Legal Documents to A.D. 535* 3 vol numbered consecutively (London 1966) 90–2.

19 Ibid 472–3

20 Ibid 382, 472 ff, 495 ff, 501, 533 ff, 571 ff, 627 ff, 635, 642 ff, 713, 1008 ff, 1099 ff. See also F.E. Vokes 'The Opposition to Montanism from Church and State in the Christian Empire' F.M. Cross ed *Studia Patristica* IV pt 2 (Berlin 1961) 518–26. Vokes finds references to strong Montanist activity down to 722, but notes: 'It is somewhat surprising to find that though the laws and anti-heretical writers so often deal with Montanism, the canons of the Councils are so rarely concerned with it' (526). So eminent a pillar of orthodoxy as Athanasius did not regard Montanism as heretical. See also J. Pelikan 'Montanism and Its Trinitarian Significance' *Church History* XXV (1956) 99–109.

Schneemelcher argues, on the basis of the Montanist sayings, that they were a prophetic and not an 'apocalyptic' group. This view appears to be based on an artificial contrast between an ethical prophecy and a speculative millennium.[21] He says that 'specifically apocalyptic notions do not appear in the forefront in the Sayings.'[22] But the descent of the New Jerusalem at Pepuza and Maximilla's assertion that she is the last prophet before the 'consummation' argue against his conclusion. Such a conclusion, in the face of the sayings, seems to view millennialism as a vagary to which various groups fall prey but which be skimmed off, leaving the 'true' content. I have tried to show how impossible this is, given the historical evidence. A slightly different approach has been taken by J.M. Ford, linking Montanism firmly to Phrygia and to that province's large and eccentric Jewish population.[23] The large Jewish population of Carthage, with its links to the apocalyptical Rabbi Akiba, is taken as the seed-bed for the North African variety of Montanism. Ford views Tertullian's position on the soul as Jewish; but surely it is more parsimonious to see his Jewishness in this matter as that of the earliest Christians, before the Hellenistic notion of the soul began to be resorted to in Christian propaganda.[24] Ford admits that 'the Phrygian eschatology seems but an exaggeration of that which one finds in the Apocalypse.'[25] It is a conscious

---

21 The impossibility of maintaining such a distinction has been shown by Russell, among others. See Russell *MMJA* 73–103; also the very conservative R.H. Preston and A.T. Hanson *The Revelation of St John the Divine* (London 1949) 43 ff.

22 *NTA* II 688

23 J.M. Ford 'Was Montanism a Jewish-Christian Heresy?' *Journal of Ecclesiastical History* XVII (1966) 145–58

24 R.A. Norris *God and World in Early Christian Theology* (London 1966) notes of Tertullian: 'The world in which he lives mentally is a framework of decision and action, ordered primarily, not in space, whether physical or metaphysical, but in time' (102). This does not prevent Tertullian from speaking in Stoic terms at a number of points, including the materiality of both God and the soul, in his attempts to oppose immaterialist philosophy and its anti-historical denigration of matter. A Jewish-influenced Tertullian would not have been driven to that particular shift in order to make his point.

25 Ford 'Was Montanism a Jewish-Christian Heresy?' 147. Ford also pursues a promising though finally overstressed line of enquiry in connecting Jewish practice to the rigorism of Montanism – and perhaps in noting the influence of the Jewish calendar on the Quartodeciman controversy which vexed Asia Minor (and Rome) for many generations. Quartodecimanism – apparently a harmless decision to celebrate Easter three days following the Passover, rather than always on Sunday, as others preferred (see *NE* #125, 147–151) – attracted the same sort of virulent denunciations as Montanism, with even less obvious reasons. See Coleman-Norton *Roman State and Christian Church* 90–2. The two phenomena are not otherwise related, so far as I know. For a possibly wider significance to Quartodecimanism, see C.W. Dugmore 'A Note on the Quartodecimans' F.M. Cross ed *Studia Patristica* IV pt 2 (Berlin 1961) 411–21 where it is argued that the issues were Christian Passover versus an emphasis on the resurrection and the authority of the apostles versus the authority (and universal applicability) of the Roman tradition. Both Ford and Dugmore point us toward a much more thorough consideration of the significance of

revivification of elements central to early Christianity, but now being submerged in the practice, if not the formal belief, of Christians. The historical affirmations of the Apostles' Creed take definitive shape in this period. These statements are not primarily propositions but dynamic. They emphasize verbs: born, suffered, crucified, buried, rose, ascended, sits on the right hand of God the Father; from thence he will come to judge. The period ought not to be read in light of the established church of the fourth century.[26]

Montanism was, it seems, difficult to live with. It was pronounced against and persecuted with some rigour. No doubt Montanists reflected on the irony of the opponents of laxity being persecuted in the same fashion that the empire before Constantine had persecuted the whole church. Whatever the truth of Apollo-

---

Asian-Phrygian Christianity than it has yet received. This would be more usefully pursued without the gratuitous prior assumption that we are dealing with heresy.

26 The influence of Augustine in the period and for the medieval period is, of course, anti-millennial. See R.A. Markus *Saeculum: History and Society in the Theology of St Augustine* (Cambridge 1970); and N.H. Baynes *The Political Ideas of St Augustine's 'De Civitate Dei'* rev edn (London 1968).

Some well regarded controversialists upheld the early Christian emphases on the Parousia, the historical millennium, and the general picture of the new world pictured in Revelation – in particular Irenaeus and Lactantius from the second and fourth centuries respectively.

Irenaeus, in his five books *Adversus haereses*, anchors himself in the Old Testament and takes Jesus as the focus of its expectation. Once raised and at the right hand of God he 'sums up all in himself' (III.21.9–23.8; III.16.6; III.24.1). The careers of Adam and Jesus are made more completely parallel than Paul had shown in Romans 5 (v.23.2); Mary undoes the sin of Eve (III.18.1; v.19.1). Biblical apocalyptic is displayed at length to show in detail the climax of this age dominated by apostasy; the picture of the Antichrist absorbs most of what is said here. Satan's comparative mildness prior to Jesus' earthly career is due to his ignorance, till then, of his punishment (v.25). The result of the Parousia will be – in a mode that can be left to God – a new earth and heavens (v.33.1–35.2) with 'the creation itself ... renewed to its old condition' (v.32.1). This last, often taken to be a reference to Edenic splendours, is Keble's translation (London 1872). The Anti-Nicene Christian Library translation (Edinburgh 1868) is more definite: the world is 'restored' to its 'primaeval' state. It is not clear that Irenaeus does mean a new Eden. The new heavens and earth are historical in character, not a departure to another plane. 'It is just that in that very creation in which they toiled or were affected, being proved in every way with suffering, they should receive the rewards of their suffering; and that in the creation in which they were slain because of their love to God, in that they should be revived again; and that in the creation in which they endured servitude, in that they should reign. For God is rich in all things and all things are his' (v.32.1). Irenaeus's sense of God's purpose in time is paralleled only by Joachim of Fiore (see ch 11).

Lactantius is a distinguished Latin stylist, voluminous writer, and tutor to Constantine's son Crispus. Lactantius held firmly to the millennialism of the early church. The seventh and last book of his *Divinarum institutionem*, a vigorous polemic against non-Christian philosophy and religion, emphasizes the end-time in a New Testament fashion. This is reconfirmed in his *Epitome of the Divine Institutions*, written many years later (ch 71–2).

nius's claim about Phrygian evasion of martyrdom, this was not true for those whose spokesman was Tertullian. Montanism experienced centuries of persecution by both pagan and Christian empires.

THE MONTANIST TRANSFORMATION OF MILLENNIALISM

There is an unavoidable reliance on speculation here; we are dealing with a movement deprived of its voice by its opponents. Yet it is important to attempt to reconstruct the intentions of Montanism and to speculate about its relation to later millennialism. The Montanists represent the last great millennial movement for many hundreds of years. When millennialism reappeared in the Christian west it most usually surfaced as an underground or protest movement directed at the Christian powers of both church and *regnum*. Often it was a movement of an élite who were the secret carriers of the meaning of history. Medieval millennialism often looked for a more or less imminent end of the unsatisfactory present era and for its replacement by a new era of gentle contemplation, Adamic innocence, radical social levelling, or the biblical Parousia. How millennialism survived and generated powerful new forms must receive at least an attempt at explanation.

We note that the Montanists made heavy use of the fourth gospel's portrayal of the Paraclete. But this use ran against the grain of that gospel's existential preoccupations. For the Montanists, if the Paraclete really has come there really is in us, now, the power to live a risen life. Montanists prophesied, worked miracles, despised mere organization, and behaved militantly against the forces of this world, so soon to pass away. The gifts of the Spirit are signs. The Montanists had a lively sense of the periodized workings of redemptive history; and they saw the approach of the consummation as an event to be marked by an increasing level of conflict.

As a movement of renewal, Montanism was a failure, frustrated by opposition, limited by its own nature, and bound to the dialectic of conflict which was supposed to bring in the Parousia. The Montanists did not seek to become isolated bands; but the circumstances of the period – their opposition to the institutionalization pursued by others – drove this movement in on itself. Its attention was already focused on the church; history became *church* history, restricted history, at one remove from ordinary world existence. And because of the workings of the Paraclete, there is much reference to a kind of supernaturalism: one's power comes from another realm layered somehow over this one.

This position thrust into prominence those who most conspicuously gave evidence of having the gifts of the Spirit – the *visible* gifts such as speaking in 'tongues' or prophecy. These people, in turn, gave to the whole movement a colour that prevented any easy coexistence with other ways of being Christian. There was no way by which Montanism could curb this bent toward extravagance. And polarization probably led Montanists to defend statements and actions that in other circumstances they might have criticized.

Yet there is evidence that Montanism possessed a hierarchy of its own. We are not simply to read into Montanism the presumed tendencies of sectarianism or of ecstatic instability. Vokes suggests[27] that the Montanists' framework is that of the larger church at the time of their separation, schism, or expulsion. Montanism was no novelty but, at least in intention, a radical conservative movement. But we know too little of the second-century church to specify which parts of later Montanism were fossilized remains and which were distinctive adaptations and new growths. Certainly the actions against them forced them into clandestine operations, which would encourage the growth of separate institutions. And there is ample time for this growth; the earliest to the latest notices of Montanism cover a period of almost 500 years, from the second-century Anonymous into the seventh century.

It appears likely that the new prophecy split local groups; inevitably the gifted, in such situations, would pity – perhaps openly – other Christians whose leaders did not have the Spirit. When Montanists were reproached for unsteadiness, they no doubt retorted that the objectors did not understand Christian freedom. Very likely, in making other Christians defensive about their own second-century adaptations, they helped to create the rigidity and caution that they criticized. Montanists were convinced that, even when rejected, it was they who were the heart of the church, the inner church. Beneath the heavy institutional framework and government by committee there existed the true temple of the Spirit. God knew who were his own.

This framework constitutes a considerable, if subtle departure from the millennialism of the earliest church. It will be convenient to set this comparison in terms of our three motifs – the sense of hidden, dialectical drama, of periodization, and of redemptive history.

In Revelation, as in earlier apocalyptic, history is not simply the story of the increasing elimination of evil and the incremental triumph of the good. The faithfulness of the covenanted people will itself stir up the forces of evil to greater activity. It must be so, so long as the organizing principle of the era is man's rebellion against God. The proclamation of Jesus' messiahship and his Parousia, and the existence of the new Israel, provide men with the opportunity to find

27 F.E. Vokes 'Montanism and the Ministry' F.M. Cross ed *Studia Patristica* IX pt 3 (Berlin 1966) 306–15

their true life; but men are not forced or inevitably led into the kingdom. Indeed, as the prologue to Isaiah reminds us, the proclamation may cause men not to hear, to stop their ears. There is no way out of this historical contradiction until evil's own actions have forced men to choose clearly for or against the present world-order (6:9–12). Only at this point does God act decisively to end a world-order which has completed its role in history. Only in these historical actions of God at the end of this age does what has been hidden become plain to all men.

Among the Montanists, despite their own intention to reform the church, the thrust was inward, so that the hidden drama of history referred instead to the paradoxical state of the Montanists themselves. Those deemed mighty in the world – or in the church – are as nothing beside those whom the Spirit has provided with gifts denied to the mighty and wise. There is little sense here that both the mighty and the Montanists are parts of God's historical project. There is little reflection about the world-order. Rather it is the larger church, under the aspect of worldliness, which is the polar opposite to Montanism. The focus is on the hidden merit of the Montanists.

The earlier millennialists had periodized in the following way: old covenant; new covenant fulfilling the old and opening the way to the fullness of the kingdom; and the third age inaugurated only as God's answer to the completed historical contradictions of the second period. Till then the creation groans like a woman in labour (Rom 8:18–25).

The neo-millennialists have cut this tension. The third age is effectively present, in the activities of the Paraclete and of Spirit-filled men. It follows that the previous ages were those of Father and Son; but such a conclusion appears not to have been drawn, because of its relation to modalist heresy.[28] Even the opponents of Montanism usually granted its steadfastness against recognized heresy. The fourth gospel itself had guarded against a modalist conclusion by stressing the 'procession' of the Spirit from both Father and Son. Most especially the Paraclete's function is to explicate and to render present and effective the work accomplished for all men in Jesus' glorification.

But the fourth gospel also promises, through the mouth of Jesus and in connection with the sending of the Paraclete: 'He who believes in me will also do the

---

28 Modalism was the attempt at a historical rationalization of what came to be known as the Trinity (the equal god-ness of Father, Son, and Spirit as one God). Modalism said there has always been one God and that he has been *successively* Father, Son, and Spirit. In addition to the simpler problems it raised, modalism found it difficult in principle to explain why just three modes and not five or six. To answer this by resort to divine fiat is fatal to modalism, which arises in the first place as an attempt to replace the divine fiat by a rationally apprehensible process. See also below, in the chapter on Joachim of Fiore, an extended discussion of the Trinity and history.

works that I do; and greater works than these will he do' (14:12). However the Montanists may have sought to emphasize the continuity of the new age with that of Jesus, they were led in practice – perhaps influenced by their sufferings – to equate Spirit-possession with the novelty of the third age. The existence of the new prophecy and its gifts becomes the sign of the new age. The Montanists have somehow exempted themselves from the historical judgment. Once again, the attempt to restore the earlier version of redemptive history has led to a narrowing of focus from the world to the sectarian setting.

The older millennialism was firmly attached to the Hebrew notion of a historical fulfilment of God's project of redemption. It is not transcendent 'values' which are 'realized,' but historical goals pursued and accomplished by historical means. Even at the extremity of history, the new world is not really beyond history. It is not a shift to a new or higher plane: it is the new heavens and a new earth. And it must be emphasized that alternative modes of conceptualization and expression were readily available to these writers, had they meant to say something other than that God will redeem the *world*.

Montanism remains fully within this mode. Its opposition to the Hellenization of the church was against the turning of Christianity into a religion, into a realm of values or ideals not open to historical inspection, correction, or validation. 'What,' asked Tertullian, 'has Athens to do with Jerusalem?' This and all subsequent forms of millennialism, including the secularized versions, insist that the fulfilment of history must itself be historical.

Despite this clear linkage to the earlier millennialism, there are significant differences between the earliest proclaimers of Jesus' Parousia and the Montanists. And these differences are passed on to succeeding millennial movements. We have seen how the inward reference of Montanism's sense of the hiddenness of the drama had led the new prophecy to deflect the earlier periodization; the future fulfilment becomes uncritically present in the Spirit-demonstrated merit of the Montanists themselves. So too this new periodization altered their sense of history as the arena of the fulfillment of the redemptive drama. The Montanists are not living in a difficult and dangerous interim in which the will of God is being carried out in many, often paradoxical, ways by many different sorts of people. Instead the Montanists themselves are the major sign of the new age. Other people lack a certain reality in this conception. This becomes clear when we ask the questions, How would the fulfilment of history look, in the context of this periodization? Is everyone to enjoy the gifts of the Spirit? The Parousia has, after all, been removed as the beginning for the third age. What characteristics are we to look for as the fullness of the third age? Only the triumph of Montanism would demonstrate the fullness of the new age. There seems here no way to accept as real, as usable by God, the forces, institutions, and men who are not possessed by the Holy Spirit.

The reconstruction above is speculative. But the millennialism of the earliest church was powerfully revived in the second century. Montanism – or what was taken to be Montanism – was disapproved of repeatedly, thus testifying to its survival. Disapproval was felt seriously in a body of people to whom unity was important. But church disapproval in the period up to ca 322 included no civil penalties. These, beginning as soon as Christian authorities could influence official edicts, turned 'Montanism' into an underground movement. Together these two forms of pressure must be counted as very important in creating the changes in Christian millennialism and in making it the radicalized complex of critical concepts which later emerged from this underground.

TOWARDS MEDIEVAL MILLENNIALISM

Neo-millennialism's descent into the underground is only the prelude to medieval millennialism.[29] If Montanism carried millennialism up to its permissible bounds, it required only a modest further step, in the overheated and ungoverned world of the underground, for the Spirit-possessed to become the élite. The naming of the present age as the new age can produce the conviction that the rules and institutions of the past applied only to a previous age. New rules will apply to the men of the spirit – or perhaps no rules at all – but not in any case rules open to a critique from the historic past. Those who have the spirit – few as they are – who live in a state of freedom from the old, have the historic mission to bring the whole world, by means of their power, into the new age of freedom, whether the world wishes it or not. This reasoning was used again and again in medieval and modern times by people whose roots reach back to the struggles in the Christian movement in late antiquity.

The peculiar relation of Montanism to the dominant wing of the church illustrates the dialectical or paradoxical development of history shown so clearly in

---

29 It must be remembered that other groups were driven underground as well. The old paganism, the last remnants of the academics, Manichees, gnostic sectarians, and newer varieties of heretical Christians were also outlawed. We are justified in presuming the existence of a somewhat hazardous twilight world in which all views appeared somewhat gray, or at least with more in common than the knowledge of passwords and safe lodgings. Certainly a depersonalized and dehistoricized 'spirit' came to be appealed to in later protest movements of the medieval period. But we must also remember that quite orthodox folk – though not a majority of them – continued to hold to the plain sense of the New Testament apocalyptic, without becoming subject to the pressures experienced in the underground.

Revelation. We have seen how Montanism arose at least in part as a reaction to the institutionalization of the church, and that further institutionalization followed as the response of a church disturbed by the effects of the new prophecy. But the descent of at least some millennialism into élitism appears to have been a response to the decision[30] of Christianity to become not only a legal cult but the only legal religion and to declare other groups illegal. By being driven underground, the Montanists lost contact with the continuing life of the official church and were driven further in on themselves and on their fellow-outlaws. Justification was thereby supplied for their suspicion that they were the only ones who really understood the issues of the age. By the time of the high Middle Ages, it was the official church or the 'Christianized' society which could be called the Beast or the bloated whore of Revelation, sitting on her seven hills. Henceforth both reformers and the most radical revolutionaries could and did deck themselves with the gifts and the privileges of the spirit-filled.

Norman Cohn has provided[31] a richly coloured portrayal of medieval millennialism, concentrating on those aspects which, in his view, help to illustrate and to originate the psychological and sociological mechanisms he sees at work in modern totalitarianism. Totalitarianism, like these earlier fanaticisms, persecutes Jews and wants to identify itself as being the élite of the last age. Cohn traces millennialism back to Jewish and early Christian sources and notes its survival, in post-Montanist times, in the Christian Sibyllines and other documents,[32] but he tends to cut millennialism off from these sources and to stress its dependence on conditions of social deprivation and dislocation.[33]

He has produced vivid accounts of medieval messiahs, of outbreaks of antinomianism, and of the horrors of popular anti-Jewish campaigns associated with the crusading fervour of the poor, denied a place in the official crusades. But the vividness of these accounts makes it somewhat difficult to see how the sources of

30 The process of so deciding remains obscure. We do not know if it was debated or what the options appeared to be for those who took this decision. It does appear that substantial initiative was taken by Constantine. No doubt the transformation was in part an uncritical reaction to the persecutions of Diocletian, prolonged by some of his successors, particularly in the east. As late as the fifteenth century, an English memorial alabaster panel now in the museum of St Peter Hungate, Norwich, shows the martyr St Erasmus being disembowelled while Diocletian looks on, a demon mounted on his head.

31 *Pursuit of the Millennium* (London 1957). Cohn is particularly helpful in epitomizing the Antichrist tradition and in tracing the motif of the emperor, long dead, who returns when he is needed. For a more benign view of medieval heresy, see J.B. Russell *Dissent and Reform in the Early Middle Ages* (Berkeley, Calif, 1965).

32 Cohn *Pursuit* 1–21

33 Ibid 22–30

this anti-Jewish activity can be related to the elements whose history I have been tracing. The organization of the book tends to atomize millennialism and to obscure the commitment of the official church to at least a formal millennialism of its own. Before proceeding to the great medieval formulations of millennialism, we must deal with the relations of Cohn's picture of millennialism to the present work.

Even Augustine's equation of the millennium with the period of the church by no means abolished the Parousia as a vivid expectation. It was customary to decorate church walls with paintings of the Last Judgment or of Christ crowned in glory. Such pictures formed the backdrops to celebrations of the sacraments and to medieval preaching.[34] And heretical millennialists were far from unique in using apocalyptic imagery against the church when it identified with worldly success or condoned and practiced moral laxity.

Cohn is correct to stress the variegated origins of popular millennialism. But we must stress two common tendencies in it: the dualism which, under cover of denouncing 'laxity,' actually declared itself against the material world as such[35]; and the tendency to abolish the present age's dialectical tension and to declare

34 Often spread on apse walls because of the space needed, they were often lost in later recon-structions (a different form of piety dictated the destruction of apse walls and the addition of 'Lady chapels'). Those on chancel screens were frequently lost with the destruction of such barriers at the Reformation. A very late example can be found on the crossing arch of the church of St Thomas of Canterbury, Salisbury. The Last Judgment, of course, is not the sole element of millennialism, and was combined, from the time of Lactantius, with Hellenistic con-ceptions of the soul and a present heaven layered over this world. But the resurrection of man and the judgment are by no means wholly spiritual in the period. Thomas Aquinas rebukes that sort of spiritualization, saying that it is 'contrary to the truth of the faith to accept a spiri-tual resurrection and decry a bodily one' (Summa contra gentila IV.79.6). He vigourously defends the immortality of the soul, but makes this doctrine 'demand a future resurrection of bodies' (79.10), which will be 'flesh and bones of this kind as he has now' (85.5). The reward or punishment of souls will not await the resurrection of the body (91), 'but there will be another retribution when the bodies are assumed again ... determined for all at the same time' (96.1). It will be carried out 'visibly'; Christ will execute it in his 'form of humanity, which all may be able to see, both the good and the wicked' (96.3). The final state of the cosmos is not one in which only 'spirit' exists: 'The bodily creation will at the last be disposed in harmony with the state of man ... even the bodily creation will achieve a kind of resplendence in its own way' (97.7). Many of the essential concerns of millennialism are argued for. (For a somewhat different effect of the combination of Hebrew and substantialist motifs, see below, 120 ff).

35 Despite the oft-repeated lore to the contrary, official church pronouncements consistently declared against denigration of the flesh or of the married state. Among the earliest of such declarations, the canons of the fourth century council or synod of Gangra rebuke asceticism which exalts itself at the expense of the holiness of ordinary life. See canons 9, 10, 14, 15, 16, 19, 20 in C.J. Hefele History of the Christian Councils from the Original Documents (Edinburgh 1871 et seq) 330–6, hereinafter cited as HCC.

that the perfected sectarians now live in the end-time and possess its privileges. Only the second of these can be traced to millennialism at all; the first arises from gnostic or Neo-Platonic thought. But both have a relation to the anti-Jewish activity which Cohn sees as somehow directly related to millennialism. Cohn makes this connection through the link he believes he has shown to exist between Revelation and the Antichrist legends, and between the sleeping emperor motif and the general Christian-imperial nostalgia among insecure medieval peoples. But these connections are of the most general kind.[36] Cohn's major explanation for anti-Jewish activity is psychosocial; and since he tends to explain millennialism as a psychosocial phenomenon,[37] the conceptual link between millennialism and anti-Jewish activity is not established with any persuasiveness.

I believe this anti-Jewish activity must be linked to the sectarian millennialists' attack on the official church. The persisting and qualified millennialism of the church, though it portrays the Jews as a superseded community, does not provide any grounds for attack upon them.[38] But the syncretistic millennialism of the high Middle Ages had ample reason to attack medieval Jewry. As the ancient custodians of God's will in history, as a community surviving continuously in hope of the not-yet-fulfilled ancient promises, Jews constituted a standing challenge to all declarations that the third age is impending or that it has arrived in its fullness. The official church could be the community of the second age, within which the new age could be awaited. The new millennial groups, dedicated to the proposition that in the group itself the third age was upon us, were always small, unstable in organization, and often anti-sacramental. But where church institutions could not be attacked directly (and sometimes they could be), the Jews were vulnerable. The group whose life said most eloquently that history cannot be overleaped – this group could be eliminated, sometimes by the fiat of manifestos, sometimes by physical attack.

Millennialist language can cover a dualism of spirit versus matter foreign to the older millennialism. 'Spiritual' millennialism often masked its attacks on the flesh by attacking instead the worldliness and lax sexuality of many of the functionaries of the medieval church. Here too the Jews offered a special target – not

36 Perhaps Cohn's reluctance to allow millennialism a central role in Jewish life itself, both ancient and medieval, can be related to an implicit acceptance of the notion of normative Judaism, with its stress on 'Judaism' as an ethic.

37 *Pursuit* 58–74. This line of analysis is taken further in his *Europe's Inner Demons* (London 1975).

38 Modern revivals of millennialism often lay stress on the role of the Jews in the Parousia and result in a kind of philo-semitism. In both the seventeenth and nineteenth centuries there were efforts made by Christians to hasten the Parousia by inducing Jews to emigrate to Palestine – well before the rise of modern Jewish Zionism.

because they professed asceticism but practiced carnality – but because popular Jewish life was frankly material and historical. Its concern, in Law and practice, was with this world's daily occurrences; and its age to come was no Hellenized 'spiritual plane' or 'other world' but an age materially like this one, yet made right.[39] This devilish doctrine, held by a degraded and defenceless people, deserved to be extirpated by the spiritual virtuosi of the new age.

Neither syncretistic, spiritual millennialism nor peasant and *lumpenproletariat* millennialism – fuelled from various traditions and springing from different social contexts – was capable of providing a coherent intellectual base for the great edifice of medieval millennialism. This role was taken by Joachim of Fiore.

39 I do not overlook the Jewish mystical tradition, with its use of emanational gnostic categories, which would have received the approbation of syncretistic millennial movements had they known of it.

11

Joachim of Fiore and the third age

A revived archaic millennialism and a syncretistic élitist millennialism had found a conceptual framework by which to build a critique of the official church. Yet this apparatus remained unsystematized and for the most part in the hands of marginal people until the advent of the abbot Joachim of Fiore. He provided a sophisticated theological and historical structure, grounded in the authority of the scriptures. It could be used, by the educated and the simple alike, to articulate their criticisms of society and to project an inevitable future in which they or their successors would play key roles.

Joachim (ca 1135–1202) founded a small order of rigorous discipline in Calabria seeking a more simple and apostolic communal life. Joachim was a serious biblical exegete in a period when theology was dominated by the allegorical mining of biblical texts and the citation of texts from earlier medieval authorities. Christian truth, as delivered by scriptures, councils, and Fathers, was taken to be both the foundation of all truth and its proof.

The most important elements in Joachim's work are his 'discovery' of the detailed correspondence between the eras before Jesus and after and his construction of three *status* or periods of human history which can be linked successively to the persons of Father, Son, and Holy Spirit. Since it could be shown that the two testaments covered the whole of human history[1] from creation to consummation, the inner movement of human affairs had been graciously and decisively disclosed. By means of the correspondences and of the scheme of three successive

---

1 That Daniel had predicted the entire Old Testament period, and perhaps far more, was axiomatic by this time. (Porphyry, the third-century pagan opponent of Christianity, had demonstrated the flaws in this notion.) Joachim is perhaps more conservative than many other commentators in restricting Daniel to coverage of the era before Jesus. His schemes of correspondence allow him to project historical parallels from it. He also apparently took the genealogy of 1 Chronicles 1–3 as bringing the generations down to just before Jesus.

periods of world history, the present – ca 1200 – was shown to be the close of one great act of history and the preparation for the decisive period in the human drama. This dual scheme and its problems will be dealt with first. Then we shall consider the far-reaching use made of it by radicals and others of the thirteenth and fourteenth centuries. Finally, we shall view Joachim's work and that of his successors against the older millennialism and later millennialism.

JOACHIM'S CORRESPONDENCES

Joachim tells us[2] how, in the midst of his labours on the scriptures, he received the sudden insight of the fundamental correspondence between the era of the Old Testament and that of the New. When he sought confirmation of this in detail, the whole of human history began to unfold its orderly sequence before him. Rigorously controlled – and thus the more powerful as a tool of analysis – in the hands of Joachim himself, this scheme of correspondences was pursued after his death in many popular writings.[3] As result, Joachim obtained a reputation as the seer of the new age of mankind, about to dawn. In the great conflicts of the age, the doctrine of Joachim became a weapon in the hands of controversialists and revolutionaries. Easily secularized, his schema provided the basic shape of the later doctrine of progress.

Joachim's schemes of correspondence are historical in character. Despite his eagerness to use numbers to point to the precise nature and location of these correspondences, Joachim is fundamentally concerned with the actual events of

---

2   *Expositio apocalypsim* f 39[v], quoted in M. Reeves *The Influence of Prophecy in the Later Middle Ages* (Oxford 1962) 22 (hereinafter IPLMA); and M. Reeves and B. Hirsch-Reich *The Figurae of Joachim of Fiore* (Oxford 1972) 4 (*FJF*). Joachim's principal works are his Revelation commentary *Expositio apocalypsim*, the *Liber concordie*, the *Psalterium decem chordarum*, and his *Tractatus super quatuor evangelia*. His views were long obscured by the existence of a number of later works ascribed to him. The relation of the undoubted illustrative figures by Joachim in his own work to the figures in the different versions of the *Liber figurae* is a complex and important problem, since his schemata are often better perceived synoptically in diagrams and figures than in his running text. Significant English-language works on Joachim will be cited throughout this chapter. The present generation of scholarship draws a firmer line between Joachim and his successors than did older scholarship; cf K. Löwith's chapter on Joachim in his *Meaning in History* (Chicago 1946) to M. Bloomfield and M. Reeves's 'Penetration of Joachism into Northern Europe' *Speculum* XXIX (1954) 772–93 and the later work of Reeves and her collaborators, which constitute a solid and indispensable point of departure for the next generation.

3   *Joachimist* refers to the work of Joachim and to the views of his immediate circle, and *Joachite* to later work that distorts Joachim's own work, or that prepares new writings of this sort as from his hand, or that uses his outlines to quite different ends from his.

history and not with superterrestrial truths. This alone, quite apart from his conclusions, marks him as a radical in his period, heretofore dominated by a debased Neo-Platonic treatment of biblical texts. Joachim's discovered concordance between the testaments (taken as historical documents) and the eras is not a matter of allegory; it is 'a similitude of proportion between actual historical facts ... which exist in their own right, each in its own dispensation.'[4] His studies on Revelation gave him this insight.

It became clear to him that the history of the world, as given authoritatively in the Old Testament,[5] was in seven periods from the beginning to the time of John the Baptist and Jesus, and that the history of the world from that time forward was given in the New Testament – he understood Revelation to contain all future history between the first century and the consummation – and was also divided into seven periods. Each period[6] or *tempus* in each of the two eras was brought to an end by a war or persecution. The end of the Old Testament era was signalled by the climactic persecution under the satanic Antiochus. The New Testament era will be brought to its end by the advent of the Antichrist at the end of the sixth *tempus* and by the world figure of Gog at the end of the seventh, prior to the consummation. Each era thus ends in a great question mark, which is answered by God himself, who is in full control of redemptive history. The consummation, standing beyond the scope of the revealed history, remains in this sense beyond history.[7] Within world history as given, Jesus Christ stands as its undoubted centre. He is the pivot of the eras; the Old flows toward him as its answer; the New flows from him in a dialectic fashion, as Satan struggles still, till Jesus' status as the final answer is confirmed at the consummation. The detailed parallelism of the sevens apart, this scheme is orthodox and follows the general bent of Irenaeus's late-second-century justification of redemptive history.

But Joachim articulates also a system or pattern of threes, based on the Christian Trinity. This destabilizes the firm structure of the two eras. If the Old Testament era of seven *tempora* is identified as that of God the Father – as it was – then the second is clearly that of the Son. This leaves the natural but awkward question of the temporal place or role of the Holy Spirit. Joachim's identification of temporal symmetry between the first and second eras was detailed and definite. He worked out the generations in detail, from precursor to modal figure to conclusion, in elegant repetition and symmetry, thus providing a pattern within each

---

4 *FJF* 6
5 His Old Testament contained the apocryphal books I and II Maccabees.
6 Or each of the first six *tempora* in each era, since the seventh is a kind of sabbath
7 But this must be specified most carefully. See below, n13.

era.[8] But this dual scheme leaves the Holy Spirit without a temporal base of the same sort. The 'omission' cried out for an alteration of the scheme of concords to include a third age.

It has been customary, reading Joachim through later Joachite materials, to find that he yielded to this need for a perfect Trinitarian temporal symmetry. M. Reeves has consistently argued that the double seven concord is fundamental; she has attempted recently to show that Joachim did not provide a third age for the Holy Spirit, at least not of the sort provided for Father and Son.[9] The Spirit's role is not temporal, she now maintains, in the same way as those of Father and Son. Rather the Spirit's role is one of raising men to yet higher levels of insight and purity of life, in a fashion somewhat independent of the pattern of temporal concords.[10]

Joachim's deep rooting in the scriptures, almost unparalleled since the early Fathers,[11] and his grasp of the particular shape given there to redemptive history

8 Joachim's number emphasis goes beyond the use of two, three, and twelve. His twelves are often elaborately divisible into fives and sevens (see *FJF* 16 ff). But there is little to suggest that his concern with numbers was due to the influence of Kabbalistic conceptions of number (see G. Scholem *On the Kabbala and Its Symbolism* London 1968). These may have originated in rabbinic discoveries of the sorts of correspondence found by Joachim, but they were soon pursued on the basis of theosophical systems. The one point of contact between Joachim and Kabbalistic scholarship appears to be Petrus Alphonsi, a Spanish Jewish convert, who apparently influenced some of Joachim's *figurae* – but not the numerically dependent ones. See *FJF* 40 ff. Nevertheless, Joachim's fascination with numbers is noteworthy – they are pointers to correspondence and validations of it. They are not themselves truth, however, as they came to be for some Kabbalists and non-Jewish theosophists, particularly in the Renaissance, who believed themselves to be resuscitating Pythagoreanism. The later thinker most like Joachim in his handling of numbers is Charles Fourier, on whom see below, ch 27.

9 *FJF* 11; cf Reeves 'The Liber Figurarum of Joachim of Fiore' *Medieval and Renaissance Studies* II (1950) 57–81, in which she finds him oscillating between assigning the primacy to the two and to the three (75 ff).

10 *FJF* 11 ff. On Joachim's orthodoxy, see *IPLMA* 126–32, and below, n 13. Reeves finds it necessary to defend him *tout court*, which involves her in a defense of the third *status* of the Holy Spirit as being enclosed within the New Testament's compass of seven *tempora*. I do not believe this tactic necessary or that the third *status* can be so securely lodged within the *tempora* of the New Testament half of the two-age scheme. There is no doubt that Joachim aimed at being completely orthodox and faithful to the concords as shown to him by the sacred scriptures which were, of course, incapable of leading him astray. But it is not so clear, as I have argued below, that his teaching could remain orthodox independently of the precise history implied in his schemata.

11 But note also that, in the twelfth century, the *Apocalypsis goliae* could use Revelation 5–8 as the reference point for a parody of the corrupt church. See F.X. Newman 'The Structure of Vision in "Apocalypsis Goliae"' *Medieval Studies* XXIX (1967) 113–23.

would certainly have made him aware of the dangers involved in any removal of Jesus from his pivotal position in that history. He recasts history in terms of two eras, but what happens then to the Spirit? The fourth gospel's emphasis on the Paraclete, and the Montanists' actualization of this emphasis, produced relatively modest consequences. But Joachim's system brings to history a drastic reorientation if Jesus is displaced from his central position.

THE PROBLEM OF THREE 'STATUS'

Any temporalization of the Spirit's work into eras such as those of Father and Son creates grave difficulties. A temporalization of the fourth gospel's emphasis truncates the era of the Son to the few short years of Jesus' career. The fourth gospel clearly does not intend this result and provides little basis for it, since its doctrine of the pre-existent *logos* (John 1) extends the Son's era over the whole of cosmic history. Joachim has undertaken to show out of the divine scriptures how God has shaped history into eras, dispensations, movements, and periods and how God has provided the most remarkable and intellectually satisfying correspondences between the two eras linked to the activities of Father and Son respectively. Joachim has shown how the second era has grown out of the first and is predicated on it. He is speaking here of the real history of the world, of its institutions, and not merely of patterns visible only to intellectuals.

The era (or perhaps the only quasi-temporal *status*) of the Holy Spirit is all too likely to be seen as having a structure and a temporal duration just like the eras of the Father and Son. Joachim appears to have understood this problem. He places his own time in the fortieth 'week' of the present (New Testament) 42-week era, but cautions against construing the last 2 weeks in the same 30-years-to-a-generation fashion as the previous 40. As we near the climax of the era and God's action takes more direct control of events, the chronology of the sixth and seventh *tempora* may be curtailed or stretched to accommodate the divine action. Joachim has also noted an anomaly at the end of the first era, which can be taken as a clue to the end of this one as well. Each of the Old Testament *tempora* had been marked by a single, dominant war or persecution. But the sixth had undergone a double persecution, thus leaving the seventh *tempus*, without a persecution, as a kind of sabbath. So in the present era, Joachim foresees the occurrence of a double persecution to end the sixth *tempus*: by the ten kings (= ten horns, Rev 17:12) and by Antichrist himself. This leaves the seventh *tempus* – and its indeterminate length – as the 'era' of the Holy Spirit.

Thus far the scheme is fastened securely to the scheme of the two eras through the seven seals on the scroll of Revelation 5. The seals are taken to have been applied in the first era, one in each *tempus*. They are successively opened in the present era, since it is axiomatic for Joachim that the New Testament covers and explains all human history from Jesus onward. Thus if the seven tempora of the Old Testament era can be correlated with the application of the seals, then their opening can be correlated with the successive *tempora* of this present era.[12] When the seventh seal was opened, 'there was silence in heaven for about half an hour,' unlike the circumstances attending the previous six. Joachim has squeezed the 'age of the Spirit' into the seventh, sabbatical tempus of the second era. Maintaining the correspondence between the old and the new and between two eras only has prevented the age of the Spirit being freed from the revealed history. But this depends on a most careful reading of Joachim and on drawing the far from obvious conclusion that 'in the conception of the Sabbath Age, the double sevens, the single seven and the three *status* all come together.'[13]

There are profound difficulties in this reading of Joachim. Once he has embarked on a correlation of history with the persons of the Trinity, his system must logically provide the Holy Spirit with an equivalent age and *status* to those of Father and Son. It cannot be left as a featureless sabbath. There is abundant speculation in Joachim on the excellence and importance of the third *status*, which suggests that age is a historical equivalent to the first and second *status*.

Joachim has involved himself in two enterprises difficult to reconcile. The first is a historical rendering of the *status* of Father and Son (that of the Spirit being

---

12 *FJF* 133 ff.
13 *FJF* 123. The single seven is that popularized by Augustine (*Civitate Dei* XVIII.18) in which the entire history of mankind is divided into seven periods. The seventh *etas* here is a sabbath. But Reeves is particularly insistent on identifying the third *status* as the sabbath of the Augustinian system or as an atemporal condition. This contention is supported by one of the *figurae* (*FJF* Pl.9) though not unambiguously; and it certainly defends Joachim against the contention that he encouraged the later speculation on the third age. In this one figure he clearly projects an 'eighth day' – an orthodox expression for the final kingdom on the other side of Gog's persecution (see also *IPLMA* 296 ff). But Reeves is concerned to describe this final state as timeless or ahistorical (see *FJF* 10–12, 123, 138, 152; *IPLMA* 299, 303, 494). It is not clear that this in fact corresponds to Joachim's intention (as she recognizes in *FJF* 154 n1).

The timelessness asserted for the final kingdom, by Reeves on Joachim's behalf, implies that history is the arena of sin – irremediably so. But *is* history to be overcome? The view taken in Genesis 1 is that history is a created good, made prior to sin. Daniel and Revelation do not finally collapse history into eternity or equate victory with escape from time into eternity, though the conceptual vocabulary was available to them to say this.

Reeves in these passages (see also *IPLMA* 390) speaks of optimism and pessimism being at stake here in the marking off of the third status from the final kingdom by means of Gog's persecution and the change from history to eternity. Joachim is alleged to be pessimistic in this and his followers optimistic in projecting an unbroken transition. The terms are misleading. Any optimism of this latter sort is actually a deep pessimism about the capacity of history to embody the redeemed life of mankind. But the terms are alien and would be better avoided.

circumscribed by the doctrine that the Spirit proceeds from, and refers back to the work of, Father and Son). Further, the final persecution by the mysterious Gog[14] follows the third status, which is thus not an ungoverned leap into freedom from the limits of history as we have known it.

The second enterprise of Joachim undermines this schema. The era of the Son is a historical advance upon that of the Father. Its institutions are better, more fully in accord with the final intention of God than those of the first era, just as Jesus is a far fuller revelation than the Old Testament Law. Similarly, the men of the third status, or at least the central figures of that era, represent more fully the completion of the intention of God than do the modal figures of this present age.[15] Joachim attempts to limit the third age by providing the revolt of Gog at the end of the third status (or of the seventh tempus of the second era). But this feature permits Joachim's interpreters to render the third status more historical than he may have intended, for it is now set within history. Combined with the two ages, the emphasis on development suggests a third age soon to dawn, marking a judgment upon and a break with the second, just as the present era made such a judgement of and break with the first status. Despite his apparent intention, then, we arrive at a three-age schematization of human history (see Table 1 and Figure 1).

14 The third status is here made equivalent to the millennium of Revelation 20. Joachim emphasizes the role of Gog, taken here as a person (cf Rev 20:8: 'the nations which are at the four corners of the earth, that is, Gog and Magog'), in contrast to Revelation, for which the unbound Satan is the principal actor. But the medieval Gog had grown by feeding upon the careers and rumoured accomplishments of barbarian, Muslim, and Mongol conquerors. Gog is an individual in Ezekiel 38–9, 'chief prince of Meshech and Tubal,' who will lead a great host from the ends of the earth against Israel, there to perish by direct action of God, who will then vindicate himself before all men (38:16, 23; 39:7, 27–8). In the early medieval period, Gog has become a demonic figure.

15 They do not represent better the will of God, however. The institutions of earlier eras are in accord with the will of God as revealed in those eras. Joachim does not suggest that some perfect pattern of characteristics and institutions hangs over all history by reference to which we can declare that earlier men fell short of God's will and that we approximate more closely to it. The modal men of the Old Testament are truly declared to have been righteous before God by following his revealed will.

For Joachim, we cannot hoist ourselves out of history; we cannot penetrate behind revelation. To suppose that we could is to suppose that we possess some standard external to God by means of which we can think God's thoughts before him. Such a standard would enable men to judge God as well as history. It would enfold God within a cosmos taken to be totality. Such a conception lies at the foundation of utopianism, but it is alien to millennialism. On Joachim's strictures against any essence of divinity behind Father, Son, and Spirit, see below, 123 ff and 126 n28.

TABLE 1 Conflation of Joachimist schemata

Age or status corresponding to person or modality of God	Dominant principle	Institutional order or social relationship	Social value	Dominant characteristic among men	Modal class	Initiator or germinator	Fructificator
Father	Law	Slavery	Labour	Knowledge	The married	Adam	Jacob
Son	Grace and faith	Sonship	Learning and discipline	Wisdom	Celibate parish clerics	Uzziah or Hezekiah	Christ
Holy Spirit	Freedom, joy, and love	Liberty	Contemplation	Fullness of spiritual intellection	Contemplative cloistered monks	Benedict	?

Figure 1   Temporal schemata and concords

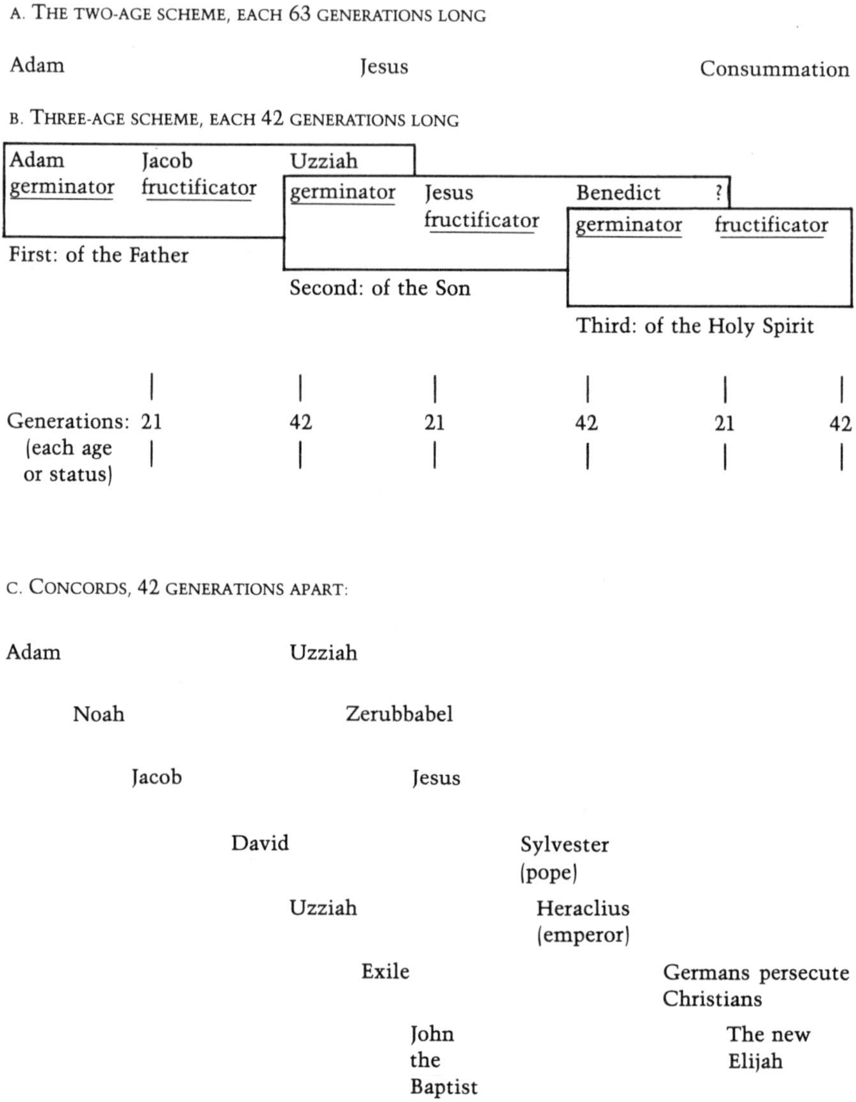

A. THE TWO-AGE SCHEME, EACH 63 GENERATIONS LONG

Adam   Jesus   Consummation

B. THREE-AGE SCHEME, EACH 42 GENERATIONS LONG

Adam	Jacob	Uzziah			
germinator	fructificator	germinator	Jesus	Benedict	?
			fructificator	germinator	fructificator
First: of the Father					
		Second: of the Son			
				Third: of the Holy Spirit	

Generations: 21	42	21	42	21	42
(each age or status)					

C. CONCORDS, 42 GENERATIONS APART:

Adam   Uzziah

      Noah   Zerubbabel

          Jacob   Jesus

              David   Sylvester
                                            (pope)

                  Uzziah   Heraclius
                                            (emperor)

                      Exile   Germans persecute
                                                    Christians

                          John   The new
                          the   Elijah
                          Baptist

The mobilization of long-lasting social movements depends on an intellectual strategy far removed from mere crankiness. Arbitrary eccentricities can give rise only to restricted sectarian developments. Joachim's achievement was his unfolding of the inner movement of human history by unlocking the plain but hitherto undiscovered meaning of the scriptural calculations. Yet his significance was not tied to one single chain of logic following from one isolated postulate. He did his work several times and in several ways; concordances of many sorts existed. The system was not only complex; it was fertile. And once exhibited, it could be employed by others. All that was required were literacy and the belief – axiomatic in the period – that what could be proved from the scriptures needed no other warrant. Further, Joachim's method was self-justifying; it brought disclosures of contemporary history that could be shown to match or express the Bible's own internal mathematics of history.

Methods of the period

Joachim's intentions and his work in progress were scrutinized by three successive popes with whom he had face-to-face encounters. His revival of millennialism was not due to some psychic peculiarity or to any special crisis in Calabria. At most, one can suggest that Joachim found the exegetical practices of the period inadequate to support his need to understand the shape of the scriptures as a whole. The 'historical' or plain sense of the scriptures was included as one of the four standard ways of exegesis; but it was commonly used as a mere starting point for feats of allegorical, anagogical, and tropological expertise, that is, the discovery of metaphorical meanings, mystical insights, and moral teachings – all these to be found in any passage. The biblical books were less interpreted than handled as chests of mosaic tiles: small, unrelated bits of colour capable of yielding many different patterns. The principles of design are not in the tiles but are derived from elsewhere.[16]

16 Aquinas, among others, insisted upon the primacy of the historical, at least in the sense that it could not be disregarded or defied. His admonition was needed. And even his defence tells us of the salience of the other senses: the historical is the foundation; the others are walls, roof, and ornamentation. They are the things that surround us in our business within the house, which shelter us, and which give employment to the greatest craftsmen, as distinguished from the humble, rough work of the foundation-layers. See his preface to his *Allegoriae in sacram scripturam*, cited in C.A. Patrides *The Grand Design of God: The Literary Form of the Christian View of History* (London 1972) 42 n 31. See further the relevant sections in *St Thomas Aquinas: Theological Texts* selected, tr, and with notes and intro by Thomas Gilbey (London 1955). McGinn, citing de Lubac and Grundmann, says that Joachim does not follow the 'four senses' method; 'The Abbot and the Doctors' *Church History* XL (1971) 31.

It should be remembered that history was not taught as part of the proper curriculum of medieval schools. It was carried on by individual chronographers and occasionally by men of very large ambition to describe the shape of their own and earlier times. Very little of this, however, was taught to that small minority of men who achieved literacy. The biblical history as such was perhaps communicated better to the illiterate masses through the miracle plays and other representational cycles. Joachim thus worked a large change by reintroducing historical argumentation, by making historical insight central to the interpretation of the scriptures, and by making it possible for historical argumentation to be used as the vehicle for a critique of the present age and conditions. Even the masses were capable of grasping the historical-numerical structures by which he explained the shape and significance of the times.

The vitality of Joachim's method is displayed by its persistence in the face of the failure of the years 1260 and 1290 to bring in the seventh *tempus* or the third *status*. These failures no more discredited the new method of historical understanding and interpretation than had the failures visible in the revisions of Daniel 12, to which the Joachite predictions are exactly parallel.[17] The point was not really the ability to predict a given day but to have the means to understand history as a whole and one's own role in it.

This ability was indispensable to combat the period's hierarchy of spiritual and secular powers which drew its strength from a dominant plane of heavenly transcendence that formed and validated the arrangements of this earthly plane. In this scheme spiritual essences can be communicated sacramentally; and social truths can be shown to derive logically from the privileged realm of eternal truth

17 The numbers from Daniel in question are 12:7 – 'a time, times and a time and a half,' to be taken as 3½ years, 42 months, or 1260 'days'; 12:11–1290 days; and 12:12–1335. These numbers were translated into calendar years dating from Jesus' birth or from the year of his death and resurrection. Such a programme yields dates of 1260, 1290, 1320, 1335, and 1365. Jean de Roquetaillade, in the mid-fourteenth century, was prepared to predict a literal millennium to be inaugurated in 1415 (*IPLMA* 228, 322).

Later writers were less likely to set dates but quite ready to compare the configuration of current events with that established (in the received tradition) for the Last Days. On that basis it could be announced that Charles VIII of France in 1494 or the Emperor Charles V, in 1519, 1527, or later, was the Emperor of the Last Days. The motif of the last emperor, whether as good or bad emperor, is not from Joachim; but it had become attached to the Joachite structure at a relatively early period (*IPLMA* 311).

Was Campanella a millennialist influenced by Joachim? Reeves claims that 'his ardent expectation of a new world was founded on a Joachimist structure of history' (*IPLMA* 387). Though he is in full command of the millennialist vocabulary and stock of images, and displays them in millennial-sounding projects for various kings and popes, he was equally at home with astrology and with utopian patterns of thought, though he handles nothing consistently. See below, ch 19.

above this temporal realm. So long as doubters, dissidents, and reformers accepted this picture, they could hope to make only marginal changes, showing by accepted methods that their versions of social truth could be derived more logically, more directly, or more securely from the mutually acknowledged realm of atemporal truth. The new Aristotelian logic of the thirteenth century was to become popular because of its superior value to both reformers and defenders of the existing formulae of Christendom.[18] But the gains from this method remained marginal because truth was believed to be self-consistent and unchangeable, propositional and ahistorical.

A second mode employed was boldly to assert a counter-truth and to argue from it to new conclusions. This way was followed by submerged groups with a secret or higher truth. These alternative truths, however, were often too subtle to hold their followers in the face of determined counter-attacks by people such as the Dominicans. Supra-temporal truth posed against supra-temporal truth tends to leave the last word to that truth able to wield secular power most effectively. Whoever wins, the result is not seen as one of change but of the establishment or vindication here of a supra-temporal reality.

Joachim and the Trinity in history

Joachim's profound contribution is to introduce a third course of analysis: the notion of historical truth. The orders of each age are coming to be and then passing away in favour of an order most completely expressive of the fullness of God himself. Joachim is able to show development,[19] as from the order of married men to that of spiritual monks, or from slavery to sonship to free autonomy. But his Trinitarian scheme prevents any simple declaration that early modes of existence are inferior and later ones are superior by the mere fact of temporal succession alone. What God the Father ordained for Abraham is not evil or even 'primitive'; it is an order appropriate to its place in the single drama of redemption. Earlier acts in a play are neither better nor worse than the later by the mere fact of their temporal priority.

Joachim's scheme is developmental in the way that drama is developmental. In displaying this sense of history, Joachim has advanced well beyond the mere

18 The careful working out of the implications of the formulae of the early councils and Fathers also continued in this period, of course, especially in the eastern church. The latter existed in more obvious continuity with the earlier conditions than did the west, somewhat cut off from the east by poor communication and by the advent of aggressive Islam.

   For a review of the handling of the historical themes of Parousia and end-time in the rather ahistorical mode of the Greek Fathers, see G. Florovsky 'Eschatology in the Patristic Age: An Introduction' K. Aland and F.M. Cross ed *Studia Patristica* VII (Berlin 1957) 235–50.

19 See again Figure 1 and Table 1, above.

succession of events as given in the popular play cycles, and equally beyond the medieval chronicles. His scheme is developmental in another sense, however, that stands in some tension with his Trinitarian emphasis. The successive ages are improvements on their predecessors. It is finally better to be a son than to be a slave, and better still to be a free man of the third *status*. Law and sonship properly yield to freedom. Each successive set of institutions is closer to the final state of beatitude that God has prepared for his own.

Joachim guards against a simplistic progressivism, however, in two ways. First, the presence of Antiochus, Antichrist, and Gog shows us that the drama has its antagonist; within the permissive will of God, Satan has his role to play until the end of the historical drama as it is disclosed in the scriptures. Each age closes in a mighty challenge to God, mounted by Satan through his historical agents. These challenges are answered by the yet fuller disclosure of God and the shape of his intention for men, by means of a deeper engagement of God in the drama.

Second, the orthodox notion of the Trinity provides no grounds for any denigration of the Father in favour of the Son; and the Spirit is not more fully God than the Son. This battle had been thoroughly fought in the early church against gnostics who identified the God of Genesis with an inferior being – else why would he have created matter? – whose work is remedied by the sending of Jesus from the true Father, pure and remote from the unfortunate creation. It was found necessary to state the identity of the true Father as the creator, and the consubstantiality of the Son and the Father, in order to establish God's saving actions in history and in Jesus as his final and complete disclosure. If the Son were a creature, the way was opened in principle for further revelations through other creatures. The seemingly obscure arguments in the fourth and fifth centuries, over whether the Son is of *like* substance or of the *same* substance with the Father, turn on the need to ground the uniqueness and finality of the saving events of Jesus' execution and resurrection. Only if he is 'fully God'[20] can this be guaranteed. Similarly, the Holy Spirit is God, God in the world, present in the new Israel, moving in his church, the guarantor of the true communication to us of Jesus and his saving work.

Sabellius, in the fourth century, attempted to rationalize this complex of utterances by proposing that God was *successively* Father, Son, and Spirit. This attractive solution was rejected[21] because it ran against the grain of the drama of redemption. Jesus will come again, the same Jesus: the Lamb slain yet alive, who

---

20 This assertion occasioned a further series of controversies about how to declare his full humanity without denying his divinity.

21 Sometimes, as it seems, on narrow grounds, such as those implied in the question, 'Then to whom was Jesus praying?'

sits now at the right hand of the Father who sent him. The Spirit communicates the completed work of the Son and maintains in Christians the lively hope of the consummation. If God has been successively one thing, and then another, the structure of that drama has been abandoned; and Christians cannot know that God will not transform himself into something yet different. The objection that the consubstantial Trinity might be only a Trinity of perception, that it could logically be a quaternity in itself, was rebutted by emphasizing the ministerial role of the Spirit; he testifies not to himself but to the Father and Son and their historical work. We are sure of his efficacious work because we are put into the presence of the living Father and Son through the Spirit. Thus he is one God, consubstantial as Father, Son, and Spirit.

Joachim was a conscious defender of this orthodox conception of the triune God. His one brush with authority was his vigorous objection to the Trinitarian formulation of Peter Lombard, which he viewed as implying a divine essence behind Father, Son, and Spirit. Joachim's concern for guarding the orthodox formulation of the Trinity and his labours on the shape of history belong together. Truth is historical, embodied, not abstracted from history.

But, quite against his intention, Joachim's conviction both undermined the authority of the papacy and provided the Holy Spirit with a world-era superseding those of the Father and the Son. The scheme of concords and *status* links God to history far more closely than any theology or philosophy since those of Irenaeus or the apocalyptic classics of late antiquity. By Joachim's day, Christian civilization and its directing institutions were underwritten by a very different picture of the divine relation to the world of human events. God the Father presided over history as Creator and as Final End; the Son was to act as judge at the consummation; the Holy Spirit acted as sanction for the authority of the institutions of salvation. But the notion of planes or levels of existence left a gap between God's eternity and man's history. This gap deprived historical life of that reality which modern man takes for granted and which the older Hebrew conception of the redemptive drama had expressed so confidently. The Holy Spirit empowered and legitimated ecclesiastical structures. But this activity was no substitute for his intimate presence with men as Israel had experienced the Father or the apostolic generation Jesus. The claim that the Holy Spirit was moving freely and unchannelled as the divine will had proved destabilizing in the period before Constantine and subversive when the great authoritative institutions were being built.[22]

---

22 The tradition of the east is rather different, in that the Spirit continued to be explicitly emphasized. But he was declared to manifest himself publicly in the unity of imperial throne with orthodoxy. The emperor was charismatic; and his will had the force of canons of church councils. Constantine's position as both emperor and theologian established this claim. His son

In the west, the claims of the bishop of Rome for jurisdiction over other western bishops – and all Christians everywhere – could not be based on so doubtful a matter as a claim to a greater portion of the Holy Spirit for Rome's bishops. Such a claim was too easily challenged. It had to be, and was, based on a claim deriving from Jesus himself and his alleged choice of Peter to lead the apostles, on the transfer of Peter to Rome, and on the succession to Peter's primacy. This unique complex of claims was maintained with increasing insistence by the Roman bishops and was rewarded with some success, at least in the west. It came to be an indispensable element in the later structure of public life in the west.

The claims for the Holy Spirit – to be as involved with the full life of mankind in this age as Father and Son had been – had to be denied in practice. Any person or institution empowered by the Spirit could come into conflict with Rome – the Spirit in conflict with the Son. In the developed phase of the Roman claim (1075–ca 1268), it was also employed to deny that kings had an independent status as agents of the divine king and that they were directly responsible to him for the maintenance of his creation. The logic of the Roman position required that there be no possibility of conflict between a legitimate representative of the Father's orders of creation and the monarch of the Son's sole order of salvation. Hence all earthly power, earlier admitted to have a co-ordinate status with the power of the papal keys of Peter, was finally declared to be ministerial and granted from the pope; kings were his agents.

The issue here is not the background or propriety of these claims, but their effect in the west on the doctrine of the Holy Spirit and on the whole matter of God's relation to the historical process. The prime effect was a rather formal relation of the Father to the present age and a subordination or relegation to private or sheltered space of the Spirit. But the Son's role, too, was made distant from living events; he was heavily, though not exclusively, identified with his establishment of an authoritative succession through Peter. The Son, too, must not be allowed to come into conflict with himself. In all these ways a space is opened up between the historical world and the plane of the divine Trinity. The sacraments and the cults of the saints provided the means of making transactions across the gulf between the two planes.[23] For a comparative few there were also

Constantius claimed it as right. Within the ecclesiastical structure as such, the activities of the Holy Spirit were emphasized most strongly in the monastic establishments and in the theology anchored in these institutions, and not in parish, family, or public life.

23 Joachim failed to provide a prominent place in his schemata for the virgin Mary. She appears briefly in the tree *figurae* (Pl. 16–17, *FJF*) as the node from which the new shoot of the second age takes its continuity from the first. Even Irenaeus had made more of Mary; and the medieval monastic magnification of her role provided Joachim with many models which could have led him to establish correspondences. But his rigorously historical approach yielded few places for the expansion of her significance. See *FJF* 166 n5, and 168 n12, for a listing of his handling of Marian themes.

the ways of ascetic discipline and mystical practice, cultivated in the cloistered environment.

But by Joachim's period the enforcement of this structure was becoming difficult. The imperial Innocent III achieved the apex of papal power. He did not, however, make the extreme claims for world dominion to which his successors felt driven in their struggles with Frederick II and with Philip the Fair of France. An over-identification with institutional imperatives opened up further the gap between church and popular life. The Dominican preachers did not feel obliged to challenge the concepts that gave rise to this gap. But many people were attracted to the alternative form of Christianity so vividly exhibited by Francis and his circle.[24] The human Jesus or the Holy Spirit could be set against the claims of the remote Son and his vicar the pope. The *new* claim is precisely that God is not remote from us but intimately and directly involved in our life.[25] It was Joachim's structures of thought which could legitimate this conviction.

Less directly traceable to Joachim are the convictions of apologists for the imperial, royal, and ordinary secular authority. In Joachim's scheme, patriarchal and kingly authority are superseded but not annulled in the second *status* by that of parish priests and ecclesiastical power as such. Joachim shared the long-standing papalist distrust of the Hohenstaufen emperors and would have been profoundly shocked at the career of Frederick II. Yet it is at least a parallel quest that Joachim and apologists for the *regnum* have embarked upon.

Against the quotation of proof-texts in anti-imperialist documents, the imperial chancelleries and royal bureaucracies gradually learned to deploy their own proof-texts. The papal citation of provisions of the ancient law codes of Theodosius and Justinian prompted secular[26] controversialists to point to these codes' assumption that the state is an order of Nature, not a device created by papal delegation. The controversy was always conducted within the framework of Christian assumptions, however.[27] The advocates of co-ordinate authority of both *regnum* and

---

24 Large numbers joined the 'third orders' of both mendicant bodies. These were committed to following the Rule so far as was compatible with marriage and other secular pursuits. See Cohn *Pursuit* 163.

25 Even before the Franciscan movement, heretics were found in the aftermath of the fall of the heresiarch Amaury or Amalric, ca 1206, who followed a doctrine in which God was incarnated in history: in Abraham as the Father, through Mary as the Son, and in these men as the Holy Spirit. The successive régimes were of Law, of grace and sacrament, and of the new works to be performed by the new men. Those folk apparently also believed that their children would be born sinless. See W.W. Wakefield and A.P. Evans ed *Heresies of the High Middle Ages* (London 1969).

26 Here and elsewhere 'secular' refers only to non-ecclesiastical authority. In the case of 'secular clergy' it refers to non-monastic clergy, those not 'regular' or under a rule.

27 Exceptions to this are some of the more worldly ministers of Frederick II and the later, somewhat isolated, example of Marsiglio of Padua who, viewing the ruin of Italian institutions result-

sacerdotium over men were arguing over the present impact of God's ancient grant of kingly authority as an order of Nature or, at least, as a means of preservation, given the fallen condition of mankind. Joachim, too, however papalist he was, cannot allow decisions of the present age to discredit the integrity of God's action in other periods.

The paradox of development

Here we reach the paradox of Joachim's notion of development. (A corresponding difficulty will be encountered in the modern notion of progress.)

A picture of steady, linear development is impossible without allowing the past its own reality on its own terms. Linear development requires this reality of the past; otherwise we run the risk of the present and the envisioned future being purely mental constructs. The past is given, not constructed; it may even have had a constitution inimical to that which we see approaching from the future. But we must accept this situation in order to safeguard the reality of the future. As we did not make up our past, so we have not made of the future a convenient projection, but have discovered it to be thus-and-so, in the same manner as the past disclosed itself to be what it was. We have to accept the givenness of history. Only then can its correspondences be accepted as real and trustworthy.[28]

Yet some means must be found to account for the supersession of the past, with its givenness. Joachim does not want the abrogation of the past, which the spirituals and later folk so desired to establish. His linkage of the *status* to the persons of the Trinity, who are one God, guards against any annullment of the past. But the successive eras are developmental.[29] The passage of *tempora* and *status* takes the drama of redemptive history closer and closer to its conclusion. Each era's institutions and characteristics are a more perfect embodiment of God's ultimate intention for men. The only conceivable means for marking the successive eras, for Joachim, is through the persons of the Trinity, who are revealed successively in history. Thus far, Joachim has retained control of his notion of the structure of history. The persons of the Trinity are the same Triune God and are mutually referential; both these convictions prevent the notion of annullment from creeping into his succession and development.

But the particular character of the development he shows us leaves his system vulnerable to the sort of handling it received at the hands of his successors. The

ing, as he believed, from papal campaigns against the revival of imperial authority in Italy, utilized Aristotelian premises to argue, in his *Defensor pacis*, for a popular sovereignty unfettered by any ecclesiastical power; in his state, the church was a department of state.

28 Perhaps Joachim's attack on Peter Lombard's Trinitarian formulation was determined by his desire to eliminate a hidden entity or principle behind the actual Father, Son, and Spirit as they disclose themselves to us in their particularity.

29 See *FJF* 168, and the whole discussion of three-status *figurae*, 146 ff.

movement from married men to secular clergy is to be completed, in linear fashion, by the succession of contemplative monks. This crowning order of men is to be supported by the continued presence – each in its place and function – of married men and secular clergy. They uphold the new order as supporting pillars.

But what if the modal men of the second *status* resist the arrival of the men of the third *status*? It was argued that this is what happened when the claims of the spiritual Franciscans were resisted and suppressed, when the new movement was – as it believed – forced back into the mould of the second *status*. At this point it became very difficult for the new men to avoid painting their opponents as agents of the Antichrist or to avoid claiming for themselves a role that annulled the second *status*. And as they were persecuted, they were deflected further from Joachim's vision of a new contemplative order, without losing any of their sense of being new men.

12

Joachim's successors

Joachim's notion of the characteristics and men of the third age was formed by his understanding of the developmental logic of God's revelation. Contemplative monks are to be the new men, the characteristic figures, the centre of the meaning of the third *status*. Despite his own labours as a monastic reformer[1] and his reputation as a great seer,[2] Joachim did not identify himself, his order, or any other existing men as the spiritual men of the imminent third age. And he did not prophesy directly that the papacy was to be superseded in the third age. But circumstances immediately after his death led others to do what Joachim had refused to do.

The tendency of the three *status* to find successive world-historical equivalents was seized upon by the Joachites, centred in the embattled 'spiritual' wing of the Franciscan order of mendicant monks. Arguably they subverted Joachim's intentions. But even in the way Joachim handled his own insights there is an analysis profoundly subversive of the established ways of justifying the major institutions of the period.

We shall see more clearly what Joachim meant when we mark out the departures from his analysis by those who employed his work in their own projects. We shall also see that what I shall call his sense of 'historical truth' undermines his own strong commitment to the papacy. The chapter concludes with an account of the further uses and transformations of Joachim's work through to the period of the Reformation.

---

1 At the canonization of St Dominic, the Florensians are named, along with the Cistercians, Dominicans, and Franciscans, as pillars of the church (*IPLMA* 146).
2 Richard I of England arranged to see him on his journey to the third crusade.

THE JOACHITES AND THEIR USE OF JOACHIM'S WORK

Predicting the third age

The Joachites identified the new men and the Antichrist, declared the papacy to be the little beast of the Revelation, and fixed the date of the advent of the third age more firmly than Joachim himself appears to have done. This last was important in the mobilization of opinion as to the identity of the players in the millennial drama. If the year 1260 can be fixed upon as the end of the present age,[3] the long-established roles in the drama can be assigned to existing men and institutions of the mid-thirteenth century. Further, Joachim's careful demonstration of the identity of the new men as contemplative monks is easily swept aside; for surely any man who perceives the obsolescence of the present institutions is a true man of the third *status*.

Joachim's detailed calculations of the generations and contents of the earlier ages could easily be used to show that the present age cannot endure longer than the period of the Father had lasted. The Daniel and Revelation numbers of 42 periods or 1260 'days' provided both the key to Joachim's calculus and its validation by scriptural authority.[4] His use of individuals as the chief figures of both series of *tempora* similarly led to the nomination of this or that person as the chief figure of the sixth and seventh *tempora*. Joachim, of course, had done no such thing.[5] The circumstantiality of Joachim's system cried out for completion.

3 And that is the natural result of using Joachim's calculus of generations without heeding his strictures about the elasticity of the last generation.
4 The day–year equivalence is established in Ezek 4:5. In Daniel, days and weeks are handled in different ways, the day-calculus of 8:14 even requiring to be halved to find the correct base number to be turned into weeks and years. The peculiar 'time, times, and half a time' of Daniel 7 (in which period the little horn seems to be triumphant) is construed as 3½ years and is the source of the 42 months or 1260 days of Revelation 11–13, where the topic is the same as that in Daniel 7. With the advent of the conviction that Revelation had prophesied the entire future history of the world, the way was opened for day–year equivalence to be applied to the number 1260, and its multiples used to cover the entire course of history. Joachim's 30-year generations actually function here, in terms of the divine arithmetic, because 30 days is the month-unit presupposed in the original calculus of Daniel and John. Providentially, 1260 years, working forward from the time of Jesus' career, confirms the normal millennialist's conviction that he himself lives at the close of the next-to-last period of human history. For a review of 'allegorical arithmetic,' see Russell *MMJA* 194–202.
5 Joachim stops well short of his own period. In one version of the concords, the emperor Heraclius, of the seventh century, is the last person named. In other versions, the parallel figures in the second seven do not proceed past Christ. In the working out of the third *status*, however, St Benedict is cast as its germinator. In the final period of the second era, the second Elijah is a *role*, not a person about whose identity Joachim is inclined to speculate (see *FJF* 142 ff).

The developmental emphasis in Joachim's Trinitarian history is given concreteness by finding the germinator of each *status* well within the temporal frame of the previous one. Thus the ancient Israelite king Uzziah or Hezekiah[6] is taken to be the germinator of the second age, though he lies 21 generations before the end of the first era or *status*.[7] Similarly St Benedict is the germinator for the third *status* developing within the womb of the second *status* since the sixth century. Joachim himself saw the married men of the first *status* and the secular clergy of the second as components of the third, even though its principals are to be the regular or monastic clergy: contemplatives. But the anti-ecclesiastical bias of some Joachites, based on personal experience of repression, could stress a Constantinian 'fall of the church' and a papal role as little beast.

The hidden nurture of the new order, since St Benedict's day, could be taken to demonstrate the illegitimacy of the post-Constantine church. This church had reached the zenith of its worldly power in the splendid reign of Pope Innocent III (1198–1216) and had produced its own antithesis in Francis of Assisi, espoused to 'my lady poverty.' The later partisans of Franciscan poverty were given a weapon

---

The Joachimist *figurae* (with their assumption of Revelation's full coverage of post-New Testament history) attach names to the seven heads of the beast from the sea, as the persecutors of the seven New Testament *tempora*. The order of the first ones became fixed, and Antichrist is sometimes sixth, sometimes seventh. In this last case, Gog has to relinquish his place as a head and to become the stinging tail of the beast, here assimilated to the dragon of Revelation 12. Later Joachite documents revised the names and order.

The Joachimist documents' persecuting emperor Constantius (believed by his fourth-century orthodox contemporaries to be an Arian heretic) was replaced in a later Joachite list of persecutors by Constantine, now taken to be the seducer of the early church away from its poverty. In one version, the emperors Henry I and Frederick I appear; and Frederick II was taken to be the Antichrist. He died inopportunely in 1250 and was left in a position as seventh head; Antichrist was relegated to the tail (*FJF* 273 ff). St Francis was made chief person of the sixth or seventh *tempus*, the new man of the third *status*, or the new Elijah.

6 In different versions of the generational calculus, Joachim has followed either the listing in I Chronicles 1–3 (making Uzziah the twenty-first generation after Jacob) or that in Matthew 1, in which the twenty-first falls on Hezekiah. The genealogy in Luke is divergent from David onward, touching the others only at Shealtiel and Zerubbabel. It has its own base-seven structure, with 21 generations from David to Zerubbabel and from him to Jesus; Joachim accordingly has a series of subsidiary concordances involving Zerubbabel.

The abbot was fully capable of building his own genealogies. Thus, in *FJF* p1.12 (if it is his), he follows the Matthew scheme down to Matthan (three generations before Jesus) then substitutes, for Jacob, Joseph, and Jesus, the names of Zachariah, John, and Jesus. Here his typological interest and the weight of legend have intervened. Many of his correspondences, of course, are created without reference to genealogies at all.

7 This places him at the mid-point of the ubiquitous 42 (generations, in this case) between Jacob and Jesus, between whom Joachim sees important parallels.

by which to declare not only the subsumption of the older orders, under the new[8] but also their annulment. Few took this line so long as there was a chance of the papacy upholding poverty as a binding obligation on Franciscans. But the proponents of poverty had stretched Joachim's scheme, and when it became clear they would get no aid from the popes, they mounted papal heads on the beast of Revelation.

The doctrine of development of one *status* from another, well integrated within orthodoxy in the hands of Joachim, is now used in two ways: to point to the spiritual party in the order as the spiritual men of the new age, and to turn the development doctrine upside down by using it to deny the legitimacy of the established triumphalist church. The latter move substitutes catastrophism for development. One of Joachim's *figurae* (*FJF* pl 16, 17) shows a branch as large as the parent tree trunk growing out, then taking root and growing upward (the second age or *status* legitimating itself in history while yet remaining nourished from its original Jewish roots). The third age or *status* is similarly pictured as growing out from the second. The rebellious spiritual Franciscans and their supporters wanted to identify themselves as the third tree – without recognizing its organic dependence upon the second and first. They denied legitimacy to the second tree's growth beyond the point at which the third had branched off from it. One could now leap from Jesus and the Fathers to the foundation of the new era in St Benedict – an age present in seed until it sprouted into vigorous growth in the Franciscan movement. The merely ecclesiastical church – which legitimates and sanctifies all other parts of life – is effectively denied its own historical legitimacy.

This style of argument can only be undertaken by men and women who have assimilated the modes of thought we have found to be central to early apocalyptic and to later millennial movements. A more common argument was that monasticism and the new mendicant orders represented a more perfect way of realizing the way of salvation on this earthy plane. That the spiritual radicals argued as they did is not owing merely to the fact that they encountered opposition, that they were marginal folk lacking power, or that they attracted a disproportionate number of psychically less stable people. The history of early and medieval heresy and sectarianism provides many examples of resort by marginal people to quite ahistorical conceptualizations of their conditions and prospects. But few major movements in Western society have ever been able for long to avoid making a historically based defence of themselves. Failure to do so has most often meant permanent marginality or a very short life for such movements.

8 See *IPLMA* 176 ff, 194 ff, 210.

Dramatis personae of the third age

The great mendicant orders were both genuine novelties and, as they quickly demonstrated, quite central institutions in the medieval world. Nothing more enhanced Joachim's later reputation than his supposed prediction in detail of both Dominicans and Franciscans. The Dominion preachers revitalized the communication of the gospel. In the English provincial city of Salisbury, for example, four great open-air preaching stations were set up, from which Christian preaching at an engaging popular level could be directed to market-day crowds. But it is among the Franciscans that Joachim's schemes were to have their greatest effect.[9] The question among the Franciscans, in the mid-thirteenth century, was the extent to which the movement was tied to the bold simplicities of Francis himself. Was the contrast between apostolic poverty (dependent on daily charity) and the giant institutions of the triumphalist church merely a point of departure, of historical interest, as doors opened everywhere to the new movement? Was Franciscanism to capitalize on its many opportunities or was it to become something permanently new and different: a body of men like Francis, and so more like Jesus than any men had ever been?

The view among the spirituals[10] was that apostolic poverty was essential if the order were to maintain its freedom from involvement in traditional church structures and from the entanglements of worldly success. If the order failed this test, it had no reason to exist. The issue remained long unresolved, though the spirituals were increasingly on the defensive. The work of Joachim was seen as a support by this party; and both groups were willing to see the order as that prophesied by Joachim.[11] New documents were prepared and fathered on Joachim. Both John

9 But later Dominicans, after the upheavals of institutional Christianity in the fourteenth century, were capable of taking up Joachimist positions. St Vincent Ferrer, in the early fifteenth century, preached *renovatio* in the face of papal schism, proclaimed the imminence of the Antichrist, and concerned himself with a new world-church whose dominion would be revealed in twelve *status*, the eleventh of which is like Joachim's seventh New Testament *tempus* and Augustine's seventh *etas*. On Ferrer, see *IPLMA* 171, and M. Reeves 'The Abbot Joachim and the Society of Jesus' *Medieval and Renaissance Studies* v (1961) 167. On Joachim's impact in other orders, see *IPLMA* 251–90, M. Reeves 'Joachimist Expectations in the Order of Augustinian Hermits' *Recherches de Theologie ancienne et mediévale* xxv (1958) 111–41, and the excellent article of B. McGinn 'The Abbot and the Doctors' *Church History* xl (1971) 30–47.

10 For the most recent review of the literature on the early Italian Franciscan spirituals, see A.M. Ini 'Nuovi documenti sugli Spirituale de Toscana' *Archivum Franciscanum Historicum* LXVI (1973) 305–77. See also M.D. Lambert *The Doctrine of the Absolute Poverty of Christ and the Apostles in the Franciscan Order, 1210–1323* (London 1961) and J. Moorman *A History of the Franciscan Order* (Oxford 1968).

11 As were the Dominicans. Both orders had made this application to themselves before 1260. In time, a highly circumstantial legend arose that, before the careers of either Dominic or Francis, Joachim had appeared at Venice to direct that the insignia of the two orders be included in the

of Parma and St Bonaventure, his successor as Franciscan general, were influenced by Joachim's work.[12] But it was only with the appearance of the 'Eternal Evangel' of Gerardo Borgo San Donnino in 1254–5 that the possibility of the third *status* was fully realized as a controversial device. Here Joachim himself appears as the angel of the sixth seal; the Franciscans are the new men; and 1260 will mark the appearance of the Antichrist. Joachim's own works are the gospel of the new age, in which the institutional church will be superseded.

This document was effectively suppressed. An investigation was launched at Paris by the secular clergy of the university in part as a means of discrediting the Franciscan penetration of teaching positions. The papacy ultimately conducted its own proceedings, in which the mendicant orders were defended even as Gerardo and his work were condemned. Joachim's work on redemptive history had first come under scrutiny in 1184.[13] It escaped official censure until the provincial synod of Arles, in 1263, by which time spurious works were circulating and the Joachite tidings had spread across Europe.[14] At Arles, the schema of the three *status* was censured along with Joachim's works, which seemed to be the source of the heretical notion that the old gospel had been replaced by the new. This action, perhaps brought on by the spurious writings, was the first time Joachim's work had ever been condemned. Joachim himself remained free of censure; the books could be attacked, but not yet the sage and seer himself.

The spirituals' dependence on briefly reigning popes may have led some of them to produce the portrait series of *vaticinia de summis pontificibus*: descriptions of popes dead, living, and yet to come, with their specific roles in the drama

new mosaics at St Mark's. His actual predictions of active and contemplative orders in the new *status* are discussed in *IPLMA* 142 ff. The indispensability of Joachim to the Franciscans lies in his correspondence theme, in which Francis himself can be seen to correspond to Jesus, in a suitably subordinate fashion which yet raised him above all other men. Francis is no mere founder. He is the New Man; and the extraordinary gift to him of the stigmata, the wounds of Christ, is meant to point up his status as the God-designated inaugurator. Innocent III is alleged to have died before his time because he frustrated the friars. See D.C. West 'The Re-formed Church and the Friars Minor: The Moderate Joachite Position of Fra Salimbene' *Archivum Franciscanum Historicum* LXIV (1971) 273–84 (NB 277 ff).

12 See *IPLMA* 176 ff. John was later brought down by baseless accusations that he had been implicated in the notorious 'Eternal Evangel' of the Joachite Gerardo. Bonaventure drew back from historical extrapolation from the pattern of threes. See also *IPLMA* 67.

13 See M. Bloomfield and M. Reeves 'The Penetration of Joachimism into Northern Europe' *Speculum* XXIX (1954) 772–93; E.R. Daniel 'A Re-examination of the Origins of Franciscan Joachitism' *Speculum* XLIII (1968) 671–6; *IPLMA* 76–95.

14 In 1215, his criticism of Peter Lombard's Trinitarian formulations was reproved. Here too he himself remained unrebuked, though there was no strong body to defend his views. Joachim followed a line of attack on the Lombard initiated at the third Lateran Council of 1179 but not carried through at that time. See below, 123 and 126 n28.

of the end-time – good popes and evil. Though Celestine V shone like a candle in darkness, it was the wicked popes who fascinated men's minds. There was an all-too-believable suggestion – contrary to anything taught by Joachim – that 'Rome' and 'Babylon,' Satan's seats and those of his Antichrist, could refer not to the wicked emperors but to evil popes as well. Is a pope to be the *reparator* of the new age? (as Jean de Roquetaillade suggested). One luckless visionary (Guillaume Postel) nominated himself as the 'angelic pope.'[15] The rigorist movement of Fra Dolcino cast the papacy itself, and not only particular incumbents, as Babylon. The real, true power of the institutional church of the second age has passed to the Apostolic Brethren in their radical poverty.[16] The brethren were sufficiently militant that a crusade was declared against them by Clement V, and there were a number of burnings; but the movement was not suppressed. The removal of the papacy to France for most of the fourteenth century was followed in 1378 by the spectacle of two popes, each the sole vicar of Christ. The notion of false popes or of the supersession of the institution appeared more and more likely. A second series of *vaticinia* appeared. As late as 1370 new spurious works were ascribed to Joachim,[17] whose general schema survived the failure of any and all dating schemes. The Protestant claim that the papacy was the Antichrist or Babylon was thus far from novel;[18] it had more than 200 years of history behind it. The last portrait of the second series of *vaticinia de summis pontificibus*, ca 1355, shows the pope as a beast and quotes from Revelation 13.

One of the other elements to survive was uncertainty about the identity of the *reparator* of the new age. The traditional papal antagonism toward the imperial Hohenstaufens had been enough to enlist the loyal Joachim among those who saw the Germanic dynasty as the great persecutor – the prophetic 'Rome.' Hence his sudden appearance to admonish Henry VI.[19] In his system of seals, Babylon and Rome are the empire.[20] Babylon-the-Germans are the persecutors of the fifth opening seal. In the early dragon's heads' sequences of the *figurae*, the successive heads from the fifth to the seventh and last are Meselmutus,[21] Saladin, and

15 *IPLMA* 238; also W. Bouwsma *Concordia Mundi; The Career and Thought of Guillaume Postel (1510–1581)* (Cambridge 1957)

16 *IPLMA* 217 ff

17 Ibid 243–8

18 Ibid 107

19 *FJF* 11

20 An understanding of his prophecy to Richard I, that already Antichrist had been born at 'Rome,' must begin from this identification of the empire, as Reeves has pointed out.

21 Meselmutus or Muthselmutus is the otherwise obscure Muslim conqueror of the farther reaches of the Mahgreb, of whom Joachim had heard by the time of his interview with Richard I in 1190–1. See *IPLMA* 7 ff.

Antichrist. Later versions replace Meselmutus by emperor Henry IV, Saladin by Frederick Barbarossa, and Antichrist by Frederick II.[22]

But the exigencies of controversy in later years not only enrolled the papacy among the Babylonians, but also rehabilitated the reputations of kings and emperors. The 'sleeping emperor' tradition from early medieval apocalyptic could be joined to the third-age materials to produce the imperial *renovator*.[23] Apologists for the French royal house of Capet spoke of a French royal renovator, heir of Charlemagne.[24] As the conduct of the papacy made it difficult to consider any longer the possibility of angelic popes, reformers of the Church began to look elsewhere. Royal and imperial publicists, too, had gained great sophistication from having to cope with earlier propaganda on behalf of papal authority. Now these royal publicists were able with some justification to claim a positive role in the new age for this or that king – even for Frederick II,[25] or, half a century later, for Frederick of Sicily.[26]

Trinitarian history without the Trinity

Soon after Joachim's death, the Joachites were already adrift from that role which alone to Joachim guaranteed their identity as possessing the *spiritualis intellectus*. But once a group identifies itself as Joachim's new men and is deflected from the specifics of that prophecy, the group has more reason to identify itself as new men than to conform to those specifics. For Joachim, the specific character of the new men was inseparable from the concordances and from the orthodox Trinitarian structure of history. The Joachites jettisoned his conclusions when these no longer fitted the perceived reality of their own situation; they could abandon neither the belief that they were the new men nor the structure of supersessory eras – even if this structure made nonsense of the orthodox notion of the Trinity

---

22 *FJF* 273 ff; also 133 ff, 146 ff
23 *IPLMA* 170
24 Ibid 216, 310. See also E.F. Jacob *Essays in Later Medieval History* (Manchester 1968) ch 10, especially 188–94.
25 *IPLMA* 170
26 Ibid 247, 309–17; also see Cohn *Pursuit of the Millennium* 103–23. The Spanish kings' conquest of the Muslims, their (temporary) inheritance of the Portuguese route to India, and their possession of the Americas opened the way to a millennial interpretation of their role. The gospel can now be preached to all men. The Spanish Franciscan Geronimo de Mendieta, in his *Historia ecclesiastica indiana*, held that, within this general picture, the Indians were the 'ten lost tribes' of Israel. Thus their conversion would in fact be the 'conversion of the Jews,' long sought as one of the signs of the end. For a careful account of Franciscan missionary millennialism, see J.L. Phelan *The Millennial Kingdom of the Franciscans in the New World*, 2nd edn, rev (Berkeley, Calif, 1970).

on which Joachim's whole structure depended for its stability and historical realism. Once this was lost, there was no control upon the uses to which Joachim's structure of history could be put.

This loss of control was not immediately apparent. For the most part, Joachites believed themselves to be orthodox Christians and used the familiar language of orthodox controversialists. Thus people who had been pushed into being political activists and revolutionaries no doubt felt little incongruity in applying to themselves the Joachimist vision of the *ordo psallendo*, ordo *contemplantium*, and ordo *quiescientium* of the third age. Perhaps the affective link is Joachim's description of this new order of life as one of *jubilatio*.[27] The persecuted spirituals were conscious of their own status as new men; and they rejoiced at having been so chosen. This sense of *jubilatio* remained with the elect no matter how far they drifted from cloistered meditation.[28] But with the loss of the direction and coherence imposed on this structure of expectation by Joachim's orthodox sense of the Trinity, it is no longer clear who is choosing the elect, to whom they are accountable, or how the content of the final age is to be derived. The motive force for the succession of the ages, to be sure, was still God.

The problem was to grow acute when the progress theorists of the eighteenth century wished to assert the increasing perfection of historical development and, at the same time, to relieve themselves of the constraints of the orthodox Christian conception of God. Where then does the motive power originate for the continuous ascent of man and his institutions? We shall first consider in part II the development of utopian thought from its origins in Plato to its joining with millennialism in the modern doctrine of progress.

LATER MEDIEVAL TRINITARIAN HISTORY

The principal issues were well articulated in the movements of Joachim's successors. The assignment of roles in the drama of the end-time continued, especially of political leaders to the role of last emperor. The advent of the Turks into central Europe in the first half of the sixteenth century gave a strong impetus to

27 See *IPLMA* 136; cf Olivi's Joachite version of the three eras as characterized successively by *labor, lectio,* and *jubilatio, IPLMA* 197; also D. Burr 'The Apocalyptic Element in Olivi's Critique of Aristotle' *Church History* XL (1971) 15–29.
28 The spirituals followed Joachim and Francis in two convictions: their vision of an order which was the key to *renovatio* and their picture of the papacy as a divinely protected instrument of that renewal. In so doing they set themselves the task of reconciling theory (which alone could justify their role in history) and the intractable facts of history itself. Thus when they encountered popes who frustrated the fixed vision of renovation, it became clear to them that such popes were not true popes at all.

this process, with the Ottomans themselves being cast in the role of the hordes of Antichrist or of Gog[29] formerly given to the fabled peoples penned up by Alexander, or to the Tartars.

Protestants were more concerned with the papacy and of course identified it as the seat of Antichrist. Protestant reformers had to abandon or modify the anti-historical interpretation of Revelation which they had circumspectly adopted.[30] They felt obliged to interpret the Reformation and counter-Reformation struggles as being between true Christianity and false. It was useful to refer to the 'false lamb' tradition in which Rome was the agent of Satan. In the military and ideological struggles of the period, millions of simple people had to be provided with a clear picture of the issues. Some on the Protestant left wing had long since taken up Revelation as their model for radical social revolution. The original peasant uprisings of 1525 had been moderate, with quite traditional and limited aims. But Thomas Muntzer's revolution had explicitly justified its program by millennialist conceptions. And the extreme and bizarre fanaticism of the Münster Anabaptists of 1534–5[31] had profoundly shocked Protestant as well as Catholic opinion. Thus the Protestant use of millennialism had to avoid literalism. The influential Second Helvetic Confession of 1566 denounced literal millennialism as 'Jewish' – an old charge against late classical millennialism by its Christian opponents and one often revived in medieval times.

Catholic polemic had a similar difficulty. The implicit chronology of Revelation accepted since Joachim's day could be used to point to Luther as the fallen angel of chapter 9 who opens the pit and looses a horde of terrible locusts on the earth. There it is promised that this plague, though painful, will be short. However, to admit the application of Revelation to present events opened the way to the Protestant identification of the papacy with the beasts or with Antichrist. This assumption had taken root in popular radicalism since the spirituals, the

---

29 A short review of the period is provided in P. Toon's introduction to P. Toon ed *Puritans, the Millennium and the Future of Israel: Puritan Eschatology, 1601–1660* (Cambridge 1970). See also W.R. Jones 'The Image of the Barbarian in Medieval Europe' *Comparative Studies in Society and History* XIII (1971) 376–407 (NB 399 ff).

30 Toon ed *Puritans* 6. As early as 1520, well before the final break with Rome, Luther had already edged into the language of millennialist anti-papal polemic. His 'Babylonish Captivity of the Church' does not refer to the sojourn of the papacy in France in the fourteenth century but to the Roman establishment as itself Babylon – the Babylon of Revelation drunk with the blood of the saints: 'Our Babylon has so done away with faith that she has the impudence to deny that faith is necessary in that sacrament, nay with the blasphemy of Antichrist she lays it down that it is heresy to assert the necessity of faith' (*DOCC* 199). A similar view is suggested in the early versions of the English Prayer Book, 1549 and 1552, of the prayer for deliverance 'from the tyranny of the Bishop of Rome and all his detestable enormities' (ibid 236).

31 For a vivid account of this strange episode, see Cohn *Pursuit* 256–80.

vaticinia de summis pontificibus, and the revival of the tradition of emperor as chastizer.[32] Further encouragement of such views was not in the Catholic interest.

After the Peace of Augsburg in 1555, pronouncements on both sides tended to moderate, though Anabaptists – persecuted by Catholics, Lutherans, and Reformed alike – retained a lively sense of the end-time and of their enemies as agents of Antichrist.

The postponement of all English reform issues in the long reign of Elizabeth meant that her death in 1603 opened the way to a much delayed consideration of issues long since settled on the Continent. There was a growing use of apocalyptic for polemical purposes from the early seventeenth century; and the civil war period, 1640–60, provided the freedom necessary for publication of such efforts.[33] These colourful treatises and tracts did not, for the most part, make any significant advance upon the millennialism of the Continent. Those very important cases where they did will be considered later, in chapter 21, in connection with the development of the doctrine of progress, to which they made an indispensable contribution.

We have now completed our consideration of the basic forms of millennialism. Their roots lay in the fundamental categories of thought and experience arising out of the Exile, crystallized in the ambiguous period of the return and in the response to Hellenization. These elements were constitutive of the early Christian proclamation of Jesus and of the significance of the imminent end-time. The Montanists revived the orthodoxy of the earliest period and collapsed these basic elements inward. Montanism thus provided the basis for the millennialism of the early medieval period, so deprecated by the ecclesiastical establishment but impossible to suppress.

32 Frederick the Wise of Saxony, Luther's protector, was accordingly identified as the evil Frederick (following the anti-imperial, anti-German tradition of Joachim himself) and by Protestants as the good Frederick of the last days, the chastizer and *reparator* (see *IPLMA* 378 ff). To connect him with the good imperial tradition, men were reminded that Frederick the Wise had actually refused to be a candidate in the imperial election of 1519. His modesty could thus be likened to that of Jesus, contrasted with papal arrogance, and made a particularly reassuring attribute in a chastizer.

33 See B.S. Capp *The Fifth Monarchy Men: A Study in Seventeenth-Century English Millennialism* (London 1972) 23–52; also W. Haller *Foxe's Book of Martyrs and the Elect Nation* (London 1963). Foxe frames his lengthy accounts of the martyrs of Mary Tudor's reign with an interpretation of Christian history that includes a Hildebrand-style fall of the church and the portrayal of Elizabeth as both martyr and new Constantine, divinely preserved from death for this role.

Joachim's structure of historical-biblical thought attracted elements of the older millennialism and could justify the struggles of reform movements of many sorts in the later medieval period. His school of thought provided a means to project a future better than the present and, because connected to the present, part of real history. The future order is thus not a projection of thought, like a utopia, but that which is coming, within history, *our* history. The later development of this theme was conditioned by the parallel tradition of utopianism, to which we must now turn.

PART TWO

Utopianism

13

Utopia as a type

This part is not a history of utopianism – that would require a much more extended and complex treatment. It deals rather with the origins and persisting elements of the utopian enterprise itself. It examines the emergence of utopia into a genre, the character of More's *Utopia*, the relation of 'utopianizing' to complex social reality (in Campanella's *City of the Sun*), and finally the rational utopias of the age of reason, before the genre was transformed by progressivism.

The importance of Plato and More for utopia requires perhaps no advance justification. I have included a treatment of Campanella in some detail not only because his work is still largely unobtainable in English, but also because he provides such a vivid example of a utopia fully responsive to all the currents of his period. His identification of issues and some of his solutions are remarkable examples of sensitivity. His final failure to encompass everything in a single structure is more impressive and more instructive about the utopian enterprise than the polished productions of so many of his more balanced successors.

Utopianism is the search for the good pattern of life in an ahistorical cosmos. Despite the development of utopianism within a society conditioned by Hebrew historical categories, utopianism is committed to the notion of a cosmos in which historical development fundamentally adds nothing. Pattern, cycle, and hierarchy (of values, if not of social structures and roles) are the prime realities. The best way to live may thus be discovered; it is 'there' already; it could have been discovered at any prior time.

This best pattern of life is rational and is discovered rationally. Historical conditions may have influenced the mode of discovery; but, once this has been done, time ceases to have any further significance and becomes an undifferentiated plenum within which meaningful existence takes place. This rational pattern is the best form of life for men together because it participates (in a manner appropriate to flesh and blood) in the pattern of the cosmos itself. To seek elsewhere for guidance than in the eternally true only compounds the problems of men caught in finitude. Mere custom, mere egotism, and mere identification with animal existence or with the mutable are obstacles. They frustrate the attempt of true human nature to recognize itself as an analogue to the rational pattern of the cosmos and to fashion itself after that pattern. Only in this recognition shall we realize our true individual and corporate potential. Having done so, we participate in eternity.

Utopia as a type arises on Greek cultural soil; it could have arisen nowhere else. Attempts have been made to declare Greek thought inherently ahistorical and to contrast it sharply with Hebrew thought, the origin of millennialism.[1] I will not argue thus, and such a demonstration is not necessary in order to establish the distinctive character of either type. Greek culture produced historians, after all, even though their preoccupations were very different from those historians working within the framework of history developed in Christian late antiquity. And however much Aristotle may differ from Hebrew thought in dealing with time, he also differs from Plato. Utopianism does not arise from a homogenized or arbitrarily selected 'Greek view,' but quite simply from *a* Greek view of the cosmos and of man's place in it: the Platonic view.

Nonetheless, utopianism has a general consonance with most of the presuppositions common to the Greek cultural world: it is not dependent solely on Plato. Plato's key role in the development of utopianism is his bringing together, out of the generality of Greek assumptions, of several themes into an enduring unity. But even in the *Republic*, Plato is not himself a utopian in the mould exhibited in later Western history.[2] Utopians, however, are securely linked to the Platonic presentation of what is at stake in the human situation, and these common characteristics – not speculation about the 'Golden Age' or the Primal Man, and not the modern quest for 'fulfilment' – provide the principal marks of utopia as a type.

Utopia then is the result of a human penetration of the plane of eternal truth. This plane is the fundamental reality of the closed cosmos (ie, the totality of all that is) in which we live on the plane of temporal, mutable existence. This latter plane is in some fashion derived from the plane of more fundamental reality. We can penetrate to this reality and participate in it because we share in both planes;

---

1 See T. Boman *Hebrew Thought Compared with Greek* (London 1960). A discussion of the controversy and a refutation of Boman's thesis on linguistic grounds is given in J. Barr *Biblical Words for Time* 2nd rev edn (London 1969).

2 See Frye in F. Manuel ed *Utopias and Utopian Thought* (Boston 1967) 33 ff; also Lewis Mumford in ibid 7: 'It is Plato's influence that comes first to mind when we think of later utopias,' even though Aristotle is more politically concrete in the matter of the 'ideal city.'

our essential nature transcends the merely temporal, mutable, and material. What we discover, then, corresponds to a reality in which we each share. Thus there is a link between the structure of human personality and the fundamental structure of the eternally true, from which all else is derived. The process of discovery may thus be described as a process of recognition. Correspondence is the validation of truth; and truth is one and self-consistent. Having recognized or discovered truth, we work for its embodiment in human institutions. Success in this task is confirmed by harmony. This harmony is vertical correspondence between the transcendent and the world of temporality and change. Harmony is shown within the temporal world by balance, complementarity, and integration into one social whole. The means of discovery (ie reason) of course also governs this whole. Utopians differ as to the scale on which embodiment is possible. But because of the direct correspondence between the higher plane and the higher faculties of man, the individual is at the very least able to exhibit the discovered reality.

We begin with a problem that vexes all accounts of utopianism. More's *Utopia* begins the genre proper; but any substantive discussion of utopianism must deal with Plato.[3] Sometimes the genre is antedated by 1,900 years to include Greek constitution-mongers and fabulists of the Fortunate Isles among the utopians[4] – along with Plato.[5] It is my thesis that the utopian enterprise was set on foot by Plato long before the genre achieved its characteristic form in More's *Utopia*. We shall not understand utopias without some scrutiny of Plato.[6] And we must first

3 *Laws, Statesman,* and other works are relevant to what we see in *Republic,* which is here made to stand for the rest. The differences among these works are important in tracing Plato's changing hopes for rational reformation of his society. But for the present purpose, all presuppose the relation between the realms that is identified in *Republic.*

4 See G. Negley and J.M. Patrick ed *The Quest for Utopia* first pub New York 1952 (Garden City, NY, 1962) 250–7; also W.W. Tarn *Hellenistic Civilization* 3rd edn rev with G.T. Griffith (London 1952) 122 ff.

5 Plato's concern is not with abundance or with the abolition of toil, ill-health, sexual deprivation, or death – the stock-in-trade of the Hellenistic paradises. The merely commodious life is explicitly put to one side in *Republic* as not germane to what is at issue. To move beyond mere sufficiency to the commodious life, without considering justice in the particular way *Republic* does, Socrates says, is to deal only with a fevered society: 372e.

6 There is a view that the notion of progress itself existed in ancient times. The case (for classical Greece) is given most persuasively by L. Edelstein in his *The Idea of Progress in Classical Antiquity* (Baltimore 1967), a work truncated by the author's death. J. Passmore's *The Perfectibility of Man* (London 1970) attempts a somewhat parallel enterprise in its early chapters. The cogency of this thesis depends a good deal on how progress is defined or on how perfectibility is related to larger social doctrines. Edelstein adopts the definition of A.O. Lovejoy and G. Boas in *Primitivism and Related Ideas in Antiquity* (Baltimore 1935): 'A tendency inherent in nature

look at the background to Plato's work: the decline of justice that profoundly troubled him.

or in man to pass through a regular sequence of stages of development in past, present and future, the latter stages being – with perhaps occasional retardations or minor regressions – superior to the earlier' (xi). If progress is to be defined in this way, Edelstein can indeed show at least some ancient progress-doctrine. But there are two difficulties here. First, this definition obscures the difference between a recognition of social development (and an expectation of more of it) and the modern doctrine with its need for a motive power within history, its notion of an open-ended future, and its desire for the human conquest of nature. Second, Edelstein consistently takes an openness to innovation as being equivalent to holding a doctrine of progress. (See, inter alia, 31 n 22, where this is made explicit.) Even on his own definition, this is pressing his texts too hard. For a critique of Edelstein's work, see E.R. Dodds *The Ancient Concept of Progress and Other Essays on Greek Literature and Belief* (Oxford 1973).

The notion of a pattern in the cosmos and in human affairs is not evidence by itself of a notion of progress. Passmore has been more circumspect in his choice of terms, in this connection. In the classical period, perception of a pattern, even a melioristic one, is nearly always conditioned by the assumption of an immanent and finite goal or 'end' to any action. The pattern unfolds itself toward one of these and according to its inherent structure. (See below, 173 ff.) Edelstein's 'inventors' are, as he occasionally shows, discoverers rather than inventors, the latter a role usually restricted to the gods.

14

The decline of Greek justice

Sometimes overlooked in the study of Athenian life is the complex of problems surrounding the decay of the notion of *nomos*.[1] The issues here have been clouded by the habit among modern liberals of drawing parallels between liberal bourgeois freedom and Athenian individualistic democracy, as well as parallels between the archaic regimes of Athens and the authoritarianism over which modern liberalism claims to have triumphed.

Further, *nomos* has been equated too easily with modern notions of law as either particular enactments or a command enforcing, by means of sanctions, a course of conduct. The uncongenial austerity of the latter provokes men to a consideration of rights instead of the nature of law. And despite the fact that we have learned to mistrust the sophists, their interpretation of law as arbitrary, class-biased, and a mask for privilege has been very influential.

In the archaic sacral world, however, the role of law had in fact been different. In the unified cosmos of the period, the bonds of law were both necessary and personal. The gods themselves were both persons and the expressions of the necessary structure of the cosmos – as that structure was visible in natural cycles and human order. Human order expressed both the givenness of the cosmos and the personal web of relationships through which this givenness was experienced. The shape of this experience was *nomos*.

The dramatists, writing in the early democracy, give us evidence of the incompatibility of this conception of *nomos* with the experience of democracy. The imperatives of honour, which led to the Trojan war, are set against the necessity for mother-love to avenge the war leader's sacrifice of his daughter, itself necessary to remove a god's withholding of a favourable wind. The mother's murder of her husband, in turn, must be avenged by the son of both, whose action is divinely

---

1 See Erich Voegelin *The World of the Polis* vol 2 of *Order in History* (Baton Rouge, La, 1957).

sanctioned by Apollo. Yet this son must necessarily be pursued by the ancient Furies whose right it is to torture and kill all who murder their own kin.

Aeschylus, in his *Oresteia* series, resolves the problem on two levels. Throughout the plays, he insists that there is an over-arching Justice in the cosmos. This Justice is that of Zeus, who is not directly implicated in the contradictory imperatives of the generations-long tragedy. Yet even Zeus himself is impugned. Did he not succeed to supremacy by violence against his father? The weary Orestes, still pursued by the furies despite his fulfilment of every ritual of purification, comes at last to Athens, directed by Apollo, to accept the judgment of Athena.

Aeschylus here connects the drama to the recent history of his own people. The resolution of the problem of incompatible imperatives within the ideas of Justice and *nomos* is made dependent upon Athens as the embodiment of perfected human society, vindicated by its victories over the Persian empire.[2] Athena convenes a jury of men, before whom the cases are argued by Orestes and the various deities. The jury divides evenly, and Athena's tie-breaking vote gives Orestes his freedom. Yet the baulked Furies are placated by being given what they have never had – a home and honour from men; they are enshrined in an Athenian cave. The generosity and confidence of the Athenians, who need not choose between alternative demands of justice, have resolved the imperatives of justice. Aeschylus delicately balances the divine and human claims to be the origin or validation of *nomos* and justice. Had the court produced a majority vote in the matter of Orestes and the furies, Athena would have pronounced its verdict her own. But it did not; hence the need for recourse to the divine tie-breaking vote.

Through the succeeding period, both aspects of Aeschylus' solution were undermined. The general instability, if also the prosperity, of the Hellenic world produced oligarchies and tyrannies as well as democracies; and democracy was by no means always seen as wholly good. The wandering scholars attacked the gods themselves; that they are so differently conceived, in different places and by different sorts of men, was taken to demonstrate that they are constructed out of human desires and limitations. Xenophanes, who observed that Ethiopian gods are black and that if horses had gods they would be like horses, did not intend thereby a sceptical conclusion. There is a supreme god; but he is wholly other, unlike men and unlike the Homeric gods and their scandalous conduct. Xenophanes knows what the supreme god ought to be like. The sophists, out of their observations of the marvellous variety of human institutions, produced a new

---

2 For a somewhat different view of the Areopagus section of *Eumenides*, see E.R. Dodds *The Ancient Concept of Progress and Other Essays on Greek Literature and Belief* (Oxford 1973) 45–63.

sense of human choice, a choice determined not by the givenness of the will of the gods but by human advantage.

The dramatists illustrate the same sort of movement. Aeschylus' Orestes is caught tragically between conflicting divine imperatives. And these imperatives take their particular shape because of a lengthy history over three generations. The curse on the house of Atreus gives a weight and density to the context of Orestes' choices; he may embrace or avoid his duty, but his duty is presented to him. Sophocles maintains the givenness of Orestes' duty, but concentrates on the 'dramatic possibilities' within it, in Electra's long years of suffering, the relations between her and her mother and sister, and the climactic recognition scene. Euripides' drama explores for their own sakes the inner lives of Orestes and Electra; the grip of her fate on Electra is treated as neurosis. The shattering recognition scene in Sophocles is treated by Euripides as a means of exploring Orestes' self-doubt. The curse is gone; and the space thus opened up is used to reflect upon extraneous matters such as the relations of the classes. On this latter, Orestes is made to observe that one must take men individually; noble and base are often disguised by wealth or poverty: 'there's no rule.' Aeschylus had written in the full vigour of Athenian democracy. Euripides writes while the Sicilian disaster is draining Athens of its last strength. There are no divine sanctions to such enterprises. From Clytemnestra's mouth we are told that its great predecessor, the expedition to reduce Troy, was undertaken only because 'Helen was a whore; her husband didn't know how to handle a randy wife.' The reasons for human actions are to be sought in the uncertainties and caprices of the passions.

Nomos can only be conceived now as arbitrary enactment. The order of the day was disorder; hence nomos is the balance of natural forces or the balance of advantage. Justice, in the words of Thrasymachus in Plato's Republic, is the interest of the stronger.

15

Plato: divine and human order

Plato attempts to deal with this decline of Justice in his dialogues, and most sustainedly in his *Republic*. Plato agrees with Xenophanes that the old gods are no source of Justice.[1] But he is not content with the facile solutions of his contemporaries to the problem of meaning in human society. The sophists, in discrediting the ancient gods, had implied that the cosmos all lay on one level. Plato reinstates a level of transcendence, which may properly be called divine, while admitting a good deal of the force of the sophists' interpretation of the plane of human affairs. The higher realm is that of the Forms – eternal, not subject to change, hence perfect – yet constitutive of the realm of men and objects in space and time. This latter realm is subject to change and hence to decay, for departure from likeness to the Forms is necessarily a move farther away from perfection and truth.

The Forms[2] are in a sense patterns, on the basis of which, within the limits of materiality and mutability, objects are made. These objects are real to the extent

---

1 See the long section joining books II and III, from 377e to 391e. Plato is particularly concerned to eliminate the transcendent realm as a source of evil. 'We cannot allow Homer or any other poet to make such a stupid mistake about the gods, as when he says that "Zeus has two jars standing on the floor of his palace, full of fates, good in one and evil in the other"' (379d–e). 'God is the cause, not of all things, but only of good' (380c). Quotations here and following are from the second revised translation of Desmond Lee (Harmondsworth 1974).

2 See 476–85b; 505a–517c. The notion of the Forms is made more difficult because Plato nowhere expounds it very directly, but always in the context of the projects of the various parts of *Republic* or in *Timaeus*. Vision of the Forms is a matter about which Plato is reticent – necessarily, since according to him the end of the philosophic quest remains incomprehensible to those who have not reached the stage of *noesis* or penetration behind ordinary life and ordinary scholarship or expertise. Indeed, even to speak of the possibility of *noesis* is apt to inflame the ordinary pursuer of worldly satisfactions and lead him to scorn the seeker or do him an injury.

that they participate in the Forms which are their origin. Men uniquely bridge the two realms. Their possession of reason enables them to penetrate behind the mere appearance of things to their true nature. Thus men approach and participate in the realm of the Forms. Further, their superior endowment of spirit or higher passion enables them to respond in love to the vision of the good or the beautiful and desire to possess it. But, Plato observes, few men do this. More often they mistake mere objects for reality. Material passions, when ungoverned, lead men to dissipate their energies on the finally unreal. The institutions within which men live predispose them to overvalue the pursuit of gratification, advantage, and acclaim. But it need not be so. It is possible for men to ground themselves in the realm of the Forms, where their true origin lies, and to live their lives (so far as is possible within the conditions of time and space) according to what is eternal, unchanging, true, and good.

The principal question in *Republic* is the extent to which life based on the Forms can be institutionalized. How can a society be shaped in this fashion? If such a structure can be created, to what extent can all men in this society share in the project which defines its existence? And if such an institutionalization is impossible or unlikely, what is the role of the man who lives his life according to the Forms?

Republic opens with Socrates – against the sophist Thrasymachus and reminders of the strength of common sense and utilitarianism – demonstrating the reality of the transcendent source of reality and value. But this solution sets up the problem of perfection and its relation to the human social order.[3]

This problem did not exist previously. The archaic gods had not been perfect in this sense. They were simply an unchallengeable reality whose incursions, demands, and influences shaped decisively public and private life. But the realm of the Forms is not arbitrary. It contains no contradictions. It is not subject to passion or alteration. It is an orderly hierarchical realm, on which the world of men and objects depends for such coherence as it can have. But the world of men and objects as we know it is arbitrary, full of chance, change, passion. It is full of death. There is thus a profound discontinuity between the two realms; the world of the Forms has been given its transcendence, its incorruptibility, at the cost of raising it above the realm of time and space. Our origin, our true values, our goals are now unchallengeably valid, beyond the reach of corruption. But how do they become effective in life? What is their institutional shape? How can the corporate life of men share in the perfection which alone makes life significant?

---

3 J. Passmore *The Perfectibility of Man* (London 1970) writes perceptively on the origins of perfectionism among the Greeks and follows this theme through the classical period (28–67).

The characteristic goal of utopia is the embodiment of perfection in social institutions. Plato's answers do not constitute a utopia, but they helped to determine the shape of later utopias; Plato is thus the progenitor of the genre. Truth for Plato is non-temporal, given not in historical events but in penetration, by those suitably equipped, to the realm where truth, goodness, and beauty are ultimately and unchangeably one. Truth never appears nude to us, unclothed by the garments of circumstance and period. But its seeker must learn that these garments obscure reality, and he will try to avoid mistaking the garment for what it clothes. He will discipline himself to disregard the circumstances with which truth presents itself to us. The truth is 'there' both for Plato and for later utopians, waiting to be discovered at any time.

Though Plato is deeply convinced of the close relation of goodness to truth, finally the good society or pattern of life is apprehended rationally. It is the disciplined reason of the good man that can penetrate farthest into what is indisputably true. The subsequent problem, how to convince others, is rational in character. The utopians believe that one publishes the rationally persuasive; and men are convinced rationally before they follow the plan existentially. Hence the form of utopian argument is always the book. The book, for utopians, displays the necessarily true form of human society; it also criticizes the existing society, stripping it of its pretensions to adequacy. Truth must be shown to exist independently of particular circumstances; it must be ahistorical in this sense. But truth, in order to move men to action, must also be related to the institutional life of men now; it must criticize that life and present the truth as an alternative order.

In Plato utopianism is not complete, for Plato lacks the naïve faith in reason so conspicuous in the seventeenth- and eighteenth-century utopias. For Plato, the perception and institutionalization of truth are determined by the place of reason in the human makeup. He sees it as ranking above the higher passions – honour, duty, and the like – which are superior to the manipulative, acquisitive, and physical passions. This framework distinguishes Plato from the later, classic phase of utopianism. The later writers supposed that the many – yeomen, craftsmen, merchants, clerics, civil servants, and nobility – were equally capable of making a rational response to the truth embodied in the utopia. This conviction, that all men were intellectually similar in this respect, was largely owing, I think, to the influence of Christianity. The revived Stoic ethic influenced the anti-religious who sought to ground Christian equality in a non-Christian fashion; indeed, the Stoics believed that Christianity had prevented men from realizing their true rational equality.

Plato does not believe in this equality; not all men are capable of apprehending the realm of the Forms. This inability is not because many men are insufficiently intelligent (although he believes this is the case); rather, many clever men are drawn to other pursuits. There is no point wishing it otherwise; it must be accepted as a given. Plato is ambiguous on this psychology of type. On the one hand, there is nothing ignoble about craftsmanship; throughout Plato's dialogues we are treated to examples of intellectual effort modelled on the praiseworthy results of the craftsmanship of the potter, the shipwright, the carpenter, and the like, as well as the skills of the navigator and other professionals. On the other hand, the range of psychological types, of men who are fulfilled by different sorts of pursuit, is ranged hierarchically, made illustrative of the differing capacities of men to approach to *noesis*. In the classic utopias, it is often found sufficient to have a place for every man and to have every man in his place; social order, in this sense, *is* rationality in institutional form. For Plato, however, the only appropriate order is that which corresponds to the ability to apprehend, dimly or directly, the realm of the Forms.

The passions of manipulation, acquisition, and gratification are good in themselves and necessary to any society. Yet for any society to be based solely upon them is fatal to the possibility of that society achieving truth.[4] At best it is likely to be a society of Philistine peasants and small merchants. And if it expands, if it seeks to be the commodious society, it encourages the rise of the higher passions for adventure, glory, and the like, which, if ungoverned by any still higher vision, produce the 'fevered' city on its way to self-destruction. A small, non-acquisitive society based on the passions for discipline, honour, and glory-seeking will fare little better, for the large number of such societies would produce perpetual war and would ultimately reduce all to the level of devastated, depopulated savagery.

Yet the search for honour and the willingness to submit to discipline and to undergo peril are, in themselves, good things. The higher and the lower passions are bad masters but good servants. This conclusion is not a simple prescription for social hierarchy, for each of us has these qualities, characteristics, or leanings within him. No man is solely noetic or solely acquisitive or totaly preoccupied with considerations of honour. The balance among these qualities or the dominance of one characteristic determines one's type as a person. A subsidiary but not negligible conclusion of Plato's *Republic* is that one is genuinely fulfilled when he is allowed full scope to employ his basic nature. But finally, there is no hope for the permanent achievement of a stable structure for such fulfilment until and unless noetic men are allowed – and constrained – to govern society as a whole.

As inherently fulfilling as manipulation, acquisition, and the physical passions are, they leave little room for discernment of true reality behind what merely presents itself to us. One becomes the prisoner of mere opinion or of belief unable

---

4 Plato argues in book IX that happiness, as well as truth, elude this society and one based on honour. Gratification and achievement do not by themselves produce happiness, however important they are in themselves or however significant a place they take in society as a whole.

to demonstrate its own grounds. It is not simply that one has 'no time' to devote to higher pursuits. It is that one's fundamental commitments are given to matters which are material, mutable, merely circumstantial – lacking reality and thus untrue.

The higher passions do transcend this level of life. The man of honour directs his life by a standard not oriented to objects and to personal gratification. He is capable of disciplining body and mind in the service of what he knows to be a concept and set of relations larger than himself – something with claims on him and on his fellows. In this sense, the man of honour and public service has passed beyond opinion and belief to a dim apprehension of that which is eternal and true. Not only the man of honour but also the teacher is in this position. The shipwright has his rule-of-thumb formulae and their associated techniques; but the teacher of mathematics understands these formulae. He can prove them; he can generate them from mathematical axioms – he can reason.

But there is a higher realm, in which the disciplined mind, prepared to sacrifice everything to this quest, can penetrate behind the axioms of honour, of mathematics, and of geometry to account for the axioms themselves, to generate new axioms, and to provide an assured basis for the embodiment in human society of institutions derived from the realm of the Forms.[5] Just as the craftsman is fulfilled in his craftsmanship and just as the man of honour gladly subordinates all else to the obligations of honour, so the noetic man counts both things and honour as nothing beside the pursuit of the eternally true.

Plato has often been accused of 'slotting' people into social roles in his *Republic*. In this view, people are put into productive roles as part of a master plan or in order to free the upper class to pursue its own ends. This can only be maintained if one ignores the *self*-selection into types which Plato has emphasized. Men will be unhappy and restless until each is enabled to fulfil himself in what he does best. The function of Plato's universal public education (including women as well as men) is precisely to uncover each person's native bent and to encourage him accordingly. So far from being a scheme to perpetuate arbitrary inequality, this educational scheme opens the way for each child, of whatever background, to identify himself as primarily concerned with tactile and manipulative pursuits or those of honour and discipline.[6] Within the latter group, successively more difficult tests are set (412d–414a), so that the very few who are capable of noetic

---

5 The similes of the sun, the divided line, and the cave (507–21) outline the epistemological hierarchy referred to in the paragraphs above.

6 The offspring of the guardian classes are to be assigned homes in the productive classes if they fail to respond to the tests which locate 'gold' among the children. And the universality of education in the scheme is mandated by the observable fact that gold is where you find it. See the so-called 'myth of the metals' (415a–c).

pursuits may be identified and aided on their arduous progression to the status of philosopher-ruler.

At this point arises a paradox which accounts for the concentration on the philosopher-rulers and the relative neglect of other groups in *Republic*. To the degree that the apprentice philosopher-ruler achieves genuine insight into the realm of the Forms, the 'normal' incentives to social responsibility become inoperative in his case. The life of things has no attraction for him; prestige and precedence are not his goals; the exercise of power is, for him, merely an entanglement in affairs in which he has little interest. This state of affairs is symbolized and made into an institution in the communal life of the guardian class as a whole: the philosopher-rulers, the administrative class, and the professional army. As a group, they have all the power, yet few of the perquisites of power. Only the productive class – by far the majority of the populace – is allowed to marry, to own property, to possess money, to raise its own children. The guardian class is denied all these things. It serves the commonwealth out of mere duty, for it possesses nothing desired or held to be of high value by the producers. If the administrative class and army enjoy a certain precedence, it is one dearly paid for, viewed from below.

But while the guardian class as a whole may serve out of a sense of duty or honour, its directing intelligence, the philosopher-rulers, must sacrifice the most, for its members must return to public life after direct noetic experience of the realm of the Forms. Plato supplies them with no inducements; he only argues that the noetic man must take up rule, or, indeed, there is no hope at all for a truly good society. 'What we need is that the only men to get power should be men who do not love it' (521b). But in order to move such men actually to take up power, only a plea is likely to succeed. Despite his talk of compelling noetic men to take up rule, Plato's Socrates in fact addresses the products of his educational system in these terms: 'We have bred you both for your own sake and that of the whole community to act as leaders ... to combine the practice of philosophy and politics. You must therefore each descend in turn and live with your fellows in the cave ... And so our state and yours will be really awake, and not merely dreaming like most societies today' (520a–b). But will this plea produce the necessary result? 'They cannot refuse,' says Glaucon, 'for we are making a just demand of just men' (520e). But the only force in this appeal is in the recognition that, if this appeal should fail, 'there is no one else' (521b).

The actual mandates for a new society that Plato lays down for the guardian class – communism, eugenic breeding, and the like – have attracted a good deal of attention, from Aristotle's pained consideration of them in *Politics* through to the present day. Often enough, the critic has looked at these provisions and rejected them as unworkable for a whole society – thus refuting a position Plato never took. Other provisions – censorship and control of the arts – which are put forward in *Republic* as necessary for the whole society are denounced as illiberal and self-defeating even when it is granted that they might be enforceable. This rather misses an important point for Plato's presentation. The whole *Republic* is put forward as Socrates' discussion with young men who can be rescued from mere sophism and saved for genuine philosophy. But the best man who ever lived – Plato's description of Socrates – had in fact been killed by the restored democracy of Athens. What hope exists, therefore, for the young men who are to be encouraged to take up the philosophic life? The question involved in the elaborate discussion of civic justice is, on an important existential level, 'What would be necessary to do, or to change, in order to have a society that would not kill a Socrates?'

This profound problem explains the elaborate discussion, in books VIII and IX, of the existing types of public order. All types are spoken of as degenerating from the perfect society created in the dialogue; and each declines into the one beneath it, until democracy and tyranny are reached. This established, Plato then shows that the happiness of the philosophic man is superior to the delusive felicity even of those who are best placed in the inferior sorts of society. The argument of books VIII and IX is made to work in both directions. Other forms of society are shown to be inferior, and the necessity of surmounting them is established. But in the case of each inferior type – the ambitious society, oligarchy, democracy, and tyranny – Plato has also spoken at length of its modal type, the sort of man who most characterizes or epitomizes that sort of society. We end up having returned to a consideration of the sort of man who most exemplifies the truest and best society: the philosopher-ruler. The discussion of the inferior sorts of society shows us how much would have to be changed in order to bring about and then to perpetuate a society in which Socrates – or Adeimantus or Glaucon or the reader – would not be killed.

Books VIII and IX are introduced by a reminder that the discussion of the provisions necessary to identify, educate, and maintain the philosopher-ruler is completely theoretical. As we reach the bald summary of the education of philosopher kings, Socrates reminds his hearers that 'we are amusing ourselves with an imaginary sketch' (536c). And at the end of book IX, Glaucon alludes again to the theoretical character of the city they have founded in words: 'I doubt if it will ever exist on earth.' Socrates does not dispute him, but counsels that it be 'laid up as a pattern in heaven, where he who wishes can see it and found it in his heart.' But it does not matter whether it exists or ever will exist; 'in it alone, and in no other society' could the philosophic man take part in public life (592b). That we have been amusing ourselves, however, is far from true. The discussion has been concerned with what the young participants in the dialogue may expect from life. The answer is that, short of the completely radical transformation of society – the importance and urgency of which changes have been so convincingly demonstrated – they will face the fate of Socrates if they venture into public affairs.

Though it is impossible to make Plato a utopian, he has established the ground plan which governed later utopias. There is an alternative social order, apprehensible by those with noetic power. This order is based on man's inner nature; its provisions express in institutional form the right relations among men of differing capacities and gifts. As the best men are those in whom reason disciplines and guides the strong horses of gratification and the desire for achievement, so in the social order as a whole the same relation of harmony must prevail. This order of rational harmony is true precisely as it penetrates behind the mere circumstances of historical existence to what is unchanging and incorruptible. This transcendent truth, logically available at any time, has now been discovered and offered as man's only hope for happiness.

But Plato has no hope that this order can be institutionalized permanently. If it is apprehensible by penetration to the realm of the Forms, it must be realized on the material plane, where mutability largely comes to mean corruption. The material plane produces error precisely as men take its undoubted goods as supreme goods. This inevitable error, so long as men are not directed by noetic reason, deprives men of happiness and even of these created goods themselves, for when taken as supreme goods they breed the conditions of their own destruction. Even if the commonwealth created in the dialogue were to be achieved, it would eventually decline and enter into the cycle of ever more degraded societies pictured in books VIII and IX. Plato's argument is obscure at this point. He suggests that the means of this decline will be failures in the calculation of 'the right and wrong times for breeding.' But in fact this failure is but an instance of a general law implied in the very conceptions of the two planes of the Forms and of mutable materiality: 'All created things must decay, even a social order of this kind cannot last for all time, but will decline' (546a). All things that exist on the plane of materiality are finally doomed. It would have been better had this world not been made and that souls had remained unencumbered by materiality. Plato is able to depict the harmonious, fulfilled society in which philosophers are not killed though he realizes the insuperable obstacles in the way of achieving this society.

16

Christianity and utopia

So long as Plato's conviction that a harmonious society was impossible was maintained, utopia could only be a discussion of the philosophic man's existential problems or the scaffolding for a discussion of the nature of justice.[1]

Christianity reconceived the whole relation of man to a transcendent realm. In its original Hebrew form, as we have seen, it did away with such a realm entirely. When Christianity did seek to commend itself philosophically, it pictured the immaterial realm as equivalent to the kingdom of God attained after death by the individual soul who has been united with Christ in this earthly life. The substitution of death for the resurrection of the saints as the effective beginning of this transformed life meant the admission into Christian thought of a distinction of realms or planes; there must be a now-existing heaven where the souls of dead Christians already enjoy the bliss of the presence of God. The final kingdom of God could not differ greatly from what already exists 'above' this earthly plane. But there was no implied denigration of this present life and its conditions. Christianity had already fought that battle against gnostic speculation; it knew how and why it differed from philosophic thought on the goodness of the created cosmos. God has established this world and heaven and has provided the means of

---

1 Stoicism surmounts in theory the Platonic duality; all men are part of the cosmos, which is the extended body of God; they are thus particles of deity. But in practice Stoicism built its fulfilment of this nature upon the philosophic man's indifference to – and thus superiority over – the objects of desire and fear. Later Stoicism pursued a unitary virtue accessible to the man of full rationality. Only possession of or identification with this unified notion of virtue could be called good. All other objects are evil, along with those who pursue them and those who fall short of the attainment of virtue.

See J. Passmore *The Perfectibility of Man* (London 1970) 53–60 for a characterization of the various strands of Stoicism. I shall argue in ch 21 that the Stoic doctrine of Nature – the Stoics invented it in this capitalized sense – is very important in the development of the doctrine of progress. Passmore, it seems to me, rather underestimates its significance.

transit from one to the other; no implication can be drawn of a necessary inferiority of one plane. It may be that God is immaterial,[2] but he created the cosmos freely and out of mere goodness; he sent his Son to live under its conditions. The means of salvation are not esoteric but quite material and worldly.

Once this picture of the cosmos and of man's destiny became universalized through the formal Christianization of the world of antiquity and northern Europe, and once it became formalized institutionally, there was little ground upon which utopianism could germinate. Early and medieval Christianity contained a great many sanctions for men to conform their conduct to the precepts of the gospel. But it provided no incentive for men to attempt to create the plane of heaven on earth. This world, if a vale of tears, had already received such a measure of redemption as was proper. It could not be classed as evil, for it was the scene of the drama of redemption, already substantially accomplished. Finally, the millennialist doctrine of the end-time had not been lost. The whole cosmic structure lay subject to the promise of transformation into something completely new, as the completion of the story of redemption.

But Christianity was not simply an obstacle to the rise of utopianism; it played a constitutive role as well. For utopianism did not arise in the pockets of antique pagan culture that survived the establishment of Christianity; and it did not develop in underground medieval spirituality.

What utopia gained from Christianity was a sense of this world as a world of human process. Aristotelian theology was used to rationalize the institutions of the age; it de-emphasized the divine fiat, reduced the impact of revelation, and produced in its place a sense of regular law.[3] The Joachimist and Joachite movements in contrast, stressed the immediate divine activity, well articulated within each *status*. This activity, however unmediated, was not capricious. God could be seen to work by his own methods, which had a regular shape of their own through time. From quite different perspectives, then, both groups produced the picture of a universe that was *reliable* in character. Further, both the established group's picture and the sense of crisis arising from the protest groups drew men's attention to actions in this world, and not to an escape from historical action or a disregard of it. I believe that this sense of a reliable universe, in which response is required, was necessary for the emphases of Plato to be turned into the making of utopias. Also required, of course, were the breakdown in cogency of the answers, in the patterns of behaviour, and in the promises that characterized the conflicts of the thirteenth to the fifteenth centuries.

2 Tertullian, as we have seen, and the Stoics, for somewhat different reasons, held otherwise.
3 See above, 120–3.

Here, too, Christianity supplied some of the solutions to its own problems. For Christianity was an organized movement theoretically distinguishable from institutions serving the needs of men for food, companionship, shelter, and safety. Christianity provided an example – in both its established forms and in the Joachite and other movements – of an independent movement organized for the achievement of tasks transcending the mere maintenance of the social machinery. If, by the sixteenth century, the church – in either established or protesting forms – was to a growing number no longer believable as the means of achieving human felicity, both its picture of the reliable universe and its style of independent organization could be joined to other visions of the purpose of human existence.

17

The Hermetic tradition

This account of the conditions for the revival and definitive creation of utopia must consider the revival of magic, alchemy, and astrology in the fifteenth century. No account of the taking up of Plato's emphases in the sixteenth century can be economical unless it discusses the extent to which the revival of 'ancient lore' influenced the new utopianism.

Further, a significant theoretical issue must be addressed: if it has been necessary to deal in detail with the historical conditions which are the matrix for millennialism, why is it not necessary to do the same for sixteenth-century utopianism? Is not our contrast – ahistorical versus deeply historical – too simple unless we can be certain that utopianism is not as deeply dependent on its social matrix as is millennialism?

Frances Yates and others[1] have shown how alchemical and, above all, Hermetical lore had become important in the sixteenth centuries. T.O. Wedel traced a fairly continuous history of astrological studies.[2] Each of these soundings of the period

1 Yates's work includes, most notably, *Giordano Bruno and the Hermetic Tradition* (London 1964) and *The Rosicrucian Enlightenment* (London 1972). See also P. French *John Dee: The World of an Elizabethan Magus* (London 1972). On the later William Lilly, see *Mr. William Lilly's History of His Life and Times from the Year 1602 to 1681* (1715), repr with notes and intro by K. Briggs as *The Last of the Astrologers* (London 1974), and D. Parker *Familiar to All: William Lilly and Astrology in the Seventeenth Century* (London 1975).

   A useful review of contemporary scholarship on this tradition is that of S.A. McKnight, 'The Renaissance Magus and the Modern Messiah,' *Religious Studies Review* v 2 (1979) 81–9. McKnight perpetuates, however, the confusion of categories I seek to distinguish in the present work. Throughout his essay the terms messiah, messianic, and apocalyptic are used to describe persons, ideas, and movements concerned to embody on earth a natural, primordial, or transcendent order that is 'true' independent of historical events.

2 T.O. Wedel *The Medieval Attitude toward Astrology, particularly in England* orig pub New Haven 1920 (1968).

before Thomas More proceeds by its own notion of what is important. Wedel neglects the Hermetic corpus and stresses the constant attempt in the medieval period to distinguish between dark, manipulative magic and the more rational and 'scientific' fields of astrology, astronomy, and natural science. For Yates the influence of the Hermetic materials is paramount, and she seeks to trace the means by which this supposedly primordial lore influenced the drama, court life, and general intellectual life of the period.[3]

What then does More owe to Plato and what to the alchemical tradition? I believe that Wedel is correct to isolate the macro–micro equation as central to astrology and alchemy. But this sets up a problem, for this equation is fundamental to Plato's *Republic*. And the humanist circles influential on More were also concerned, as we see in Marsilio Ficino, to employ alchemical studies.

We may begin by noting that the macro–micro equation is used in the alchemical and astrological traditions to influence events and bring changes in the world. More is not interested in this endeavour; nor are the classical utopians of the succeeding 200 years. The apparent exception is Francis Bacon – but his greatest influence has been in the twentieth century, and I shall try to show, in chapter 30, that the emphasis in Bacon on manipulation and transformation is better traced to non-utopian roots. This cannot be demonstrated, however, until the fundamental characteristics of utopianism have been established. More's period saw the beginnings of a new and open reliance upon the Hermetic tradition – but More and his utopian successors were but little affected by that otherwise quite pervasive mode of thought.

The appeal of the Hermetic materials requires a somewhat different treatment. A good deal of the literature and practice of theosophy (wisdom about the 'divine') and thaumaturgy (the working of wonders or miracles) has origins quite independent of early Christianity and rabbinic (ie post-70 AD) Judaism. But these latter, after some hesitations, set themselves firmly against conjurations of 'powers' and against the world-view that gave rise to organized theosophy, thaumaturgy, and theurgy (the seeking of divine action, particularly in Neo-Platonism). Diocletian, in the final struggle against new religions, ruled impartially against both Christianity and the late-classical efflorescence of 'lore.' When his efforts failed and the Christian empire began to legislate against its competitors, Theodosius and his successors included in their proscriptions the groups associated with these types of theanthroposophical lore (about the linking of the human and divine).

3 She perhaps insists on what 'must have' been the case where statements of strong probability would have been more prudent. Her general conclusions are highly probable. To distinguish, as she has done, the influence of the Hermetic corpus from the general acceptance of alchemical notions is a significant service.

The Hermetic materials recovered in the sixteenth and seventeenth centuries appear on internal evidence to date from the fourth-century competition between Christianity and these alternatives. They were conscious alternatives to Christianity and Judaism. Earlier there had been a spectrum of views and practices not clearly differentiated from Hellenized Christianity and late-classical Judaism and ranging from Neo-Platonism to thaumaturgy. But both Christianity and rabbinic Judaism gradually set themselves against most manifestations of these traditions.[4] There was thus a substantial population for whose allegiance there was now serious competition. The balance had shifted against astrology and theanthroposophical lore by the time the present Hermetic corpus was pulled together in late antiquity. The corpus thus constitutes a self-conscious alternative to ascendant Christianity.

The Hermetic material portrayed itself as originating with the Egyptian god Thoth – the Hellenistic Hermes – and was expanded over time. Its attribution to Thoth-Hermes may indicate an older tradition. The germ of the whole enterprise may have come from Clement of Alexandria, the Christian theologian who discussed a body of genuine ancient text associated with Thoth: 42 books – 42 being a number associated in ancient Egypt with settings of solemn judgment. Perhaps the late-classical writers of the new materials intended their texts to stand as a judgment upon the period so increasingly hostile to their own enterprise.

By the time these Hermetic materials, somewhat fragmented, appeared in the later middle ages, they were accepted as products of Egyptian antiquity. Their vicissitudes cannot be traced here. But Yates declares roundly that 'Renaissance animism is ultimately Hermetic in origin.'[5] In animism 'the world' is alive and, because it includes all that is, is self-referential and without need of what can now be called an 'exterior' explanation. This notion owes its persuasiveness in this period to the Hermetic corpus and to those who employed it as a counter-gospel. This loading of so much that was central to the Renaissance upon one body of text may well require a good deal of qualification; astrology, alchemy, and some forms of theanthroposophy can be shown to have other origins and other channels of transmission, despite their attribution to Hermes in the sixteenth century.

In a general way, any non-Hebrew world-view can support the utopian half of the typology. But where, as in China and India, there is a kind of politics of Nature or

---

4 The obvious exceptions are the Christian Neo-Platonism bequeathed to the Middle Ages by the Pseudo-Dionysius and the quasi-underground Jewish activities that came later to be known as Kabbala.

5 *Giordano Bruno* 381

a unitary system, utopia is unlikely to arise. Such a divinized cosmos must, it seems, lose its self-evidence before we have the conditions for utopianism. In democratic Athens and, more generally, in the whole empire in the first century AD, we have such conditions. But any incipient utopianism was stifled by the rise of Christianity as a mass religion. However, utopianism renewed its challenge as the Christian world-order grew infirm in the later middle ages. Yates is only the latest to document the creation among the intelligentsia of the period, including the humanists, of a covert, unorganized, but potent reappropriation of a world-view inimical to historic Christianity but perhaps hospitable to the development of utopianism.

To what extent is the lore associated with the Hermetic corpus an indispensable social precondition for utopianism? Does this tradition, by appealing to a remote antiquity, indicate that the rigid distinction I have made between historical and ahistorical world-views is untenable?

The answer to the latter question opens the way to a clearer determination of the former. The elements brought together in the revived Hermetic tradition do not, in fact, make a historical case. The appeal to the remotest Egyptian antiquity is not made in order to argue from the shape of history. Rather it is to lay hands on the primordial. The primordial is not historical; it is original and basic in and of itself. Clement may have unwittingly supplied the germ of the Hermetic project. His earlier fellow-Alexandrian, Philo, had already affirmed that Moses was both prior to and the inspiration of the Greek philosophers – not a historical argument but an appeal to the dignity of priority. But Philo could make this case because his version of Moses could be made the decisive influence on men whose work Philo also wished to affirm and incorporate.

The fathering of their works on a prestigious ancient figure by the writers of the Hermetic corpus is of a somewhat different character. They do not wish, like the Alexandrian gnostics, to fold Christianity into their own system; they wish to propose a counter-system. They may ape Philo in the mechanism they adopt, the appeal to priority. But now priority must be affirmed for its own sake, in order to establish primordiality – its own sufficient recommendation. What is revealed by Thoth-Hermes is a range of truths and manipulative techniques that in no way depend on anything that has happened in human history. Judaism and Christianity are thus treated merely as mistakes or as mantles obscuring the eternal truths of the divine cosmos. This cosmos is the real object of devotion, even as it is manipulated by adepts in command of secret techniques.

The appeal to Hermes cannot be the same, however, when it is made by men of the Renaissance. They are heirs of a Christian civilization that at bottom has always explained itself historically. They will have to argue on behalf of Hermes in a 'historical' fashion. Thus the priority of the Hermetic lore could give it standing when compared to fading Christianity, while, at the same time, the two were co-ordinated in a gnostic fashion. This strategy concealed the fact that some Hermetic revivers rejected Christianity's central affirmations. For them the primordial dating of the Hermetic corpus established perhaps the primordial *status* of this lore. Men conscious of their own marginality could feel themselves in direct contact with the ultimate revelation about the cosmos – to say nothing of the powers this knowledge promised to confer. But the consciousness of possessing truth in a world of error is by no means the same as making a historical argument, in which the meaning of the world is disclosed in its history. To be one of a secret brotherhood of adepts is not at all to be one of the 'saving remnant.'

As we shall see below, the utopian tradition, while ahistorical in style, is notably free of obvious Hermetic influences. Whatever the currents of thought in their times, the Hermetic materials simply did not furnish them with a useful scaffolding or with building blocks. The major exception, Campanella, tends to demonstrate the case. The formal contradictions introduced into his *City of the Sun* by the attempt to join astrological lore to his borrowings from Plato and More threaten to tear the work apart.[6] Many writers, including utopians, employ language drawn originally from astrology and thaumaturgy. Imported from Italy, with the Hermetic elements – embedded in the whole, plot devices, themes, and literary structures – this vocabulary had become conventionalized, as poetic and dramatic language does, into stock images.[7]

Thus the conclusion remains – though it must be demonstrated further below by actual analysis – that the utopian tradition is remarkably independent of theanthroposophical lore and alchemy. It arises instead from the elements laid down in Plato's writings, preeminently in *Republic*. The utopian tradition did not falter when the Hermetic corpus was shown, in 1614, not to have originated

6 Campanella is dealt with below, in ch 19. Yates, in *Giordano Bruno* (360 ff), treats Campanella almost exclusively as an extreme representative of Hermetic enthusiasm. But it is possible to place Campanella's theological activity well within the main-stream of Christian theology in the period; see B.M. Bonansea *Thomas Campanella: Renaissance Pioneer of Modern Thought* (Washington, DC, 1969). A third view is that of G. Bock *Thomas Campanella: Politisches Interesse und Philosophische Spekulation* (Tübingen 1974).

7 The 'new vocabulary follows the teeming but subtly articulated medieval iconography and symbol systems. One can point to its continuity with the Christianized 'chain of being' imagery and language of the Middle Ages. But the new vocabulary draws its elements from the pre-Christian classics. This intention correctly provides the point of departure for Yates, Levin, and others.

with a primordial Hermes Trismegistus.[8] And despite the conscious vocabulary changes and Yates's tantalizing evidence of a political character for this program, it failed at every point to cohere. The utopian style of analysis throughout remained true to its own, distinct origins.

8 See Yates *Rosicrucian Enlightenment* 30 ff, 103–4, 145 ff, 182 ff.

18

More: the first utopia

In the previous two chapters we have considered the roles of Christianity and of the revived Hermetic tradition in the formation of utopianism. Christianity, I suggested, provided the rationalist epistemology and a pattern of social order which could be used or adapted by utopians at a time when Christianity itself was undergoing a severe crisis. This was true despite the basically un- or even anti-utopian bias of Christianity. In contrast, the Hermetic tradition, while essentially ahistorical in nature like utopianism, did not provide a useful intellectual, political, or social framework for utopian speculation.

These conclusions concerning the heavy influence of Christianity and the relative insignificance of Hermetic lore certainly apply to the first true utopian, Thomas More. However we can also learn much about More's thought by contrasting it with two other major intellectual forces more specifically tied to the period in which he was writing. These are, first, the literary-political tradition of the 'mirror for princes' and the new genre of 'courtier' literature, and second, the 'urbane' humanist thought of his period. Even the discovery of America played a role in the inception of Utopia.

Clearly the 'mirror for princes' tradition is reflected in book I of More's *Utopia*, but only to be rejected, as J.H. Hexter has shown.[1] For More the problem of 'the commonwealth' is too deep to be addressed simply by offering advice to the prince for his own conduct. The prince and the men of his council are so deeply caught in systemic corruption that merely model patterns of behaviour are beside the point.

---

1 See ch 2 'The Utopian Vision: Thomas More. *Utopia* and Its Historical Milieux' in his *Vision of Politics on the Eve of the Reformation: More, Machiavelli and Seyssel* (New York 1973). I had reached the conclusions on More outlined below before reading this magisterial essay and the incisive essay of R.C. Elliott 'The Shape of Utopia' *English Literary History* xxx 4 (1963) repr in R.M. Adams tr and ed *Utopia: A New Translation, Backgrounds, Criticism* (New York 1965).

The courtier tradition, well exemplified by Baldasar Castiglione's *The Book of the Courtier* (1514), shifted the emphasis from the prince to his counsellors. There is no doubt that Elizabethans made significant use of this tradition. But Castiglione was not translated into English until 1561. The problems addressed by Castiglione presuppose a less robust – not to say less lethal – environment than the ones in which both Castiglione and More found themselves. Castiglione certainly produces portraits of ideal men and women of Renaissance courts. And many of More's humanist friends were acutely aware of opportunities and problems inhering in princely patronage. But a considerable gap exists between this literature (and this occupational hazard for wandering humanists) and the issues faced by More in 1516. The humanists faced the necessity of moving on or, at most, the possibility of personal disgrace; More believed the important issues were larger than those of urbanity or reputation.

The 'humanist' members of the Academy in Florence in the fifteenth century sought consciously to build a new definition of civilization on models not drawn from the established Christian world-view. In the main they looked back to classical civilization, through the lenses of their newly edited Augustan texts; these provided their models. Urbanity was to replace fanaticism and barbarism. The new Latinity, based on a recovery of the old, was contrasted to the living Latin of the medieval period, with its many accretions and changes since Cicero and Virgil. The Kabbala was used by some as a continuation of antique Pythagoreanism. And while few of the Italian Renaissance figures were overtly pagan, their enterprises often bore little relation to the Christianity they at least formally professed. They had faced the shattering of all political hopes as the fragmented Italy of the period was devastated by internal wars and finally by the advent of the French into Lombardy at the end of the century. By this time also the shift of political gravity away from Italy had been accompanied by the development of the Atlantic trade at the expense of Italy's former central position in commerce.

The tone of northern humanism, if not always devout, was much more in favour of reform of both church and society. Fewer nobles, perhaps, but certainly more of the bourgeoisie were involved in patronage of learning and in the endowment of new universities, colleges, and schools by which the benefits of humanism might be spread further. It was in the nations bordering on the Atlantic that the impact of the new discoveries was greatest and there that Amerigo Vespucci published the accounts of his voyages in the Americas. The inhabitants of the Indies, in his stories, mixed repellent habits with customs worthy of emulation by civilized Europe, a combination which became quite popular in the utopian genre.

Thomas More[2] took up the ancient device of the distant island and the new theme of uncorrupted savages in his reworking of the themes of Plato's *Republic* and created the new genre of the utopia. *Utopia* is much concerned with the question agitating Plato in *Republic*: the place of the philosophic man in public life. Despite its carefully maintained air of being a humanist *jeu d'esprit*, *Utopia* is a sustained enquiry into the possibilities for both personal and corporate fulfilment. Book II, the actual 'utopia,' was written first, in Flanders; but it now follows what More wrote after his return to public life in England. The whole work's proper title is *The Best State of a Commonwealth*. Published first in Latin at Louvain in 1516, and later in Paris, Basel, and Florence, it was translated into English in 1551. In order to exhibit the work that establishes the utopian genre, to deal with its differences from Plato's work, and to respond to some of the less appropriate interpretations of *Utopia*, I shall summarize the work and discuss its intent together.

Book I is largely taken up with the efforts of More and Peter Giles to persuade Raphael Hythloday, the traveller returned from Utopia, to take up service with some monarch, the better to influence public policy and carry through on his own views and the admirable example of the good society he had found in Utopia. Raphael responds with a number of reasons why philosophers will always find public office worse than useless. The rationality and moral cogency of the philosopher's advice is contrasted to the weight of passion, tradition, and intrigue at court, which will doom his own efforts. Raphael rejects the palliative role which is the most he could attain; for while one problem was being dealt with, a dozen

2 More was a new man – one of those profiting from the diversion of lands by the Tudors and, accordingly, no longer constrained by the values of the old order. More had been raised in part in the household of Morton, one of Henry VII's chief instruments. The young More managed to serve all three of the new forces: the new learning, the new commerce, and the new centralized royal authority. He also wrote one of the earliest pieces of Tudor propaganda, a highly coloured biography of Richard III. More rose rapidly in both mercantile and political establishments. He was a lawyer, privy councillor, MP, arranger of commercial treaties, and long-time public office-holder. At age 38 he was part of a delegation to Flanders in 1515 on behalf of the textile industry. There and later in England he wrote *Utopia*. Minor ministerial office and the Speakership were followed by his appointment as Chancellor, at that time the king's principal officer. More was punctilious in his conduct of the king's business, including the suppression of heresy, but felt unable to aid either the royal divorce or the preparations for the Act of Supremacy. At length, pleading ill-health, he left office. His subsequent silence on the royal supremacy over the church was felt to be an affront when maintained by so eminent a man. After a lengthy confinement, he was found guilty of treason and beheaded: 'the king's loyal servant, but God's first,' as he put it on the scaffold. It was discovered that throughout his adult life he had practised the monastic mortification of wearing a hair-shirt next to his flesh.

others would grow worse. The remedy lies in a radical attack on private property. 'More' is made to contradict him (all the radical statements in *Utopia* being put in Raphael's mouth), but Raphael confutes him by pointing to the existence of Utopia: 'You should have been with me in Utopia and personally seen their manners and customs as I did ... You would ... admit that you had never seen a well-ordered people anywhere but there.'[3]

Two issues are thrust to the fore here. One is the tension between the real and the ideal – here given additional point by the insistence that in this case the ideal *is* real. The other is the attempt to convince not through explication of principles but through description of how 'the best state of a commonwealth' actually works in practice. Plato's *Republic* is substantially restricted to the first issue; its elaboration of institutions is conducted in the knowledge that, whereas all institutions change and die, the soul is immortal. It is the soul's destiny which is at issue.

Raphael, in contrast, though he makes use of Plato's arguments and Plato's experience of the futility of dealing with unphilosophic princes (I 39), cannot simply take over the Platonic argument. Utopia is not simply 'laid up as a pattern in heaven where he who wishes can see it and found it in his own heart.'[4] It does matter, in contrast with Plato, 'whether it exists or ever will exist,'[5] for a mere ideal cannot compete with the brute facts of how public life is actually conducted. Raphael emphasizes the systematic nature of public affairs: how passion is necessarily reinforced by bad advice, which drives out good (I 18–19, 40–5). Utopia, we are given to understand, really does exist. That the whole enterprise is conjured up out of the head of More is neither in question nor to the point. The evil More opposes is not an illusion or a mere mistake, but quite real. The counter-reality he proposes must be endowed with the same sort of reality; it cannot simply be a hypothesis; at least it cannot be *spoken of* as a hypothesis.

More and his friends, in the letters attached to various editions of *Utopia*, no doubt amused themselves and their readers with the *verismo* with which they discussed Raphael's present whereabouts and the possibility of getting from him the actual location of the island, a reference they had missed due to a distraction at that point in the actual conversation in Giles's garden. But the literary japes both conceal and give point to the necessity to pose an actual solution to the problems addressed in the book.[6] It is necessary at least to seem to offer a histori-

---

3 *Utopia* tr, ed, and with notes by E. Surtz, SJ (New Haven 1964) 55. Subsequent citations are from this edition unless otherwise noted.
4 *Republic* tr Desmond Lee (Harmondsworth 1974) IX 592b
5 Ibid
6 P. Turner, in the introduction to his racy translation of *Utopia* (Harmondsworth 1965), argues for the influence of Iambulus and of Lucian's satiric accounts of travellers' voyages on the composition of *Utopia*. But More resists the temptation to satirize or caricature England within the

cal reality in place of the evils of sixteenth-century England which are discussed at such length in book I. 🖙

More is concerned not about our attitude towards a society that has killed Socrates, but about what we shall do about systemic misery, greed, brutality, vainglory, and folly. A city that kills Socrates reveals itself to be untrue, and, to that extent, unreal. But More does not attempt to convict his society of unreality; his goal is not to keep philosophers from being sacrificed but to lead men to change their society for their own sake. Lacking Plato's psychology of types, More cannot localize the crucial element of society's problem in this group or that. If all men are victims, in their various ways, of the present social organization, so all men are responsible agents in its reform. The elaborations of humanistic literary conceit are employed in *Utopia* – including putting in Raphael's mouth both the critique of England and the defence of utopian institutions – in order to distance More from the fundamental seriousness of what he is doing.

Book II completes the movement of the whole enterprise. It shows us 'the best state of a commonwealth' in action, rather than in a blue-print. Its point is not simply to illustrate the felicity of its inhabitants (as with ancient descriptions of the Elysian fields) or to outline proper principles (as in such predecessors of More as Doni and Fabrizi). More's point is to show us a counter-reality – in Frye's words, 'what a society would be like in which the natural virtues were allowed to assume their natural forms.'[7]

This is not to say that rational-deductive imperatives are absent from Utopia. The sameness of the cities, the plainness in clothing, are defended on the basis of a Philistine reasoning about utility. But the dominant mode of exposition in book II is simply to let Raphael describe the life and institutions of the Utopians.

Somewhere in the southern hemisphere, once attached to the mainland but now supplied with an equivalent to the English Channel, Utopia is an island shaped like a fat crescent moon, some 200 miles wide across its thickest part. It has 54 cities distributed as equidistantly as possible throughout the island. Its

pages of Raphael's description of the customs and people of Utopia. The high humour of More's style, to which Turner does more than justice, ought not to lead us to take the style for the matter. No doubt Utopia is a practical joke, but it is exceedingly practical as a joke.

7 F. Manuel ed *Utopias and Utopian Thought* (hereinafter *UUT*) (Boston 1967) 26. More does not adopt the device, so popular in later utopias, of the traveller who arrives in utopia and is 'shown around it by a sort of Intourist guide ... The narrator asks questions or thinks up objections and the guide answers them' (ibid). He does exhibit what Frye describes as the first of two 'literary qualities which are typical, almost invariable, in the genre, [namely that] the behaviour of society is described ritually' (ibid). A rational, deductive defence of Utopia is not necessary; but it is necessary to show 'the natural virtues' behaving naturally. So deployed, they explain and defend themselves. More feels little need to *forestall* scepticism about his proposals.

government, based on householder franchise, is representative in character, with an ascending pyramid of elected officials. The extended household is the basic social unit, with up to 16 adults permitted in each city household and up to 40 in the country units, which are given over entirely to agricultural pursuits. The country districts are populated by two-year shifts of city folk, with staggered terms of service, so that the new group can be trained by experienced people. Thus no distinctive, separate town or rural cultures can grow up, to the disadvantage of either. The barter system prevails, with free distribution of essentials. There is no private property in goods, transport, dwellings, or means of production. There is universal education, a flexible apprenticeship system, and an effective oversight of movement in order to ensure that all persons, male and female, do productive labour.

The commodiousness of Utopian life is stressed. With all hands at productive work of some sort, and with no costly luxuries to distort economic and social values, labour need be no longer than six hours per day. The rest of each day is devoted to decent and rational pleasure. Utopia is defended by means of bribery, the stirring up of sedition among its enemies, the employment of mercenaries, and, only as a last resort, the use of the Utopian popular militia, which goes into battle with entire families. But the large surpluses of goods and food created by Utopian industry are widely distributed among the Utopians' mainland neighbours and usually suffice to prevent aggression against Utopia. War apart, the Utopians shrink from all shedding of blood, employing sentenced criminals and slaves – usually refugees from hardship elsewhere – to act as butchers. Utopians are monogamous, with affianced persons being exhibited to each other naked, so that misrepresentation and illusion may have no place in the founding of families. Prohibition to marry is the punishment of premarital sex; adulterers are usually enslaved; but divorce, though closely restricted, is possible.

Utopian philosophy is an informed and moderate hedonism. In religion the widest tolerance obtains, save that no one may profess what would be destructive of society as a whole: that the soul is mortal, that the world is the outcome of chance, or that there is no reward or punishment after death. Those who do profess one of these forbidden doctrines are not persecuted but only prevented from propagating it in public. Private advocacy of them to priests and other significant persons is positively encouraged, in the hope that their advocates will thereby be converted. Public worship is maintained without concrete images of deity, so that no particular sect need be constrained by obtrusion of the doctrines of another.

Raphael does not believe that the Utopian example, as persuasive as it is, will convince men to adopt it. Even though self-interest – to say nothing of the counsels of Christ – would lead us to follow the Utopian way of life, pride stands in the way as 'one single monster, the chief and progenitor of all plagues ... preventing and hindering them from entering upon a better way of life' (II 150). Yet he is comforted to know that this way of life actually does exist in the world and is so secure that it is unlikely ever to be overthrown.

The More of the dialogue then tells us how many things seem 'absurdly established'; in a few phrases he appears to cover most of Raphael's account, and 'most of all in that feature which is the principal foundation of their whole structure. I mean their common life and subsistence – without any exchange of money.' With wide-eyed irony More tells us 'This alone utterly overthrows all the nobility, magnificence, splendor and majesty which are, in the estimation of the common people, the true glories and ornaments of the commonwealth' (II 151).[8] Yet even the dialogue's More is constrained to admit, in the concluding sentence of the work, 'that there are very many features in the Utopian commonwealth which it is easier for me to wish for in our countries than to have any hope of seeing realized' (II 152).

I have asserted that utopia was the search for the good pattern of life in an ahistorical cosmos in which historical development fundamentally adds nothing to pattern, cycle, and hierarchy. The device of the island functions, for *Utopia*, as the realm of the Forms does for Plato. If it is eu-topia (the good place) it is also ou-topia (no place), outside the world that More addresses. The Christianity that More professed – and practiced so rigorously in his private devotions – was not markedly historical in character. If More resented its corruptions, these were institutional corruptions and personal failings, not those of doctrine. The piety of More was deep, but it was a piety that did not question the great medieval theological formulations or the ahistorical character given to the sacraments.

More had acquired a sound and fluent knowledge of the classic pagan writers who were known and valued by the humanism of the day, especially the Latin writers influenced by later Stoicism. The notion of *nature* is important for More, as it was for them. The Utopians 'define virtue as living according to nature ... That individual, they say, is following the guidance of nature who, in desiring one thing and avoiding another, obeys the dictates of reason ... Nature herself, they maintain, prescribes to us a joyous life or, in other words, pleasure, as the end of all our operations. Living according to her prescriptions, they define as virtue' (II 92 ff). 'Not nature, but custom causes men to accept bitter things for

---

8 Cf Turner's translation at this point: 'The laws and customs of that country seemed to me in many cases perfectly ridiculous ... There was the grand absurdity on which their whole society was based, communism minus money. Now this in itself would mean the end of the aristocracy, and consequently of all dignity, splendor and majesty, which are generally supposed to be the real glories of any nation' (132).

sweet.'[9] Christian theology, and the life marked by earnest participation in the sacraments, do not contradict the dictates of nature, but perfect them.

For More there is an inherent shape to human nature and human society, given in the cosmos. For Christian theology this shape ultimately depends on the fiat of God at the creation and is controlled further by the end to which the creation is proceeding. Yet with the near-disappearance of any lively sense of the end-time, the dramatic structure of created history was largely lost. Human nature is to be perfected to the degree possible in this life and finally presented to God after death, in the afterlife. The structure on which the sacramental life rests is nature. One lives firstly according to nature. One is counselled to follow nature. The natural structure of the cosmos is enveloping and directing. The new world revealed by the explorers was a world untouched by Christianity (or by opposition to Christianity); it was expected by many that the new world would exhibit a pure nature which, if requiring the addition of Christianity to be complete, was nonetheless perfect in its own way. To the degree that both medieval Christian theology and the older classic-Stoic notion of nature were systematic and philosophic, they could function for More as the equivalents of Plato's realm of the Forms.

At the same time More's society of natural justice can be used to imply very strongly the presence of Christianity as the real source of those values he holds up to his contemporaries. The absence of revealed Christianity in Utopia is really its presence, in a way that could not have been brought about by the composition of a pious, 'improving' Christian commonwealth – such as J.V. Andreae's *Christianopolis*, written a century after the *Utopia*. By positing a people of pagan natural virtue More disarms the reader's resistance to being didactically improved. Having thus engaged his readers, More can then deal with them on two levels in comparing everyday society to *Utopia*. Many features of Utopia will commend themselves to the reader on the basis of their reasonableness. When other equally reasonable provisions are found objectionable by the reader, it can be urged in mitigation that the Utopians are, after all, only pagans. A third group of provisions exploits the reader's objection to them by making him put his own society on trial. The Machiavellian prudence with which the Utopians conduct foreign conflicts begins by discomfiting the reader; it ends, so More intends, by disconcerting the reader even more as he is forced to compare the results of the Utopian approach and the carnage visited by Christian nations upon one another. Surely Christians, with the aid of Holy Spirit, scriptures, Fathers, and sacraments, should be able to improve on the merely natural justice of unaided pagans.

---

9 G. Negley and J.M. Patrick ed *The Quest for Utopia* first pub New York 1952 (Garden City, NY, 1962) 274 (Robinson's 1551 translation)

If it is denied that More was serious about the communism of the Utopians, *Utopia* rather loses its coherence. In response to a Marxist appropriation of More as a socialist forerunner, some have dismissed the advocacy of communism as a youthful jape or a piece of literary dialectic; or it has been admitted that he was serious but has then been argued that his communism was directly related to monasticism rather than being an early anticipation of Marxism. More was 37 years old when he wrote *Utopia*, a mature man of letters and a responsible public official. And he knew and valued monastic rules – if not always monkish practice; but monastic communism drew its sanctions from the commands of Jesus – the 'evangelical counsels of perfection' – and from the example of the earliest Jerusalem church group, not from the judgments of reason. This conclusion does not assign More to the Marxists. His analysis of acquisitive behaviour bears little resemblance to Marx's critique of the functioning of capitalism; correspondingly, the Utopians' communism does not arise out of the historically conditioned functioning of class antagonism. It is the natural product of reasoned thought, neither imposed nor struggled for, but adopted freely.

Utopia's communism is not a piece of literary impudence. Too much turns on it, structurally. And it appears that More quite seriously intends his readers to feel the force of the Utopian example. More's moral strategy, as outlined above, depends on Utopia making sense as a society. It is true that the advocacy of communism is all put in Raphael's mouth.[10] But what are the arguments against it, and where are they placed? There are just two counter-arguments in the book.

The first objection occurs after Raphael has concluded his indictment of contemporary European society and has maintained the hopelessness of attempting to reform it by advising any of its princes. Rather we must go to the root of the problem, which is the institution of private property. Raphael expands Plato's provision for the guardian class and universalizes it for all men. There is no hope of a fundamental attack on men's most serious problems until and unless commonality of goods is insisted upon. Here the dialogue's More brings two prudential objections to making communism work: Where is the source of authority in a

10 Turner, in his translation of *Utopia*, 8, has noticed that Raphael is named after the Jewish angel whose name means 'God has healed' and who, in the non-biblical Book of Tobit, takes Tobit on a journey that concludes with the blind Tobit now able to see. And it may be one of More's many jokes that his own real position is put in Raphael's mouth. In the example of Utopian poetry obtained by Giles, the Utopian word *he* means *I* in English. And Giles says, of More's work, in his letter to Busleiden: 'I honestly believe there's more to be seen in his account of the island than Raphael himself can have seen during all those five years that he spent there' (included in Turner's translation, 33–4). Broader still perhaps is an earlier comment: 'By reading his words I seem to get an even clearer picture of it than I did while Raphael Nonsenso's voice was actually sounding in my ears – for I was with More when the conversation took place' (33).

radically egalitarian society? and What are men's incentives to continue producing goods? Raphael responds that these may seem to be cogent objections, 'but you
should have been with me in Utopia and personally seen their manners and
customs as I did.' Had More done so, he, like Raphael, would have had to recognize that he 'had never seen a well-ordered people anywhere but there.' From this
climactic assertion we are conducted straight into book II where it is precisely
these questions of More that are answered in the lengthy description of Utopian
life.

The second objection to communism is also put in More's mouth, at the end of
book II. Here, more tellingly, the objection is put with heavy irony. If what
Raphael has finished demonstrating were really true, then we should have to
abandon what everybody knows to be the best things about our way of life:
aristocracy, dignity, splendour, and majesty. With such a rejoinder all that is
possible, Raphael is in fact left in possession of the field. The communism of the
Utopians is thus central to the structure of the book itself and to More's strategy
of moral argumentation in writing the book at all.

Most explicitly, More's communism is not that of *perfecti* or of a class, but of
plain men and women living in a productive society. If, as Turner puts it, Utopian society is 'communism minus money,' More offers his own society communism plus Christianity. There is no way to reduce this communism in the
book to the level of those other elements, like military practice, which are
intended to goad Christians, armed with revelation, to surpass the conduct of
mere pagans. This communism is a matter of natural justice which Christian
revelation has all the more reason to adopt and to complete with Christian virtues. It is the institutions of private property which make a mockery of the practice of Christianity. To rid society of these institutions would be to rid Christians
of the daily need to violate in practice what they profess. Only thus, also, would
the existential problem of book I be solved – a problem that remains unaddressed
in book II except by Utopian practice. Only in such a society could the advice of
the best men be accepted and used.

Yet Raphael holds out no hope for such a resolution of his problems and those
of Christian Europe – however real and persuasive the Utopian practices. Pride
stands in the way. Men actually prefer to see others worse off than themselves;
invidious distinction is the root of their own self-esteem. And pride is inveterate,
'too deeply fixed in men to be easily plucked out.'

The gracefulness of the whole document and its exuberant wit should not obscure
for us the fact that More concludes on this pessimistic note. It may be, of course,
that More is perfectly right here. But much of his discussion is conducted in quite
medieval terms: the traditional vices, with their traditional names, are employed

to deal with the destruction of the open land[11] and the consequent dangerous spread of vagabondage, the growing gaps between rich and poor, the concentration of power in king and council, the encouragement offered to the courtier mentality, the eye for the main chance, England's first serious inflation, the new chaos of international relations, and the ubiquity of the merely clever. The terms of analysis at More's disposal did not provide him with useful access to many of these problems or enable him to recognize their novelty and structural characteristics.

Yet out of his own resources and background More created a new genre. And if others later employed it in a flat and simplistic fashion that obscured the deeper problems and paradoxes of human existence, the same was not true for More or for his mentor Plato. The marks we saw in Plato are visible in More, translated into the idiom of scholastic theology and humanism. Utopia is a self-generated, self-subsistent, self-contained, and perfect society (so far as it goes). It is held up over Christian Europe as an example. Achieved by natural reason, it is to be understood and emulated by reason also.[12] Though More's piety was profound and flexible, it was based on a thoroughly conventional theology which, as we have seen, had largely lost any sense of being a faith based on historical interpretation. Its general tendency was to ground itself in propositions communicated from the atemporal realm of heaven to that of this earthly existence.

Thus More offers the pattern of Utopian life[13] – itself effectively removed from any linkage to real-world history – as a perfect pattern for human life. Utopia for this life, and the conventional medieval heaven for the life above, after death. In More himself this picture is saved from over-simplicity by his clear-eyed sense that life was a great deal more complex than this. His existential problems, his humanism, and his piety all came together to produce a harvest of ambiguity, irony, and high humour and to give a rich flavour to what he created in *Utopia*.

11 More shows no awareness in *Utopia* that it was precisely the men of his own class and background who led the move to convert the agricultural economy to a money economy by means of the enclosures.

12 No doubt the Utopians were inspired by God, even if they understood him imperfectly. And More certainly expects feelings of guilt to operate on Christians who see what felicity is possible when virtuous pagans act on their imperfect knowledge. But in both cases men are wrestling in a reasoned fashion with the gap between what is now and what they perceive. This process is not at all like being smitten with a sense of sin by the direct action of the Holy Spirit, or with an infusion of grace, accomplished by action of the sacraments.

13 Like most utopians – for he was followed in this, too, as in so much else – More has all the dirty work of establishing Utopia done off-stage, as it were. Utopus conquers the original inhabitants, turns the peninsula into an island, ordains laws, and founds cities – all in the decent obscurity of a period separated from the 'present-day' Utopia by 1,760 years.

19

Campanella: a 'marginal' utopia

Before the utopian genre produced the flatness and relentless didacticism of many later seventeenth- and eighteenth-century writers, there came the illuminating eccentricity of Tommaso Campanella and his *City of the Sun*. Prepared in various versions from 1602, it was finally published in Latin at Frankfurt in 1623. Campanella was a Dominican agitator and author of numerous revolutionary schemes for world order which were meant to be implemented by various powerful princes. *City of the Sun* is perhaps the first utopia by a marginal figure. Thereafter, utopia would be used as a means to float a great many schemes; but it is not clear what relation *City of the Sun* bears to Campanella's own revolutionary plans. Its importance in the development of the utopian genre is owing not only to its dependence on both Plato and More and to its relation to Andreae and Bacon, but also to its vivid exhibition of the relation of the writer and of his situation to the shape of the work.

A monk in an age coming to distrust religion, Campanella is the very model of marginality. He proposed political novelties to an age worn out by a century of them. He was a Dominican at a time when the Roman church valued learning much less than the brilliant obedience of the Jesuits. His sense of timing was fully in keeping with this out-of-phase career. He prepared a scheme for the Spanish king to become universal emperor; but the Protestant north had never been stronger than just at that time. He played some role in a revolution against the Spanish Catholic rulers of his native Calabria and attempted to engage the Turks in the plot. He proposed that the pope take the leadership of a European federation in a period when papal diplomacy was never more inept. He ended his career, typically, by casting the French king in an imperial role – at a time when a great alliance of European nations was arrayed against France.

He also shared much with his contemporaries, including a deep interest in astrology, a faith in science as it was then developing, and a readiness to consider new modes of education. Although intensely committed to the new, he shared membership and belief in three ancient universal societies: the church, the community of scholars, and the Holy Roman Empire.

What characterizes his *City of the Sun* above all else is its quest for unity, for underlying principles of unity amid multiplicity, complexity, tension, and contradiction. He aims to do justice to all realities; and he can have this aim because he believes so firmly in the existence of unities underlying the multiple phenomena. Three particular ways of achieving this are highlighted below: the relation of science to a monolithic if multi-faceted society; his educational innovations; and the role of astrology.

A general summary of Heliopolis (the 'city of the sun') will place these in some perspective. Heliopolis lies on the equator in a great plain. More than two miles in diameter, the city rises at its centre to a great hill. Internally it is divided by seven concentric walls and connected by four avenues oriented to the compass points and piercing each wall. The houses, or rather palaces, form a continuous series of dwellings around the circumference of each section. Within the last wall and in the centre of the flattened hill top stands the Temple of the Sun. Domed and perfectly circular, it contains an altar with a celestial globe and a smaller terrestrial sphere. All the stars are located exactly and their influence on human affairs is noted precisely. The temple is lit by hanging lamps named for the planets; and an internal dome over the altar contains the cell within which a voluntary 'human sacrifice' meditates on the higher cosmological mysteries before being returned to human society. Sol, or *Metaphysic*, the chief priest and principal ruler, is assisted by three executives: *Power* deals with defence and justice; *Wisdom*, a polymath, is assisted by the heads of each science or craft except those reserved to *Love*, who rules agriculture, preparation of food, manufacture of clothing, and, most importantly, the breeding of animals and people.

All goods are held in common; and the people dine in common halls, one in each circle. Sexual intercourse is forbidden men till the age of 21 and women till 19, although special arrangements are made for the incontinent. All mating is controlled by *Love* and his assistants, who breed people according to genetic theory and only at the astrologically propitious hours. The same considerations rule animal breeding. Children go into communal care at the age of two and are ready for their first scientific studies by six, subsequently going on to their apprenticeships. The care in breeding assures that harmony prevails among those drawn to particular pursuits. Subordinate magistrates are elected; laws are few and simple; justice is swift, the *lex talionis* governing all penalties, save when voluntary confession precedes discovery of crime. General confession of non-criminal sins to one's superiors assures Sol of hearing what is amiss. Religion and philosophy are a remarkable mixture of astrology, natural theology, Stoic cosmology, and elements from Parmenides and Plotinus.

The relation between Campanella's Temple of the Sun and the 'Salomon's House' of Bacon's *New Atlantis* is not clear,[1] but the borrowing is likely to be Bacon's. Campanella's scientists differ significantly from Bacon's narrow investigators and controllers. Campanella's scientists do not live in a world in which it is axiomatic that the possible ought to be tried. They are the central and controlling force in the city, but are themselves in the service of a conception or system of human good that exists prior to and independently of what may be discerned about the natural world. Their positions as politicians, priests, and managers are not an outgrowth of their status as scientists but are precisely a limitation on their science. Science exists in the service of a human good that is defined independently of technological possibility. But Campanella has clearly identified both elements of a polarity that increasingly occupied his successors, though few of them before the twentieth century exhibited his sensitivity to both sides of the problem.

Campanella's debts to Plato are plain on every page, but never more clearly than in his notion of education.[2] His system is Platonic in its centrality to the society, in its universality, that includes females, and in the attention to nurseries. But Campanella breaks with the typical school of his own day, with its authoritarian régime, discipline, memorization, and drill, relieved by lengthy sermons and prayers. Children are hardly romanticized in Campanella's work, but there is a clear sense that they are a distinct class of people with their own requirements and tasks. Only among isolated groups in northern Europe was there anything like what Campanella proposes as the normal mode of education for all people.

The community itself is the classroom. The curriculum is the living, adult world. Students are not segregated from society; they start early to identify with adult roles, in the adult setting. His scheme of letting children and young people try out various sorts of work is a specification of something latent in *Utopia* and was copied by many subsequent utopians, though its practice has been discouraged by child labour laws. Campanella's concentric city walls are each painted

---

1 The circulation of manuscripts among the learned complicates the problem of priority and influence. Bacon's work will be dealt with in ch 30.

2 More had been rather vague in *Utopia* on the formal education of the young and had concentrated his few comments on education on the continuous self-education of adults. Campanella was the first utopian to deal systematically and radically with the nature of the curriculum and with the best ways of communicating it to children.

topically, like a completely visualized *Encyclopaedia Brittanica*.[3] Play space and teaching space are one, before these walls. One absorbs the environment, both before the walls and in one's various apprenticeships, though neither process is without explicit guidance and supervision.

Campanella's reliance on astrology is owing in part, I think, to astrology's promise that it can make sense of a wide variety of seemingly unrelated phenomena. Campanella is by no means out of step with the times in his dependence on astrology. Only some sort of determinism can hold together his geometrical inclinations and his distinctive openness to the future: 'Our age has more history in it in a hundred years than the whole world in the preceding 4,000 years' (341).[4] The stars do determine, but they do so in very long cycles; at the end of each age there is an interval of openness in which new orders of freedom may be set up, to determine the shape and to govern the next long cycle.

Campanella very clearly wants to break free from the static hierarchical universe, which is all that his theological and philosophical background has provided for. Of the Christianity that offered so much to a Joachim, Campanella can say that it 'adds to the laws of nature only the sacraments.' And Roman Catholicism in the Counter-Reformation period was much less able than Protestantism to argue from history. The new Protestant establishment could argue that a providential movement of history had resulted in the replacement of the Roman Catholic church by Protestantism; sectarian Protestants could conjure with the Constantinian 'fall of the Church' and picture themselves as recovering the central meaning of God's plan for this age. Historical argumentation appeared to be a Protestant device; and most recent 'examples' – since the decline of the imperial papacy – from which 'lessons' could be drawn were not encouraging to a man of

3 The order of presentation gives us some insight into the characteristic utopian attention to detail. From the temple wall outward the representations are: stars and astrological powers, mathematics, geography, minerals, liquids, botany, fish, reptiles and insects, mammals, the mechanical arts, and, finally, the great founders and lawgivers, their codes and constitutions. Moving inward from the outer wall toward the temple, it is by no means a progression from complex human events to first principles. The various fauna are out of order for this. I suggest that the arrangement is in part determined by wall space. First principles are logically placed in the centre; but also take the least space to portray. Mammals take up both sides of the second-longest wall. The extensive and vital topic of the mechanical and practical arts takes up the inner surface of the outermost and longest wall; the inhabitants see these matters as they go out in the morning to their labours. And as one approaches the city, one sees representations of the world's great lawgivers whose work undergirds and is completed in the City of the Sun.

4 The citations in the text are to the translation of *City of the Sun* in G. Negley and J.M. Patrick ed *The Quest for Utopia* first pub New York 1952 (Garden City, NY, 1962) 307–42.

sincere if eccentric attachment to Roman Catholicism. In any case, Campanella's training seems to have left him without a Christian historical sense; and his maladroit schemes show him as perhaps not over-concerned to build upon the real events of the period.

Yet he gropes for something his background will not let him say clearly. At the end of the present cycle, when the iron determinism of the stars relents, and when amendments to the constitution of the cosmos become possible for a brief interval, then 'a new monarchy will arise, and a reformation in laws and arts will come about; there shall be prophets and renewment, and they say a great gain is portended for Christianity. But first there will be plucking and rooting out, then building and planting' (341). This Joachite-sounding statement in fact has no conceptual underpinning in Campanella: its force is vitiated by his resort to the influence of the stars and to the truths of reason. 'He who follows feeling more than reason' is more subject to the stars than is the steadfast philosopher. Hence the rule of women in his own time has been productive of great mischief; it has been fecund of novelty. And he lists the roll of female rulers. It is the stars which have predisposed northern Europe to 'heresy, a horrible thing of lust, disposed to bestiality' (342). Different stars and signs – 'Sagittarius and Leo' – have influenced Spain and Italy to doctrinal purity. This naked determinism, by itself, would undermine the notion of truth and virtue as held by his Christianity.

Campanella tries to balance off the influence of the stars by the influence of reason. The influence of the stars operates 'slowly and at a distance.' The man of clear and steadfast reason can resist this influence. Thus the propositional truths of the Catholic faith are not the result of astral influence and they are not imperilled by the stars. His final word on this matter goes further still: 'The stars incline sensual people to the thing toward which their own nature inclines them.' And heresy is sensual; the received explanation of the Reformation was that it arose from Luther's lust, Henry's lust, Calvin's pride, and so forth. But 'in the case of rational men, the stars incline men to the rational, true and holy law of first reason, the word of God' (342).

Lacking either a historical sense or a doctrine of autonomous reason, Campanella was unable to ground his own urge to justify genuine innovation. And his ambition to unify in *City of the Sun* the disparate tendencies of his own time could perhaps only be achieved with the aide of astrological determinism. Within this collection, the central structure is that of reason – reason enhanced by astral influence and consonant with Catholic doctrine. Prior to the eighteenth-century rise of progressivism, utopians must finally obtain reliability by adherence to a fixed ahistorical structure of some sort.

20

Classic 'rational' utopias

The uses of historical argumentation were not to be rediscovered for some time; but reason was soon freed from its dependence upon dogma, either Catholic or Protestant. The tentative religious settlement of Augsburg, in the mid-sixteenth century, was preserved with some strains and some alterations until 1618, when all of central and northern Europe north of the Alps fell into the almost uncontrolled and unrelieved ferocity of the Thirty Years' War. Begun as a limited attempt to consolidate the Counter-Reformation in Bohemia, it became a general European war of religion, in which the very existence of each faith seemed to be threatened by the other. On both sides it was felt that true Christendom was at stake, threatened by the minions of Satan. It was thus not a war decided by a few set-piece battles, but by long campaigns supported by popular enthusiasm at least in its first decade and after the crusader-like irruption of the Swedish forces into the conflict. Under these conditions, the numbers of dead, the depopulations, and the desolations approached in impact the effects of the Black Death of three centuries before.[1] And even this cause lost its force when, for reasons of state, alliances began to shift and Protestants and Catholics together made war on their co-religionists. The peace of 1648 was one of exhaustion. One of its results was a reaction against politicized religion, against the notion of an authoritative Christendom, against enthusiasm of any sort – *pas de zèle*. Religion, in both its Catholic and Protestant forms, had managed to discredit itself for many of those best placed to see its social costs when it was taken as a direct guide to the conduct of public affairs.

Was what followed the 'age of reason'? Not if one means the unchallenged reign of the power of reason in determining the means of human felicity. The

---

1 The elaborate punctilio of the later dynastic wars, so absurd to modern men, was a reaction to the terror of these earlier wars.

traditional tag does, however, point to the fact that, throughout the period, it was reason which was the central issue; it was reason which was attacked or vindicated anew.[2] Faith was appealed to on both sides. On the one side, it was asserted against speculative metaphysics that nothing could be known or conclusively demonstrated, though knowledge may indeed be organized usefully in the absence of metaphysical certainty. Hence, Gassendi argued, we should accept as reliable the faith that God gives on matters where metaphysics offers only false assurance; and we can get on with practical science without either faith or metaphysics. On the other side, Descartes refuted the radical sceptics by out-doubting them, as he thought, until he found what could not be doubted: the existence of the doubter. From this he built up a demonstration of the necessity of God to guarantee that the results of reasoning, by means of 'clear and distinct ideas,' deal with the real world and not with an illusion or with a delusion sent by a malevolent demon.

The utopians of the period, most often not metaphysicians but men concerned more directly with public conduct, were decisively men of reason. Their utopias were commonly islands, following the examples of More and Campanella, or were placed safely in the past.

Antangil, published in 1616 by an unknown IDM, speaks of its continent as having been 'owned by various kings, princes, lords and republics. Because of the bad order which prevailed in their government ... the rulers were continually involved in unending wars and disputes. They had rendered the land almost desert.[3] This description of France following the wars of religion (and of the Europe of a generation hence) was prudently located south of Java and set 2,200 years before IDM's day. The problems of Antangil are solved by a great assembly which takes a kind of tennis court oath and prescribes a new constitution. The estates general elects a king and an executive but remains sovereign itself. The class structure is simplified, with the ruling classes unified by compulsory education of their sons at the state military academy. Conscription prevails, along with Protestantism, in this first French utopia.

The tradition of utopian satire was started by Joseph Hall, in 1605, in his *Mundus alter et idem*, first published in Frankfurt. His bitter tales of the people of the south Indies were followed by two Caroline accounts of extraterrestrial monstrous societies and by French tales of interplanetary extravagance, doubtless also

---

2 For a concise discussion of the period and its issues, see R.H. Popkin 'Introduction' in R.H. Popkin ed *The Philosophy of the 16th and 17th Centuries* (London 1966) 8–22.

3 G. Negley and J.M. Patrick ed *The Quest for Utopia* first pub New York 1952 (Garden City, NY, 1962) 301

inspired by Rabelais.[4] This tradition can be excluded from consideration here, even though, in the form of modern science fiction, it has sometimes rejoined the mainstream of utopian endeavour. Satire, while eminently a rational enterprise, exploits the utopian form without making substantive proposals for reform. However clearly its strange islands and planets fulfil the notion of something that stands over against the present world-order, there is seldom a clear pattern that would guide the philosophic man or the comprehensive reformer. It is enough for satire that it pillories what is.[5]

English writers after Hall produced highly practical utopias, beginning with Robert Burton's offering in the introduction to his Anatomy of Melancholy (1621), a systematic program of attainable reforms. The Civil War stimulated a large number of programmatic utopias, as advice in the immediate task of building a middle-class Puritan England. Some, such as Harrington's Oceana, used the most minimal utopian scaffolding around their real contributions, which were model constitutions. Many English writers, whether utopians or, as we shall see, neo-apocalyptists (see chapter 22), were inspired by the possibility of a genuinely new and godly society, which would completely realize the idea of Christendom or the perfected rule of the saints. With their republican convictions, these writers tended to assume that all men could be governed by the prescriptions of godliness, either from inner motivation or from the force of godly institutions shaping their lives.

In France, the régime of Richelieu and the lengthy reign of Louis XIV, at first a constructive period supported by substantial public goodwill, did not provide the conditions for the offering of utopias as solutions to public problems. But by 1676, Gabriel de Foigny, a Campanella-like figure who disgraced himself in both Catholic and Protestant eyes, published at Geneva his account of Terra australis incognita. The people of this great continent are eight feet tall and hermaphroditic. They had imposed a uniform governmental system on a land also made regularly flat by the elimination of all irregularities. Each 'Australian,' in addition to his sexual self-sufficiency, is strongly attached to equality: 'Our glory consists in being all alike' (401).[6]

---

4 See M. Nicholson Voyages to the Moon (New York 1948) for a review of this sub-genre.
5 The modern dystopia (Zamiatin's We, Huxley's Brave New World, and Orwell's Nineteen Eighty Four) differs from the older satiric tradition. Satire is concerned with hating what it satirizes and is convinced that bitter laughter will bring down the false, grotesque, and harmful. Dystopia terrifies precisely because it offers the vision of the omnipotence and persistence of evil unless we act now.
6 The references to Terra australis incognita are from Negley and Patrick ed Quest 392–413.

The point of the narrative is not the wonders of 'Australia' or the novelty of antipodean sexuality, but the Australian views on reason and religion. Beginning from a scholastic definition of creaturely perfection accepted by Foigny's narrator as well as by the Australians – 'Reason taught us a being was perfect when it wanted nothing that constituted its nature, and that therefore to add to it what good things another possessed would not make it more perfect, but rather make it monstrous' (399) – the hermaphroditism of the Australians confirms and perfects on the bodily level the autarkic principle at the root of this definition.[7] Bodily functions, including eating, are performed privately, so strongly do the Australians identify their true, social, life with that of reason.[8]

The narrator presents European thought on God as being of two sorts, 'the one natural, the other supernatural.' The latter is ignored after this admission, and attention is given exclusively to what nature (that is, reason) tells us: 'Nature instructed us that there was a Sovereign Being, the Author and Preserver of all things.' The natural order, to a man of reason, discloses 'a Superior Cause,' whom the narrator 'is obliged to acknowledge and adore' as the cause of the narrator's own being and all else. 'When my reason conducted me to this first principle, I concluded evidently that this Being cannot be limited, because limits suppose a necessity of production and dependence' (405).

His Australian interlocutor finds all this the first real evidence – apart from the narrator's fortuitous hermaphroditism – that he is a genuine human. But the Australian goes on to confine 'this Being of Beings' to the origination and supervision of the most general and universal causes; he works only through what he has made, being 'too far above us to manifest himself otherwise.' And 'if his conduct was particular, I should be at a loss to persuade myself that it was His, since an universal being ought to act after an universal manner' (406).

Here reason is no longer discovering the Superior Cause, but legislating the character of 'this Being of Beings' – an entirely proper activity, given the assumptions of this deistic enterprise. Reason's god must obey the laws of reason in order to be recognized as deity. It follows also that public worship consists entirely in assembling 'to acknowledge His Supreme Greatness and to adore His Sovereign Power' but never to pass beyond this to particular praises, which are undemonstrable by reason and which tend only to discord. The narrator finds that this

---

7 'The more perfect a being is, the less need it has of any assistance from without' (401). The Australian sexuality does not offer the opportunity of sexual activity with all other Australians, but rather means that one generates children by oneself. Love, on the other hand, is non-carnal and consists in a universal regard.

8 The dualism hidden in all this is further evidenced by the fact that the Australian infants hardly excrete at all (408). Cf Swift's anguished reflections on the unacceptable fact of his beloved's bodily functions.

provision 'impresses on the mind an admirable respect for divine things' (407–8).[9] Deistic religion was to remain a favourite theme of utopians, surviving even the advent of progressivism and appearing as late as 1840 and 1845 in Cabet's *Voyage to Icaria*.

But the utopian genre could equally well serve the purposes of Fénelon, bishop and tutor to the heir of Louis XIV. Fénelon's *Telemachus* (1699) takes the son of Ulysses (here standing in for the young duke of Burgundy) through Egypt, Tyre, Boetica, and Salentum, in each of which different aspects of utopian virtue are illustrated. Mentor, the guide of the young prince, actually reforms an ailing Salentum, thus providing the bishop's charge with a practical example of how to conduct his anticipated reign. The noble prelate was highly critical of the extravagance, artificiality, ambitious wars, and corrupt manners of the court of the aged Sun King. Accordingly, simplicity, industry, frugality, modesty, and a sense of duty dominate the various antique societies visited by Telemachus and Mentor.[10]

For purposes of instruction and uplift, Fénelon could make use of the utopian form quite as easily as could the recorders of fantastic voyages. The distant island or the location in remote antiquity served equally well the comparative purposes of both earnest improvers and satirists.

Simon Berington's *Memoirs of Signor Gaudentio di Lucca* (1737) carries forward the preoccupation with Nature, natural justice, and natural law, in its descriptions of the central Africans descended from the ancient Egyptians. On the one hand, we see the familiar faith in the discernibility and immediate applicability of the laws that 'Nature' has provided: 'Their laws therefore are nothing but the first principles of natural justice, explained and applied by the elders in the public hearing of all who have a mind to come in when the facts are brought into dispute' (439).[11] A sort of Platonic myth of character types has come to be believed among the Mezzoranians and is justified: 'It is of very great benefit to keep them

---

9 Cf L. Holberg's once-popular *Niels Klim's Journey under the Ground* (1741), where the same line is taken. See Negley and Patrick ed *Quest* 452, 455.

10 Negley and Patrick, the editors of *Quest*, hold that *Telemachus* 'is unique in seventeenth-century utopianism because its setting is historical rather than geographic' (414). Strictly true, the statement is yet misleading, for the late sixteenth and seventeenth centuries had seen a revival of golden age and arcadian speculation, within the conventions of which there had been an extended enquiry into the true nature of man and the authentic foundations for reformation of custom; see on this the valuable work of H. Levin, *The Myth of the Golden Age in the Renaissance* (Bloomington, Ind, 1969). Fénelon's uniqueness in his setting is to wed this tradition to the developing utopian form.

11 References below to *Memoirs* are to the version in Negley and Patrick ed *Quest* 431–48.

within the bounds of reason' (436). Consequently, they must be 'always watchful and upon their guard against their own passions' (436–7).

But with this by then traditional rationalist emphasis, Berington has a peculiar sensitivity to problems of the emotions. He has a notable mistrust of females; the presence of brutal (animal) souls is much harder to detect in women than in men, since, as it seems, their natures are less noble to start with. But this mistrust is not simply misogyny, and his is not a strictly patriarchal government. Berington has as little faith in mere repression as he does in the abandonment of all attempts at restraint: 'If you allow them liberty, you must depend on their honour, or rather caprice, for your own; if you keep them under confinement, they will be sure to revenge themselves at the first opportunity; which they will find in spite of all you can do' (446). Despite the fact that 'solid reason' does not persuade women, they are no negligible factor in the good society: 'So far from being an indifferent thing in the commonwealth, that much more depends on the right management of them than people imagine' (446).

Within the general Mezzoranian system, the foundation of female satisfaction is her unrestricted right of choice of spouse: 'making the woman, rather than the man, happy and fixed in her choice.' These choices are elaborately tested for their constancy; then, 'when we are well assured of this, all obstacles are removed' (447). Berington is even willing to call his Mezzoranians 'a nation of happy lovers.' This state may be rather the persistence of Eden than the unfolding of a progressivist or romantic motif: 'Among this people nature seems to have kept up to its primitive and original perfection' (445).

But neither the conventions of Arcadia nor Miltonic musings on the right relations between the sexes can accommodate completely the improver's emphasis so characteristic of English utopias after Bacon; in Mezzorania, public statuary tends to be of inventors, with 'usefulness' of the invention being translated into size of statue.

Berington shows us the utopian genre straining at its traditional limits. The rationalist utopia cannot contain a dynamic idea of nature; it is of little help in exploring the notion of emotional fulfilment; and it cannot encompass continued innovation. And it must be observed that the rationalist utopia, in comparison with the deftness of More and the vivid struggles of Campanella, is rather a pale form, and one that deteriorates over time. If Telemachus is a rather didactic opera, its successors were libretti in search of music.

PART THREE

The formation of the doctrine of progress

21

God become Nature

A great social truth, the doctrine of progress, appeared rather suddenly; this in itself is noteworthy. More remarkable, it was brought together out of two incompatible traditions – of rational utopia and of millennialism – which not long before had been the province of literary conceits, political cranks, and heated visionaries.

The abrupt appearance of the progress doctrine in the second half of the eighteenth century is made possible by what took place in England and France in the half-century before. In the 'age of reason' few utopias are produced. What has happened? As we shall see in the present chapter the linguistic usage of the period shows the successive stages in the depersonalization of the traditional God. He must become something like a process before we can have the notion of automatic improvement executed by the (mere) passage of time. This significant shift in language provided a major part of the conceptual foundations for the progress doctrine.

In the remainder of Part III we shall trace the changes in and ultimate margins of contradictory millennialist and utopian elements in the doctrine of progress. Chapter 22 reviews the changes in English millennialism brought by seventeenth-century controversy and discusses how the Cambridge Platonists and deists further altered it. Chapter 23 outlines its transmission to France by deist publicists at a time when the régime of reason had begun to come under challenge. Chapter 24 focuses on the early French progressivists Turgot, Mercier, and Condorcet. And in chapter 25 I consider what utopianism and millennialism brought to progressivism and how elements from each were modified by those from the other.

Why did men feel it necessary to add historical argumentation to the rational designs of the seventeenth century? A notable linguistic shift in the high culture of the period can help us understand this process. The need for historical argumentation made itself felt most acutely after this shift had been accomplished.

In the immediate post-war period of the seventeenth century, God is still almost universally referred to as God. But too much of the uncontrollable dynamism of the God of holy will clings to this usage and makes it out of place in the new setting. There is a gradual substitution, in the eighteenth century, of a more appropriate name, reflecting more accurately God's new role in the order of things. God becomes regularly referred to as Providence.

This term focuses attention on the most agreeable and least offensive activities of the historic God. In the beginning, he created the well-ordered world we see; and he peopled it with rational creatures. Now he maintains it by a general and benevolent superintendence. The means of this Providence are visible in the regularities and symmetries of nature. He does not interfere arbitrarily in the affairs of the rational creatures who return to him the gratitude owed to such benevolence.[1] As a term, Providence can of course refer to a personal being and no doubt was so taken in folk culture and by intellectuals within the orthodox tradition – perhaps more commonly in England and Germany than in France. But Providence, as a term chosen deliberately, emphasizes a function or role. 'The Provider' would have served this prupose and kept the personal reference as well. But it is significant for us to note that 'Providence,' and not some other term, began to replace 'God.' It is the function of providing that is important: providing metaphysical underpinnings and providing the agreeable system of nature that seemed so to confirm the reasonableness of the conceptual and moral worlds as well. This providing is essentially passive; the conception leads directly away from any consideration of *will*; providing is what Providence is *for*, without, one may say, much remainder.

This identification of deity with one of its functions modulated easily into the yet-more-impersonal 'Nature.'[2] Now benevolence and regularity are immanent

---

1 As does the creation itself, when viewed with a Newtonian eye. Addison's 'spacious firmament on high,' with its related effects, 'their great original proclaim.' As for the stars and planets:

> What though in solemn silence all
> Move round the dark terrestrial ball?
> What though no real voice nor sound
> Amid their radiant orbs be found?

> In reason's ear they all rejoice,
> And utter forth a glorious voice,
> For ever singing, as they shine,
> 'The hand that made us is divine.'

2 See from Shaftesbury's apostrophe to Nature in his 'The Moralists' (1709): 'O mighty Nature! Wise substitute of Providence! impowered creatress! Or thou impowering Deity, supreme creator! Thee I invoke and thee alone adore'; quoted in D.B. Schlegel *Shaftesbury and the*

in the cosmos. Jefferson's phrase 'Nature and Nature's God' brings together the whole process of linguistic development and it is itself far from being an innovation, even in America. The discussions on the relation of orthodox Christianity to civil government in New England reiterated the earlier justifications of the bourgeois revolution of 1688 in England: 'nature having set all men upon a level and made them equals.'[3] Here intentionality is imputed to nature in a fashion that has endured into the present. And it is a benevolent intention that is so imputed. But whereas the public men of godly New England no doubt intended little more than a vivid metaphor, Jefferson, a redoubtable deist, probably added 'Nature's God' to his 'Nature' as a harmless redundancy that would render his intention acceptable to his more orthodox fellow-rebels.

The more remote a place is assigned to God, the more necessary it is to speak of a benevolent intention in Nature itself. Looking 'through nature up to nature's God' was Pope's pious counsel; but Bolingbroke's version, in his *Letter to Mr. Pope*, became more influential: 'One follows nature and nature's God – that is, he follows God in his works and in his word.' As with the rationalist utopians, so with Bolingbroke; it is more 'modest,' less 'presumptuous' to accept the truths revealed in Nature and not to aspire to speak of the being of God. This pleasant irony conceals the instability, or at least the ambiguity, of the counsel to follow nature. It is one thing to counsel men of the benefits of living according to Nature. But Grotius followed Seneca in asserting that even God obeys the laws of Nature. Having once (only) commanded, now he obeys, said Seneca. For Grotius, the law of Nature is unchangeable, even by God. This hard saying is justified in the rationalist tradition by means of the argument that the Perfect Being must necessarily have created perfect laws – otherwise he would stand convicted of imperfection. But it results in the effective banishment of God from this world and the attribution of his (still necessary) personal qualities of benevolence and foresight to his laws or to the result of those laws: to Nature. Bolingbroke's counsel to 'follow nature' becomes imperceptibly the statement of an imperious and

---

French Deists (Chapel Hill, NC, 1956) 78. The Stoics had long since referred to the immanent Logos of the world as God, as Providence, and as Nature. And this teaching remained more or less continuously available to educated Europeans through their study of Cicero, Seneca, and Marcus Aurelius. But the Stoic use of these terms is neither consistent nor systematic in development; the immanent Logos is a notably slippery concept, and one with different levels or aspects. The words used by the Stoics to refer to it may have influenced the later declension from God to Providence to Nature, but I do not believe that Stoic influence is important, much less decisive, in a society so saturated with Christian concepts. The depersonalization of God is not a matter of words but of a program or movement. The later repersonalization of Nature, however, may well owe something more directly to Stoic concepts as well as to words first used interchangeably by the Stoics.

3 Joseph Wise *Vindication of the Government of New England Churches* (1717), quoted in H. Kohn *The Idea of Nationalism* (New York 1944) 270

unavoidable demand; we are commanded: Follow Nature! Two things mitigate this harsh requirement. The demands of Nature are regular, fixed, and known; they do not require fidelity to a divine Will whose requirements have never been predictable. And the demands of Nature are in fact benevolent, intended to guarantee the commodiousness of human life.[4] But the prospect of commodiousness if one willingly adapts to the laws of Nature is not by any means the same thing as a doctrine of progress. For that to come about, the new notion of Nature had to be joined to a renewed access to historical argumentation similarly freed from its dependence on a directly personal God.

But the shift from God to Nature had difficulty surviving the onset of cultural relativism, even in the rudimentary form it assumed in Montesquieu's *Persian Letters* (1718) and *Spirit of the Laws* (1748). The older scholastic distinctions between natural law (*jus naturale*) and law of nations (*jus gentium*) had presumed that, however the actual customs of folk might differ, there was at least normatively a bond established by observably common usages and prohibitions. And over the *jus gentium* stood its informing source, the *jus naturale*, derived from and supported by the arguments for the existence of God and thus demonstrably valid for all men, at all times, however poorly it was apprehended or followed among a given people or at a particular time.

The new cultural relativism undermined the status of these distinctions and terms and substituted others. Out of the complex reality of human behaviour, one may build up principles or one may intuit them after viewing the variety of human institutions (it is not clear in Montesquieu how these two processes are to be related). Here the distinction between the empirical and normative begins to be broken down, for it is observed that cultures maintain their own continuity through time, that this survival is dependent on their own distinctive ways, and that these ways are different from those of others; societies have a collective nature. This leads Montesquieu to offer a tripartite analysis of the relation of the corporate structure of a society to the 'spirit' of its 'laws,' or to the 'tone' of a people that the observer gathers from assembly of the empirical data and reflection upon them.

Montesquieu describes three natures and gives them traditional names: despotic, aristocratic, and republican. But he has not arrived at them in the traditional way, and they provide us with the unsettling reality of three natures, and not one. That one – the republican – is better than the others does not rescue Montes-

---

4 Hobbes outraged his contemporaries no less by his notion of God as unconditioned *will* than by his now better-known statements that fear-ridden, invidiously proud natural man makes life, apart from the saving artifices of will, a nasty, though perhaps fortunately short, nightmare.

quieu, for it is impossible simply to leap out of one's natural history, one's climate and economic resources, in order to establish by fiat a government that is abstractly best when all other things are equal; they never are – that too is nature. The advice to 'Follow Nature' has led us into a situation in which Nature speaks in different voices and has different shapes.

Montesquieu struggled against this conclusion. God is brought in as the basis for something similar to the old *jus naturale*. But the clock-making God is insufficiently close to his creation. At most, his providence guarantees the stability of natural processes and the stability of the human power of reasoning. These facts are made to yield the conclusion that at least in principle there is a stable notion of normative justice behind the plurality of fact. There is, that is, a state of nature. By taking thought we can penetrate behind the empirically given and the merely historical and can consider what laws would exist in the state of nature. These laws, then, have a normative and regulative character which cannot be arrived at by following the mode of empirical analysis. This conclusion, however it may have encouraged investigations of the state of nature by Diderot, Rousseau, and others, is only tenuously connected to the rest of Montesquieu's program. Nature, insofar as it was identified with astronomy and physics – as it had been since the Cambridge Platonists and the circle of the Royal Society and its publicists – spoke in many voices, or whispered from too great a distance, or yielded only a speculative original state open to quite different interpretations.

Voltaire's studies in human history emphasized the pluralism of the human condition. His work offered a contrast to the comprehensive providentialism of Bossuet's attempt[5] to encompass all history within the scope of the Christian drama of redemption. But if Bossuet had omitted China and other societies as irrelevant to his purposes, Voltaire wished to ignore the great bulk of the past. It was hopeless to expect to penetrate to the truth about ancient times; the medieval period is best passed over as barbarism and superstition; and only the most recent 150 years ought to be taught to the young at all, for only then does history begin to furnish us with illustrations useful for the improvement of human conduct – which is the real point of history. The writing and teaching of history, so conceived, is quite as much an 'improving' enterprise as anything conceived of by Bossuet. Actual improvement of society would come about through the enlightened use of power. Voltaire, though impressed by English political institutions, held that the innovative despots of the period were the agents of positive change. The royal power was evil only as allied to the maintenance of church privilege, medieval superstition, and – very much the same thing – Christian dogma.

5 *Discourse on Universal History* (1681)

Voltaire was far from being alone in this attitude toward the enlightened monarchs. But it was these princes who quite 'rationally' destroyed the liberties and then the existence of Poland, a nation whose possibilities for reform and whose love of liberty, as interpreted by able and winsome exiles and pretenders to its elective throne, had given it a special place in the affections of the *philosophes*. And it was to be the amiable Louis XVI who first brought the progressive intellectual Turgot to office with a mandate for reform and then succumbed to counter-pressures and dismissed Turgot in circumstances indicating clearly that experimentation was at an end.

A very serious problem thus confronted the *philosophes* with respect to Nature. Cultural relativism, when combined with the Newtonian physics and the deistic God, could not be made persuasively to yield a single doctrine of Nature. And scepticism about the accurate recovery of the ancient past, together with the consignment of the period of Christendom to the realm of meaninglessness, required that modernity carry the meaning of history and disclose men's true nature. This it could no longer do when those rulers best fitted, by their *philosophe* sympathies, to realize the meaning of modernity turned instead to dynastic aggrandizement or to the craven dismissal of enlightened ministers. A much wider understanding of Nature and of historical argumentation was required in order for the *philosophes* to see any hope for their society.

Finally, on the argument from linguistic usage, it must be said that, by concentrating on innovation, I have neglected the continuation of older language in its long-established senses. Despite the blows received from Protestant reformers and from philosophical radicals, the language of the substantialist metaphysic continued to be used in theology and even in the new philosophy. Similarly, Christians continued to use the term God and to mean by it either the dynamic God of the Bible or the divine Author of men's being, whose attributes could be so edifyingly catalogued. In Germany, a new use was made of God-language in the Pietist movement. Here an intense language of personal relationship and dependency was put forward by those dissatisfied with the deity of the Protestant scholastic theology.

The material achievement of the movement conveniently symbolized by the God–Providence–Nature shift is nonetheless its substitution of a new vocabulary to replace or at least compete with the dominant theological vocabulary. So long as this task remained only a project, it was almost impossible to develop an effective rival to either the established metaphysic or to the older Biblical worldview. As we have seen, the attempt to deal with Christianity appeared to be possible without making a break with the rationalist and substantialist metaphysic. But the substitution of Nature for God involved this project in difficulties that the substantialist metaphysic could not surmount. To gain access to genuine historical argument, renewed application had to be made to a source which had remained more continuously related to Protestant biblical Christianity.

22

Puritan millennialism transformed

To see how historical reasoning entered the process of the transformation of God into Nature, we must return to early modern millennialism. In mid-seventeenth-century England, the outpouring of millennialist scholarship and speculation was vast in comparison with the production of programmatic utopias. The millennium remained a central datum of English intellectual consciousness, in one way or another, through the Puritan period, the Restoration, and the early Hanoverian years.[1] One might expect that the Puritan period would exercise itself over a 'theological' question. But many of the issues of the Restoration, of the Roman Catholic succession, of the wars in the Low Countries, and of the Hanoverian settlement also turned not alone on narrowly political or economic grounds but on the identity of the Antichrist and of the placement of current events in the drama of the end-time. The placement of the millennium – before one's time or after it – had a direct bearing on present conduct.

The slow, tortuous course of the English Reformation – never allowed full course, never completely frustrated – meant that historical arguments drawn from the undoubted authority of church and Bible retained their full, naïve force in England long after they had become stereotyped or discredited elsewhere. Indeed, in England, it was scriptural argumentation that fought against and over-

---

1 'This was not a ... fantastic preoccupation of the lunatic fringe in theology ... It was a deadly serious business which concerned Lutheran, Calvinist and Anglican of every variety. It involved the rightness of the cause on which they had staked their careers, their lives, and their souls. It involved finding the answer to the terrible mystery of why the seamless coat of the Church had been rent by a bloody dissension, causing wars and calamities without end. Eventually, it involved the relation of classes within the state and the very nature of all authority ... For almost two centuries the prophetic books were the mirror of Western European history'; E.L. Tuveson *Millennium and Utopia* (Berkeley, Calif, 1949) 29–30. This volume is still the best single means of access to the materials of the period as a whole and to their connection with the development of the doctrine of progress.

came the loss of nerve among more courtly folk after the souring of the Elizabethan visions of a secularized renaissance for England.[2]

So far from running down, proclaimed George Hakewill's *Apology*[3] (1627), the
world discloses no decay. The gloomy predictions of the early Fathers (newly
scrutinized, as Protestants sought to link themselves to the earliest church) can be
disregarded – these men were over-impressed by the troubles of their own times.
They lacked, that is, historical perspective. Our works are not inferior to those of
the ancients; and in many cases of knowledge we have achieved greater insight.
But Hakewill can speak only of a 'kind of circular progress,' apparently using the
word in its literal sense, as in Elizabeth's tours about the realm. It required something more authoritative than such arguments to straighten out the line of history
and to provide inevitability to the notion of history.

MEDE AND HIS FOLLOWERS

Joseph Mede (1586–1638) of Cambridge profited by the previous century's Protestant scholarship upon the text of Revelation and reaffirmed that the millennium
is a this-worldly event and one yet to come.[4] Augustine's doctrine of a millennium coterminous with the era of the church, if not itself fully persuasive to
Protestants, had provided them with a means to identify the papacy with the
Antichrist. One of the features of the end of the millennium, it will be remembered, is the loosing of Satan. If the binding of Satan and the onset of the millennium could be set at some time in the fifth or sixth century, then the disorder of
the Reformation era, the onslaughts of the Turks, and the resistance of the papacy
against Protestant purifications could all be explained as the loosing of Satan
before the final battle preceding the new heavens and new earth. All this seemed
to commit men to a Christian version of 'renaissance pessimism.' All we can do
now is endure to the end.[5] But none of the predicted dates given by Mede's

2 This movement had itself succeeded the fervour of early Elizabethan end-time prophecy, discredited by its dates having failed to see in the kingdom of God.
3 See Tuveson *Millennium and Utopia* 72 ff.
4 His *Clavis apocalyptica* (Cambridge 1627) went through three editions before 1643, when it
   was translated by R. More.
5 This is by no means always a Christian version of the decay theme, however. The sense of
   crisis in a Luther or in the English apocalyptist John Dove or their conviction of perilous
   moments, in contrast to past temporal tranquillity, is based on one of the principal insights of
   Revelation: the approach of millennial events causes Satan to step up his efforts to destroy the
   people of God. His own efforts bring about what he most hates: the clear identification and
   steadfast endurance of the holy ones. As Dove puts it, 'the nearer he is to his judgement the
   more he rageth' (Tuveson *Millennium* 50). In anticipation of his judgment, he creates – against
   his will but by his agency – the specific conditions that bring about the end he fears, that
   mean his doom.

predecessors for the final overthrow of Satan had been fulfilled.[6] Mede's merit was to deal not only with the text of Revelation afresh but also to pose the question of the mode of the end: Is it to be a literal battle or a long process? Is it gradual or catastrophic, by direct action or through secondary causes?

Mede breaks completely with the tradition that sees the millennium as past. He is prepared to see the Reformation as one of a series of events – not as the only ray in darkness – which constitute improvements in the world, victories over Satan. So far from being newly loosed, Satan has never been weaker than now. In Mede's hands, the terrible judgments of the seven bowls are not signs that harden men already far gone in rebellion; they are the successive victories of God's people over the forces of darkness. The millennium is yet to come as the last age.

Revelation and its pre-Mede interpreters provide no basis for viewing the people of a single nation as the saints. Often enough, the perilous position of small embattled minorities led them to view the winnowing process of the end-time as being so rigorous that no particular Christian body – much less a nation – could expect to emerge from it whole. But the partisans of holiness in the English Civil War were prepared to make an exception in their own case. Utopian constitution-publishers, Leveller democrats, Fifth Monarchy men, Presbyterians, many Independents, and lone visionaries all subscribed to the possibility of England becoming a fully godly commonwealth. The most persistent and persuasive of them all, the Fifth Monarchy men, could rely on a remarkably high state of biblical literacy when they conducted their propaganda in the army and in the streets on behalf of an English theocracy. Very substantial efforts had to be made by Cromwell's authorities to refute, outwit, and finally to suppress Fifth Monarchy activities. Much of the argument, sometimes conducted as regimental debates, turned on detailed exegesis of Daniel[7] and Revelation.

Parliament, in 1643, had found Mede's arguments so agreeable to the Parliamentary cause that it ordered his work on Revelation to be 'Englished' and republished at public expense. From it, radical purifiers could argue for their program for the final messianic kingdom to be established in England. But this program faltered on the intractability of public events and on the radicals' consequent suspicions that it was Cromwell, rather than the dead king, who was the little horn of the beast.

---

6 As late as the Restoration period, the widespread belief that 1666 – the *annus mirabilis* – would bring in the end was based on taking Jesus' birth as the starting point of the binding of Satan. To that 1,000 years one added 666 years: the years equivalent to the 'number' of the beast in Revelation 13.

7 Daniel, of course, attempts to guard against so simple a program. The Maccabean clan is not mentioned. The holy ones are not identified as the whole nation.

The problem of language becomes important here. Mede was thoroughly the master of the vocabulary of Protestant biblical scholarship and polemic. He made it possible to discuss broad systemic improvements in society and the relation of the Protestant world to the rest of society or to changes in that relation through time without abandoning the vocabulary of Protestant zealotry and without mortgaging the use of this language to the conclusions of Protestant catastrophism. The men who adopted this vocabulary are intellectual analysts of politics quite as much as Harrington, Locke, Hobbes, Bolingbroke, or Shaftesbury, whose vocabulary is so much more congenial to modern ears.

We should not let our preference lead us into positing a clear seventeenth-century division between theologically based writers and those of a more secular persuasion, with the latter being designated main-line thinkers. And we do not meet this caveat by treating people such as Mede as significant because they 'influenced' a main-line thinker or put forward a position occasioning a refutation by one of the masters. Such treatment is perhaps the last surviving remnant of Whig history, faithfully carried on by some academic political theorists long after its abandonment by most historians. Indeed, the supposed replacement of the theologically based analysts by a positive political science only illustrates the extent to which Mede and others succeeded in laying the foundations for the modern idea of periodized progress and in making it the inevitable framework for other men's thoughts.

Mede and his successors, then, could use a vocabulary of great authority, subtle and well nuanced for the discussion of the shape of human history. But they did so in such a fashion as to free it from Catholic metaphysics and from either Protestant zealotry or Continental Protestant ahistorical scholasticism. They made the vocabulary of millennialism available, fresh and new, to public men generally.

When Mede wrote, and for a generation thereafter, the most direct public consequences were drawn – at least by some – from the discussion of biblical apocalyptic. Freed from Augustine's notion of a millennium coterminous with the era of the church, the events of the end-time no longer had primary reference to the individual existence and its transition from this life to an after-life on a higher plane. These events had to do with dateable, worldly events. The Second Coming or the convulsions of the end-time could leave no one untouched. The present was directly related to these events; one might expect to meet a minion or dupe of the Antichrist in the street.[8] These notions were not an aberration that had to be

8 The Diggers established themselves on a bit of waste land which was theirs because in the end-time all private titles to land had lapsed. Public men were the subjects of exegesis to determine whether the number of their names yielded the 666 of the beast. The direction and even the

got over before real political and historical analysis could be begun. They were an integral part of such analysis. A generation of intense discussion of the coming shape of society, conducted by means of an authoritative vocabulary, and engaged in a very wide public, habituated men of all sorts to regular reflection and discourse on the basic questions of political philosophy.

Further, any discussion of the events of the end-time by men who still, for the most part, believed in Christendom and in the duty of all men to act on conclusions that could be clearly drawn from the scriptures, took place in a context of anticipation quite different from that of the New Testament millennialists who proclaimed the end-time to a hostile, pagan world. We cannot now gauge the extent to which large public events provided men with insight as to the proper interpretation of scripture and the extent to which the opposite movement obtained. Neither movement of interpretation seems reliable to more modern generations. It appears arbitrary and subjective to move from this or that public event to fruitful scriptural insight. And the labelling of public events by reference to Revelation or Daniel seems unlikely to us to produce competent guidance about public policy. But we have seen that the medieval period had not extinguished the conviction, now newly fanned by the Reformation, that the events of the end-time were quite as dateable and world-historical as the Hohenstaufen emperors or the Reformation itself or the battles of the Thirty Years' War, still not concluded when Mede wrote. The wise man, accordingly, could expect world events and scripture each to shed light on the other.

Mede's clear identification of events from early medieval times to the Thirty Years' War as successive defeats for Satan accomplished very important things in the freeing of historical argumentation for its later joining with the utopian enterprise. Mede distanced himself from the numerical calculus and from its debilitating record of erroneous predictions based on a past millennium. He read Revelation correctly and at least placed his bowls before the millennium. But by his bold reversal of the meaning of the bowls – now victories of the saints rather than judgments on a rebellious world – he provided a concrete historical basis, rather than a philosophic framework, for the notion of improvement in history.

Mede provided also a new division point between this age and that of the millennium. This new point owed nothing to biblical numerology; but neither was it the sort of political or public event that, according to Mede, had made up the series of bowls. This event was the conversion of the Jews. Mede imported

control of national policy in the early commonwealth years remained uncertain so long as any regiments had not yet made up their minds about certain contentious propositions about Daniel and the Fifth Monarchy.

this from Paul's letters rather than from the more usual apocalyptic sources.[9] Such an event could not be programmatically carried out, like Digger or Fifth Monarchy manifestos. But the possibility of its occurrence could be enhanced. Cromwell's régime lifted Edward III's banishment of the Jews; this change marks the beginning of the sporadic western Christian interest in the recolonization of Palestine by Jews.

In other ways, too, England's delayed Reformation was to plays its key role in the climax of the ages. Satan has never been weaker; hence our opportunities have never been greater. This judgment is buttressed by appeal to the sorts of evidence cited earlier by Hakewill. But in Mede's hands, the scientific, cultural, and political achievements of modern men become evidence of positive advance over the past, and of advance towards the goal of the millennium. This millennium is not introduced by catastrophe and does not have, for Mede, those characteristics of saintly domination of an unredeemed world that are in fact implied in the text of Revelation. The progressive binding of Satan and the vigorous advance of the Protestant cause lead us without a serious break into the final epoch of mankind. Here too Mede appeals to science, to the new conviction that in nature there are no radical discontinuities. Even Mede's views on the last judgment and on the 'new heavens and a new earth' are subjected to this understanding. The heavens, never having been corrupted, need no reconstitution. And for the 'new earth' we need understand perhaps no more than revolutionary social changes.[10]

THE CAMBRIDGE PLATONISTS

The Cambridge Platonists[11] fall between the English millennialist tradition and the deist emphases on rationalism and historical argumentation. Mede had

---

9 See Romans 9–11. In Paul this conversion appears to have two roots. Paul is reluctant to see his own people abandoned. But more importantly, he believes that God's ancient promises must be fulfilled; his word is never given in vain. Despite their increasingly clear rejection of Jesus – which Paul does not see being reversed in the near future – the Jews will one day, in the providence of God, once again play a role in the economy of salvation, at the end-time.

10 See Tuveson Millennium 76–85 on Mede.

11 Different lists are given of those who may be accounted Cambridge Platonists. But all agree on their founder, Benjamin Whichcote, five years senior to the others, on Henry More (of Christ's, rather than Puritan Emmanuel), and on Ralph Cudworth, author of True Intellectual System of the World (1678), all substantially contemporaries, dying in their seventies in the 1680s. Introductory surveys of their work may be found in G.R. Cragg ed The Cambridge Platonists (New York 1968); C.A. Patrides ed The Cambridge Platonists (London 1969); and E. Cassirer The Platonic Renaissance in England tr J.P. Pettegrove from German edn of Leipzig 1932 (Austin, Tex, 1953; repr New York 1970). The first two volumes above contain extensive and representative selections from a number of the major figures.

released English millennialism from its habit of fastening the whole apparatus of the end-time on the events of any given year in the Interregnum. But it is a long way from the substantial orthodoxy of Mede to the latitudinarian divines and to the principal deists. The Cambridge Platonists are mediating figures in a number of directions.

Trained at Puritan Emmanuel and remaining orthodox at least in intent, they insisted on yoking to Protestant Christianity the full apparatus of Platonism, as they understood it through Neo-Platonism and through the Florentine Academy. They did not simply seek what today might be called liberation; they were opposed to the Baconian program and abhorred Hobbes. Yet with their rejection of the program of Bacon went membership in the Royal Society for More and Cudworth. Cassirer locates the link between their anti-Calvinism[12] and their anti-empiricism in their rejection of knowledge being simply at the disposal of the will, either of the Christian or his God. 'There is that in God that is more beautiful than power, than will and Sovereignty, viz. His righteousness, His goodness, His justice, wisdom and the like.'[13]

Their positive contribution in the present context is their insistence upon a unifying doctrine of Nature, an emanational doctrine. Thus Nature is not a mere *res extensa*. The divine is the medium of the particular in Nature. Man is thus no *tabula rasa*. But '*Nature* is not the Deity itself,'[14] as it perhaps is for Shaftesbury. Instead, both More and Cudworth, in somewhat different ways, saw Nature as having a logic of its own development. More will be taken up below.

The distinctive doctrine of Ralph Cudworth (1617–1688) is 'the Plastick Life of Nature.' What appeared to him, in Hobbes and the Cartesians, as a doctrine of nature unduly dependent upon the moment-by-moment activity of God was combatted by something like a Nature somewhat apart from God, unfolding itself under his superintendence. The world was not made – probably not as a whole and certainly not in its particulars – by divine fiat and not through the execution of commands but by a 'Slow and Gradual Process that is in the Generations of things' (292).[15] The world was not made 'as an Artificer makes an House, by Machins and Engins, acting from without upon the Matter ... but by a certain *Inward Plastick Nature* of its own' (296). This is by no means the Platonic demi-

---

12 For both Cassirer and the Cambridge Platonists, Calvinism is centred intellectually on predestination and ethically on self-discipline.

13 Whichcote *Sermons* II (Aberdeen 1751) 244, quoted in Cassirer *The Platonic Renaissance* 82

14 Cudworth *True Intellectual System* I.3.xxxvii in Patrides ed *The Cambridge Platonists* 302

15 Page references in this paragraph are to Cudworth's *True Intellectual System* in Patrides ed *The Cambridge Platonists*.

urge, however. 'It is a thing that cannot act Electively nor with discretion' (311). Yet neither is it a mere principle. It is a life and 'must needs be *Incorporeal*; all life being such' (311). This life 'must of necessity, be either an Inferiour *Power* or *Faculty* of some *Soul* ... or else a lower *substantial Life* ... depending upon a *Superiour Soul*' (313). This latter is then specified as 'depending immediately on the *Deity* it self' (321). This 'life' is responsible for the particulars of the world; but 'there must also be a general Plastick Nature in the *Macrocosm* the whole Corporeal Universe' (316).

The Puritan millennialists saw the unfolding events of their own period as a drama in which they were themselves principal actors. Henry More (1614–1687) speaks of 'the Theatre of the world' in a different sense; this theatre is itself 'an exercise of Mans wit.' This comment occurs in a lengthy apologetic section on the providential 'signatures' of plants whose outward forms indicate their medicinal use. But some plants have no such signatures; thus room is left for 'the exercise of Mans wit.' There are risk and consequence to human action (he writes during the turbulent Cromwellian period). 'Therefore all things are in some measure obscure and intricate, that the Sedulity of that divine Spark the Soul of Man, may have matter of conquest and triumph when he has done bravely by a super-advenient assistance of his God.'[16] The accent falls not on the dialectical creation of a drama by the actors finding sides in the great conflict of redemption, but rather on the human discovery of the underlying and unfolding character of the world of man and Nature. In this sense, man is now spectator as well as actor in the theatre. The Fall has been reworked. It is no longer the ever-present premise of all historical action. The will is not in bondage. The emanationist doctrine of Nature allows no room for a decisive gap between man's present state and the final kingdom. All things in More's world are matters of degree. Hence salvation unfolds in an orderly progression of discoveries – or enlightenment.

Natural history and its gradualism now begin to determine the view of human history as a whole. Gradualism (or at least non-catastrophism) is the mark of this history, which can be explicated rationally now while one remains relatively orthodox theologically. Unmoved by saintly triumphalism, More equally distanced himself from the main-line Protestant view of sin as radically disabling and as providing history with an ever-clinging taint. Now the Fall is no longer an unmitigated disaster; it is the very means of beginning man's upward quest for maturity, goaded by the conditions imposed on him at the Fall. The catastrophic

16 *Antidote against Atheism* (1653) II.6 in Patrides ed *The Cambridge Platonists* 262–3

Fall is turned into a paradoxically merciful divine pedagogy.[17] But one of the consequences of this conception is that God, having arranged all things well, has no need to interfere with these excellent provisions. It is rather for man to discern and to realize the divine pattern which thus stands as the immanent meaning of life. The arbitrary Hebrew God who makes himself known in history by his free actions has become something very like the realm of the Forms.

BURNET'S 'DIVINE DRAMA'

It is Thomas Burnet (1635?–1715) who exhibits more fully the mediatization of God into Nature. Burnet is eager to show how the scriptural prophecies of wonders, formerly thought to require the direct hand of God, can now be seen to be the results of perfectly natural, immanent processes. But revelation is not limited to wonders. It could also be put that examination of the structure of the cosmos, since it is created by God, will reveal to us the direction of nature – how the world will unfold. This does not lead Burnet directly to a theory of progress. Instead, he employs the famous simile of God as the clock-maker who so contrives the apparatus that, once given its initial impetus, it requires no further intervention on his part. This simile suggests that the perfection of God may be judged from the perfection of his works. It is a short step from here to judge what is possible for God, or what it is possible to say about God, on the basis of what natural scientific investigation will admit as possible.

Burnet is not ready to take such a step. He holds firmly to the existence of the millennium as the culmination of the temporal process. His cosmos requires not only a maker but also a goal toward which it aspires. The mechanism is so contrived that when the millennium has run its course, the cosmos contains within it (and not imposed from outside the natural process) the forces that will bring about its purgation and dissolution by fire. But more than self-destruction awaits the cosmos. Its purgation results in a new creation on a yet-higher plane of perfection; a kind of cosmic Royal Society will result, with yet enough aesthetic appre-

---

17 More's notion of divine pedagogy should be distinguished from the doctrine of the 'fortunate fall.' In many of these interpretations of Genesis 3, autonomy is good for its own sake, and God is held to have been culpable in 'withholding' knowledge, which creates the power that gives point to autonomy. It is not altogether clear how far this differs from the serpent's interpretation of what is at stake. (For one of many contemporary expressions of this tradition, see that of Erich Fromm in his foreword to Edward Bellamy's Looking Backward, 2000–1887 first pub 1888 [New York 1960] vii–viii.) More is genuinely concerned with knowledge and the wholeness of self-realization that is possible, and not with autonomy as such, or with manipulative power.

ciation that Burnet can envision 'the whole Theatre resounding with the praises of the great Dramatist, and the wonderful art and order of the composition.'[18]

In fact, the 'theatre' that best expresses Burnet's conception is not that of a dramatist but the lecture theatre of the Royal Society.[19] The image of drama is largely debased by the notion of further progression to begin on the far side of the great purifying conflagration. A drama whose content is not on stage but is provided by the ardours of adoration on the part of its spectators is not much of a drama. Such a conception is very much in line with the medieval notion of the beatific vision in the after-life; but that conception is the abandonment of the dramatic conception of life contained in millennialism.

Burnet's conception here is a piece of speculation not supported by the archaic conception of testimony to the historical actions of Yahweh, and it is not a conception to which he was driven by the force of revelation or by the church's historical experience. The necessities that impelled Burnet to put forward his suggestions about successive levels of post-millennial progress are necessities imposed by his own speculations, following Mede and More, about necessary development in the present era. To the degree that this kind of systemic necessity is contained in the clock-cosmos, the figure of drama and Dramatist is unreal, a convention. We are a long way from the real drama of Daniel or Revelation or of even the Fifth Monarchy men. Burnet and his successors were ready, in fact, to criticize certain reported acts of the Dramatist as unworthy of him: these actions were not really actions, but parables devised by religious geniuses in order to impart high truth in a form suited to our rude forefathers.

CONCLUSION

It appears to be but a short step from the conviction that certain biblical events are parables to the stand of the French rationalists and *encyclopédistes* against religion as a shameful imposture. But these Englishmen did not take that step. They felt it was not self-seeking charlatans, but men whose intuitions outran their science, who told these stories of God. We can show scientifically how these facts about the cosmos, then ascribed to the direct agency of God, take place as part of a perfectly articulated plan immanent in the cosmos itself.

18 *Theory of the World* IV.9, quoted in Tuveson *Millennium* 125.
19 J.W. Yolton, in his *Locke and the Compass of Human Understanding* (Cambridge 1970) 44–75, provides numerous excerpts from these adepts and virtuosi which describe their own programs. Their notion of Nature neither is exploitive in the fashion of Bacon nor does it lend itself to the fervid hypostatizations of Nature that we see in Shaftesbury; Nature is not an idea or a person, but a realm of investigation, the motives for which, in the cases of people such as Boyle and Newton, were predominately theological in character.

The role of the future has gradually become important, not, as before, for the sake of its determinate content but simply because it is the future: it provides the arena in which the immanent process has time enough to fulfil itself. This staged development is a kind of intellectualized Joachimism, minus much of its Trinitarian anchoring. In Burnet, the third age is clearly that of those millennial savants, whose fullness of intellect and absolute contemplation become the dominant characteristics of the new age. In Lord Monboddo's bold conception, the Holy Spirit becomes the soul of this present world. Civilization is realization or, as Tuveson puts it, he 'transferred the whole process of salvation to cultural evolution'[20]

'The future' is also required in order to deal with evil, a problem given only glancing blows by intellectual Joachimism. Burnet dealt with evil by means of his fiery purgation of the whole sublunary world. But catastrophists such as Burnet were losing the field to those influenced by the new doctrines of Nature. Burnet's clock showed its maker's perfection by destroying itself when its appointed tasks were done; this appeared to be a wanton sacrilege to men for whom the demonstration of mathematical regularity in natural and cosmic process constituted proof of the clock's embodiment of eternal perfections.

More subtle thinkers abandoned the clock image and replaced it with an organic model. In Adam Ferguson, for example, the whole argument from design was superseded by one based on the accumulating experience of the human race.[21] It is important to note that even this shift does not precisely dispose of evil or provide a secular salvation; it provides only the indefinite extension of time necessary to carry forward and capitalize upon the improvements of our own past and present. The arguments are quite interdependent. An indefinite future offers salvation only if improvement has already been demonstrated; and improvement requires its own indefinite extension if it is not to be futile. Improvement, at least in knowledge and control, is demonstrated most readily in science. Science, as then conceived, could not rest with the partial, the incomplete, or the ambiguous. Present labours and achievements can thus only finally be justified in the future, by the future. We labour for the future. The assurance and hope it offers us has been provided at some cost; the future must in return be venerated.

20 Tuveson *Millennium* 191
21 Ibid 195 ff

23

Fair wind for France

We have seen that the new questions of eighteenth-century France could not be addressed satisfactorily without a new mode of historical argument. J.B. Bury has reviewed the famous late seventeenth- and early eighteenth-century battle between the upholders of the superiority of antiquity and those insisting on the superior development of modern knowledge. He has shown that the moderns established the possibility of cumulative knowledge at the expense of any theory of social progress. Changes in society are viewed as either hindrances or passive aids to the independent accumulation of the results of intellectual labour and artistic production.[1] As for Montesquieu, his 'treatment of social phenomena ... abstracted them from their relations in time. It was his merit to attempt to explain the correlation of laws and institutions with historical circumstances, but he did not distinguish or connect stages of civilization.'[2] Nor did his successors, whose own projects for reform shattered against the preference of the enlightened monarchs for dynastic aggrandizement instead of rational programs. The prestige of Newtonian science provided both incentive and a model for one sort of cumulative progress. But the prevailing theories of human nature, above all Lockean sensationalism, produced no means by which scientific and technological progress could be linked to a developmental theory of society. Both Locke and the anti-technological Rousseau produced rather static good societies.[3] And the French materialists who followed the deists tended to believe that rational enquiry led by scientific methods rather than a continuous process of social change could produce the correct social solutions.[4]

1 *The Idea of Progress* first pub London 1920 (New York 1932) 78–126
2 Ibid 148
3 The dynamism in the notion of the general will was perhaps not appreciated in the generation within which *The Social Contract* was published.
4 See S. Pollard *The Idea of Progress* first pub 1968 (Harmondsworth 1971) 44–53.

But there was no automatic or simple taking over of available English historical argumentation despite the tidal flow of English ideas and achievements into France in the century before the French Revolution. English freedom was cautiously extolled; English science was wholeheartedly admired; English political philosophy was a point of departure for most French thought.[5] But some English ideas were met with incomprehension or hostility. The English preoccupation with the little horn or with other ventures in the correlation of Daniel with contemporary public events was brusquely rejected. Early eighteenth-century France suppressed any hint of the Protestantism it had tolerated until 1685. That suppression had been answered by Protestant visionary enthusiasm and by an alarmed official Catholic response that extended to the execution of Protestants accused of hindering conversion of their fellows to Catholicism. The *philosophes* too rejected what could only seem to be irrational fanaticism. The notion of the holy commonwealth did not cross the Channel in strength; and the English historical argumentation used in France had little direct connection with scriptural concerns or with the need to demonstrate that one's enemies were dupes of the Antichrist.

Certain Englishmen regarded with suspicion at home were the primary agents of the transmission of English historical argumentation to France. They were unwelcome, for the most part, in official France as well; these unreconciled 'commonwealthmen,' over-bold deists, and free-thinkers operated principally from the Netherlands via agitation and correspondence. Franco Venturi has shown[6] the peculiar influence of John Toland and his relations with luminaries so different as Leibniz, the Electress Sophia (the Protestant heiress to the English throne), and the great enemy of Louis XIV's old age, Prince Eugène of Savoy. A master publicist, Toland appears to have been used to test public opinion and prepare the way for a number of projects, in England as well as on the Continent. He was supported by the first Lord Shaftesbury, who had close relations with Anthony Collins, early in life a disciple of Locke. The relations of these men, the younger Shaftesbury, and other publicists such as Trenchard and Gordon, editors of the *Cato Papers*, and Molesworth, who also maintained Toland, were complex and extensive.[7]

---

5 Even the great *Encyclopédie* was undertaken originally as a French edition of Chambers's *Cyclopedia* of 1728. On the general sense among the French that they were epigones to the English giants of reason, see G. Tonelli 'The "Weakness of Reason" in the Age of Enlightenment' *Diderot Studies* XIV (1971) 222.

6 *Utopia and Reform in the Enlightenment* (Cambridge 1971) 49–67

7 See C. Robbins *The Eighteenth Century Commonwealthmen: Studies in the Transmission, Development and Circumstance of English Liberal Thought from the Restoration of Charles II until the War with the Thirteen Colonies* (Cambridge, Mass, 1959); on Toland, see 125 ff.

The influence of English deist-related thought on eighteenth-century Continental thought is a complicated and controverted question. But, because of its key role in the transmission of historical argumentation to France, this question must be addressed here.

The current state of opinion is conveniently summarized by Ira O. Wade.[8] In his view, the cross-Channel journeyings from both sides (with their attendant narratives), the activities of exiles after the revocation of the Edict of Nantes in 1685, the extensive publishing efforts directed mainly from Holland, and the clandestine circulation of these and of underground deist writings generate a strong presumption of significant influence on France by English deist-related thought. Yet his final judgment is that, after an early phase of interest, French circles show little trace of English deist influence again until Diderot's translation of Shaftesbury in 1745. The strong deist stream of underground literary production in France he attributes, though without corroboration, to Spinozist influence.

This judgment appears at first impression to block my attempt to show a direct stimulus from the English thinkers responsible for the flowering of progressivism proper. There are two problems here: the relation of the central figures of the Enlightenment to progressivism and the relation of French 'deism' to Spinoza.

This study is no place to examine in detail the first question. But I have been able to proceed without major reference to most of the principal Enlightenment figures. I focus below only on Voltaire and Diderot in the generation prior to the advent of Turgot and Condorcet with the full doctrine of progress. Voltaire is perhaps not precisely an Enlightenment figure, though his influence is pervasive, particularly, as Wade notes, in bringing together into intellectual coherence the observations on England he and others had made and the impressions on the French made by English thinkers themselves. Wade's interpretation of Voltaire's retirement at Cirey, coinciding with the official reaction to publication in 1733 of his *Lettres philosophiques* and extending to 1750, is that he put himself through a régime of intellectual anglicization. It is not without significance that it is in the post-Cirey period that deist influence in his work becomes prominent. Diderot's work, beginning with his translation of Shaftesbury, is noticed separately below.

The issue of French 'deist' opinion and Spinoza calls for more extended comment. First, much of the underground religious radicalism antedates Spinoza's principal work of direct interest to deists, the *Tractatus Theologico-Politicus* (1670). Second, the philosophical work of Spinoza, while perhaps occasioned by

8 Most recently in *The Structure and Form of the French Enlightenment* 2 vol (Princeton 1977). See especially I 120–76. Wade has spent a lifetime assessing the origins and character of the Enlightenment, particularly the influences on Voltaire and his impact on others. His most recent views do not always take account of his earlier ones.

that of Descartes, made little directly traceable constructive impact in France. Leibniz insisted on the connection between Spinoza and Cartesianism, but for polemical reasons. And Spinoza himself found occasion to deny similarity between his work and that of Descartes. Third, then as later it was useful to use the term Spinozist as a label. It requires careful inspection to see why this label is applied: as a short-cut condemnation; as a means of identifying oneself with the lonely man of integrity who has for the honour of truth suffered at the hands of the Philistines; or as an accurate description of some conceptual affiliation. Fourth, while the *Tractatus* undoubtedly contains much to interest deists and free-thinkers, there Spinoza also insists that it ought not to be understood apart from his *Ethics*, a document upon whose metaphysical base it is difficult to erect a systematic deism. Toland's latent or late-blooming pantheistic tendencies must count against this judgment, of course. But no one among the deist publicists appears to have been happy with Toland's alleged shift into pantheism.

The supposed dependence of French 'deism' upon Spinoza remains singularly difficult to demonstrate, unless one is content to lay an unwarranted weight on the use of his name as a bugbear, as a totem or emblem, or as one known to favour tolerance. As an alternative explanation either to native growth or to English influence this dependence seems highly speculative.

The most parsimonious explanation of French 'deism' is, of course, that it is a native growth. And there is much to recommend this view. The vigour of French philosophical thought, the problem of French political Protestantism, and the convulsive Catholic controversies over Jansenism and over the activities of the Jesuits called forth, among the different responses, free-thought convictions and pleas for religious and political toleration. It will not do, however, simply to label as deists all writers making either response.

Free thought has its own origins, in simple anti-religion and in simple revulsion against the horrors perpetrated in the name of Jesus. Abundant historical documentation lay to hand, culminating in the Thirty Years' War and the more recent theological and political controversies. But free thought, as a radical notion, was all too likely to clothe itself in the more reputable garb of pleas for toleration. The relation is not symmetrical, of course, since tolerationist convictions, both theological and political, could be maintained by those repelled by the *enfants terribles* of free thought. And neither free-thinkers nor tolerationists need automatically be denominated as deists. Neither free-thinkers nor tolerationists automatically or inevitably put their arguments in the form of a lengthy historical argumentation, as the English deists commonly did.

We must look to the political and cultural context for some guidance in assessing the relative importance of native 'deism' and the proto-progressivism carried to France by English deism.

The expansionist wars of Louis XIV and his gradual abolition of even limited toleration for French Protestants provoked his foreign opponents to unite against him again and again. The period ended with France exhausted by Pyrrhic victories, her overseas empire curtailed, and first her great enemy William of Orange, and next his Protestant heir, Anne, on the English throne. Domestically France was weakened by the Jansenist controversy. This debate was heightened in 1713, the year of the general peace, by French reception of the pope's anti-Jansenist edict, *Unigenitus*, thereafter used as a cover for political intrigues by the many factions in Louis XV's long minority. So late as 1746 a policy was initiated of refusing the sacraments to non-jurors to *Unigenitus*. This high-water mark of Jesuit political intrigue brought about the reaction of 1759 and thereafter, when the Jesuit order was expelled. But, equally, the *Encyclopédie* was suppressed in 1759, followed by the attempt to ban Rousseau's *Émile*.

We turn now to the topic of direct English-French relations to attempt to account for the relatively easy intercourse of the Locke-Toland-Shaftesbury period, the apparent lack of direct influence in the post-1713 period, and its revival in the Enlightenment proper. Locke's *Essay Concerning Human Understanding* had been translated into French in 1700; and Locke was personally involved in bringing his work before the French. His controversy with Malebranche (in 1706 and 1720) engaged him with a man whose own works had first appeared in English in the same year, 1695, as his own *Reasonableness of Christianity*. The writings of the deists proper were circulated from the Netherlands through long-established, quasi-underground publication networks in France. Shaftesbury enjoyed an early vogue in France. But then the French turned inward during Louis XV's minority and Fleury's ascendancy. The intrigues of faction were absorbing to would-be élites now freed from the constraints of the earlier absolutist era.

But the death in 1727 of George I removed the last survivor of the anti-French coalition responsible for the terms of 1713. And the only French diplomatic and military successes of the period, modest though they were, had been achieved with the aid of English naval strength. English governmental stability was compared to the incessant intrigues that prevented coherence in either French society or French policy.

Voltaire published his *Lettres philosophiques* in 1733, three years after the peace that sealed the only French gains of the period. Voltaire's emphatic contrast of England and France and his remarks on orthodox religion brought official condemnation to the book and a warrant for the author's arrest. Though the ban was lifted in 1735, Voltaire remained in residence beyond the French border for 15 more years. The atmosphere in France, given the censorship and the ease with which epithets such as 'Jansenist' could be made to stick, was not conducive to public free thought or deism.[9] Then we have the *Encyclopédie*, originally intended as a French translation of Chambers's *Cyclopedia* (1728), falling, after remarkable editorial and financial chicanery, into the lap of the willing Diderot. He engaged more than 100 contributors, some very radical, and contributed nearly 1,200 articles, excluding those on the mechanical arts. The first volume appeared in 1751. The eighth was in the press when the order of 1759 was issued. Eventually 35 volumes were produced.

Thus by the late 1740s it was possible to contemplate the full, public espousal of the ideas incubated since the attempted suppression of Voltaire's *Lettres philosophiques*. Voltaire himself felt able to do this in his post-Cirey period. The *encyclopédistes* were prepared to use the series as cover for a full statement of 'deistic' ideas. And Voltaire himself contributed eight volumes on topics arising from the *Encyclopédie*.

This is by no means a full demonstration of the impact of ideas carried by English deism into the lives of those who first proposed the modern idea of progress. But it clears the way for an investigation, which cannot be carried on here, of the precise mechanisms of transmission. The substitution of Spinoza as a principal influence is quite unlikely to be demonstrable. Native 'deism' decomposes into what may be a 'mere' free thought and into advocacy of toleration, both probably responsive to the problems thrown up by the régime. Neither Spinozism nor native deism seems likely to have produced a comprehensive view of developmental history like that produced by Henry More and others like him.

There was a link in some English deists' minds between their religious views and republicanism, in which there was much interest in France in the troubled years after 1713. England was not merely a survival of antique republicanism, like Venice or Genoa; it appeared to be a demonstration of stable development. Or so it seemed in the propaganda of the English republican deists, who urged con-

---

9 Wade presents presumptive evidence for Voltaire being influenced by English thought in these years through the studies of Mme de Chatelet, his companion and hostess of the Cirey period. She read Tindal and Woolston and was writing a revisionist commentary on the Bible. 'There is just no reasonable way to avoid the assumption that Voltaire must have known the English deists, especially Woolston and Tindal and, of course, Bolingbroke, during the Cirey period'; Wade *Structure and Form* I 188. The question of 'influence' is bedeviled by the absence of books in the period that could document it precisely. During Bolingbroke's residence in France in 1724, for example, he was in regular contact, through the Club de l'Entresol, with Saint-Pierre, d'Argenson, and a variety of others (ibid 316 ff). Abbé Prevost complained in 1734 that 'for the last thirty years' they have been engaged in subversion, according to V.S. Spink *French Thought from Gassendi to Voltaire* (London 1960) 224. He notes also that Voltaire did at least read Tindal, Woolston, and Trenchard and Gordon during his English visit (ibid 316). There was a large program of translation of English deists into French in the period after 1760.

stantly on their fellow countrymen the completion of the settlement of 1688–89. The deism of the English publicists and exiles was welcome in France as an attack on revealed religion and on its alliance with privilege. This alliance grew closer in the eighteenth century as the nobility systematically engrossed higher ecclesiastical offices that had heretofore been open to men of ability from other classes. More importantly, English deism supplied an account of the fall of primitive religion. Toland's work of 1696 was titled *Christianity not mysterious, or a Treatise shewing that there is nothing in the Gospel contrary to reason nor above it and that no Christian doctrine can properly be called a mystery.* The primal religion of mankind was not mysterious, though it was soon made so as a means of producing docile populations. What Jesus preached was conformable to this original religion; he is a liberator in this respect, though his work too was stifled.

Toland's argument is not the ahistorical one that religion is imposture and that malevolent priestcraft has at all times been responsible for the suppression of truth and reason. Rather, truths knowable in principle were simply not yet known – quite apart from the work of wicked suppressors. The experience of mankind, as Adam Ferguson was to put it, had not yet been able to render many phenomena 'not mysterious' and open to reason. This lack of historical experience, in fact, provided the opportunity for imposing a system of mystery on events, truths, and ideas where such an attitude was less warranted, where progress could have been made. The fight for demystified religion was inseparable, for both Toland and his French readers, from the fight for rational, demystified government.[10]

But while the historical argumentation thus introduced was to remain influential in France, the republicanism of the English publicists was not. Indeed, it even lapsed with Toland who, under pressure, declared the succession of Charles II and the settlement of 1689 to be compatible with his earlier dogmatic republicanism,[11] which he was now prepared to treat less as a program than as a Platonic Form, an informative and regulative utopia. The *encyclopédistes* were not well able to advance historical arguments. They were outflanked by the popularity of

---

10 This connection persisted through the eighteenth century. The dogmatic republicans in revolutionary America, the Paines and Jeffersons, were equally dogmatic deists. In England, the radical Richard Price followed Toland faithfully in his *Observations upon the Importance of the American Revolution and the Means of Making It a Benefit to the World* (London 1785). Both deism and republicanism were necessary to the progress of mankind: 'Perhaps I do not go too far when I say that, next to the introduction of Christianity among mankind, the American revolution may prove to be the most important step in the progressive course of human improvement'; quoted *in extenso* in R.E. Richey 'Counter-Insurgency, An Historical Homily' *Drew Gateway* XLI (1971) 83–93.

11 Perhaps also his increasing involvement in the intrigues to secure the Hanoverian succession made it unwise to continue being labelled an unreconciled republican.

Rousseau's new republicanism, which was based on seemingly antique models rather than on English examples or on reform of France's existing constitution – the project increasingly favoured by *philosophes*. Rousseau's work on Geneva, on the Corsican and Polish constitutions, and in *The Social Contract* was felt, in contrast, to be a kind of utopian enterprise.[12] Diderot's article on political authority for the *Encyclopédie* was used by the *parlements* in the run-up to the abortive period of reform that ended with Turgot's dismissal in 1776. In neither Rousseau nor the reformers was the actual republican emphasis of the English publicists followed up.

While Rousseau used the state of nature in *The Social Contract* as a point of departure on the way to actual society – a merely conceptual device, Diderot, in his *Supplement to the Voyage of Bougainville*,[13] pictured an actual society – contemporaneous with his own – living in the state of nature. Tahiti may represent a prior stage in society, but it is none the worse for that. It provides him with living proof of the laboured, deathly artificiality of his own society. It is the point-by-point contrast with popular Paris, bourgeois Paris, and official Paris that occupies Diderot. But this project could go no further once Turgot had been dismissed from office – and with him the *philosophes* to whom he had distributed sinecures. And it could not be radicalized, even after the Revolution; Babeuf's violent attempt to turn primitive communism into a program[14] presented a temptation to very few.

Tahiti works as an example for Diderot because he is working with man come of age, who now has no need of his past and its institutions; he has outgrown them, especially religion. Mature man is generic or universal man – treated quite as universally by Diderot as by medieval philosophers or Protestant theologians. But he is not conjuring with an archetypal utopia that might have fallen from the skies; he is working with ethnographical evidence even if, as in this case, he felt entitled to manufacture some of it. Similarly, the arguments about priestly imposture, in Diderot's hands, become historical arguments at least in intent – he is under the necessity of explaining how and why the world fell into a thousand years of darkness after the flourishing of the classical years.

C. Kiernan has pointed to a correlation between Diderot's deism and his dependence on the Newtonian sciences, on the one hand, and, on the other, his later

---

12 Venturi *Utopia and Reform* 77

13 Bougainville had published his account of the south seas in 1771. Diderot prepared his *Supplement* in 1772, but it was not published until 1796.

14 'I shall now offer you the great lucidities of nature'; from his newspaper, the *Tribun du peuple* no 1, quoted by G. Niemeyer *Between Nothingness and Paradise* (Baton Rouge, La, 1971) 39, from M. Dommanget *Pages choisies de Babeuf* (Paris 1935)

atheism, use of life science models, and greater political radicalism.[15] In 1746, we are told, Diderot proved God via the physical sciences; by 1749 he proved atheism via the life sciences. In his later period he was prepared to draw political conclusions from the sciences. Mathematical insight is unevenly distributed; to the degree that the Newtonian sciences are venerated, hierarchy necessarily follows. But life itself is more democratically distributed; and many more of us can contribute to its understanding by introspection, experiment, and action. Diderot is struggling here with a relation he cannot yet clarify; the influence of the Cartesian separation between Nature and culture has not yet been overcome. As Kiernan puts it, in Leibniz, the two clocks are providentially synchronized; in Diderot, they interact directly, but are still two clocks.[16] Diderot was not a revolutionary and did not produce a unified theory of dynamic social growth and change. He has not fully grasped the uses of historical argumentation. Like him, the materialists sought a means of unifying the realms of the two clocks, but their solution, after removing the clock-maker from the scene, was to reduce culture to Nature, to Newtonian nature. Diderot, in contrast, is moving toward a unification under culture.

Diderot's uses of language in *Supplement to the Voyage of Bougainville* show a considerable shift in this direction. Nature is still 'the sovereign mistress of all things.'[17] His Tahitians 'follow the pure instincts of Nature' (227), however. Naïve, yet wise, they respond to the voice of Nature, unlike the French, in whom prejudice has entirely stifled this voice (238). Nature here is portrayed in an immanent fashion, not with the attributes of a distant deistic God or with the austerities of Newtonian science, but as possessing a wooer's intent. No doubt there is Nature's other aspect: 'the eternal will of nature' (236). And there is nothing 'in the whole universe, whether in the sky above or the earth below that can either add anything to or subtract anything from the laws of nature' (236). But the Parisians can flout them, to their cost in self-imposed suffering (238). Nature does not pronounce Mosaic dooms; she impels, she incites (246 ff). Men perplexed may put the question to her, and she will respond (243).

Perhaps the movement from Fifth Monarchy millennialism to Diderot's warm, immanent Nature is fairly straightforward. The crude, date-fixing Puritan millennialism exhibited the confidence of a unified dynamic world-view, in which Nature and culture did not appear as separate or separable entities. They are swallowed up in redemptive history. And both God and Satan are seen in proxi-

15 'Additional Reflections on Diderot and Science' *Diderot Studies* XIV (1971) 113–42
16 Ibid 129
17 In *Diderot's Selected Writings* selected, ed, intro, and notes by L.G. Crocker; tr D. Coltman (New York 1966), 231. Quotations in this paragraph are from Coltman's translation.

mity; their partisans clash in the streets. This simple identification of *dramatis personae* and of current events with the purpose and culmination of all history proved to be overly ambitious.

God was therefore next said to operate through secondary causes; and the failure of the end-time to arrive encouraged the already existing tendency to be concerned with the course of the world and of possibilities within it rather than with the end of the world. To the degree that the whole notion of redemptive history was found to be restrictive, the movement to leave God as a remote prime mover or 'Superior Cause' could cover, in theological but sub-Christian language, a determination to remove him from any effective relationship to human history at all.

But – the most arrant deists apart – English political philosophers and natural philosophers did not abandon the notion of a unified historical teleology. This concept, carried over into France by even the deists,[18] began to influence French thought, which had reached something of an impasse. Yet Cartesian dualism gave way only slowly before it. Either Nature or culture tended to become the encompassing term. It was not clear what was meant by Nature: the Newtonian sciences or the life sciences. Both Diderot and Rousseau reacted against the assimilation of culture – particularly of politics – to the reigning Newtonian science. Rousseau's non-Newtonian version of Nature was criticized as being unrelated to concerns for reform.

Diderot succeeded in making Nature immanent and making it winsome. The God–Providence–Nature equivalence was no help to Diderot so long as Nature was deist Nature, as remotely conceived as deism's God. Diderot completes the movement away from the 'crude' millennialism of the Puritans by returning to something very like it. A benevolent Nature works with men in their institutions, perfecting both in a unified fashion. But Diderot is not a progressive in the sense that his successors were. For him, human nature was too much determinate to allow for the endless vistas of change that we see in Condorcet. In Diderot, there are still 'eternal relationships that exist between men,'[19] which inhibit, at least for him, the formation of an open future of continuous improvement.

18 Shaftesbury, who was a decisive influence in *philosophe* France, enjoying a second vogue in the years 1745–72 (so Schlegel *Shaftesbury and the French Deists* 11), was uneasy about 'cold' deism, its over-rationality and its tendency to hide more radical conceptions under the prudent cover of language about God. He insisted on the necessity of an affective relation to God and Nature and of a mover and originator behind Nature. See S. Grean *Shaftesbury's Philosophy of Religion and Ethics: A Study in Enthusiasm* (Athens, Ohio, 1967) 50–72, especially 61 ff. Grean holds that Shaftesbury's God is better described as an artist than as a maker or mover (65).

19 *Diderot's Selected Writings* tr Coltman 243

24

The first progressivists: Turgot, Mercier, and Condorcet

Turgot[1] began from the central French problem, the contrast between Nature and culture. Nature is the realm of the regular and repetitive. But human culture is the realm of progress. His version of progress has an oddly pointilist origin: men of genius rise above their fellows and present us with their new achievements, which are an improvement on what we have possessed as our common heritage. This improvement is most visible in technology, though it is traceable in pure science, aesthetics, and morals. These developments move at different rates in different sorts of society, as Montesquieu had taught.

But the cumulative effects of the work of individual geniuses take on a mass and an inertia which guarantee that progress as a whole is now impossible to stop. In our time it has achieved 'critical mass' and is now self-sustaining. The notion of a normative state of nature is thus disposed of. The accounts of savage or archaic societies tell us where we have been in our past, not where we should be. And as the influence of present progress diffuses over the earth, these pockets of backwardness will be wiped out. Their peoples will take their place in the structure of development which prepares the way for yet further progress in the future. The problem of the origin of past innovation is rather sidestepped, by means of reference to the nearly unanalyseable notion of genius – though Turgot does tell us a good deal about conditions for the discovery and nurture of genius.

1 See F.E. Manuel *The Prophets of Paris* first pub Cambridge, Mass, 1962 (New York 1965) and the second bibliography contained in the notes. See also *Turgot on Progress, Sociology and Economics* tr, ed, and intro by R.L. Meek (Cambridge, 1973). In moving to Turgot I am ignoring some anticipators of the progress notion, such as the abbé Saint-Pierre, well-covered in Bury *The Idea of Progress* London 1920 (rpt New York 1932) and other histories.

The question of evil is recast, for the passions of mankind, and its irrational hopes, have been motive forces for progress. Mere reason, on the models current only a generation earlier, could have produced a static society like that of China. But by means of the passions, men have heaved themselves up out of mere nature. It is conceivable that – given unlimited, self-sustaining progress – we shall in the future be able even to see the conquering of our most inveterate passions, for once we have, as now, reached the stage of self-sustaining progress the passions will gradually become superfluous and so will be confined to smaller and smaller areas of human life.

Turgot tells us, anticipating Comte, that the philosophic period, itself the successor of naïve anthropomorphic theology, would give way, and was already doing so, to a mathematical stage, in which that supple realm of symbolism would be able to catch and preserve all previous human achievements in all areas. His work merits fully Manuel's description of it as 'a new conception of world history' and 'the first important version in modern times of the ideology of progress.' Turgot throughout his life remained a Christian, at least by *philosophe* standards. But his notions of progression owe little to Christian formulations; as we have seen, their origin is simply asserted from their existence through the medium of genius. And the open vistas leading to the mathematization of human achievements of all sorts are an anticipation more of his labours as intendant and controller-general than of the kingdom of God. Yet Turgot has decisively shifted the question of progress away from the mechanical-natural models which squeezed the matter of human progress to one side. Further, Turgot's notion of progress did not rest upon the kind of sentiment we see in Diderot – progress that may falter before the dark works of the passions. He has shown that even the passions have their role to play in the march of inevitable progress.

Before considering the form given to progress by Turgot's disciple, Condorcet, it will be useful to see how the doctrine of progress, in its ambiguous forms or in the clear version of Turgot, affected the production of classic utopias.

MERCIER

Mercier, fellow-member, with Condorcet, of the National Convention, survived to prosper in the Empire. In 1770 he wrote the first utopia to be placed in the future, *L'An 2440*.[2] It would no longer do, apparently, to tell us how well some distant islanders are governed, or to let this picture stand over European society, as

---

2 Its full title, *The Year 2440, a Dream of What Will Never Be*, was rounded off in the English translation (1772) to *Memoirs of the Year 2500*, perhaps from a dislike of finicking French detail. Quotations are from the excerpts in G. Negley and J.M. Patrick ed *The Quest for Utopia* first pub New York 1952 (Garden City, NY, 1962), 466–88.

Diderot had done, in order to show how the Western perversion of sexuality produced only hypocrites, unfortunates, imbeciles, and abnormal creatures.[3] Utopia can no longer stand over us as merely an uncorrupted world of Forms. Displacement of this concept by a reference to the future is indicative of the new commitment to the historical process itself, to a gradually more articulate faith that the future holds the salvation of the present.

Mercier's use of terms recapitulates the vocabulary of the whole century. In 2440, 'justice has spoken by the mouth of nature, sovereign legislator.' The notes of both the classical utopia and the newer accents of Diderot and Rousseau are heard together in the fact that justice is 'founded on reason and humanity' (471). The Supreme Being is still adored without discussion of his characteristics and without ritual. But Mercier balances the elements of the old and the new, of the classical utopia and of progress. 'We teach them little history, because history is the disgrace of humanity, every page being crowded with crimes and follies' (470). Here, history is apparently still thought of didactically as a source of examples; and formal kings-and-battles historiography yields only bad examples.

Social progress is clearly evolutionary in character: 'Nature in all her operations tended to the formation of man; and ... she endeavoured, by various essays to arrive at the gradual term of his perfection' (479). Mercier, like Turgot, distinguishes his own new age from that of 'metaphysics,' for which the people of 2440 'have a sufficient contempt' (470). But he holds to 'physics, that key to nature' as the means of understanding 'the wisdom and power of the Creator' (470), rather than to the life sciences or to Turgot's sociology of innovation. Yet the universes of the older mechanists of nature are explicitly condemned by Mercier as cold, cruel, and unpitying (478). Reason is extolled in the old manner; but Mercier asks, 'What is reason itself without sentiment?' (485). And we are treated to a concern with sublimity, with the heart, with innocence (473 ff, 484 ff), and with the utility of the passions (486).

Nature, however, remains the key word in L'An 2440. Nature provides continual examples for emulation (472); the attempt to flout nature's laws is sin (473); nature has a voice, and art consists in repeating that voice (476); she has intentions and carries them out (479). This nature is no construct of reason, though she is reasonable and perceptible by sympathetic understanding. No merely inert pattern, nature ought to be followed, and when this is not done, the result is aptly described as sin.

Every effort is made to ensure that men enter into a devotional relation with nature. When a young person shows signs of this capacity he is guided into his

---

3 *Diderot's Selected Writings* selected, ed, intro, and notes by L.G. Crocker; tr D. Coltman (New York 1966) 238

first communion, the pivotal sacrament of *2440*. By means of the telescope and microscope, the young person's spiritual director discloses to him his true relation to the universe, an overwhelming experience that establishes forever the direct bond between the child and the cosmos: 'God is manifest to me; my eye has visited Saturn. I find that my being is more noble than I imagined, since the Supreme has vouchsafed to establish a relation between my nihility and his greatness. O! how happy am I to have received life and intelligence! I begin to see what will be the lot of virtuous men' (474 ff). This day marks his initiation 'to the rank of thinking beings.'

All of life in *2440* is organized to reinforce this relation. The entire philosophical and literary output of the past has been reviewed. All that was found harmful – contrary to nature and reason – has been consigned to flames, with the good bits anthologized into 'a small duodecimo' (477).[4] The arts have been similarly purged; the plastic arts are now engaged in 'faithfully repeating the voice of nature' (476). 'Our dramatic authors have no other view than the improvement of human nature' (475 ff). The offender against these canons is classed as a criminal, visited daily by re-education teams until his thinking is reformed. 'Then he will be re-established; he will even acquire from the confession a greater glory; for what is more commendable than to abjure our faults and to embrace new lights with a noble sincerity?' (469). 'We leave nothing to chance' (479).

Thus encouraged, the community of *2440* is only a temporal segment of the greater community. The different planets and stars are the successive superior planes reserved for the souls of the virtuous devotees of nature in this life (472). 'By perceiving the degree to which they could ascend, they have been stimulated by glory to pursue the boundless career that is set before them. The life of a single man is too short; and what have we done? We have united the force of each individual; they have acquired an immense empire; the one finished what the other began. The chain was never interrupted ... This chain of ideas and successive labours may one day surround and embrace the universe' (479 ff).

This vision is set in the context of man's technology. Mercier has visited the great temple called 'An abridgement of the Universe' in which the remarkable insight of the book is given exemplary display by the arrangement of myriads of natural specimens and created objects; the places of honour are given to the great inventors and their works. The scene concludes with the governing intention of the whole: 'Our end is to know the secret cause of each appearance and to extend the dominion of man' (480). This last is a close paraphrase of the credo of Bacon's *New Atlantis*.

---

4 Mercier does not blink at the historical parallels: 'This tremendous mass was set on fire as an expiatory sacrifice to veracity, to good sense and true taste. We have therefore done from an enlightened zeal what the barbarians did from one that was blind.'

These two emphases in Mercier – the devotion to nature and the Baconian program – are not brought together conceptually. On the one hand, we are to *follow* nature with ardent devotion. On the other hand, nature is conceived as passively supplying a pattern and raw materials for man to realize the goal of universal dominion – in Bacon's words 'to the effecting of all things possible.' This latter goal is not given in the mere laws of nature as we know them, or in the cosmos viewed through the instruments of the first communion, or in the mystic, raptured knowledge of the young man, no matter how often 'he returns ... to feast on these sublime objects' (475). And the goal of universal dominion is not given in the record of man's feats of technology, which can be seen as governed by the maxim to follow nature. The program of dominion arises from a smuggled imperative which is never spelled out in any utopia or any early theory of progress.

CONDORCET

It was Condorcet who put the modern doctrine of progress into a form useful to the great projectors of social progress.[5] Secretary of the Académie des sciences, disciple of Turgot, biographer of Voltaire and Turgot, eminent mathematician, educational reformer, member of the National Convention, and finally fugitive from the Terror, Condorcet produced his testament to progress, *Esquisse d'un tableau historique des progres de l'esprit humain* (The Sketch of a Historical Picture of the Progress of the Human Mind),[6] while in hiding in 1793, just prior to his capture and death while in detention. The National Assembly of the régime that succeeded the Terror distributed thousands of copies of his *Sketch*, 'symbolic recognition that his theory had become official revolutionary doctrine.'[7]

The *Sketch* shows us ten stages of the rational self-development of mankind, which, though often frustrated or slowed by the intrigues of religion, superstition, and ambition, has no bounds, is 'above the control of every power that would impede it,' has 'no other limit than the duration of the globe,' and 'can never be retrograde' (4). Nine epochs carry us to the present, the ninth being the period from Descartes to the establishment of the French republic. Thus we are con-

---

5 His *Sketch* 'was the form in which the eighteenth-century idea of progress was generally assimilated by Western thought' (Manuel *Prophets* 61). Cf L. Edelstein *The Idea of Progress in Classical Antiquity* (Baltimore 1967) where Condorcet is said to have 'inaugurated modern progressivism' (175).

6 It was published in 1795, in Genoa in 1798, in Germany in 1804, in England in 1795, and in the United States in 1796. See Manuel *Prophets* 323 ff for fuller publication details. Quotations below are from the anonymously translated first English edition, *Outlines of an Historical View of the Progress of the Human Mind* (London 1795).

7 Manuel *Prophets* 59

ducted, as by almost every other seer, to the threshold of the final age (an aspect of millennialism now taken into a utopian or progressivist enterprise).

Condorcet's efforts are directed to showing us why future progress is inevitable and illimitable. In the original, it is spoken of as *'une grande probabilité'*;[8] and it is true that most of Condorcet's most provocative statements are put in the form of questions; but these are the very model of the rhetorical question and admit of only one answer, the one which he labours in so many ways to render unquestionable. His method is one of 'combination,' in which ethnographical evidence, the continuous history we possess of our own society since the days of the Greeks, and introspection are brought together. The mathematical calculus of probabilities, to which he was a contributor, provides us with the assured means for extracting the proper elements from which we may confidently extrapolate the curve of the future.

But Condorcet does not rest with the results of even so sure a method. He demonstrates as well that even the opponents of progress have unwittingly and unwillingly contributed to it; like Satan's struggles as seen by John, those of religion and despotism in the view of Condorcet only hasten the day of their own demise. Recklessly futile in their attempt to clog the wheels of progress, they succeed only in delivering their new weapons into the hands of men who are on the side of history instead of flailing against it. Further, there is the combinational and inertial effect of previous innovations:[9] together they are simply too much for any single set of enemies to thwart; if stifled in France, they will break out in England. The sheer spread of those two languages and cultures around the world makes it impossible for even the most energetic enemy of progress to search out all the places where its friends may be operating. Thus 'no vicious combination can effect the infelicity of a great people' and 'everything tells us that we are approaching the era of one of the grand revolutions of the human race.'[10]

Condorcet believes that, in his assemblage of facts and hopes, and in his selection and exhibition of their combination, he is avoiding grand constructions of theory and, instead, finding truths scientifically. Theory as such is not to be shunned; our task in relation to theory is to reduce the amount of error in it (290). In this task, 'algebraic language ... alone is accurate and truly scientific' (271). In comparison with the unaided 'natural processes of the human mind,' it 'certainly includes the principles of an universal instrument applicable to all possible combinations of ideas' (272).

8 *Esquisse* ed O.H. Prior, first pub 1933 (rev edn, Paris 1970) 203
9 To Condorcet, innovation is progressive; the unprecedented actions of those he dislikes are not innovations.
10 *Outlines of an Historical View* introduction

The use of algebraic language in politics and morals is not only permissible, but mandatory, for there is a direct link between scientific blunders and moral errors, which are 'connected with physical errors,' that is, with errors in the hard sciences: 'There does not exist any religious system, or supernatural extravagance that is not founded on ignorance of the laws of nature' (298). The undoubted advances in the physical sciences therefore guarantee similar advances in nonscientific fields; and these fields need not remain unscientific, for the application of algebraic language will, through time, remove their imprecision. Chance, which heretofore has bulked so large in human affairs, is not a mysterious residuum after we have exhausted the assignment of causes; chance is itself a 'necessary and unknown cause' – to which we give the name of chance, 'a word the sense of which can only be known with precision by studying this method' (293), the calculus of probabilities.

But Condorcet is not arguing for the mechanical application of physical law to human affairs. In art, for example, though there are 'universal rules of reason and nature' which apply in matters of taste 'for all peoples and languages' (364), these rules are to be modified just as 'the other laws of the moral and physical universe when it is necessary to apply them to the immediate practice of a common art' (305). It is not the simple conformity of human life to uniform law that Condorcet wishes to demonstrate, but the possibility, which somehow becomes the inevitability, of progress in the tenth epoch. The necessity for this progress is stated in his summary of progress to date: 'The exertions of these last ages have done much for the progress of the human mind, but little for the perfection of the human species; much for the glory of man, somewhat for his liberty, but scarcely anything yet for his happiness' (310). Progress must transform the lives of ordinary men or we have, in the end, accomplished very little (313 ff).

The tenth epoch, then, is the point of progress. Here we must have the fullness of life for mankind as a whole. Accordingly the elimination of inequality is of the first importance. Inequality among nations receives sustained attention. A partisan of the American Revolution, Condorcet eagerly awaits the freedom of the whole of the Americas. The Asian and African subject areas will appropriate what is best from their masters and join the rest of the world. Already, in 1793, revolutionary principles are too widely diffused to be suppressed. 'Then will arrive the moment in which the sun will observe in its course free nations only, acknowledging no other master than their reason' (327). He is not, however, prophesying a common culture or the universal adoption of merely Western values. Differences may well endure, and are no doubt useful, but not inequality of access to the good things of life.

Again, in his section on the progress of equality within the nations, he is careful to warn against a mechanical levelling. There are inequalities of wealth, inequality between those who can pass on masses of land and capital and those who cannot, and inequality of access to education. All three must be diminished; but some inequality is natural; to suppress it would lead to greater evil (328).[11] Among his tenth epoch visions is a modest social security system. The threat of want must be removed so that men may direct their attentions, as their talents allow, toward the attainment of happiness.

Condorcet estimates that only 2 per cent of the able now study in such a fashion as to reveal or employ their talents. He follows Turgot in stressing the significance of genius and seeks to maximize the opportunities for its manifestation and its social utilization (333 ff).[12] But a higher level of common education will open careers to greater talent generally and will provide a powerful check to the credulity of the common people and prevent their being led easily into plausible schemes. Education is a powerful prophylactic against imposture.

The prospect of a nation teeming with *savants* raises the question of their exhausting the knowable and thus bringing progress to an end. Here Condorcet's experience of the power of mathematics is called upon to demonstrate – or rather to assert – that when new rational methods of doing everything are put into effect, these new methods together will produce a new possibility of combination hitherto obscured. And these new possibilities will in turn call forth still newer methods for dealing with them (338 ff). This process will become self-sustaining or even increase the rate of future progress. 'The methods by which genius will arrive at the discovery of new truths, augment at once both the force and the rapidity of its operations' (340).[13]

The rational allocation of resources, so as to produce sufficient for everyone, is not simply a means of distributive justice. It is the precondition for the employment of these resources in ways not possible to envision today. On the land, 'not only the same species of ground will nourish a greater number of individuals, but each individual, with a less quantity of labour, will labour more successfully and be surrounded with greater conveniences' (334).

This productivity raises the spectacle of a world teeming with people. Could this put a ceiling on the advance of progress? That he raised the question is to his credit; Condorcet wanted no cheap or rhetorical victories, but to prove decisively that progress was quite simply illimitable. His answer provoked Malthus's memorable essay on population as a refutation.[14] The prospect is too far off to be worth our present concern. And if it ever did arise as a problem, something would

---

11 But sexual inequality, so far as it is not simply natural difference, must be suppressed; see 355.
12 Also see Manuel *Prophets* 63.
13 See also 349 ff for the flexibility his method provides.
14 The full title of the first edition, in 1798, was *An Essay on the Principle of Population as It Affects the Future Improvement of Society. With Remarks on the Speculations of Mr. Godwin, M. Condorcet, and Other Writers*.

by then have turned up; it is idle to anticipate what, since our ability is very small to forecast what powers as well as what problems will be on hand in that distant day. What we can predict with certainty is that the solution will be in the exercise of restraint and rationality and that it will not be artificial or against nature (345 ff).[15]

The method of argument by rhetorical question is increasingly employed as the essay reaches the question of the moral improvement of mankind. 'Does not the well-being, the prosperity, resulting from the progress that will be made in the useful arts, in consequence of their being founded on a sound theory, resulting, also, from an improved legislation, built upon the truths of the political sciences, naturally dispose men to humanity, to benevolence, and to justice?' Without pause he continues, 'Do not all the observations, in fine, which we proposed to develop in this work prove, that the moral goodness of man, the necessary consequence of his organization, is, like all his other faculties, susceptible of an indefinite improvement? and that nature has connected, by a chain which cannot be broken, truth, happiness, and virtue?' (354 ff).

The sciences are the vehicle of the most assured sort of progress. Their reciprocal action with education, with its geometric advance, is the surest spring of progress. One means of securing to everyone the results of this advance will be concise tables showing the interrelation of different sorts of knowledge. This will be facilitated if men can invent a universal language of signs, to be learned with science itself. This notation will provide us with a rigour and precision 'that would facilitate the knowledge of truth, and render error almost impossible.' This Orwellian insight into language extends to work in every science, so that the results of all can be 'as infallible as that of the mathematics, and the propositions of every system acquire, as far as nature will admit, geometric demonstration and certainty' (366); this proposition was resubmitted with the early claims of twentieth-century symbolic logic.

Having proved indefinite improvement, even with human nature taken as a constant, Condorcet goes on to speculate about changes in the very structure of the human condition. Why should not better diet, longer life, and improved sanitation and medicine lead us to the indefinite prolongation of human life? 'We are bound to believe that the mean duration of human life will forever increase' (369).[16] And as we can pass on our improved physical constitutions, so we may hope to do the same for our improved intellectual and moral faculties. 'Analogy,

---

15 Similarly, on art, he is willing to face difficulties. We may well lose in the future the delight of seeing one work of art surpass its predecessors and itself be surpassed. But the general excellence of all art will make up for the loss of this particular gratification.

16 The proposition that there may or may not be a limit, but that we can progress indefinitely whether or not it exists, aroused the most withering response from the mathematical Mr Malthus, equally wedded to geometric demonstration.

an investigation of the human faculties, and even some facts, appear to authorize these conjectures' (371).

What is at stake is mankind 'emancipated from its chains, released ... from the dominion of chance.' The present is to be justified by this future. The wise man of the present, the last *philosophe*, hunted by the police, is thereby consoled and rewarded, for he, with his generation, 'becomes the associate of these wise and more fortunate beings whose enviable condition he so earnestly contributed to produce' (372). Thus ends the labour of Condorcet, but not before he has raised, among his difficult questions, the most difficult of all. Is the present difficulty to have not greater justification than its status as the foundation of the bright tomorrow? If the beatific vision, in the individual's after-life, as conceived by medieval theology, is merely made the corporate possession of our descendants, has Condorcet produced more than a civil theology with the same moral defects as the one it replaced? Condorcet's successors were not to answer this question, but turned rather to more proximate questions.

25

Millennialism, utopianism, and progress

I have taken the position that progress, as an idea, is directly dependent on both utopianism and millennialism. But it is remarkable that anyone should have thought of joining these two incompatible sets of assumptions; and, indeed, no one may have done so, consciously.

To the working assumptions of millennialism, the phenomenal world is the only cosmos there is; there is no structure behind it, only the free will of God. The question of *truth* does not arise; it is rather the question of adequacy to the will of God, historically revealed in events. The question of permanence does not arise; the project of redemption of God's people, and his vindication of his promises, mean that change and impermanence always, and properly, challenge any existing structure. Nothing can be sacred, as an object or practice, in the sense of being derived from a higher, fixed, privileged reality. The historical process *is* reality, for its dynamic is not one of truth versus illusion but of open response to God versus rebellion.

In the assumptions of utopianism, history is chained to illusion. It is propelled by material passions and ambitions. To the degree that men take this plane of existence as real, they are disabled from ever correcting themselves and seeing the truth. Instead, we become real by participating, as we are able, in the true. The recognition of truth carries its own necessity and is beauty. When once we see beauty, we recognize that it cannot be other than it is. 'God' is the sum, or perhaps the central substance, of that which is true, therefore good and beautiful. There is that in man which is akin to this substance, or else we could not recognize it. And this within us is the real substance of man, which must, accordingly, survive the accidents of flesh and history and be united to that which now stands over us as actuality to potentiality.

Utopia has a spatial orientation and is dominantly cognitive. It has no place for history as conceived or experienced by millennialism. Millennialism is radically temporal and is characterized by will. Each excludes the other. And neither, by itself, can give rise to the doctrine of progress. That men so commonly think otherwise demonstrates only that the accepted reading of the texts has been done through progressivist spectacles.

Millennialism proper cannot be separated from the dialectic of open response and rebellion so vividly portrayed in Daniel and Revelation. This dialectic will continue and heighten until it envelops and eliminates all ambiguity from history. At that point, God himself will vindicate his promises. Thus there is no immanent force in history making for automatic improvement. 'Things grow worse as they grow better' is the most that can be said. The age is to end catastrophically by a complex interaction of human wills and that of God.

Utopianism also does not generate progress. It is cognitive; and the truth is what is at stake. There is no necessary development in truth. The Platonic psychology is based on the notion of hierarchy in ability to recognize and love truth. But this is a precarious hierarchy. One may surmount one obstacle only to fail at the next. One's children must start the course at the beginning and may stumble at the first hurdle, through their own inability, through mischance, or through the malice of others who create structures which institutionalize and encourage passions rather than the truth. Utopia is the attempt to institutionalize the truth, to cope with this psychology, to create the conditions which will encourage the greatest number of people to surmount the largest number of hurdles, to guard against the commonwealth being dominated by those who nonetheless fall short. But utopia is not, in its classic phase, the construction of a launching pad upon which our descendants may build vehicles worked by principles unknowable to us, in order to travel to now unguessable goals. We already know what the truth is. As the perfect, changeless object of cognition, as the principle according to which our own souls have been constructed if we but knew it, the truth is discernible now. It is logical and consistent in structure. He who knows it in part can be led to see it in its totality, unless he be unable by mental infirmity to grasp its deeper principles of unity. It is precisely change which is ruled out in utopia.

How then did these quite opposed sets of conceptions become joined to produce the doctrine of progress? It is important to note how little that was taken into the doctrine from other sources became vital to it. The Lockean sensationalist epistemology, for example, influenced the *philosophe* tradition heavily, but never became essential to the notion of progress.

The great thinkers did not play major roles in the articulation of progress and they regarded both utopianism and millennialism as of little consequence. Utopia was a charming diversion or, at most, a half-serious vehicle for serious ideas, as was the case with *Oceana*: a permissible popularization for ideas better expressed in serious essays. Millennialism, of course, was Münsterite fanaticism or the effluvium of ecclesiastical quarrels which had so disastrously upset the balance of Europe.

I have tried to demonstrate, to the contrary, that millennialist motifs were in constant use throughout the early modern as well as the medieval period and that their influence on thinkers, controversialists, and publicists was substantial and continuous – even when these persons rejected any particular orthodoxy. Similarly the utopian mode was influential. It was well adapted to exploration, to synthesis, to concretization of ideas, to persuasion – and it could be camouflaged as a literary conceit if it offended the powerful. It could be used by the cultured, by lonely autodidacts, and by cranks.[1] But it retained, throughout its classical period, the basic assumptions summarized above.

The direct influence of utopianism on general political thought is somewhat harder to demonstrate than that of millennialism. Millennialism, after all, was a part of the official documents of Western man – however inconvenient a part. The faith linked to these scriptures was backed by great institutions whose claim to antiquity and authority was at least as good as that of any given state. Theorizing about the *regnum* began from the fact of the empire as well as from the scriptures; but Platonic thought was not central to either, however important it was in other areas. In the investiture controversy, beginning in 1075, it was scripture, the imperial legacy, and Teutonic tradition to which men appealed. Publicists hurled scripture, Roman law, and Aristotle at one another in succeeding centuries. The nominalist logic, reducing substance and hierarchy to matters of either convention or will, underlay the new secular definitions of state authority in the conceptions of men such as Bodin. It was left to the utopian tradition to preserve the neglected Platonic political thought. And the utopian writers influenced one another more obviously than they did the major controversies of the period. But utopianism thereby preserved its own coherence; and we must remember that as a popular literature it was available to shape the genesis of progressivism, tenaciously held as a popular, and not an official or academic, doctrine.

We thus have two coherent traditions of great antiquity arriving together in the eighteenth century. In response to the cumulative effects of the break-up of the enclosed medieval cosmos, the bankruptcy of religious politics, the rise of the new science, the delayed Reformation in England, the development of new economic thought and its practice, the loss of nerve of the Enlightenment, and the persistence of the *ancien régime* in France we have a confused, unsystematic, but quite perceptible bringing together of these two traditions and the creation of the

1 See Frye in F. Manuel ed *Utopias and Utopian Thought* (Boston 1967) 39 ff.

doctrine of progress. The elements of the doctrine of progress are more obviously and parsimoniously traceable to utopianism and millennialism than to other sources. The doctrine of progress tells us that the human world (and perhaps the whole cosmos) is in a demonstrable state of unilinear improvement. Man is at once his own master in all this and is following the promptings or the dictates of Nature. We can demonstrate our progress from ancient times through to the present and can project the future development of the race to its destined state of perfection. This movement is irreversible and irresistible.

The proper work of mankind is to take part in progress and to advance it. This notion in the progressivist faith is traceable to neither tradition. But it is not a re-appropriation of elements only ambiguously present, at best, in obscure Hellenistic writers. It arises precisely out of the combination, in the hands of progressivists, of elements from the two incompatible traditions we have scrutinized. To see how the distinctive progressivist doctrine arose conceptually from these two is the task now at hand.

Which elements in the idea of progress are to be derived from utopianism and which from millennialism? How is each modified by the other? Are these changes in each produced by earlier interactions and changes? What logic, if any, brought these two traditions of social thought together and produced the doctrine of progress?

Elements from utopianism include the 'state of perfection,' the strong preference for order and pattern exemplified in the level of detail to which utopian writers, both classical and progressive, take us.[2] Being perfect, the utopia discloses its perfections as its provisions and their articulations are disclosed. To the callous outsider or to the unconvinced this level of detail appears wearying. But to the utopian writer, this perfection is winsome; the arrangements of the utopia are perfect in all their detail because they so fully accord with the requirements of the fullest employment of all men's best powers. The Platonic microcosm–macrocosm equivalence is fundamental here; and this does not alter in progressivism merely because the vocabulary of economics may be substituted for one more intellectual.

It appears at first glance that far more is taken from millennialism into progressivism: the concentration on the realm of history as that of the real and the implicit abandonment of the spatial metaphor of planes and transcendence; linearity and one-way development, ie an anti-mythic understanding of history as a once-only story or drama; the sense that the whole world is the field of

---

2　See B. de Jouvenel's comments on this in Manuel ed *Utopias* 220 ff, 233. The millennialist minutiae of historical argumentation should not be confused with this utopian motif.

action; the feeling that the final state of mankind is not simply a conformation of microcosm to macrocosm but a confirmation and conclusion or resolution of the drama and of all the issues raised in it; and – the key assumption in the 'conquest of nature' motif – the desacralization of the cosmos, a notion derived from the Hebrew picture of the cosmos as created and contingent, a staging for man's own story.

Some aspects of utopianism are altered by contact with millennialism. The cycle was always a difficult, disturbing part of classical utopianism, yet an unavoidable one. Once perfection had been pictured clearly, any anticipated change – inevitable in a mutable universe – could only be seen as decline and disorder. In progressivism the cycle is straightened out and assimilated to unilinearity, to the sense of a single, over-arching drama. The fixed vision of the final state gives way to a notion of the fullest employment of man's powers or, as we should say, of freedom.[3]

There is a sense of hazard in the classical utopia. One's children, by the luck of genetic endowment, may lack that full grasp of the Ultimate which entitles the people of utopia to full citizen status; hence Plato's and Campanella's anxious fiddling with eugenics; one may assure oneself that one would certainly follow these prescriptions for outwitting the unsatisfactory randomness of genetics. For progressive utopias this problem is removed. In the democracy of progress, we are all subject to historical laws of irreversible development. Similarly the hierarchy of roles and types, and consequently the description of utopia in terms of institutional arrangements, give way in progressivism to the millennialist sense that all the saints are on the same footing, all holy ones, all mature. Accordingly the progressivist utopia of the nineteenth century typically does not so inevitably focus on the details of the system but instead offers us a picture of what the people are like.

Millennialism, in turn, is modified by its contact with utopianism. The fixed periodization is opened up. Even the Joachimist scheme of overlapping stages is displaced by an indeterminate span of years in which development is broadly upward and which can be periodized in a number of ways. The 'hard' dialectic of Revelation is softened by the utopian cognitive or epistemic hierarchy: it is not now ultimate good and ultimate evil which are at stake, but insight and ignorance; and these two are not so much opposed as distinguished by a series of gradations. Millennialism's final state, fixed by the determinate will of God, is modified by utopianism's sense that the structure of the cosmos is fixed from

3 In Rev 2:17 we are told that the holy ones who endure will, at the triumphal end-time, each be given a 'new name' heretofore known only to God, a name that expresses one's true self, now liberated.

within itself, immanent rather than given. Thus, too, the catastrophism of millennialism gives way to the surprise-free scenarios of progressivism.

But this mutual modification of millennialism and utopianism in the idea of progress introduces us to the problem of why progressivism came into being at all. There is no obvious need in either utopianism or millennialism that makes one reach out to the other. Few classic utopias were produced after the advent of progressivism. It may be that those who might have done so were indeed convinced of the self-evident truth of progress. But this conviction discloses no prior necessity for classic utopianism to have helped to create the doctrine of progress in the first place. And the older millennialism did continue undeflected after the advent of progressivism – even, in its orthodox Second Coming version, enjoying a significant revival in the nineteenth century.

We must accordingly look elsewhere than within utopianism and millennialism for the forces that brought them together and produced progressivism. We are not, in any case, charting the immaculate conception of ideas from other ideas. It is enough to ask: Who gains? Who needs a new set of assumptions about the world? Who feels these things to be problems? Pre-eminently it is the heirs of the rational Enlightenment who experience as a problem their own age: the corruption of the idea of God by the wars of religion, the formalism of enforced Protestantism or Catholicism, the necessity always to speak elliptically in attack against established institutions lest these institutions arbitrarily crush one, the betrayal of the international culture of reason by the princes who had corresponded with *philosophes*, the complacency of existing institutions in the face of economic and social collapse. Their own prior assumptions provide insufficient answers.

The doctrine of progress has its rise in this context. Reason, of the geometrical-demonstrative sort, will no longer do. The mere presentation of truth compels no one to follow it. Utopianism of the classical sort shares in this disability. Berington's *Gaudentio di Lucca* tells us that God is 'the supreme, intellectual, rational and most noble of all beings ... It is the duty of all intellectual beings to imitate the just laws of reason in him; otherwise they depart from the supreme rule of all their actions.'[4] But it had become clear that reason required a greater sanction than its own self-recommendation. And the God of the *philosophe* generation – being too cultivated a gentleman to intervene arbitrarily in his reasonable world – was no remedy for this situation.

What was needed was a way to recover the authority of the old, coercive God without having to accept the arbitrariness of that God. We have seen the God–

---

4 G. Negley and J.M. Patrick ed *The Quest for Utopia* first pub New York 1952 (Garden City, NY, 1962) 434

Providence–Nature declension that provided the means to accomplish this feat. God's forethought and benevolence were emphasized at the same time that his arbitrary personal characteristics were devalued. His newly marked benevolence was matched by a new perception of man, who is no longer the rational microcosm corresponding to the clockwork mechanism of Foigny's God who always and only acted 'after an universal manner.'[5]

Man is active, passional; his bonds with his fellows are those of sentiment and attraction rather than resting on a common subjection to disembodied reason. Despite the greater psychological realism of this picture of man, it is in some respects only a conceptualization of the problem. Rational man needed to be inspired; affective man is *capable* of being inspired. But the problem has not been solved. And to ask 'How are such men to be organized into community?' only emphasizes the problem, for a mere principle of benevolence, whether human or divine, will not suffice. The microcosm–macrocosm notion of utopianism stimulated a deeper consideration of the new human nature, individual and social, in relation to physical nature. What was required was an immanent set of principles, dynamic principles which could direct the creation or re-creation of a society expressive through time of all that is in individual nature.

Thus we return to the last element in the God–Providence–Nature set; now immanent Nature acquires the dynamism of the old Hebrew God, without his inconvenient irrational character. He becomes an impersonal, powerful force from below, guaranteeing the progressive development of human community, providing both propulsion and pattern at the same time. Nature has become an object of faith. As we have seen, the metaphysical compliments earlier paid to the transcendent Author of our being are now transmuted into rhapsodies about beneficent Nature. But when the French Revolution has once again exposed the darker passions, and when industrialization requires to be explained, even capitalized Nature will not do. God could be depotentiated, and this process could seem but the completion of emancipation from ecclesiastical tyranny. But the immanent historical process could not forever be denied the coercive power withheld from God. This is the problem of nineteenth- and twentieth-century progressivism.

5 Ibid 406

PART FOUR

Progress and the third age

26

Saint-Simon and the age of industry

Nineteenth-century Europe inherited the fully developed doctrine of progress and, after 1815, a century of scarcely interrupted peace in which to employ it. This part examines three such programs. The new industrial system, largely built upon the stern demands of the Napoleonic era for *materiel*, was analysed by Henri de Saint-Simon and made the vehicle of a powerful vision of society. System analysis replaced Turgot and Condorcet's dependence upon individual genius or upon a generalized social momentum.[1] The mordant eccentric Charles Fourier, 80 years before Freud, produced a keen analysis of the individual and collective consequences of affective repression – the counterpoint to the story of institutional and productive development – and proposed a human future based on the carefully organized fulfilment of the passions. Edward Bellamy considered the newly mobilized forces of popular democracy and tried to bring together, under the concept of nation, the emphases of both Saint-Simon and a laundered Fourier. The nation is immortal and can become the means for humanity to surpass itself.

In inspecting the work of each man, I shall not only outline his use of developed progressivism but also show the specific contribution of millennialist and utopian motifs to his version of progress. I shall try to locate the points of strain that appear in their conceptions of the future and, in so doing, identify more clearly the crucial difficulty in the doctrine of progress: the attribution of beneficence to an automatic process.

---

1 The influential work of Auguste Comte follows lines laid down by Saint-Simon and includes a classically progressivist scheme of human history showing why a scientific 'sociology' – he coined the word – is the synthetic science subsuming all others and showing why the final age of mankind has dawned with its advent. Comte's influence on social and political thought in Latin America was considerable. His new 'religion of humanity,' of which he was the archpriest, travelled rather less well.

Mercier's censors had burned the history books: the past was irrelevant, futile, and confusing. But the new progressives were unwilling to set fire to their own past. The new present could only be defined in relation to the past. The most important thing about the present was its qualitative change from the past. But the past was more than a signpost. By seeing the processes of progress at work in the past we could learn to recognize them in the present and gain confidence about predicting what was necessarily to come.

Henri de Saint-Simon (1760–1825), a minor aristocrat, had survived the French Revolution and embraced it as a turning point in human history.[2] Though he emerged from the Napoleonic period with only a clerk's pay, he had long since begun to develop a ground plan for organizing the new industrial age that lay on this side of the Revolution. From early in his career he sought to identify and then to balance the elements and forces in the new society. His merit to Marxists, and his influence on them, lay in his analysis of classes or groups in light of their relationship to production. But his efforts to bring about a balance among these elements earned him the heavy sarcasm of Engels in *Anti-Dühring*[3] and consignment to a place among the utopians, a term which acquired its pejorative sense from Marx and Engels in the *Communist Manifesto*.

Unlike his own progressive forebears, Saint-Simon had not spent his life fighting the *ancien régime*. Following Turgot, he made a historical analysis that rehabilitated the Middle Ages as a period when the social hierarchy had reflected the relations of production; later mere privilege had maintained power in defiance of changes in the natural relations of production, thus producing the hated *ancien régime*.

A PSYCHOLOGY OF TYPES

The complexity and fecundity of Saint-Simon's thought cannot be caught by merely comparing him with his contemporaries or listing his influence upon others. His interest was in finding a harmony of human interests in the new industrial age. Like Plato, he sought the key to harmony in a theory of human nature, and, like Plato, he saw that this central problem entailed finding some means of linking man's physical nature to the moral order. Only thus could a

2 See Manuel *The Prophets of Paris* first pub Cambridge, Mass, 1962 (New York 1965) 105–13; also K. Taylor's 'Introduction' 13–29 in K. Taylor ed *Henri de Saint-Simon (1760–1825), Selected Writings on Science, Industry and Social Organization* tr K. Taylor (London 1975).

3 *Herrn Eugen Dühring's Revolution in Science* (1878) A section from it was excerpted and published separately as *Socialism Utopian and Scientific* (London 1892), from *Socialisme utopique et socialisme scientifique* (Paris 1880).

'scientific' account of progress be established; only in this way could a comprehensive and defensible program be set forth for the present age.

This program would provide at once for the rational maximization of productive capacity and for the moral unity of mankind. Production emphasizes diversity and, unregulated, it estranges man from man. Moral unity is the form of harmony. Society's failure to heed Saint-Simon evoked from his later followers their war-cry 'Progress is in danger!' But how is this diversity of productive nature and capacity to be linked to the presumed moral unity of mankind? Saint-Simon's analysis divides the past into successive moral systems rather than régimes of economic or political relations.

Félix Vicq-d'Azyr, F.M.X. Bichat, and others, who interpreted their work to him, provided Saint-Simon with the physiological basis of human diversity and with the link between these capacities and man's affective capacities. Physiology he defined broadly enough to allow himself to exhort its practitioners to 'expel the philosophers, moralists and metaphysicians,' now to be suppressed as chemistry replaced alchemy.[4] This psychological physiology will soon be taught, along with the other 'positive' sciences, in schools. Accordingly, morals will also become scientific. 'The physiologist is the only scientist able to prove that in every case it is the path of virtue that leads to happiness'[5] because 'there are no phenomena which cannot be observed from the viewpoint of the physics of inorganic bodies or the physics of organic bodies, which is physiology.'[6]

Out of this reasoning comes the classification of men into producers (producteurs), scientists (savants), and artists (artistes). But, in keeping with the ethos of the new age, all three are really producers: scientists produce their positive laws and the basis for useful inventions; artists include moralists of the proper sort; and all make a social product, whether a statue or a sentiment tending to foster social unity. In 1815, Saint-Simon introduced a new word, industriels,[7] (entrepreneurs, craftsmen, and workmen) to replace producers, thereby emphasizing producteur as the umbrella term.

This classification remains throughout the remainder of Saint-Simon's career. He gradually attracted a circle of young men of remarkable and diverse talents. In 1825 he published, with Léon Halévy, a dialogue, 'L'Artist, le savant et l'industriel,' in which the typology is maintained. Frank Manuel has interpreted Saint-

4 'Letters From an Inhabitant of Geneva' (1802–3) in Taylor ed Selected Writings 75
5 'Memoir on the Science of Man' (1813) in Taylor ed Writings 113
6 Ibid
7 In 'To All Englishmen and Frenchmen Zealous for the Public Good' (1815). See Taylor ed Writings 307 n44: 'To the best of my knowledge this is the first occasion on which Saint-Simon used the term "industriel."'

Simon's public career as successive attempts, each different, to found social harmony on the initiating role or precedence of one psychological type over the others.[8] I employ Manuel's account in presenting the aspects of Saint-Simon's thought relevant to the present study.

At the beginning of his career, Saint-Simon was very much the successor of Condorcet in his preoccupation with the role of scientists, the *savants*. They neither own property nor labour for entrepreneurs. Yet their work fuels the new developments of our times. In his early proposal for a Council of Newton he displayed his faith in the scientists' ability to be both a balance wheel and a disinterested central directorate for society. Over time he became detached from the enthusiasm of Burnet and Condorcet with the delights of co-operative rational science. It was observable that the exuberance of the *industriels* was soon outstripping science and undermining scientists' independence. This enfolding of science within the entrepreneurial ethos was producing not harmony but hegemony. Science had shown itself insufficiently dynamic to take leadership in society. A dynamic and not a hierarchical harmony was required if progress were to continue and to accelerate.

Here we must consider Saint-Simon's three human types: motor, rational, and emotive. It is important to compare them to Plato's typology in the *Republic*. Plato's readers often overlook the fact that his appetitive men included not only labourers and minor artisans, but large-scale craftsmen and merchants as well. So with Saint-Simon, whose authorities have convinced him that the motor-orientation of entrepreneurs and managers is sufficient warrant to group them with their employees and with peasants. But Saint-Simon, unlike Plato, does not correlate appetitiveness with the lowest position on the cognitive scale and in the hierarchy. For Saint-Simon there is no real cognitive hierarchy. Talents do differ, and combined with other factors they produce a wide inequality of fortune among men. But Saint-Simon does not regard this disparity as evil. His *industriels* are the most numerous and powerful of the three types, and there is nothing to fear from their activities: Saint-Simon's journal was called *Le Producteur*, and an important theoretical piece was *L'Organisateur*.

8 See especially F. Manuel *The Prophets of Paris* 113–24. This scheme, though perhaps overly neat, has been supported by Henri Desroche in a detailed outline of the movement of Saint-Simon's thought. For Desroche a utopia-millennialism typology plays a determinative role in Saint-Simon's work; see *Les Deux Rêves: theisme et atheisme en utopie* (Paris 1972) and *Saint Simon, le nouveau christianisme et les écrits sur la religion* (Paris 1969). Similarly, Jacqueline Russ, emphasizing Saint-Simon's 'precursor' status, finds stages in his development conformable to those stressed by Manuel; see her *Pour connaître la pensée des précurseurs de Marx* (Paris 1973).

For Plato each of the three elements had been present, in greater or lesser amounts, in each person. Saint-Simon tends to treat *industriel, savant*, and *artiste* as exclusive labels, no doubt as a result of an overly neat reading of his physiologists. But there is no cognitive hierarchy in Saint-Simon; there is thus no need to insist that each individual share some 'higher' faculty. The *industriels* fulfil themselves as producers, whether at the work-bench or on the Bourse.

Since the concept of power is discrediting itself, the three types do not dispose themselves into a new power pyramid. Saint-Simon does not deny the fact of exploitation, particularly in the past. But the issue of power is no longer the sub-text in discussions of human capacity or of social organization. The functional order of production is transforming the very basis of the older power relations. Further, the sloughing off of dogma and ritual from religion, freeing it to take its true place as morals, was removing the ideological underpinnings from political power.[9] Science had long since been anti-political in character. Thus the relations among the three types would not be political in character. Politics has been superseded, or will be when the realities of the post-revolution world are properly understood.

What group is to take the place of scientists as the leading element in society? In his middle phase, Saint-Simon believed the process of social development to be sequential, with the motor types implementing what the scientists had refined into concrete processes. Since Saint-Simon equates psychic types with social formations, it follows that this sequence produces self-realization. As one produces what one is best fitted to make – ideas, rational models, concretizations of these ideas, and objects or institutions which realize the models – one is making actual what one is. Only arrange the succession from initiation to response properly, and no coercion is required. Unlike the *ancien régime*, when men were forced by arbitrary command to try to be what they were not, in the new régime one need only administer the process.

Power in the old sense has now become irrelevant. No organic creation requires coercion in order to become itself. It need only be understood and let alone, to order its functions and structures naturally. Indeed, the test for the artificial or non-organic society is made by observing a society's need for the instruments of interference and violence. In contrast to the usual game of power, in which what one man gains he takes from another, now, in an organic society, all men gain, and are united even in their diversity.

---

9 Saint-Simon's celebrated 'political parable' – What would happen if our entrepreneurs and artisans all disappeared? What would happen if we lost all our political élites? – occurs in *L'Organisateur* (1819).

The remodelling of relations among the three types of persons now emphasizes the predominance of the *industriels*, even though they do not actually initiate the production process with ideas or the discoveries of science. But they lead society as a whole, because they marshal society's resources in the making and distribution of things; they realize the productive process.[10] Even though government has been superseded, we are not in anarchy; we are in a natural hierarchy which administers itself naturally.

Later Saint-Simon became convinced that the entrepreneurs could not be relied on so confidently. The lust for domination had not been driven out by the joy of self-realization. The creation of a deprived proletariat and a crass cultural tone were not parts of Saint-Simon's vision.[11] Accordingly, he now raised to social leadership the third type, the emotives or artists. The institutional form of this new leadership he called the New Christianity. He had long enjoyed cordial relations of difference with the Catholic reactionaries, such as Bonald and Chateaubriand. They too had argued for the organic society. But their emphasis on dogma and authority had repelled Saint-Simon.

Now Saint-Simon engaged in a demythologizing of dogma in the *Nouveau Christianisme, dialogues entre un conservateur et un novateur* (1825). Dogma had an inner intent now translatable into moral imperatives for lifting the ethical tone of industrial society. Earlier he had criticized Comte for advocating a spiritual supremacy in society. Now the dying leader himself projected the necessity of the artists, including the moral types, assuming the leadership of society.

Saint-Simon has reproduced the deist reduction of dogma to morals, but has not made morals a matter of rationality. To Saint-Simon, the New Christianity is in the special care of the artists or emotives. What is needed is not a matter for rational analysis; it is the promise of feeling and intuition, of the affective passions. Now brotherly love and positive science together for the first time will guarantee the organic development of the new society.

OLD ELEMENTS: NEW VISION

How can we understand Saint-Simon more clearly through reference to the major, persisting themes of utopianism and millennialism? How does the whole exercise throw light on progressivism?

10 'The industrial class is the fundamental class, the nourishing class in all society ... Thus it has the right to say to ... non-industrials: We wish to feed you, house you, clothe you, and generally satisfy your physical tastes only on certain conditions'; from *Catechisme des industriels* 3e cahier (1824), cited by Taylor ed *Writings* 43–4. But this part may be by Comte.

11 He had long allowed for the possibility of conflict between the entrepreneurs and their workmen but supposed it unlikely to become evident in France, as distinguished from England. See *De l'Organization sociale* (1825) in Taylor ed *Writings* 265.

Merely to parcel out the bits of his work into packages labelled 'of utopian origin,' and so forth, would not carry the task very far, since his thought changed over time. In general, however, I believe we can see a movement from broadly utopian premises to those more dependent on millennialism. He is, it appears, driven to this movement because he is more historically minded than his *philosophe* forebears. Their Manichaean simplicities – the march of Reason beset by superstition – led them, he sees, to falsify history and to render progress a kind of Form standing over history. In contrast, Saint-Simon can value the Middle Ages for its development of a natural hierarchy and division of labour. The succeeding period is not simply better because later and less theological in orientation. It is rather an unhappy transitional period in which the forms of the older order are exploited. The old forms have lasted so long not because of 'superstition' but because they functioned rather well as a cover for those new men who wished to exploit their fellows. Only now, with the sweeping away of the forms of the old order, do we have the opportunity to develop appropriate institutions for the new order.

This preference for taking history as it was, this acceptance of historical consequentiality instead of forcing it to illustrate a predetermined plan, existed in Saint-Simon in some tension with his liking for neat schemata. He took over Condorcet's vision of science and created a vision of the 'religion of Newton' or a republic of science. But he could not rest there; he was driven toward a plan better anchored in the development of a whole society. He seized on Bichat's psychology as a supra-historical given element in society. He developed a plan in which the orderly passing of initiative from one Bichat class to another constitutes the process of development and change. But this gave way, in the face of the evidence of post-Napoleonic France, to a vision of one people realizing a vision of practical brotherhood.

Though the categories of Bichat gradually broke down as an organizing principle for society, the Platonic correspondence between macrocosm and microcosm remained and developed. The Bichat typology, taken flatly, did not allow correspondence between any one individual and society. Accordingly, Saint-Simon made do with an organic analogy. But as Bichat's scheme was falsified by experience, the way was opened for a clearer emphasis on the correspondence between individual and society. At least the practical problem was the same by the time of *New Christianity*: the unification and mobilization of both individual and society by affective means. No utopian theme survives in Saint-Simon in its classical form.

We do not see millennialism in its original Hebrew and Christian colouration or in the motifs I have identified. Saint-Simon's sense of periodization is a mere punctuation and exhibits little persuasive character. Correspondingly, his notion of hidden or dialectical development in history is rudimentary. The idea of cultural lag is used to explain the unsatisfactory character of the period from late medieval times to the Revolution. Or the whole period of Western history is characterized as first the emphasis on universals, next the swing to particularism (with an unregulated egotism operating under cover of universal institutions), and finally, in his time, the opportunity to rebuild with both emphases together.

But two elements of Montanist and Joachite millennialism become central to Saint-Simon. The first is the search for the men of the third age, the remnant-as-élite. As the Bichat typology collapses for him, this search becomes more urgent, issuing in the *New Christianity*. But this quest goes hand in hand with something that prevents it from becoming demonic: the sense that the task of society, its reason for being, is the full realization of the potential in all people. At times this aim is put in economic terms associated with his idea of production and its values. At other times he speaks in Baconian terms: 'to make and remake nature in accordance with our will.'

But Saint-Simon's basic impulse, I think, is always the vision of man exercising all his powers: mature man. The new society, Saint-Simon agrees with Condorcet, must not make the mistake of creating a mechanical equality, a levelling of men, even in the interest of keeping the powerful from oppressing the weak. Such provisions frustrate all men in the name of creating opportunity. But men do not want equality; they want the chance to realize their full potential – their quite varied potential, a matter later taken up and made his own by Fourier.

Even the 'economic' emphasis in Saint-Simon rests on this primary intuition. Maximum production follows upon and is conditioned upon maximum development and employment of individual capacity. Variation is no threat; for organization will enable each man to make his distinctive contribution to the social whole. Similarly the domination of nature is not an exercise in power as domination, but an enterprise made possible because so many men work at it from so many different perspectives and with so many different talents.

The human machine harnessed to one corporate will to power over nature[12] is *not* Saint-Simon's vision. And though he will use organic images for both macrocosm and microcosm, the purpose of this structure is not fixed, for the future is open; it is not clear what man will be, once he embarks on the new society. If the third age is one of self-realization, it is not one in which we may feel, in advance of their maturation, the shape of the fruits of self-realization. The metaphor of organism carries us into the presence of the mystery of progress – but only just.

12 For a clear exposition of this tradition, see Mumford in F. Manuel ed *Utopias and Utopian Thought* (Boston 1967) 3–4.

SAINT-SIMON'S INFLUENCE

Saint-Simon's influence cannot be accounted for by any single element in his thought.[13] His experience was limited: a mercenary soldier in his youth and a profiteer in the Revolution. For the rest he was self-taught. His economic ideas as such are undeveloped. His challenge to the primacy of politics could be discounted because it seemed finally to rest on his claims on behalf of his new religion. He outgrew his borrowed psychological garments; but it is not clear what replaced them. He changed his mind frequently without telling us exactly where the changes occurred.

The positive effect of the whole, rather than any of the bits, is what makes Saint-Simon significant for us.[14] This significance is directional, rather than specific, despite his intent. He highlights the problems of the progress doctrine as it continued to develop. Political philosophers took over his economics and rudimentary sociology but abjured his religion; yet they too required some motive force for society. Nationalists picked up his organicism. His own disciples, without being nationalists, tried to build 'organicism in one country' on the basis of *New Christianity*.

The principal problem Saint-Simon bequeathed is the problem of what guarantees progress. His own thought is not strong enough to solve this problem or to point to a solution in a way that made it possible for others to work on his foundations. Manuel suggests that the problem of progress theories is that of an inadequate theodicy. But both Fourier and Bellamy, in their different ways, took different aspects of Saint-Simon's work and attempted a form of theodicy in their progressivist utopias.

13 For an account of the disciples, see Manuel *Prophets* 151–93. His notes identify many other studies.
14 The influence of single formulations – the administration of things; from each according to his capacities; etc – is instructive, however, and has been much traced in accounts of the development of Marxism.

27

Fourier and the age of harmony

Charles Fourier (1772–1837)[1] suggested – falsely, I think – that Saint-Simon wanted a transformation of man but took man as he is. Fourier here consigns not only Saint-Simon but also, as he admits, thousands of years of hortatory moralism to the dustbin. Moral exhortation has not only been wrong, it has also been useless: men remain what they are. Yet Fourier is no reductionist; he makes no suggestion that man is *only* this or that. Rather man is an undreamed or unadmitted abundance, upon the recognition of which vast social improvements can be erected.

Civilization's repression of man's wonderful variations and capacities has created the graveyard perversions that make up society as we see it. What is needed is a new social order fuelled by the power of these unlocked capacities. Heretofore men have seen dimly that these capacities and passions have pulled in radically different directions; accordingly they have feared for the unity of society and have repressed these opposing and differentiating passions. Thus we are all blunted, unfulfilled, living in an economy of (false) affective scarcity, competing frantically for what, in reality, exists in superabundance.

But only organize society on the basis of the complementarity, the mutual attraction, of these differing passions and we shall have full abundance and employment for all the capacities of man. Nothing need be repressed. Thus the coming state of harmonism: 'I make use of a lever hitherto unknown ... The

---

1 Fourier was a salesman and clerk. He was a bachelor, a provincial who hated Paris and was never accepted by it, and remained a marginal man all his life. Only toward the end of it did he attract attention and disciples, though these never formed a coherent body in the Saint-Simonian fashion. He founded no phalansteries, but others soon tried – in Romania; in Russia, where Dostoevsky was involved; and in the United States, where dozens were attempted. See F. Manuel *The Prophets of Paris* first pub Cambridge, Mass, 1962 (New York 1965) 197–209. I select Fourier for analysis because he works consciously in opposition to Saint-Simon and because his thought did in fact lead progressivism in quite a different direction.

contrasted passional series operates by those very disparities which so much embarrass our political sciences. By its action, the passions which now produce so many discords will be changed in their development, and become the sources of concord and harmony.'[2]

Heretofore men have been content to organize affective life on the pattern of industrial life; thus our civilization stands on its head. We must turn it upright and instead establish industrial life on the basis of the varied emotional necessities of mankind. Only then will society walk forward unassisted into the next stage of its development beyond mere civilization, which is 'for the human race a disease of infancy, like teething; but it is a disease which has been prolonged in our globe at least twenty centuries beyond its natural term.'[3] Fourier recognizes that his own labours are not without precedent; there have been presentiments, but our age 'has feared to trust its inspirations ... It has conceived the possibility of the associative order without daring to proceed to the investigation of the means of realizing it.'[4] Fourier's ground plan for the transformation is most simply explained by employing the motifs of millennialism.

HISTORY AND THE THIRD AGE

Despite the salience in Fourier's work of system and symmetry, of preposterous fantasy and utterly humourless attention to detail, characteristic of so many utopias, Fourier can only give structure to his project by a historical outline. He criticizes his predecessors for concern with abstractions such as mass, class, and system. 'Every day, philosophers, you add new errors to the errors of the past.'[5] He sees himself, in contrast, as building up his own conceptions on the basis of existing particulars, by observation of real individuals. Social progress is illusory and abstract until and unless it meets their needs. It is a sign of his commitment to this path that he devotes so much attention to women, submerged, in the work of others, in the abstraction 'Man.' His focus on the individual is not itself abstract; the lonely inhabitant of bed-sitters observed closely his fellow men in all their astonishing variety. He does not see ideal man, for Eden is not his objective. Eden

---

2 From A. Brisbane's selections from Fourier's then published works, *The Theory of Social Organization* (New York 1876) as excerpted in M. Poster ed *Harmonian Man: Selected Writings of Charles Fourier* (Garden City, NY, 1971) 53. Several other excerpts exist in English but no comprehensive translation, even from the *Oeuvres complètes* of 1841–5 and the larger work of the same name of 1967. See also J. Beecher and R. Bienvenu ed *The Utopian Vision of Charles Fourier* (Boston 1971).
3 Poster ed *Harmonian Man* 28
4 Ibid 33
5 Ibid 29

exists, in his historical scheme, but it is passed over quickly; we cannot recover it. What matters is to describe in concrete terms how we got into the hellish state called advanced civilization and how we may and must move beyond it. The way out is not back to a state of nature or out of history into some timeless present in which apples are always ripe, but forward into the next age – the third age.

Fourier's celebrated taxonomy of affective predispositions is very much related to his scheme of the successive ages: both spring from the need to build the future on observed reality. The observed need of some folk for intrigue for its own sake and the fact that history presents us with hard results and not with unlimited possibilities are accepted gladly by Fourier; he does not seek to annul them. Beginning from them is the only way to make progress at all.

The whole course of human history to date is schematized by Fourier in a developmental outline of the whole 'first age of the social world.' This outline is described as a ladder and it has three ages, with the second marked off from the first by introduction of the division of labour. We are now in the last phase – the detested 'civilization'[6] – of the second age, which will soon[7] give way to the third age. Associative labour and the associative principle in general will overcome the estrangements and perversions of civilization. There are periods beyond the full achievement of harmonism, but Fourier tells us that we can know nothing of them at present, being as yet far short of harmonism.

Fourier concentrates, in his historical analysis, on his equivalent of the biblical 'fall' – the division of labour. This fall is the disastrous but necessary precondition for the full development of mankind. We are still under the dominion of the tyrannical, estranged division of labour. Civilization, as the last and worst phase of this age, illustrates the necessity of transcending the division of labour as it has been institutionalized by our forebears, so that we can enter the maturity of mankind. Association is health and salvation, long withheld by 'sophists.' Fourier's history, then, is one of Fall and Redemption.

The division of labour sets off the second age, that of (literally) repulsive industry, from the first age, of savagery and indolence. This division of labour both creates and is created by the patriarchs. The subsequent phases of barbarism – larger patriarchal societies – and civilization simply intensify the repulsive effects of the division of labour. Men are separated by their labour and identified with their productive roles when each man has only one productive role. As a result, men over-identify with one or a few emotions and social roles. In this condition men compete for the necessities of life, further estranging one

6 'It would be impossible for the council of devils to organize the sensual persecution of the human race more scientifically than it is in this perfectibilized civilization'; ibid 107.

7 'We are on the verge of a great social transformation ... Now, indeed, is the present big with the future'; ibid 43.

another. Civilization promises us that these are the modes of life that lead to fulfilment.[8] This claim denies all we know about the complexities of the human affective life, says Fourier. Even under the stifling conditions of mere civilization, the richness of the passional order and its possibilities stand in the greatest contrast to the poverty of our industrial and formal social orders. Indeed, it is only the presence of some characteristics of the next age which keeps our society coherent at all.[9]

THE PHALANSTERY

But what are the means by which the Redemption is to be accomplished? The second age, with its authority principle, the division of labour, and the consequent mass institutions, sought to control and repress the passional life of mankind. But this project cannot be successful; the passions break out again and again. It is they, in fact, which hold society together, not institutional authority alone or primarily. But they are repressed and so deformed; therefore their influence is a deformed one which confirms to us how dangerous, how worthy of repression, they are.

We come together out of undeniable need – and then behave as mutual predators. Victimization is the mode of the passional life in the period of civilization, and the bourgeois family is its chief instrument. The same forces that repress, however, also create larger stages for the break-out of deformed emotion. Cabalism – Fourier's name for our love of intrigue – has enormous scope in mass institutions; the effect of deformed intrigues then affects vast numbers of men and women. All the deformed passions have similarly baleful consequences.

All progress now depends on the realization of the passions in their natural forms. This does not mean going back behind the division of labour[10] – nothing

8 Fourier says nothing illustrates the impiety of civilization as much as its following propositions: 'That God has subjected us to two irreconcilable and conflicting guides – *passion and reason* ... That God is unjust toward the ninety-nine hundredths of the race, to whom he has not imparted that degree of reason necessary to cope with the passions ... That God, in giving us reason as a counterpoise and a regulating agent, has miscalculated its effects; for it is evident that reason is powerless even with the hundreds of men who are endowed with it'; ibid 31 ff.

9 'The little good to be found in civilization is due only to features that are contrary to civilization'; *Théorie des quatre mouvements* 127. Quotations here and below from the original documents are taken from Charles Gide ed *Selections from the Works of Fourier* tr J. Franklin (London 1901). This volume has recently been reissued with a new introduction by F.E. Manuel (New York 1971).

10 The division of labour is transformed in the same way that the variety of the unblocked passions transforms and supersedes the drudgery of the bourgeois family. No one will have to work at anything longer than two hours per day, and he will only labour with those to whom

lies back there but savagery. And we cannot remain as we are. Fourier's metaphors of blockage suggest a social constipation anticipating Freud's notion of anal fixation: 'Today the third phase exceeds its natural limits. We have too much material for a stage so little advanced; and, this material not finding its natural employment, there is consequent overloading and discomfort in the social mechanism ... symptoms of lassitude.' Civilization, is 'besieged by the need of raising itself.'[11] If the diagnosis of repression does some of Freud's work 80 years before him, the prognosis anticipates Marx by some years. History develops, then, both dialectically and ineluctably.

Just as Daniel, John, and Joachim stand on the brink of a third age, so does Fourier. Civilization will give way to the third age by means of man's acceptance of what will, in any case, be. By accepting Fourier's analysis, however, and the proofs he offers in his demonstration project of the phalanstery, men can avoid being dragged through a traumatic period of change. The phalanstery, the economic and social institution composed of 2 each of the 810 different personality types (how poverty-stricken was Bichat!), demonstrates the reality of both diagnosis and prognosis.

But Fourier is clear that the virtues of phalanstery life cannot be realized widely in civilization. In that context they would be, as men so thoughtlessly charge, mere vice. In a syphilitic society, freer sex merely spreads venereal contamination.[12] Simplistic reform – passion by passion, so to speak – will not serve: 'These impulses entice us only to evil if we yield to them singly';[13] they create voluptuaries enslaved to a single passion. In phalanstery life, when the full keyboard of the passions lies waiting to be played upon, 'moderation ... will spring, then, from the very abundance of pleasures which today are so pernicious on account of the excesses provoked by their rarity.'[14] The great change can only come by means of recognizing the 810 types and providing for them all.

The phalanstery is not a bordello, however; it is the location of both passional and industrial life. Passional attraction creates a viable, free society of industry, with its own spontaneous division of labour, once the full range of personality

he is drawn by the different sorts of passions. The jobs no adult likes, such as emptying chamber pots and manuring the fields, will be done by bands of small children, in whom God has planted a passion for filth which, if transitory, is nonetheless intense. See *Harmonian Man* 322 ff; cf 288.

11 *Le Nouveau Monde industriel et sociétaire* 418
12 'A man is applauded in France if he succeeds in deceiving women and husbands ... A generation trained to such usages could not but abuse our extension of liberty in love'; *Pièges et charlatanisme des deux sectes Saint-Simon et Owen, qui promettent l'association et le progrès* 53.
13 *Le Nouveau Monde* 125
14 *Théorie de l'unité universelle* III 125

types has been brought together. The phalanstery is a social molecule, with tremendous forces inside, counter-balancing one another. Its equipoise is not static uniformity but the peace of fully employed forces. The sure success of the phalanstery will mark the beginning of the transition into the modes of the third age, culminating in full harmonism.

UTOPIAN ELEMENTS

I have stressed Fourier's conformity to the millennialist motifs: linear history as the locus of all meaning and existence; developmental, dramatic history; periodization; and a dialectical character to the periodized development. But this millennialism, while fundamental to Fourier, is balanced by persistent utopian aspects to his thought and expression. His third age will illustrate the matter. The third age is indeed to be equated to the third age of developed millennialism; he has no content for subsequent ages, so for practical purposes his third phase of the 'first age of the social world' is in fact the completion of mankind. Yet he is compelled to elaborate.

It seems that, while the phases of the age can be grouped into threes composed of three periods each, the periods themselves (as he illustrates from civilization) are each composed of four phases plus an apogee. Each phase, in turn, is made up of four movements and a pivot. The symphony of history is minutely divided within each movement into simple germ, composite, pivot, counterpoise, and tone. These 16 movements, plus pivots and apogee, are further unified by imposition of an organic model: infancy, adolescence, virility, and decay.[15] The dialectical movement of these moments is finally confined by the circle of the organic metaphor. So it is in the progress of the ages themselves.

Harmonism merely completes, it seems, the infancy of mankind. At some far-off time, after adolescence and apogee, and after the productive phase of virility, we shall sink into decay. The circle will be completed, presumably, with the death of the social world.[16] But as in the minor series we see the descending movements preparing the way for the next ascent, are we entitled to see the same in the master series? It hardly matters; the whole extension past the first age is formalistic in the extreme, a theoretical modification, only, of the basically historical, unilinear bent of his work.

But Fourier has a consistent bias toward system. Like Edward Bellamy, he was personally excited by the order, system, precision, and arrangement of component parts in military parades and displays. His mathematics is very important to him:

15 *Le Nouveau Monde* II 387
16 So Manuel *The Prophets of Paris* 211.

There are three groups of three periods to make up an age, and four times four movements to a period.[17] There are three distributive passions and four group passions. The threes are threes, not fours or fives. History commits few twos or sixes. The passions total twelve (the three, the four, and the five senses), probably because base twelve is the most composite and divisible of all the useful bases. There are 810 combinations or permutations of the 12 passions. Each of the group and distributive passions corresponds to a musical note, to a colour, to a mathematical exercise, to a geometric figure, to a metal.[18]

What can all this mathematics mean? It means that, while Fourier has no notion of a world of Forms, he behaves as though they existed. These Pythagorean equivalences express his belief – epitomized obscurely in his trinity of deistic God, Matter, and Justice-Mathematics – that the events of the real world, in their particularity, do correspond to something else that is true: a kind of symmetry or set of patterns. We are invited to recognize, and see confirmed, the truth of our perceptions about human affairs when we see how these perceptions parallel and correlate with the patterns of ordered numbers, which must be what they are, once we understand their properties.

Fourier cannot be content to have discovered this or that about the human passions; he has to go on and prove that there can be just twelve passions, not eleven or thirteen. It is more true at twelve, once we can see the relation of twelve to the other numbers, and once we are alerted to the presence of so many other twelves in the world.[19] Further, the thirty-two world periods correspond to rather minute phenomena in phalanstery life, like the thirty-two groups in his pear-growing collective who distribute themselves symmetrically, as by an unseen hand, in such numbers and ways as to neglect neither the hardest nor the softest pears, but also to devote the most groups to production of 'juicy' pears, one

17 Poster ed *Harmonian Man* 165 ff shows this detailed movement for the period of civilization.
18 *Théorie de l'unité universelle* i 145
19 'I do not claim that the number 10 is to be banned, but merely that it is of less importance than the integral numbers of harmony ... The number has in its favor the evidence of spoken or musical harmony. God would not have assigned this number to music had he not judged it the most appropriate to the multiplicity of accords. The same number 12 has mathematical harmony in its favor.' But Fourier is prepared to be generous: 'Must division into four or nine groups be excluded because Saint-Martin esteems only the number 4 and proscribes the number 9? ... God's genius is not so narrow.' At the end of this meditation on Providence, Fourier can tell us that 'the disparity of human character, which has so strongly disoriented science, is nothing else but a mechanism of the fifth power having twelve tetra-octaves forming 576 steps on the scale, backed by 234 steps on the sub-pivot and ambiguous in varying degrees' – the famous total of 810. 'It is fitting to foresee these immense problems, as much to attest to the attention merited by the calculus of the measured series which will explain it, as it is to point out the pettiness of civilized theories'; Poster ed *Harmonian Man* 146 ff.

type among eight, corresponding, no doubt, to the eight affective, distributist, and 'unityist' passions.

One suspects that if someone could have shown Fourier that his number – characteristic correspondences were wrong, he might have given up his whole enterprise. The merely real is insufficient for him, despite all he says about taking man as he is. The factual world requires to be underwritten by something else he recognizes as truth. The meaning of the historical world has finally to be guaranteed or confirmed by something equivalent to the world of the Forms. This, in conjunction with the cycle apparatus and his faith in the exemplary power of the phalanstery, marks Fourier's debt to classical utopianism.

CONCLUSION

Fourier is nevertheless a true progressive rather than a mere conflater of millennial and utopian themes. Though the Pythagorean correspondences are important to him, it is finally historical development which is primary – along with the dialectical psychology which drives it forward.[20] Despite the merely economic and distributive use that his immediate disciples made of his work, his long-term significance is in the linkage he established between the individual, the natural order of work and play in community, and the movement of world history. For the first time it became possible to think of founding rational, socialist communities, rather than religious, retreatist communities or high-minded communities of philosophers unable to find anyone to shift the manure.[21] Fourier had shown that

20 Niemeyer *Between Nothingness and Paradise* (Baton Rouge, La, 1971) contains a stimulating discussion of Fourier, 59–73, but assimilates his ideas too firmly to an older mechanistic view of nature.

21 Few of the 'utopian communities' which followed added anything to the stock of progressivist ideas. They usually failed for quite mundane reasons. The chief surveys at the time, those of Noyes and Hinds, were made by committed but clear-eyed communitarians; Charles Nordhoff's eye-witness accounts took him further afield than the others. See J.H. Noyes *History of American Socialism* first pub 1870 (repr New York 1966); W.A. Hinds *American Communities and Cooperative Colonies* first pub 1878 (repr New York 1961); and Charles Nordhoff *Communistic Societies in the United States* first pub 1875 (repr New York 1965). An unusually full bibliography on this period, with later, related experiments is contained in Rosabeth M. Kanter *Commitment and Community: Communes and Utopias in Sociological Perspective* (Cambridge, Mass, 1972). Divided mainly between religious and half-baked Fourierist groups, as the commentators, including Brisbane, agreed, the former communities were no longer growing by the 1870s and the latter had extremely short lives. North Americans were learning the languages of science, of world culture, and of nationalism. The communes no longer spoke to the needs of an urbanizing, newly industrialized society. And Marxism did not take early root in the English-speaking world. For an example of comprehensive, national progressivism cast in the utopian literary mode, we must turn to Edward Bellamy.

every man had his creative role to play in moving the world toward harmony. This linkage also assured the individual that, by identifying himself with the future, he was freed from the claims of the present. Fourier warned, however, that unaided self-liberation was a delusion; it could only be accomplished with an adequate number of others. And even then, the full articulation of harmony must wait on the work of time. But the individual, armed now with a set of historical tools, could begin to build with confidence, for he was the agent of history.

28

Bellamy: corporate solidarity and organic change

Edward Bellamy's *Looking Backward, 2000–1887* (Boston 1888) was perhaps the most studied and most copied book of the nineteenth century.[1] This was true despite the fact that the United States, formed as a political unit rather than as a culture or an economy, would seem to have offered little scope for the anti-politics of Saint-Simon or Fourier. But the experimentalist tradition endured and, particularly on the frontier, provided ample opportunity for all sorts of communitarianism, so long as it did not challenge the political order of the American commonwealth. The Mormons learned this lesson at very heavy cost before they moved to the desert.

The Civil War altered this civic foundation. A great act of centralizing power destroyed not only the ideological Southern rebellion but also the basis of New England and Western particularism. The central apparatus of government did not simply inherit the authority of these regional polities; it could not even hold its own war-augmented power. The war effort had required the rationalization of production, the creation of a new economic infrastructure, and the rise of a new entrepreneurial class. These realities remained and now dominated the polity at all levels. Plutocrats sent themselves or their agents to the Senate to replace the fabled statesmen of earlier generations.

The strains created by these circumstances opened the way for a reconsideration of the anti-political or supra-political doctrines of the earlier French social reformers. Bellamy can be regarded as paying his dues to both Saint Simon and Fourier. He is an economist and concerned with the largest scale, but he expresses the mid-Victorian sensibility. His people are not mere exhibitions of factors; they are individuals whose sensibilities must be served in any worthy society. The

---

1 See the comments of E. Fromm in his foreword, v–vi, to the reprinted edition of *Looking Backward, 2000–1887* (New York 1960). I quote below from this edition.

present society is unable to do this. But Bellamy finds the way to indict the society of 1887 while, at the same time, avoiding a lengthy arraignment or analysis of it.

THE 'GREAT CHANGE'

Making use of the device begun by Mercier, Bellamy has the future disclose salvation to the present. Mercier's 2440, however, had not been integrally related to the present; it stood over the present as a critique, of the classical utopian sort. But Bellamy's new society lies only 113 years in the future, and his work shows how the perfected society of the future grows integrally out of the unreconstructed present. The convention of a substantial amount of time – in Mercier's case, more than 600 years – provided both a break between the bad and the good and gave time for natural progress somehow to bring about the necessary institutional and character changes. Mercier placed his society ahead in time, by a kind of instinct perhaps, responding to a notion of progress that had not yet achieved clarity in 1770.

But by 1880, the notion of near-automatic progress had become almost axiomatic. Bellamy does not need a great length of time. Like his predecessors from Daniel to Fourier, he knows that he stands at the end of the penultimate period: the 'great change' (110)[2] is both imminent and inevitable.

The change is the greatest event ever to take place. As in the work of other progressives, it is the transition from necessity to freedom. In this case, the imminence of the change is hidden under the weight of the most striking phenomena of the old Boston: ungoverned industrialization, the near-absence of social services, contempt for the unsuccessful, the prominence of the new 'robber barons,' unparalleled public corruption, the sudden swelling of urban concentrations, the presence of hordes of immigrants. Though society is innocent yet of mass marketing, unions, and a succession of wars, there is exuberance, waste, energy, and corruption. Out of this, through the great change, arises the Boston seen by Bellamy's protagonist as he wakes from hypnotic slumber 113 years later – a Boston but one part of a new world-wide system utterly different from that of 1887.

THE AGE OF INDUSTRY

Bellamy is very much the heir of Saint-Simon in concentrating upon the city, the industrial system, and the world as a whole. After Bellamy, this new focus

---

2 See also 31, where his individualistic, bourgeois contemporaries are made to regard indefinite linear progress as 'a chimera of the imagination, with no analogue in nature.'

remains. Previous North American utopian, experimentalist, and progressivist thought had characteristically been rural in orientation.[3] Few of its constructions could have been transferred into cities. The isolation of the rural commune is a function of the classic utopian's faith in the power of successful example. The experimentalists were not complete rationalists, content with literary ventures; they were convinced, rather, of the persuasive power of good works. It was through success that the principles of utopia would recommend themselves to men in the wider world. Bellamy ended this rural idyll and emphasis on example with *Looking Backward*. He writes to persuade, but his means are not exotic principles or closet experiments. He writes directly to the whole society with a message of an imminent change that must overtake it.

It is upon the industrial system itself that Bellamy concentrates. This system is not the enemy, to be replaced by rural co-operatives. And it is not to be altered by reform of one component, as the monetary theorists were suggesting. Bellamy advocates neither a drawing back nor an adjustment of one or more parts before allowing industrialized society to move forward. He asks instead for the logic of industrialism to be allowed full course; it needs acceleration. His protagonist reports of the world of 1887: 'We felt that society was dragging anchor ... Whither it would drift nobody could say, but all feared the rocks.' His mentor in 2000 replies that 'The set of the current was perfectly perceptible if you had but taken pains to observe it, and it was not toward the rocks, but toward a deeper channel' (50). This channel is the pursuit of industrialism to its logical conclusion. Hidden in the problem is its solution: unhindered concentration of capital.

Soon after the turn of the twentieth century, we are told, 'the evolution was completed by the final consolidation of the entire capital of the nation' (53). At this point, between clauses, Bellamy somehow contrives the transformation of oligopoly into state capitalism. 'A single syndicate, representing the people' now holds title to the wealth of the nation. It is 'the sole employer, the final monopoly.' This strategem allows Bellamy to condemn ordinary capitalism as vigorously as any socialist: 'The obvious fact was perceived that no business is so essentially the public's business as the industry and commerce on which the people's livelihood depends, and that to entrust it to private persons to be managed for private profit is a folly similar in kind, though vastly greater in magnitude, to that of surrendering the function of political government to kings and nobles to be conducted for their personal glorification' (54).

---

3 With the exception of the Brooklyn outpost of the Oneida community under J.H. Noyes, American communal experiments were rural. Noyes blames this emphasis on the influence of Fourier and on the experimentalists' fixation on the European version of phalansteries; *History of American Socialisms* first pub 1878 (repr New York 1965) 266. See also his comments, 18–20, 594.

Throughout the description of the change, the verbs are characteristically passive, as in the passage above: it 'was completed,' it 'was perceived.' Thus Bellamy avoids the problems of having to identify just who initiated the changes; and the indefiniteness of reference also obscures any centres of resistance to the great change. The process is made to look inevitable. Once through this difficulty, Bellamy launches into his description of how the future works.

A DEVELOPMENTAL 'LOGIC'

Logic, system, and a kind of distributive rationalism pervade *Looking Backward*. Arrangement and creation of economical effects by organizational deployment are shown on every page to the entranced immigrant from 1887. In Julian West's nightmare vision of the *old* Boston, he sees a military parade: 'It was the first sight in that dreary day which had inspired me with any other emotion than wondering pity and amazement. Here at last were order and reason, an exhibition of what intelligent cooperation can accomplish' (212). Intelligent co-operation does not necessarily stand as a synonym for order and reason, even though the rhetoric of co-operation and the vocabulary of Victorian sentiment are constantly employed in the volume.

In many places, Bellamy spells out his attachment to a developmental logic. The opening sentence of the work speaks of 'a social order at once so simple and logical that it seems but the triumph of common sense' (xxi). The 'labour question' turns out to have been no riddle at all: 'It may be said to have solved itself. The solution came as the result of a process of industrial evolution which could not have terminated otherwise' (49).[4] Later, West is told that 'Our system depends in no particular on legislation, but is ... the logical outcome of the operations of human nature under rational conditions' (89).

The following of this logic has a foreordained character to it: the word destiny recurs throughout the work. Bellamy clearly intends more than a Platonic Form hovering over the earth; it is an embodied logic, the logic of productive industry, powered by capital. By capital he means more than money, plant, and inventory. Like Ricardo, he sees accumulated labour as capital; in Bellamy's terms, the ability to command and mobilize this labour-capital is itself a kind of capital. This concept is crucial to what he means by the concentration of capital. The 'labour question' disappears because labour is now treated as capital; it is now mobilized just as money is mobilized in the Wall Street of 1877. This process began in labouring men's blind reaction to the concentration of money capital. It is simply carried through logically in the new society in an organic fashion.

4 See also 57 ff.

Bellamy had had the advantage of working after a generation of debate on the application of evolutionary thought to the social system. Rejecting the rigours of Spencer and Sumner, he yet opted for an organic model. It is humanity which is concentrating itself, is evolving toward social 'solidarity.' Julian West's personal crisis, in *Looking Backward*, follows his hearing of a sermon contrasting the old with the new. He recognizes himself as the anachronistic representative of an inferior form of life, a superseded species. The preface to West's narrative uses the vocabulary of transformation, development, destiny, improvement – onward and upward.

Bellamy's reply to a critic of the book is itself organic in argument. He protests that the book is intended as a serious forecast, 'in accordance with the principles of evolution, of the next stage in the industrial and social development of humanity' (220). Each act of solidarity since the race began has been pushing us 'toward an ultimate realization of a form of society' (221). The sermon that so disturbs West informs him that 'the betterment of mankind from generation to generation' is the animating idea of society. 'We believe the race for the first time to have entered upon the realization of God's ideal of it and each generation must now be a step upward ... Humanity has burst the chrysalis' (194).

The imagery is beguiling, but too much is attempted here. The argument sounds evolutionary. But Darwinian evolution provides no place for 'the race for the first time to have entered upon the realization of God's ideal of it.' No stage is of higher value than any other, and no pattern or 'ideal' presides over the process. The chrysalis image is another, but necessary, intrusion. It suggests a fixed cycle and an entelechy within it, upon which we may rely.

RECTILINEAR PROGRESS

How does Bellamy derive rectilinear progress out of all this? The doctrine is no better grounded here than in any other enunciation of it. The chrysalis image has nothing logical to do with progress. The closed cycle even militates against it. But the inevitability of the change (and our belief that a butterfly is somehow 'better' than a chrysalis) are necessary for Bellamy to buttress an otherwise ill-supported pronouncement. The vague framing reference to Darwinian evolution must be in our minds before the chrysalis image can even seem to contribute to his notion of progress. And he will accept only some aspects of evolutionary thought, rejecting the Social Darwinist proposition that attempts to mitigate competition only frustrate nature's attempts to breed for social strength. This rejection denies his notion of progress the benefit of the automatic push from below contained in the Social Darwinist version of progress. The three conceptions of rectilinear progress, organic evolution, and organic cycle, on inspection, do not hold together except by the sort of rhetorical blurring at which Bellamy is so adept.

But Bellamy is led to this curious pass by his conception – unargued in *Looking Backward* – that a nation is really a single entity in process of realizing itself. It is organic, with a unity far more fundamental than any of its perceived divisions. We shall not realize at all who we are until we realize our unity as a people. The statism of *Looking Backward* is simply our social self, our best self ruling over our particular selves; it is our true self – the butterfly after the chrysalis. Like that change, the social transformation will come in the millennial manner: soon, decisively, and suddenly: 'On no other stage are the scenes shifted with a swiftness so like magic as on the stage of history when once the hour strikes' (221). 'The dawn of the new era is already at hand, and ... the full day will swiftly follow' (220). With these images the analogy of the butterfly is left behind. We are in the language of normal nineteenth-century rectilinear progressivism. Like orthodox millennialists, we do not look toward a repetition or a restoration of Eden: 'The Golden Age lies before us and not behind us, and is not far away. Our children will surely see it' (222).[5]

Nevertheless, the notion of system finally immobilizes Bellamy's vision of an open history ('ever onward and upward') propounded in the preface, in which the next millennium is required for the full development of the leap forward. Despite all that, the book itself gives few clues to any change that may be possible in the system of the year 2000. Its institutional framework is meant to be perfect; it answers all the questions that West and his mentor can put to it. Indeed, no really hard questions can be put to it, because it is good and perfect. Besides, it is inevitable.

---

5 These last three references, it must be emphasized, are Bellamy's response to criticism of the book; they are his own voice, in 1888.

PART FIVE

Progress and will

29

The paradox of progress

The difficulties of the progress tradition are fully visible in Bellamy. But neither the persuasive wealth of detail, the ingeniousness of his devices,[1] nor the serious attempt to balance individual freedom and equality against the needs of society can disguise the increasing difficulty of combining into intellectual coherence the notions of millennialism and those of utopia. Problems which can perhaps be concealed in a small-scale communal experiment become apparent when one attempts to persuade a whole society to co-operate with the inevitable and to assure that society that the inevitable will be democratic, egalitarian, personally fulfilling to every man, and tightly organized.

The need of a guarantor for progress drives progressivists toward some self-executing force characterized by a coercive logic: mathematics, capitalized Nature, physics, or the alleged laws of psychic types. But these guarantors lead us not to historical 'betterment' in rectilinear fashion but to the cycle or to a static perfection. If, however, one emphasizes linear development and the process aspect of linear history, one is led toward an acceptance of contingency and away from the notion of inevitability and guarantee. Guaranteed progress requires propulsion from some self-executing necessity, insulated from contingency. But necessity is ineluctably what it must be, no matter what the wishes of men in history. It must be insulated from 'mere' history in order for us to be able to rely on it as something not subject to the contingency that so constantly frustrates us. Yet that insulation deprives necessity, of whatever sort, of any need to guarantee delivery on what men in history want. *The doctrine that there is a blind force, uncontaminated by historical contingency, dedicated to the continued improvement of man is the central affirmation of the notion of progress.* I have no

---

1 Bellamy invents the radio (and the clock radio), the mail order catalogue, the credit card, Giro banking, and the covered shopping mall.

explanation for the persistence of this doctrine except the fact of its manifest convenience.

The offensiveness of this position is not primarily in its intellectual incoherence, but in the fact that so few people apparently perceive the incoherence or regard it as a problem. But the sheer convenience of the progress doctrine ought to give pause to critical minds. It is a curiosity that people who believe it inconsistent for a deity (if any) to care for particular men are often the same people who find it an unquestionable social truth that there is an immanent, automatic force in history that produces continued improvement in human history. Or devotees of intellectual freedom from all 'outworn tyrannies over the spirit of man' demand fealty to the doctrine of progress. One could regard these inconsistencies with detached amusement, save for the fact that this doctrine, with its central contradiction, has had the most serious social consequences.

The doctrine of progress has, of course, been criticized heavily. The events of the present century have seemed to many to be themselves a massive refutation of the progress notion. Yet it survives, and not only among the unreflective. Serious thinkers are by no means united in opposition to it; and it acquires new supporters, as we shall see. Even among its critics, however, little has arisen to take its place in the West as the ideology of liberal and social democratic politics and social theory. The same may be said for the revolutionary tradition, whether specifically Marxist or not, as the apparent competitor to liberal democracy. Perhaps in the very radical version of Frantz Fanon this may be the case. More often it is observable how dependent the revolutionary tradition is on liberal democracy – the latter serves as a point of departure and as a provider of goals for revolutionary action. Liberal democracy's problems are not markedly different in character from those of the revolutionary tradition, and the similarity in problems is deeply conditioned by the dependence of both traditions on the modern doctrine of progress.

The contradiction at the heart of the notion of progress, though seldom confronted openly, is in fact dealt with in both intellectual and public political life, resolved, as it may be, by appeals to the two notions of necessity and of human will.

This century's social experiments and intellectual fascinations have been dominantly not with freedom but with necessity, with totalitarianism and technology. Each may be said to have dominated a half of this century; each has been a means of carrying out the inner intention of progress; and each, as I shall try to show, has a direct relation to the idea of necessity. Even liberal democratic social development can be seen, under its garments of rhetoric, to be concerned with submission to necessity. Why necessity? Because, as I think appears in the representative progressives we have examined, necessity and system finally guarantee progress.

And in the end, if the events of this century convince men that the progress doctrine is defective, men must yet trust something. The transition from progress to necessity can be made all too smoothly.

The consciousness of human will as a problem is all but absent from the progressives we have thus far considered, despite the clear and well-articulated views on will in millennialism and utopianism. But there is a progressivist tradition in which will is central: the tradition of technological progress stemming from Bacon. Similarly, the notion of the general will in modern social theory has been influential in the attempted realizations of progress at the national level. Both necessity and will, then, come together in the twentieth century's dominant social movements – totalitarianism and technology.

How can the contradiction at the heart of progressivism be resolved by using the contradictory notions of necessity and of freedom founded on the human will? What are the real relations among progress, freedom, and necessity?

In the next chapters I will try to bring together technology and nationalism and deal with the notions of necessity and human will in light of the developed doctrine of progress. I shall first discuss the intention in progressivist programs for technology by discussing Bacon as the great exemplar of this tradition. Then I shall consider the problem of corporate human will in national communities, a central theme in liberal democratic society, but also in the revolutionary tradition; I think it can be shown that there is exhibited in both cases a culmination of progressivism which is at once the apex of human will and its abandonment. B.F. Skinner can then be seen as the disclosure of what is at stake in contemporary progressivist employment of technology.

30

Bacon and universal dominion

At the same time that Mede and others were opening the Apocalypse in order to disclose the historical destiny of mankind, Sir Francis Bacon was writing his *New Atlantis* (London 1627)[1] This fragmentary work, never finished, is commonly supposed to be about science; it is usually interpreted in light of *Advancement of Learning* and *Novum Organum*. This identification owes perhaps less to Bacon than to the contemporary confusion between science and technology. But if science is knowledge and technology is problem-solving by means of science, then Bacon's *New Atlantis* is the manifesto of the latter.

Science itself is of course a human activity, carried on for purposes originated by humans. But technology has a form distinct from that of science. It arises in that cast of mind which sees the world as made up of problems to be solved. What might otherwise be described as a condition or circumstance, becomes characterized as a *problem*. To define a condition as a problem invites a *solution*.

The problem-solution model is not drawn in any simple way from mathematics or from science, though its advocates often appear to suppose so. The model has been with us since ancient man wanted to keep warm and dry, to protect his village, or to shift heavy objects. But when the model is universalized and made central to what a society is for, and when science is thereby made subordinate to technology, we have something new.

Bacon universalizes the problem-solution model and makes science subordinate to technology. His message could neither be fully understood nor acted upon until this century. The rhetoric of science dominates *New Atlantis*, but the reality is that of technology. Bacon, writing at almost the same time as Campanella, does not face both ways like the Dominican. He is a modern man, prudent and

1 Citations here are from the modernized text in G. Negley and J.M. Patrick ed *The Quest for Utopia* first pub New York 1952 (Garden City, NY, 1962) 353–72.

controlled, not to be caught out in any of Campanella's quixotic ventures. Bacon will get ahead; and his concern is that all men shall be able to do the same.[2]

Bacon's utopia is not concerned to define the good man, to build the good society or to define the harmonious development of human nature. Neither harmony nor perfection appears to interest the author of this utopia. But it is a grand project, quite as much as any venture of Plato, More, or the progressives.

The central focus of the new Atlantis is 'Salomon's House.'[3] This foundation or guild is the reason for the existence of the new Atlantis. After the customary recounting of the history of the kingdom, the visitor is given a solemn disclosure of the purpose of Salomon's house: 'The end of our foundation is the knowledge of causes and secret motions of things, and the enlarging of the bounds of human empire, to the effecting of all things possible' (364). Here science and technology are conflated, just as often happens in the twentieth century. Here man's differentness from Nature is transmuted into man's *domination* of Nature. And here – against previous and most subsequent utopians – empire is argued for. The role of man is now to subject, control, shape, and dominate wherever possible. Whatever can be done should be done.

Bacon's identification of science and technology would not have been made in ancient times. Then *techne* was seen as falling within the realm of necessity. Skill, art, and craft are things we must do in order to survive. There is nothing distinctively human in *techne*, which is the tribute we pay to necessity so that we can then go on to do the distinctively human enterprises: science, politics, philosophy. In *Republic*, *techne* is characteristic of the appetitive classes, who are what they are precisely because they do not seek fulfilment beyond *techne*.

Bacon seems not to understand this distinction between *techne* and science. *New Atlantis* offers only two meagre lines about what we would term science: 'We also have a mathematical house, where are represented all instruments, as well of geometry as astronomy, exquisitely made' (370). As a whole, the document identifies, and delights to identify, the human with the exercise of *techne*. The description of the technological program is detailed and even loving, cast in an elevated or liturgical style. *Techne* is an expression – the principal expression – of what it is to be human.

We may contrast Bacon in another way with the Mesopotamian and Greek ancients; men sought knowledge of human nature or of the harmonies of the

2 Bacon's biographers ignored, explained away, or excused his place-seeking, his treachery in office, and his corruption as Lord Chancellor. Even so staunch an advocate of progress as Lord Macaulay, who also admired Bacon's scholarly labours, was incensed by this oversight. See his essay, 'Lord Bacon,' in *Critical and Historical Essays* II (London 1888) 280–429.
3 'Which house or college ... is the very eye of this kingdom'; Negley and Patrick ed *Quest* 355

cosmos in order to know their place, play their roles, in the orderly arrangements of the cosmos, of which both gods and men are parts. Man makes his place in the cosmos; he distinguishes himself from the merely natural, but he remains securely in Nature, which is not dead or inert. The Hebrew notion of the created cosmos makes possible a conception of Nature as 'there' to be exploited. But it is man's conception of God as a dominator, a competitive dominator, which leads to his Fall in Genesis. The serpent's suggestion that God is jealously or fearfully hampering man's full self-development leads to the awful moment in which the man and the woman look at each other and, for the first time, see each other as competitors for dominion.

Bacon's theme is the natural cosmos as a completely human project. Despite his commendation of orthodox religion (355 ff), religion, as previously conceived, plays no determinative role in his work. The cosmos is raw material for a human project of empire and dominion. Domination of man by man is of no interest here. The field of conquest is Nature. And it is a matter of *conquest*, which is why science is of so little help or concern to him. Science is content to know; the results of such knowing could mean our living in harmonious relations with Nature, acknowledging appropriate limits and bounds.

But for Bacon, Nature exists to be exploited. Implicit is a definition of man as exploiter and dominator. The people of the new Atlantis are said to be good and wise. But we are given no reason to believe this, no picture of human nature that would show us why they are good. And when Bacon must leave off describing Salomon's house and go on to describe the rest of his utopian society, he cannot do it; the narrative breaks off, and it was never resumed. Salomon's house exhausts the purposes of the project. The purpose of human life is to dominate more and more of Nature and to enlist it in the service of human ends. But there are given to us no human ends except that of domination.

Bacon's is a remarkable conclusion from the viewpoint of the previous Western tradition. That tradition gave us, variously, man the child of God, man the knower, man the imprisoned soul seeking release to his home in the higher realm, man who lives on the border of nature and values and knows the anguish and ambiguity of this situation. Even the sophists, who suggested that man is the measure of all things, had some picture of what they meant by 'man,' some determinate content: man the seeker of bodily pleasures, man the dominator of other men, man who out of fear is willing to be led by others. But the sophists did not seriously put forward the notion of man the effector of all things possible.

Where does Bacon's dream come from? It is true that he writes when 'Renaissance optimism' is long since dead. And the great promises of the Reformation and Counter-Reformation have issued in the savagery of the Thirty Years' War, in progress while Bacon writes. The older sources of authority and thus of definition are not determinative for him. It seems natural to see Bacon as shaped by the achievements of early modern science, technology, and exploration. But this context does not go far to explain the peculiar accent of *New Atlantis*.

When Galileo writes to Kepler, he complains that his opponents will not even trouble to look through his lenses and convince themselves: 'What will you say to the noted philosophers of our University who, despite repeated invitations, still refuse to take a look at either the moon or the telescope and so close their eyes to the truth? This type of people regard philosophy as a *book* like *Aeneid* or *Oddysey*, and believe that truth will be discovered, as they themselves assert, through the comparison of texts rather than through the study of the world and nature.'[4]

Galileo, like Bacon, has no confidence in older modes of establishing truth, and his attitude toward the traditional methods closely parallels that of Bacon. But Galileo does believe, with his opponents, that *what is at stake is truth*. For Bacon there has been a shift away from the natural scientists's concern; for him it is now not truth that is at stake but power.

Yet Bacon's is a strange sort of power – not power over other men, or power in the sense of achieving some definite program. Bacon cannot give it a name; it is power 'to the effecting of all things possible.' And man can only be defined in terms of this project; he only feels fully human, it is suggested, when he knows he can bring about 'all things possible.' But if this is the case, when indeed will man ever feel like man? Bacon has set him on an unending quest and has ensured that man will feel threatened, less than human, oppressed, so long as any aspect of the cosmos remains undominated. But what is man threatened by? Bacon has managed to define man as threatened by his own finitude.

In science we continually discover new limitations to human capacity[5] and human knowledge. These limitations have a positive role to play in delineating the shape of what we do know. They are an accepted part of the state of knowledge; they are not experienced as a reproach. But in *New Atlantis* this acceptance is precluded in principle by Bacon's effective collapse of science into technology, and especially into a technology put to the service of an impossible dream. Now all limitation has to be experienced as reproach. And to the degree that men accept Bacon's statements about what is at stake in human existence, they will perhaps be led to the peculiar insistence and imperialism of modern

---

4 Quoted in H. Reichenbach *From Copernicus to Einstein* (New York 1942) 20

5 What Galileo was doing in kinetic science, and what his successors are doing in many other fields, run against the grain of common sense. In general, sense data have not governed science, but proved to be problems for it.

technology, including alteration of the genetic base of mankind. Nothing in Bacon's definitions in *New Atlantis* would cause us to draw back from such a step. Indeed, failure to press on might lead us to conclude that we are in part defined by our limitations, or that there are such things as truth apart from the feasible, or that there might be meaning or direction to human life apart from the extension of human empire. To the degree that these conclusions are resisted, and Bacon's program accepted, the peculiarly compulsive, driven character of modern technology is not likely to be moderated or curbed.

The new Atlantis is given to us in the form of a utopia, but a truncated and deceptive one. For as soon as Bacon has uttered his project, he loses interest. He has finished what he set out to do; he has embarked on an enterprise which can only be understood by reference to millennialism. The character of human history is determined, from that perspective, by God's historical labour to overcome the effects of the Fall and to redeem man. The millennium and what follows constitute the state in which history has been not annulled, overcome, or even recapitulated but fulfilled and the fall of man overcome. In the Fall, the serpent promises that man, knowing all, will have all power. God has here been defined as power. And for Bacon, man, like God, will be without limit or hindrance. Bacon's millennial dream is the attempt to harness the cosmos itself in order to try to make come true what the serpent promised.

31

The general will

In the classical origins of utopianism, will was treated as an element to be controlled by the exercise of a directing or encompassing reason. It is clearly distinguished from reason (even though reason has its own erotic drive toward the realm of the Forms). This view of will was reinforced by the medieval traditions of substantialist reason and by the early triumphs of mathematical and astronomical science. Apart from More and from Bacon, the utopian tradition finds it sufficient to describe right order. Reason will lead men to adopt its provisions.

Only with Mercier do we find a reinstatement of will, and Mercier is a progressivist. Here the indignation of the *philosophe* generation against the past leads to the erasure of the past and to a coercive reshaping of man, a project of self-affirmation. It is the presence of secularized millennialist motifs, in progressivism, which reintroduces the will. But because this secularization has made immanent the divine will, the human will can no longer be handled critically, as was at least possible in the classical utopian tradition.[1]

1 Lewis Mumford in F. Manuel ed *Utopias and Utopian Thought* (Boston 1967) 3–24, and in a subsequent series of articles collectively titled 'The Megamachine,' argues instead that utopia begins in the foundation of cities by sacral kings. These cities are not placed rationally, ie, strategically, but are placed arbitrarily, as acts of will. They are the first displays of planned technological will. The technology is the 'invisible machine' – the organization of man for gigantic tasks determined by will. Christendom made no such foundations; it was otherworldly. Modern science in the service of absolutist kings reactivated the megamachine. The later utopias are machine-like and focused on means, not ends. In the real world, the megamachine culminates in the United States and its use of nuclear weapons. Thus the inability to feel consequences, the concentration on quick solutions, the fascination with size and power, the desire to conquer nature and change man himself.

   The virtues of this conception are many, but its flaws overwhelm it, I think.

   (1) It neglects the great commercial foundations of ancient times, and the Hellenistic foundations do not conform to his model.

We can see this inability to handle human will critically in the eighteenth-century concept of the general will. Already, late in the reign of Louis XIV, Fénelon had commented on a growing divergence between the royal aims and those of *la nation*.[2] The republican sentiment of the eighteenth century was not in program anti-monarchical, but was a search for a new basis for political authority. Turgot, in office, proposed a 'council of national instruction' to foster and supervise patriotic values throughout the schools of France.[3] But the *philosophe* progressivists found that the rational imitation of Nature provided few reasons for men in real life to be willing to sacrifice themselves for *la patrie*.

Rousseau's *Social Contract* seeks a natural order that does justice to the whole man, his passional nature, his wholeness – to man in community. Harmony is now not so much harmony with reason but with other men. As is well known, the general will has nothing to do with our wills and interests as wheat farmers, mothers, or innkeepers. We do not, as in later democratic theory, or English theory, reach an acceptable compromise among these interests. True community is achieved when we come together and consciously transcend our particularities, when we forget our ages, stations, and occupations and, instead, will what is best for all of us. When this is done and is seen to have been done, we have the general will, which is our rightful sovereign, our personal and social harmony, the means of our fulfilment – our natural selves in dynamic, unitary form.

(2) Utopianism is a Western phenomenon, and sacral cities are not.

(3) In utopianism, will is seen as a danger; and when foundation of cities is discussed, in *Republic* and in *Laws*, it is not arbitrary will which is at issue but the discovery of true order; there is no sense of *fiat*. In later utopias, though the model of Tudor, Capetian, and Italian autocrats is available to More and Campanella, their utopian founders seek natural justice or the cosmic order.

(4) Utopia is not concerned with cities. The *polis* is not a megamachine. More's cities are towns, and agriculture is the main focus of life. The City of the Sun is the only conspicuous exception.

(5) Mumford's identification of the significance of Bacon obscures for him that utopian writers prior to progressivism did not handle science as Bacon did.

(6) Mumford does not account for the disenchantment of utopians with absolute monarchs which is so visible in the advent of progressivism.

(7) Mumford does not relate the problem of arbitrary will to Christianity. Christendom interrupts his schema, which is resumed after the lapse of Christendom. I have tried to show that the human story is more cumulative than that, and that the rise of modern technological will must owe something to the influence of Christian categories. His technological imperative is too patterned to allow for Christian categories as a modification. This results in too simple an equation of modern liberal nationalism with sacral absolutism. Liberal nationalism has to do with Christendom and its values at least as much as with sacral absolutism.

2 See H. Kohn *The Idea of Nationalism* (New York 1944) 204–8, 220 ff; also Venturi *Utopia and Reform in the Enlightenment* (Cambridge 1971).

3 Kohn *The Idea of Nationalism* 222

The general will is the willed overriding, by ourselves, of our particular wills; it is not the abandonment of willing, the discovering of majorities, or even an arithmetical unanimity, which could be the result of common passion or common corruption. It only arises when each of us rises above these things and considers what measures are best for all of us. Class, locality, particular interest only corrupt the process of achieving the general will. Both its creation and its effect, if they are to be sovereign, must be unmediated. No one can represent us; the achievement of the general will is literally im-mediate. Society is now redefined: not given, but created. And this creation is the product of a purified will.

The revolutionary character of the general will can be seen when we contrast it with the notion of the 'unseen hand,' a conception of the English political economists which also is a considerable departure from earlier theory. The unseen hand harmonizes the competition of particular wills and interests. Its position 'above' the push and shove of daily life does not make it transcendent, however; it is immanent and unconscious. If it were conscious, it would cease to be automatic, which is its most valued characteristic from the viewpoint of both economics and morals. The revolutionary character of Rousseau's conception is that the general will is human and that it remains a conscious will. What that will intends to will becomes the chief problem, because the general will is, by definition, cut off from an identification with actual interests and institutions.

J. Talmon has shown how the Committee of Public Safety genuinely sought the general will in the period of France's greatest peril.[4] Despite all its efforts to exclude from these assemblies of patriots all those tainted with monarchism, foreign sympathies, and self-interest, the Committee found individual will, group will, but never the general will. The Terror was in part designed to create the conditions for the only thing that could really justify the Terror: the general will.

The interest of totalitarianism in the general will is well known. Each tradition proclaims it in different ways. Fascism is 'the expression of a universal ethical will.' Its power makes its will felt and affords 'practical proof of the universal character of the decisions necessary to its development.'[5] In Hitler's Aryan, 'the instinct of self-preservation has reached its noblest form, since he willingly subordinates his own ego to the life of the community and ... even sacrifices it.'[6]

Lenin, in his preparatory notes to *State and Revolution*, picks up Engels's proposal that communists should cease using the term state and replace it with *Gemeinwesen* as an equivalent to what the French meant by commune: an affec-

---

4 See his *Origins of Totalitarian Democracy* (London 1952).
5 B. Mussolini *Fascism: Doctrine and Institutions* from 1st English edn Rome 1935 (New York 1968) 12–13
6 A. Hitler *Mein Kampf* from 1st German edn Munich 1925 (New York 1943) 297

tive community which realizes itself and cannot be structured in a merely democratic sense. Indeed, 'democracy precludes freedom.' The dialectic leads us finally 'from proletarian democracy to none at all,' that is, into the condition of purified community will. 'Proletarian democracy is complete, universal, unlimited (quantity is being transformed into quality) ... It is not a special organ or special organs that will manage the affairs of state, but all its members.'[7]

It would be a mistake to let the Augustulan trappings of Mussolini, the German *Blut und Boden*, or Stalin's 'socialism in one country' obscure the universalism of western European totalitarianism[8] and its clear dependence on general will theory. The general will, after all, is, *ex hypothesi*, what we all most want and need when we are freed from all merely local, historical, class-based, temporary, or other *corrupting* influences. The general will arises within a given people, but becomes real as it is freed from locality, as it is universalized, as it immunizes itself against the ravages of time and other sources of corruption. A united will emerges, then, freed from conditions of time and space – no doubt a large task; and most modern agents of the general will have been appropriately cautious in their claims for realization of it. But they have moved with great energy against the agents of corruption. No punishment is too great for those who would keep the people from becoming the expression of the general will, or who would hold back the inauguration of true human history and true human nature.[9]

The distinctive elements in American nationalism have been brought within the range of the present discussion by Tuveson's *Redeemer Nation*. It offers powerful evidence for the formative influence of the motif of the holy community and of corporate messianic mission. Today's discussions of an American 'civil theology' relate this heritage to utterances such as John Kennedy's inaugural address and to the debates over the American role in Viet Nam.

---

7 V.I. Lenin *Marxism on the State: Preparatory Material for the Book The State and Revolution* written 1917, first pub 1970 (Moscow 1972) 24–5, 66–7. For the distinction between the new commune and former entities with that name, see 46. Cf *State and Revolution* 2nd rev edn (Moscow 1965) 75, 91 ff. The points in the notebook are often obscured in the completed work, published under very different circumstances from those of its initial composition.

8 In linking Marxism to Fascism and Nazism here I do not wish to blur over the important differences of Marxism from these other phenomena.

9 Hannah Arendt attributes the welter of competing jurisdictions in Nazi Germany, the non-enforcement of hundreds of laws, and the enforcement of hundreds of non-laws to a determination to let no objective standards exist which might circumscribe the work of will. She also notes that, in the war period, the campaign against the German 'unfit' was as severe as it was against any other European people, except Jews and gypsies. Even the nation itself must not hinder realization of the movement. Program itself becomes secondary to the will of the movement to realize itself, to will away the limitations of time and space. See her *Origins of Totalitarianism* (New York 1958) 398; also 320–4.

But the secularization of American life has also produced a congruence between the unique elements of American nationalism and the traditions of social democracy. The antipathy of this outlook to both totalitarianism and to the older millennialism only obscures its dependence on the tradition of the general will and on a more general progressivism. Thus a brief discussion of liberalism speaks of impulses that are important in all Western nations.

To connect both totalitarianism and the liberal tradition to the general will is not to equate the two or to suggest, with visceral conservatives, that liberalism is a step on the slippery incline to totalitarianism. And it is not relevant that in emergencies democracies adopts a form of dictatorship. Rather the issue is the increasing tendency of democratic institutions to become totalistic in aim. I do not refer here to economic centralization under state auspices, which seems to me quite a separate matter. Such a program is quite compatible with deeply pluralistic cultural institutions.

Social institutions, however, show us this thrust toward comprehensive, inclusive, mandatory aspirations. In many nations state education must not only be preferred, but private schools must be eliminated. It is apparently believed that only in state schools can the correct attitudes toward democracy be inculcated. In many cases, democracy is equated with equality; and unequal achievement in the state schools is sometimes ignored, since by definition it cannot happen. Or deficiencies in achievement are attributed to corrupt, 'undemocratic' forces elsewhere in society.

For some it is intolerable that crime continues and expands since crime is held to be caused by socio-economic conditions being overcome in democracies. Hence *treatment* of criminals replaces the imposition of penalties. The goal of treatment is rehabilitation; but when rehabilitation fails as a mass prescription, the cry is for more funding – not for an examination of the premises upon which society has attempted to construct new democratic Man. The health-disease model can be extended to encompass more and more sorts of behaviour until it becomes central to liberal social theory. The basis of this Manichaean model is of course supposed to be scientifically validated, but in fact its programs and assumptions are uninspected.

That these programs are often pragmatic and manipulative, rather than being in the service of some genuinely determinate vision, should occasion no surprise. The more determinate the program, the more its proponents must face squarely the limitations of time and space and accord them some reality. A program aimed at maximum satisfaction or happiness in the abstract may find such limitations an affront to the status of its ends as supreme and self-evident. Hence the link between 'pragmatic' means-orientation, technology, and the general will.

32

Skinner's age beyond will

The picture, familiar from the American cinema, of the pious frontier farmers putting up a wooden church is false in many respects. The Christian denominations had to make strenuous efforts to Christianize the frontier in the face of a population often lawless, anarchic, and single-mindedly bent on exploitation. The new state universities that came in time to the Midwest and West were pragmatic in character and nearly always excluded religion from their curricula. And the religion that prospered in the West was one directed almost completely to individual emotional satisfaction and emphasized spiritual technique. B.F. Skinner grew up in this environment.[1] While it is too much to attribute the rise of behaviouralism solely to these factors, it is noteworthy that Skinner's *Walden Two*,[2] the most influential utopia of the century, draws together the Baconian vision and a concern with emotional satisfaction as the sole worthwhile goal for a society. To this end is directed the transformation of the total environment of man, and man himself.

Walden Two in form is an American 'utopian colony,' but one made to function, in Skinner's novel, on the basis of that school of experimental psychology called operant conditioning. For experimental psychology, the greatest power of that school lies in illuminating the capacities of pigeons and other animals to respond to certain stimuli or inducements and to modify their own behaviour in directions desired by the experimenter. Transferred to the human situation, Skinner's work relies on utilitarian formulae about happiness in order to provide a framework for purposive experimentation. The human being is defined as the

1 David Bakan, in an unpublished York University lecture of 1973
2 *Walden Two* first pub 1948 (New York 1962). Quotations below from *Walden Two* are from the 1962 edition. Discussion of this volume and of later works of Skinner is summarized and extended in H. Wheeler ed *Beyond the Punitive Society* (San Francisco 1973).

sum of his behavioural repertoire and it is assumed that satisfaction is the goal of the operations of this repertoire.[3]

Walden Two is the community contrived by Skinner's protagonist, Frazier. Along with offering some of the more practical features familiar to students of actual and literary utopian communities of earlier times, Skinner provides his people with a small body of non-elected Planners, who determine the course that experimentation will take. The people of Walden Two, unremarkably bourgeois in nearly all their pursuits, read almost no history (115). And the Planners do not accept much guidance from history,[4] for previous human history is largely irrelevant (209, 238 ff). History 'never sets up the experiments the right way' (92); it never allows controlled activity permitting us to draw valid conclusions (175).

But in Walden Two, self-manipulation at the initiative of experts is not merely aimed at producing happiness; it *is* happiness (161, 292). Experimentation, it emerges, is designed to prune away from the people of Walden Two all that proves, now or in the future, to be dysfunctional to happiness.[5] Similarly, other characteristics can be added as the need makes itself apparent.[6] Both of these activities are possible through the practice of positive reinforcement: rewarding behaviour that is desired, so that the subject himself desires to reproduce the desired behavioural item and does so (162). None of this method needs to be kept covert; it works better when done openly. That man is nothing more than the sum of his behaviour is demonstrated for Skinner by the success of operant conditioning and by the inability of other notions of human nature to explain scientifically what people do. These alternative conceptions have neither explanatory nor predictive power, while operant conditioning possesses both.

3 'Our conception of man is not taken from theology but from a scientific examination of man himself,' *Walden Two* 199 (one of the outstanding examples of question-begging to be found). More ruminatively: 'What is the "original nature of man"? I mean, what are the basic psychological characteristics of human behaviour – the inherited characteristics, if any, and the possibilities of modifying them and creating others? That's certainly an experimental question – for a science of behaviour to answer' (175).

4 'We discourage any sense of history' (ibid 235).

5 'When a particular emotion is no longer a useful part of a behavioural repertoire, we proceed to eliminate it' (ibid 103). Similarly, the library is adjusted: 'We subtract from our shelves as often as we add to them. The result is a collection that never misses fire' (121).

6 'What do you say to the design of personalities? Would that interest you? The control of temperament? Give me the specifications, and I'll give you the man! What do you say to the control of motivation, building the interests which will make men most productive and most successful?' (ibid 292). Most of this activity, it is important to note, is carried out by mutual manipulation, not by master controllers.

Walden Two has been continuously in print since its publication and has attracted a good deal of critical comment, not only on the 'Philistine vulgarity'[7] of *Walden Two* but on Skinner's handling of the problem of will. Some of this comment has been made up of Acton-style forebodings over the power of the Planners or of expostulations over the passivity of the inhabitants. But the Planners are prevented from going wrong by the experimental framework and by the goal of happiness. Things either work or are soon abandoned. And people know whether they are happy or not. This bedrock assumption of utilitarian democracy serves Skinner as well as it did Bentham or Mill. The Planners may err, but error's response corrects the Planners. If it does not, the very framework of their power vanishes as the community disintegrates (271).[8] And the subjects of the experiments are not all that passive, since they give to one another the approval and co-operation which constitute positive reinforcement. And if the results leave all members happy, there can be, from Skinner's viewpoint, no coherent objections (270); other definitions of human nature and the pursuit of other social goals leave people demonstrably unhappy.

Neither the objections nor their rebuttals locate the real problem of will accurately. Will is not centred in the Planners and is not lacking in the other members. Will in Walden Two is general: corporate and structural. *Our unfettered will permits us to experience the least possible discrepancy between what we are and what we shall will to be.* Skinner's process of operant conditioning, in a continuous experimental framework, so reduces any possible gap that people are not exposed to the risk of failure. The process, and Skinner's notion of the utter plasticity of human nature, allow the prospect of unlimited adaptation (290). We alone know what will make us happy in any given circumstances. And since happiness is the sovereign virtue, it follows that no one can govern the Walden Two people but themselves. Mutual operant conditioning provides the means for us to adapt smoothly, with the least discernible break, from adaptation-to-circum-

---

7 This unimprovably apt phrase is that of Frye in F. Manuel ed *Utopias and Utopian Thought* (Boston 1967) 32.

8 Skinner characterizes the work of despots and totalitarians as limited to negative reinforcement. And certainly these projects have been shattered, sooner or later, by the limitations of time and space. He castigates democracy for its particularism, its flaccid theorizing, and its unwillingness to experiment rigorously. But the particularist revolts of the past decade have often been against tendencies in democracies to become wedded to universalist goals seen as repressive of Jura mountaineers, Ulster republicans, Kurds, Filipino Muslims, Nagas, bourgeois groups, Scots, French-Canadians, Shans, and Karens, those on fixed incomes, and many other groups. Even the best established of the Skinnerite communities, Twin Oaks, has refused to concern itself with the 'hard,' systematic behavioural engineering (his own term) at the centre of Skinner's work. See K. Kincade *A Walden Two Experiment* (New York 1973).

stances A to adaptation B. Thus there is the least gap possible between desire and sense of fulfilment.[9]

It is important to note here the power of operant conditioning, in Skinner's view, to prune away useless or harmful capacities and abilities. We can will ourselves not only to be other than we have been, but also less (in the conventional view) than we were. But 'less' makes no sense in Skinner's airtight world of discourse: there will be no way for the group to know its new state as a diminution, since happiness will be undiminished – perhaps even enhanced. Will, in the influential Baconian tradition, is linked to expansion and domination. But it need not be. It may also be harnessed to, or issue in, a kind of nihilism. A non-hubristic nihilism is not incompatible with happiness. As we annihilate, in Walden Two, the last determinate structures of the supposed human nature, we may express the ultimate achievements of will and the ultimate happiness. As the last successful Planner renders himself obsolete because the last experiment has rendered conscious planning unnecessary, perhaps human consciousness itself will be replaced by automatic adaptive process. The last gap between desire and fulfilment has been plugged by the abolition of the distinction between self and world – a distinction that has heretofore circumscribed will and given it its pathos. We have triumphed over time and space.

9 'What we ask is that a man's work shall not tax his strength or threaten his happiness' (Walden Two 76).

33

The end of will

How do the Baconian project, the general will, and Skinner's apotheosis of adjustment come together? What are their relations, which end in the seeming paradox that the assertion of will passes over into the surrender of willing itself?

The Baconian project could only be carried on seriously by developed progressivism. One of the shortcomings of the hagiographical tradition of the origins of modern science is its lack of discrimination among very different things: experimental science, speculative or chalk-board science in the Newtonian tradition, rationalism, early progressivism, and the project of Bacon. Most of these fields of endeavour are irrelevant to realization of Bacon's project. And it could not develop until its proponents could command men, goods, funds, and energies on a national or continental scale. Those who could do this were the believers in the developed progressivism of the nineteenth century and, specifically, those whose sense of group will was formed on a scale large enough to encompass the necessary resources.

Historically, then, the first alliance was between Baconians and the enthusiasts of corporate will in the progress tradition. This alliance produced a program that advanced the project and pleased the utilitarian progressivists whose highest value was happiness: more and more of everything for everyone.[1] This program has

---

1 An evocative bit of documentation – one example of a distinctive sub-genre of the period – is a volume, produced in 1899 by about three dozen academics, journalists, and civil servants, under the editorship of J.P. Boyd, which bore the full title *Triumphs and Wonders of the 19th Century; the true mirror of a phenomenal era, a volume of original, entertaining and instructive historic and descriptive writings, showing the many and marvellous achievements which distinguish an hundred years of material, intellectual, social and moral progress, embracing as subjects all those which best type the genius, spirit and energy of the age, and serve to bring into brightest relief the grand march of improvement in the various domains of human activity* (Philadelphia 1899).

come under cogent attack – not only for its non-performance but for its very performance and for the costs associated with delivery.

Skinner quite rightly criticized the incoherence of this program, its lack of proper controls, and its neglect of those human factors which, as he could see after two world wars, sabotaged both dominion and happiness. With a very simple technology, and an even simpler understanding of it, Skinner proposed a new alliance between rigorous experimentalists and those imbued with the hedonic calculus as their public philosophy.

For all three elements, the will and any other determinate characteristics of the human person came into focus as a problem. For the tradition within which domination was seen as fulfilment, it became possible to see the will as a so-far-intractable bit of nature which must be conquered in order to achieve the Baconian victory. For Skinner, as we have seen, the presence of determinate structures in the human being is the principal cause of the occurrence of those painful gaps between self and happiness. These gaps must be eliminated. Mass adoption of Skinner's mode of procedure would also satisfy those for whom the doctrine of equality was supported by the thesis that willing together what we will constitutes fulfilment. For it is always the particular will which frustrates equality of this sort. We can now will the dissolution of that kind of willing.

Skinner's technology has, of course, now been refined, ramified, and placed at the disposal of very large numbers of people. His methods appear crude beside the prospects opened up by genetic manipulation, cloning, and similar wonders of microbiology and chemistry. It would be most unfair to blame Skinner for these. Many of the advocates of these new procedures display a significant coarsening of tone when compared to Skinner himself. He would perhaps identify the difference as the evident belief of some of them in negative reinforcement. But it is not at all apparent that the attack of the will on the will has altered between Skinner in 1948 and the genetic imperialists of the last quarter of the century.

What would the success of the Baconian project mean, when carried through to the willed conquest of the will as limit to domination? It would mean the universal dominion of system and the absence of man. Thus only would 'Nature' be conquered at last.

What would count as the success of the theory of the general will – especially if it appeared that 'Nature' persisted in offering obstacles? The purity of our willing together constitutes our true equality and brotherhood. It is obviously better for us to will purely, and thus to make real our unity, than it is for us merely to continue willing, knowing that we shall in time be corrupted and lose our brotherhood. The solution is perhaps a single corporate act of will that eliminates the possibility of future falling away. Suicide. Corporate suicide. Not restricted to the fantasies of a Hitler in his bunker, it is a real possibility with nuclear weapons.

What would constitute the success of Skinner's plan?[2] Too clearly, it would be a different sort of suicide: the attempted elimination of determinacy and particularity in human beings. Once again the result is the absence of humans and their replacement by the experimental environment and by its subjective correlate, universal adaptability. No will remains to frustrate the conquest of – or is it by? – Nature.

With the lapse or failure of naïve progressivism, these three hard, consistent versions remain in the field, often disguised in the rhetoric of more agreeable programs. But their success is to have willed nothingness finally to reign in place of existence.

---

2 I would include here many of his 'soft' detractors in existential psychiatry and its vulgarized off-shoot, the 'human potential' movement. Self-realization, self-manipulation, and mutual manipulation are scarcely a rebellion against the omnicompetence of technique or the banality of the happiness ethic.

PART SIX

Towards a critique of progress

34

Limit and perfection

Implicit in parts IV and V has been the view that the doctrine of progress has been at least as important in the shaping of Western man and his institutions as the works of the great political theorists. These philosophers perhaps assumed, as part of the reality they were analysing, the popular beliefs of millennialism, utopianism, and progress. I have argued that these popular forces were no mere background, static and pictorial, before which the great men have played their roles; and I suggest that anyone who ignores these forces leaves himself more open to their pervasive influence – on himself or on his readers – than he supposes. He also runs the risk of having little to say when the doctrine of progress issues in the extremities I have pictured.

I do not, however, want to assign degrees of relative importance to these popular systems and to the great men of political and social theory. I have tried instead to throw light on Western public philosophy from an unaccustomed direction. If the shadows cast are of different shapes from the ones we usually see, it is because the angle of illumination shows us something that was always 'there' but obscured by other sources of illumination.

This work is not finished until we allow utopianism and millennialism to direct such light as they can on the paradox of progress, as I have posed it above. Each offers its own distinctive illumination and, perhaps, offers some direction for public philosophy today. If men find it difficult to accept this illumination, they should reflect on their reasons. That utopianism – or the roots from which it springs – and that millennialism are very old and have been with us a long time does not make them irrelevant or obsolete. If an inspection of the doctrine of progress teaches us nothing else, it instructs us to be very wary of the notion of obsolescence. And if the messages of utopianism and millennialism seem unbelievable or lead to unacceptable conclusions, have other public philosophies served us better? Does the doleful result of the doctrine of progress seem more acceptable?

From Plato's *Republic* to the most plodding scheme, the utopian genre is dignified by its insistence on objective truth standing as a limit. Objective truth is simply there; it is not for any purpose outside itself; it is untouchable and unalterable; and man does not lose his humanity or his dignity when he acknowledges it – rather he finds these things in the glad recognition of a truth beyond considerations of utility, convenience, or advantage.

In utopianism, it is human will that tends to refuse to recognize the bounds thus set to human enterprise. Plato's Socrates and More's Raphael both reflect on the destructiveness of the human will and its tendency in both individuals and institutions to work out as self-destructiveness. Unless the *polis* can be so restructured that will can be subordinated and directed, the good *polis* will surely decline into the perversion outlined in books VIII and IX of *Republic*. Whether Plato's psychology of types is adequate or not, his diagnosis has relevance to societies which have not themselves curbed will. Rendering it immanent as world-process, as the progressivists have done, only makes the problem more acute. And the levelling of the older hierarchical psychology ('we are all equally reasonable') meant that will was almost ignored as a problem. But classical utopianism continues to assert that not all things can be changed by human endeavour. The realm of the Forms is our salvation, our true home as humans, precisely because it does not yield to the demands of human schemes.

In its hierarchy of realms and in the intractability of the higher realm, utopianism stands most sharply against millennialism. In millennialism all the cosmos is indeed material employed in a complex drama; nothing is safe or privileged; for Christians, 'the Incarnation' means that even God is changed. The progressivist use of this doctrine of mutability to serve the projects of human will is guarded against in utopianism by the rigid insistence on the hierarchy of the cosmos and on the immutability of truth. 'Truth' is a word little employed in apocalyptic. But, of course, the privileged utopian realm of value is secured at heavy cost, for finally it does not care whether men submit to its truth or not. If it is unresponsive to pride, so it is also deaf to human pleas. If some men do stand as devotees, it is only through them that the higher truth can be translated into institutional terms.

The democratization of reason first seen in More declared each man potentially a philosopher-king. But institutional rigidity and public hypocrisy are the results, in modern democracies, of believing that each man can see and act upon the political truth.

Utopianism nevertheless performs the valuable service of telling us, in its own way, that there are limits to what can be willed. The renewed interest in Eastern philosophies shows us some willingness to consider – with relief – that this might be so. In these new clothes the utopian message is reappropriated. But we need not search so far for this word.

The other way that utopianism is helpful in dealing with progressivism originates in the utopian concern for perfection. The word is one that progressivism also conjures with, of course; but progressivism's notion of perfection has become curiously unstable or fluid. In classical utopianism, the perfection sought is quite determinate; it is the perfection for which the person, object, or institution (or even the cosmos itself) was designed. Not open-ended, vague, or imperialistic, it is the perfection inherent in the design, requiring only to be realized. On this matter, of course, utopianism was nourished by the teleological argumentation of medieval theology. But in utopianism its influence extended well beyond the small circles interested in Aristotelian teleology after the era of the Reformation.

Limit and perfection belong together in this view. The classic idea of unfolding design in all bodies in the universe is not compatible with unplanned, unlimited expansion. Similarly limit appears quite arbitrary apart from the possibility of the perfection of each sort of thing in the cosmos. Separate limit and perfection, as progressivism does, and each becomes problematic. In the face of much pressure to do precisely this, utopianism kept them together; and it is not clear that this insistence has been superseded or shown to be false. A most serious problem was identified and an at least partial answer was perpetuated in the utopian tradition.

35

The alienated will

The millennialist tradition has consistently undermined the world-view contained in utopianism. Views derived from 'main-line' millennialism are clearly at work in the progressivist sundering of the bond between limit and perfection.

But 'main-line' millennialism itself contains its own strictures on the developments we have seen in progressivism. Like utopianism it did not create the basis of this critique; but just as utopianism took Plato's project with the greatest seriousness, so millennialism worked out with the greatest consistency the principal convictions of the exiled Hebrews on the historical nature of the cosmos. The theological developments of the fourth century and later within Christianity compromised these positions and made it almost impossible to work them out consistently. It is no accident that the most strongly millennialist theologians were least influenced by the substantialist metaphysic. Conversely, the 'main-line' millennialists conformed their own convictions most consistently to the convictions of the Exile and to the original message of the apostolic period.

The problem of the human will is addressed profoundly by the Genesis prologue (probably prepared in its present form in the Exile as a preface to the Pentateuch). One need not be a practising Jew or Christian to listen with respect to this document. It can illuminate for us a profound problem. One section of the Genesis prologue, part of the earlier J document, propounds the problem of the human will in a manner appropriate to the situation of modern progressivism.

Characteristically the J writer tells a story, as part of his primeval history. Later millennialism consistently harks back to this story, implicitly recognizing that here the problem of human existence is most powerfully set forth. Christian millennialism sets forth Jesus' death and resurrection and the end-time as the overcoming of this problem. J shares part of the prologue with the P writer, who must address himself to a weak people in exile or surrounded by late paganism. Accordingly P must reject use of motifs from ambient pagan myths. But

J writes early enough to be able to utilize, with more freedom, pagan creation myths and to turn them to his own purposes. He creates a new myth, a story of realities that can only be spoken of in story form. His myth is of original rightness and of the Fall. The 'naïve, anthropomorphic' details, which have distressed so many high-minded readers, are, as we shall see, anything but naïve. To do justice to the intent of J, and of those who made this story central to their own view of the human situation, we cannot abstract the story into propositions; we shall have to follow the story itself.[1]

In J (as in P) man is made good and made whole, the proper lord of the created world. He is not 'innocent' in the sense of being made incomplete or naïve. There is no suggestion – despite generations of commentaries to the contrary – that he was sexually immature or inexperienced. That notion arises from our response to the statement that ends J's creation narrative: that the man and the woman 'were naked and they were not ashamed,' a statement we in *fallen* society can only apply to the immature or the 'innocent.' J means precisely the opposite. He knows no more powerful image of fully employed powers without sin than to show us what cannot be true for us: they were naked and not ashamed. No other statement could so clearly mark them off from us. Will and act were united, in the sight of God, without contradiction. For us, no one can act out all the desires of a fully empowered mature person; to attempt to try is the mark of the madman or the anti-social monster.

In chapter 3, the woman is subtly tempted by the serpent, who is not Satan. The origin of the serpent, and of his challenge, is ignored in this story. And we are not to see a veiled reference here to sexual seduction, though such a reference may well have been in the materials from which J drew this element of his story. J is the least prissy of men and, had he meant this sort of reference, would not have been vague about it.[2] His theme is far larger. It is not the origin of evil that concerns him; and he has a far more profound view of the origin of sexual disorder, as we shall see.

The serpent's artful question drives a wedge between the woman and God, and it is this point which is the focus of this remarkable scene. For man starts this scene as lord of the created cosmos, as we see in chapter two, where man names all the animals as they are brought to him: to give a thing its name is to discern, declare, and fix its nature; and of course we see this same free lordship in the man's unconstrained relations with the woman. The notion that it is 'knowledge' that is at stake in this scene, and that the acquisition of freedom depends on this,

---

1 The following interpretation of the Genesis prologue has been influenced considerably by D. Bonhoeffer *Creation and Fall* (London 1959); A. Richardson *Genesis I-XI: Introduction and Commentary* (London 1953); and G. von Rad, particularly *Genesis* (London 1961, 1972).

2 See below, n 7. The references could be multiplied on this matter.

is an interpretation of the scene that is put by the serpent, as a means of masking from the woman what is really at issue.

The serpent's first question and the woman's answer constitute, as Bonhoeffer notes, the world's first religious discussion: talk about God, as distinguished from talk with him. 'Has God said you shall not eat of any tree of the garden?' The art here is that the woman is invited to defend the justice of God, who has, in fact, forbidden only one of the trees.[3] Any response she makes will be an objectification of God and of herself: a consideration of him and his actions from a perspective of her own; a separate *standpoint* is created by the fact of her speech *about* God. Her answer is, in fact, overly zealous on God's behalf, so anxious is she to correct the serpent. She quotes God as saying not only 'You shall not eat' but, in addition, 'neither shall you touch it.' She has completed the objectification she was invited to make; and she has felt competent, in a good cause, to embroider upon God's command, to interpret it.

The serpent now rushes into the wide gap so swiftly, if so innocently, disclosed between the woman and God. 'You will not die.' This lie, or contradiction of God, itself opens up a further objectification; it is now possible to consider God's command as a piece of information or as a claim contrasted with other data or claims. The serpent secures this bold gain by offering a reason why God should have lied: God knows that if you eat, your eyes will be opened. You will become like him, knowing everything.[4] The serpent's characteristic method is here repeated; one bold step is covered, attention is deflected away from it, by another. The step of balancing God's command off against competitors (and so making oneself a judge) is covered by the invitation to examine God's motives. And a motive is offered: God is declared to be concerned over competition. Knowledge and status are treated as scarce commodities: life is a game in which what one player has or wins is necessarily at the expense of the others.

The serpent now drops out of the scene; and we see the woman before the tree in question. We follow her reasoning: 'she saw that the tree was good for food, and

3 Westermann *Creation* (London 1974) 89–90 very properly notes that this 'restriction' is not a restriction but a condition of relationship with God and a condition of freedom. No reason is given for the command. 'Consequently it can only be listened to and obeyed, if he who commands is listened to and obeyed,' on the basis of confidence in the one who thus commands. 'The command therefore opens up the possibility of a relationship to him who commands. And this is the meaning of commands in the Bible. Something is entrusted to man in the command. The command introduces him to freedom.' The equation of restriction (via command) with un-freedom is made by the serpent, not by the context.

4 Here again, generations of learned commentators were drawn off into disquisitions on ethics, on the basis of the serpent's locution: 'knowing good and evil.' But this phrase, like 'the bitter and the sweet' and 'the right and the left,' is an established construction of inclusion; it means, simply, everything. This is borne out by the woman's reasoning before the tree.

that it was a delight to the eyes, and that the tree was to be desired to make one wise.' She has apparently accepted the logic of the supremely clever questions and the breathtaking assumptions of the serpent. But why, in this packed narrative, is there room for these subjective musings? Why does she not simply eat? Here the command, which because of its non-rational character created the possibility of trust, is opposed by reasons – or by rationalizations: utilitarian (good for food), aesthetic (a delight to the eyes), and metaphysical – from that concern with an autonomy so recently glimpsed and now being enacted by this very process of rationalization.[5]

'She took of its fruit and ate; and she also gave some to her husband, and he ate.' We are perhaps to understand that it was possible for her to have drawn back, if not to live as before, then as one chastened, in a more complex and perhaps closer relationship with God. But she eats, and draws her husband along.[6]

Here we arrive at the crux of the narrative. In what happens next, the reality is revealed of what has been at stake in the dialogue and in the woman's promptings to herself before the tree. One of the serpent's promises is fulfilled: 'Then the eyes of both were opened, and they knew that they were naked; and they sewed fig leaves together and made themselves aprons.' The full reality of their separation from God is not revealed directly, and cannot be. But its effects can be shown; by concentrating on its effects in the relationship of man to man, the gravity of this wider sundering can be illuminated. 'They knew that they were naked.' But they had always been naked – and not ashamed. Not-ashamed had had nothing to do with not-aware. The man described in Genesis 2 is neither a simpleton nor a new-born puppy; the one who there joyfully embraced his newly created counterpart is the same man who discerned the essence of the animal creatures and declared their names. The man and the woman have had the full employment of their natural powers; they did not wear clothes; they were not ashamed. But now they are, and the knowledge is intolerable; they cannot proceed further until they improvise coverings for themselves.

What has happened? 'Their eyes were opened.' To what? Not, as we have seen, to their nakedness as such. The serpent had promised that their eyes would be opened to the knowledge of everything. But what they are now conscious of

5 The final and most important rationalization is curiously, but aptly, put in an impersonal construction: the fruit 'was to be desired' to make 'one' wise.

6 Was he persuaded at greater length? It is not important to the narrative how he was involved. The essential matter has been concluded by the woman; given the solidarity of family in old Hebrew thought (see Joshua 7), he is implicated. The precedence of the woman is probably adventitious here, a survival from one of J's sources, a story of the origin of evil in which women were held specially to blame; cf the story of Pandora's box. Conclusions about the status of women should not be based on isolated texts such as this in Genesis 3.

knowing is the intolerability of their nakedness. Why is it suddenly so intolerable? What has happened? What has happened is that man – the man and the woman – has accepted the opportunity to treat God as an object and to consider his claims as options instead of their being his fulfilment and horizon. Man has conceived of knowing as being directly related to power, has learned to think of power as scarce, and has sought to place himself, through 'knowledge,' in an autonomous relation to God.

Given this conception, it has become intolerable that man should remain so vulnerable before God. Armed with knowledge of all things, man will no longer be at the disposal of another. He will be able to arrange the circumstances of his life to suit his own ends – effectively to become his own deity. But when he embarks concretely on this venture, when he eats, he sees something he did not expect to see. The man and the woman, co-eaters, co-conspirators, must now consider each other as competitors. Each, after all, has undertaken to grasp at scarce knowledge for the sake of autonomy and for the convenient arranging of life around his own pursuits. But all of this necessarily involves treating the other person as a competitor in the grasping at scarce power. Each must now look on the other as an item to be arranged; the other must be regarded as having this attitude toward oneself. Each is now exposed to being made secondary or instrumental in the eyes of another. In this profound sense each discovers his (new and just-created) nakedness before the other.

Yet the fullness of sexual attraction has not abated; the counterpartness has not been annulled. Each is bound to the other. Hence this sexual attraction is now the most profound of vulnerabilities. One must open oneself to the risk of the 'counterpart' using oneself for purposes not one's own, subordinating one to that other's purposes. This is an intolerable risk, an affront to one's new status as sole master of one's own cosmos – *yet a risk to which one is compelled to submit*. The contradiction is too great. Indeed, one's new feeling of insecurity might be taken as evidence that the new project of knowledge and power was a false or unrealizable project. In either case, nakedness now means what it could not have meant before. And it must be removed, covered. The newly grasped freedom is thus first exhibited by compulsive ritual; each must be covered from the other. Then both flee from the coming of God who, it is now conceived, must be coming to put down this threat to his dominion.[7]

This last touch simply underlines the real character of the motivations of the man and the woman throughout the narrative of Genesis 3. The pathos of

---

7 The economy with which all this is conveyed is not at all uncharacteristic of tenth-century Hebrew narrative. Cf the story of Amnon and Tamar, II Sam 13:1–15, a marvel of compression in which sex is treated naturalistically and with great insight into the sexual consequences of 'the Fall.'

their new condition is not further explored. It is the mixture of the new bondage and the old freedom that concerns the rest of the biblical books. The real freedom, nobility, and power of the man and the woman of chapter 2 are not taken away. It is the new project which deforms them, the uncancelled freedom which fuels the redirected human project. Man is not deposed and another put in his place; rather his lordship is now a deformed rule over himself as well as over the created world. And if his power seems to him to be diminished it is because he will now seek contradictory ends and expend his strength on both.

This theme is not pursued again in isolation in the Hebrew scriptures. The theme soon shifts to the slowly disclosed plan of God to overcome his fallenness within history and restore man to full relationship with God. The apocalyptic writers have stated clearly what has happened, in their view, to this human will at odds with itself. It has become alienated from individuals and requisitioned by great organized forces, ie the fourth beast in Daniel. In Revelation, when the partisans of the obedient Son – the second Adam, as Paul calls him – are hard pressed by the beast and the false lamb, it is the ordinary men of the world who recognize that the beast has usurped their own wills; it wills, and they cannot: 'Who is like the beast, and who can fight against it?' The book as a whole celebrates victory over such alienated forces; and thus in this limited but important fashion it cele-brates the possibility of recovering the full humanity of humankind.

36

Towards a critique

I have pursued the problem of the human will at length because it has seemed to me that only in relation to the will has the doctrine of progress developed in this century beyond the received pieties of the nineteenth. If the present century's development of the doctrine of progress is, from some perspectives, morally distasteful or if – perhaps worse – it shows signs of foundering on the congruence of self-assertion and nihilism, these problems are traceable to the inherent instability of the notion of progress itself.

There is no pleasure in this assertion; and I have no wish to end by labelling this or that 'ism' as the root of modern man's problems. We are all too deeply implicated in the problems of the present for any of us to take so simple a position. It is sad to record the flawed development of the doctrine of progress. We can see its issue in our own time in a reductionism in which success and nothingness are almost indistinguishable. The final achievement of the will to knowledge becomes the loss of both knowledge and will – a loss so complete that its advocates cannot even recognize it as such. Such an enterprise diminishes all men. This tendency, I repeat, is not one that can be bracketed as an aberration. It seems to me central to the doctrine of progress itself.

It is therefore useful for us to have attended to the rejoinders that can be made from utopianism and millennialism, the traditions out of which progressivism was made. 'Their' rejoinders, of course, were not created within those traditions. Rather they are convictions which are integral to those traditions and which have been conserved within them. Where they are conserved and treated seriously they can be recovered and re-presented with some freshness.

I do not suggest that, in order to avoid the ruinous conclusions of current progressivism, one need become a classical utopian or adopt the doctrines of millennialism. Their rejoinders may well be no more than that and may provide us with no more than starting points for a comprehensive critique of existing popular social theory. But the seriousness, richness, and longevity of these two traditions stand in some contrast to the banality, reductionism, and fleeting character of much that passes for social theory today. Millennialism and utopianism are worthy of a deeper inspection than they have often received. I have exposed them at length in the hope of making some contribution to the comprehensive tasks of social theory in our time. One need not be a millennialist to feel that the task is urgent and that the time may be short.

Works cited

Ackroyd, P.B. *Exile and Restoration* London 1968

– *Israel under Babylon and Persia* London 1970

Adams, R.M. jr, ed *Utopia, A New Translation, Backgrounds, Criticism* tr R.M. Adams jr, New York 1965

Albright, W.F. *The Archaeology of Palestine* rev edn, Harmondsworth 1960

Anderson, B.W. *The Living World of the Old Testament* 3rd edn, London 1967

Aquinas, St Thomas *St Thomas Aquinas: Theological Texts* selected, tr, and with notes and intro by T. Gilbey, London 1955

– *Summa contra gentiles* tr, with intro and notes, by A. Pegis, Garden City, NY, 1955

Arendt, H. *Origins of Totalitarianism* New York 1958

Barr, J. *Biblical Words for Time* 2nd rev edn, London 1969

Barrett, C.K. ed *The New Testament Background: Selected Documents* London 1956

Bartsch, H.W. ed *Kerygma and Myth: A Theological Debate* tr R.H. Fuller, 2 vol, London 1953–62

Bauer, W. *Orthodoxy and Heresy in the Earliest Church* from 1st German edn 1934, London 1972

Baynes, N.H. *The Political Ideas of St Augustine's 'De Civitate Dei'* first pub 1936; rev edn London 1968

Beecher, J. and R. Bienvenu ed *The Utopian Vision of Charles Fourier* Boston 1971

Bellamy, E. *Looking Backward, 2000–1887* first pub Boston 1888; with foreword by E. Fromm, New York 1960

Berington, S. *The Memoirs of Signor Gaudentio di Lucca* in G. Negley and J.M. Patrick ed *The Quest for Utopia* first pub New York 1952; Garden City, NY, 1962, 431–48

Bettenson, H. ed *Documents of the Christian Church* second edn, London 1967

Bloch-Laine, F. 'The Utility of Utopia for Reformers' in F. Manuel ed *Utopias and Utopian Thought* Boston 1967, 201–18

Bloomfield, M. and Reeves, M. 'The Penetration of Joachism into Northern Europe' *Speculum* XXIX (1954) 772–93

Bock, G. *Thomas Campanella: Politisches Interesse und Philosophische Spekulation* Tübingen 1974

Boman, T. *Hebrew Thought Compared with Greek* London 1960

Bonansea, B.M. *Thomas Campanella: Renaissance Pioneer of Modern Thought* Washington, DC, 1969

Bonhoeffer, D. *Creation and Fall* London 1959

Bossuet, J.B. *Discours sur l'histoire universelle* Paris 1681

Bouwsma, W. *Concordia Mundi: The Career and Thought of Guillaume Postel (1510–1581)* Cambridge 1957

Boyd, J.P. ed *Triumphs and Wonders of the 19th Century* Philadelphia 1899

Braaten, C. and R. Harrisville ed *Kerygma and History* Nashville, Tenn, 1962

Briggs, K. *The Last of the Astrologers* London 1974: Briggs's introduction and *Mr William Lilly's History of His Life and Times from the Year 1602 to 1681* (1715)

Bright, J. *History of Israel* Philadelphia 1959

Brinton, C. 'Utopia and Democracy' in F. Manuel ed *Utopias and Utopian Thought* Boston 1967, 50–68

Brisbane, A. ed *The Theory of Social Organization* New York 1876

Brøndsted, G. 'Two World Concepts – Two Languages' in H.W. Bartsch ed *Kerygma and Myth: A Theological Debate* tr R.H. Fuller, vol 2, London 1962, 216–305

Brown, R.E. 'The Paraclete in the Fourth Gospel' *New Testament Studies* ns XIII (1966) 113–32

Bultmann, R. 'New Testament and Mythology' in H.W. Bartsch ed *Kerygma and Myth: A Theological Debate* tr R.H. Fuller, vol 1, London 1953, 1–44

Burr, D. 'The Apocalyptic Element in Olivi's Critique of Aristotle' *Church History* XL (1971) 15–29

Bury, J.B. *The Idea of Progress* London 1920; rpt New York 1932

Campanella, T. *The City of the Sun* in G. Negley and J.M. Patrick ed *The Quest for Utopia* first pub New York 1952; Garden City, NY, 1962, 307–42

Capp, B.S. *The Fifth Monarchy Men: A Study in Seventeenth-Century English Millennialism* London 1972

Cassirer, E. *The Platonic Renaissance in England* first pub Leipzig 1932; tr J.P. Pettegrove, Austin, Texas, 1953; rpt New York 1970

Castiglione, B. *The Book of the Courtier* first pub 1514; tr C.S. Singleton, Garden City, NY, 1959

Charles, R.H. ed *Apocrypha and Pseudepigrapha of the Old Testament* first pub Oxford 1913; rpt 1963

– *The Book of Enoch* London 1917

Charlesworth, M.C. 'Some Observations on Ruler-Cult, Especially in Rome' *Harvard Theological Review* XXVIII (1935) 5–44

Coggins, R.J. *Samaritans and Jews: The Origins of Samaritanism Reconsidered* Oxford 1975

Cohn, N. *Europe's Inner Demons* London 1975

– *The Pursuit of the Millennium* London 1957

Coleman-Norton, P.R. *Roman State and Christian Church: A Collection of Legal Documents to A.D. 535* 3 vol, London 1966

Condorcet, M.J.A.N. Caritat, Marquis de *Esquisse d'un tableau historique des progres de l'esprit humain* first pub Paris 1795; ed. O.H. Prior first pub 1933; rev edn, Paris 1970

– *Outlines of an Historical View of the Progress of the Human Mind* trn from Paris original 1795, London 1795

Cragg, G.R. ed *The Cambridge Platonists* New York 1968

Cross, F.M. 'New Developments in the Study of Apocalyptic' in R. Funk ed *Apocalypticism* New York 1969, 157–65

Cullman, O. *Christ and Time* 2nd edn, London 1962

Daniel, E.R. 'A Re-examination of the Origins of Franciscan Joachitism' *Speculum* XLIII (1968) 671–6

Dentan, R.C. ed *The Idea of History in the Ancient Near East* New Haven 1955

Desroche, H. *Les Deux Rêves: Theisme et atheisme en utopie* Paris 1972

– *Saint-Simon, Le Nouveau Christianisme et les écrits sur la religion* Paris 1969

de Vaux, R. *Ancient Israel* London 1961

Diderot, D. *Diderot's Selected Writings* selected, ed and with intro and notes by L.G. Crocker, tr D. Coltman, New York 1966

Dodds, E.R. *The Ancient Concept of Progress and Other Essays on Greek Literature and Belief* Oxford 1973

Dugmore, C.W. 'A Note on the Quartodecimans' in F.M. Cross ed *Studia Patristica* IV pt 2, Berlin 1961, 211–21

Ebeling, G. 'The Ground of Christian Theology' in R. Funk ed *Apocalypticism* New York 1969

Edelstein, L. *The Idea of Progress in Classical Antiquity* Baltimore 1967

Eichrodt, W. *Theology of the Old Testament* 2 vol, London 1961 and 1967

Eissfeldt, O. *The Old Testament: An Introduction* Oxford 1965

Eliade, M. 'Paradise and Utopia: Mythical Geography and Eschatology' in F. Manuel ed *Utopias and Utopian Thought* Boston 1967, 260–80

Elliott, R.C. 'The Shape of Utopia' *English Literary History* XXX (1963)

Evans, C.F. *Resurrection and the New Testament* London 1970

Farrer, A. *A Rebirth of Images: The Making of St John's Apocalypse* London 1949

– *The Revelation of St John the Divine* Oxford 1964

Florovsky, G. 'Eschatology in the Patristic Age: An Introduction' in K. Aland and F.M. Cross ed *Studia Patristica* VII Berlin 1957, 235–50

Foigny, G. de *Terra australis incognita* in G. Negley and J.M. Patrick ed *The Quest for Utopia* first pub New York 1952; Garden City, NY, 1962, 392–413

Ford, J.M. 'Was Montanism a Jewish-Christian Heresy?' *Journal of Ecclesiastical History* XVII (1966) 145–58

Fourier, C.: M. Poster ed *Harmonian Man: Selected Writings of Charles Fourier* Garden City, NY, 1971

– C. Gide ed *Selections from the Works of Fourier* tr J. Franklin, first pub London 1901; New York 1972

– *Selections from the Works of Fourier* with a new intro by F. Manuel, New York 1971

– J. Beecher and R. Bienvenu ed *The Utopian Vision of Charles Fourier* Boston 1971

Freedman, D.N. 'The Flowering of Apocalyptic' in R. Funk ed *Apocalypticism* New York 1969, 166–74

Freeman-Grenville, G.S.P. 'Date of the Outbreak of Montanism' *Journal of Ecclesiastical History* V (1954) 7–15

French, P. *John Dee: The World of an Elizabethan Magus* London 1972

Frend, W.H.C. 'The Gnostic Sects and the Roman Empire' *Journal of Ecclesiastical History* V (1954) 25–37

Frye, N. 'Varieties of Literary Utopias' in F. Manuel ed *Utopias and Utopian Thought* Boston 1967, 25–49

Fuchs, E. 'On the Task of a Christian Theology' in R. Funk ed *Apocalypticism* New York 1969, 69–98

Funk, R. ed *Apocalypticism* New York 1969

Gardiner, R. ed *The Philosophy of History* London 1974

Gaster, M. *The Samaritans* London 1925

Gide, C. ed *Selections from the Works of Fourier* tr J. Franklin, first pub London 1901; New York 1972

Goldstein, J. *I Maccabees* Garden City, NY, 1976

Grant, R.M. *Gnosticism and Early Christianity* London 1959

Grant, R.M. ed *Gnosticism: An Anthology* London 1961

Grean, S. *Shaftesbury's Philosophy of Religion and Ethics: A Study in Enthusiasm* Athens, Ohio, 1967

Haller, W. *Foxe's Book of Martyrs and the Elect Nation* London 1963

Hamerton-Kelly, R.G. 'The Temple and the Origins of Jewish Apocalyptic' *Vetus Testamentum* XX (1970)

Hanson, P. *The Dawn of Apocalyptic* Philadelphia 1975

Hayes, J.H. and J.M. Miller ed *Israelite and Judaean History* Philadelphia 1977

Hefele, C.J. *History of the Christian Councils from the Original Documents* Edinburgh 1871–82

Hennecke, E. and Schneemelcher, W. ed *New Testament Apocrypha* II from German edn, Inbingen 1964; ed R.M. Wilson, tr E. Best et al, London 1965, 1974

Hexter, J.H. *The Vision of Politics on the Eve of the Reformation: More, Machiavelli and Seyssel* New York 1973

Higgins, A.J.B. 'The Priestly Messiah' *New Testament Studies* ns XIII (1966) 211–39

Hinds, W.A. *American Communities and Cooperative Colonies* first pub 1878; rpt New York 1961

Hitler, A. *Mein Kampf* first pub Munich 1925; rpt New York 1943 .

Holberg, L. *Niels Klim's Journey under the Ground* in G. Negley and J.M. Patrick ed *The Quest for Utopia* first pub New York 1952; Garden City, NY, 1962, 449–66

Ini, A.M. 'Nuovi documenti sugli Spirituale de Toscana' *Archivum Franciscanum Historicum* LXVI (1973) 305–77

Irenaeus *Adversus haereses* Ante-Nicene Christian Library vol 5, Edinburgh 1868

Jacob, E.F. *Essays in Later Medieval History* Manchester 1968

Jones, W.R. 'The Image of the Barbarian in Medieval Europe' *Comparative Studies in Society and History* XIII (1971) 376–407

Josephus *Antiquities of the Jews* Cambridge, Mass, 1926

Jouvenel, B. de 'Utopia for Practical Purposes' in F. Manuel ed *Utopias and Utopian Thought* Boston 1967, 219–35

Kahler, M. *The So-called Historical Jesus and the Historical, Biblical Christ* from 2nd German edn, Leipzig 1896, ed and intro by C. Braaten, Philadelphia 1964

Kanter, R.M. *Commitment and Community: Communes and Utopias in Sociological Perspective* Cambridge, Mass, 1972

Käsemann, E. 'The Beginnings of Christian Theology' in R. Funk ed *Apocalypticism* New York 1969, 17–46

– 'On the Topic of Primitive Christian Apocalyptic' in R. Funk ed *Apocalypticism* New York 1969, 99–133

Kee, H.C., Young, F.W., and Froehlich, K. *Understanding the New Testament* first pub 1957; Englewood Cliffs, NJ, 1973

Kegley, C.W. ed *Theology of Rudolf Bultmann* London 1966

Keresztes, P. 'The Jews, the Christians, and the Emperor Domitian' *Vigiliae Christianae* XVII (1973) 1–28

Kiernan, C. 'Additional Reflections on Diderot and Science' *Diderot Studies* XIV (1971) 113–42

Kincade, K. *A Walden Two Experiment* New York 1973

Kinder, E. 'Historical Criticism and Demythologizing' in C. Braaten and R. Harrisville ed *Kerygma and History* Nashville, Tenn, 1962, 55–85

Kingdon, H.P. 'Origins of the Zealots' *New Testament Studies* ns XIV (1972) 74–81

Koch, K. *The Rediscovery of Apocalyptic* London 1972

Kohn, H. *The Idea of Nationalism* New York 1944

Kümmel, W.G. *Introduction to the New Testament* London 1966

Lactantius *Divine Institutions*

– *Epitome of the Divine Institutions*

Lambert, M.D. *The Doctrine of the Absolute Poverty of Christ and the Apostles in the Franciscan Order, 1210–1323* London 1961

Lanternari, V. *Religions of the Oppressed* Toronto 1965

Lenin, V.I. *Marxism on the State: Preparatory Material for the Book The State and Revolution* written 1917, first pub 1970; Moscow 1972

– *State and Revolution* 2nd rev edn, Moscow 1965

Lerner, R.E. *The Heresy of the Free Spirit in the Later Middle Ages* Berkeley, Calif, 1972

Levin, H. *The Myth of the Golden Age in the Renaissance* Bloomington, Ind, 1969

Lilly, W. *Mr. William Lilly's History of His Life and Times from the Year 1602 to 1681* first pub 1715; rpt in K. Briggs *The Last of the Astrologers* London 1974

Lovejoy, A.O. and Boas, G. *Primitivism and Related Ideas in Antiquity* Baltimore 1935

Löwith, K. *Meaning in History* Chicago 1946

Luther, M. 'On the Babylonish Captivity of the Church'

Macaulay, Lord *Critical and Historical Essays* 3 vol, London 1888

Macdonald, J. *Theology of the Samaritans* London 1964

McGinn, B. 'The Abbot and the Doctors' *Church History* XL (1971) 30–47

McKay, J. *Religion in Judah under the Assyrians* London 1973

McKnight, S.A. 'The Renaissance Magus and the Modern Messiah' *Religious Studies Review* V (1979) 81–9

Malthus, T. *An Essay on the Principle of Population as It Affects the Future Improvement of Society. With Remarks on the Speculations of Mr Godwin, M Condorcet and Other Writers* 1798

Manuel, F. *The Prophets of Paris* first pub Cambridge, Mass, 1962; New York 1965

– 'Toward a Psychological History of Utopias' in F. Manuel ed *Utopias and Utopian Thought* Boston 1967, 69–98

Manuel, F. ed *Utopias and Utopian Thought* Boston 1967

Manuel, F. and F. Manuel *Utopian Thought in the Western World* Cambridge, Mass, 1979

Markus, R.A. *Saeculum: History and Society in the Theology of St Augustine* Cambridge 1970

Marshall, I.H. 'Palestinian and Hellenistic Christianity' *New Testament Studies* ns XIX (1972) 271–87

Mede, J. *Clavis apocalyptica* 1627

Meek, R.L. ed *Turgot on Progress, Sociology and Economics* tr and intro R.L. Meek, Cambridge 1973

Mercier, S. *Memoirs of the Year 2500* in G. Negley and J.M. Patrick ed *The Quest for Utopia* first pub New York 1952; Garden City, NY, 1962, 466–88

Miller, J.M. 'The Israelite Occupation of Canaan' in J.H. Hayes and J.M. Miller ed *Israelite and Judaean History* Philadelphia 1977, 213–84

Minear, P. 'Rudolf Bultmann's Interpretation of New Testament Eschatology' in C.W. Kegley ed *Theology of Rudolf Bultmann* London 1966, 65–82

Montgomery, J.A. *The Samaritans* London 1907

Moore, G.F. *Judaism* 2 vol, Cambridge, Mass, 1927–30

Moorman, J. *A History of the Franciscan Order* Oxford 1968

More, T.: E. Surtz ed *Utopia* intro and notes by E. Surtz, New Haven 1964

- *Utopia* tr and intro by P. Turner, Harmondsworth 1965
Morris, L. *Apocalyptic* London 1973
Moule, C.F.D. ed *Significance of the Message of the Resurrection for Faith in Jesus Christ* London 1968
Mumford, L. 'Utopia, the City and the Machine' in F. Manuel ed *Utopias and Utopian Thought* Boston 1967, 3–24
Mussolini, B. *Fascism: Doctrine and Institutions* from 1st English edn, Rome 1935, New York 1968
Nagel, E. 'Determinacy in History' in R. Gardiner ed *The Philosophy of History* London 1974
Negley, G. and Patrick, J.M. ed *The Quest for Utopia* first pub New York 1952; Garden City, NY, 1962
Newman, F.X. 'The Structure of Vision in "Apocalypsis Goliae"' *Medieval Studies* XXIX (1967) 113–23
Nicholson, E.W. *Deuteronomy and Tradition* Oxford 1967
Nicholson, M. *Voyages to the Moon* New York 1948
Niebuhr, R.R. *Resurrection and Historical Reason* New York 1957
Niemeyer, G. *Between Nothingness and Paradise* Baton Rouge, La, 1971
Nisbet, R. *History of the Idea of Progress* New York 1980
Nordhoff, C. *Communistic Societies of the United States* first pub 1875; rpt New York 1965
Norris, R.A. *God and World in Early Christian Theology* London 1966
Noth, M. *Exodus* London 1962
- *History of Israel* rev edn, London 1960
- *History of Pentateuchal Traditions* Englewood Cliffs, NJ, 1972
Noyes, J.H. *History of American Socialisms* first pub Philadelphia 1870; New York 1966
O'Neill, J.C. 'On the Resurrection as a Historical Question' in S.W. Sykes and J.P. Clayton ed *Christ, Faith and History: Cambridge Studies in Christology* Cambridge 1972, 205–19
Parker, D. *Familiar to All: William Lilly and Astrology in the Seventeenth Century* London 1975
Passmore, J. 'Objectivity in History' in P. Gardiner ed *The Philosophy of History* London 1974
- *The Perfectibility of Man* London 1970
Patrides, C.A. ed *The Cambridge Platonists* London 1969
- *The Grand Design of God: The Literary Form of the Christian View of History* London 1972
Pearson, B.A. ed *Religious Syncretism in Antiquity* Missoula, Mont, 1975
Peel, M.L. *The Epistle to Rheginos: A Valentinian Letter on the Resurrection* London 1969

Pelikan, J. 'The Eschatology of Tertullian' *Church History* XXI (1952) 108–22
– 'Montanism and Its Trinitarian Significance' *Church History* XXV (1956) 99–109
Phelan, J.L. *The Millennial Kingdom of the Franciscans in the New World* 2nd rev edn, Berkeley, Calif, 1970
Plato *The Republic* tr and intro by Desmond Lee, 2nd rev edn, Harmondsworth 1974
Plöger, O. *Theocracy and Eschatology* Oxford 1968
Polak, F. 'Utopia and Cultural Renewal' in F. Manuel ed *Utopias and Utopian Thought* Boston 1967, 281–95
Pollard, S. *The Idea of Progress: History and Society* first pub 1968; Harmondsworth 1971
Popkin, R.H. ed *The Philosophy of the 16th and 17th Centuries* London 1966
Popper, Sir K. *The Open Society and Its Enemies* 2 vols, first pub London 1945; 5th rev edn, London 1966
– *The Poverty of Historicism* London 1957
Poster, M. ed *Harmonian Man: Selected Writings of Charles Fourier* Garden City, NY, 1971
Preston, R.H. and Hanson, A.T. *The Revelation of St John the Divine* London 1949
Price, R. *Observations upon the Importance of the American Revolution and the Means of Making It a Benefit to the World* London 1785
Prior, O.H. ed *Esquisse d'un tableau historique des progrès de l'esprit humain* (by Condorcet) first pub 1933; rev edn, Paris 1970
Pritchard, J.B. ed *Ancient Near Eastern Texts* 2nd edn, London 1955
Purvis, J.D. *The Samaritan Pentateuch and the Origins of the Samaritan Sect* Cambridge, Mass, 1968
Randall, J.H. *Hellenistic Ways of Deliverance and the Making of the Christian Synthesis* New York 1970
Reeves, M. 'The Abbot Joachim and the Society of Jesus' *Medieval and Renaissance Studies* V (1961) 57–81
– *The Influence of Prophecy in the Later Middle Ages* Oxford 1969
– 'Joachimist Expectations in the Order of Augustinian Hermits' *Recherches de Théologie ancienne et medievale* XXV (1958) 111–41
– 'The Liber Figurarum of Joachim of Fiore' *Medieval and Renaissance Studies* II (1950) 57–81
Reeves, M. and B. Hirsch-Reich *The Figurae of Joachim of Fiore* Oxford 1972
Reichenbach, H. *From Copernicus to Einstein* New York 1942
Richardson, A. *Genesis I–XI: Introduction and Commentary* London 1953
Richey, R.E. 'Counter-Insurgency, An Historical Homily' *Drew Gateway* XLI (1971) 83–93
Richter, P.E. ed *Utopias: Social Ideals and Communal Experiments* Boston 1971
Rissi, M. *The Future of the World* London 1972

Robbins, C. *The Eighteenth Century Commonwealthmen: Studies in the Transmission, Development and Circumstance of English Liberal Thought from the Restoration of Charles II until the War with the Thirteen Colonies* Cambridge, Mass, 1959

Roberts, R.E. *The New Communes: Coming Together in America* Englewood Cliffs, NJ, 1971

Robinson, D.B.W. 'II Thess. 2, 6: "That which restrains" or "That which holds sway"?' in F.M. Cross ed *Studia Evangelica* II pt 1, Berlin 1964, 635–8

Rowley, H.H. *The Relevance of Apocalyptic* first pub 1944; rev edn, London 1963

Russ, J. *Pour connaître la pensée des précurseurs de Marx* Paris 1973

Russell, D.S. *The Jews from Alexander to Herod* London 1967

– *Method and Meaning of Jewish Apocalyptic* London 1964

Russell, J.B. *Dissent and Reform in the Early Middle Ages* Berkeley, Calif, 1965

Salomonsen, B. 'Some Remarks on the Zealots with Special Reference to the Term "Qannaim" in Rabbinic Literature' *New Testament Studies* ns XII (1965) 164–76

Schlegel, D. *Shaftesbury and the French Deists* Chapel Hill, NC, 1956

Schmithals, W. *The Apocalyptic Movement: Introduction and Interpretation* first pub Göttingen 1973; tr J.E. Steely, Nashville, Tenn, 1975

– *An Introduction to the Theology of Rudolf Bultmann* London 1968

Scholem, G. *Jewish Gnosticism, Merkabah Mysticism and the Talmudic Tradition* New York 1960

Scholem, G. *On the Kabbala and Its Symbolism* London 1968

Schweitzer, A. *The Quest of the Historical Jesus* first pub Tübingen 1906; London 1910

Shklar, J. 'The Political Theory of Utopia: From Melancholy to Nostalgia' in F. Manuel ed *Utopias and Utopian Thought* Boston 1967, 101–15

Skinner, B.F. *Walden Two* first pub New York 1948; rpt New York 1962

Smart, J.D. *History and Theology in Second Isaiah* Philadelphia 1965

Smith, J.Z. 'Wisdom and Apocalyptic' in B.A. Pearson ed *Religious Syncretism in Antiquity* Missoula, Mont, 1975

Smith, M. Palestinian *Parties and Politics that Shaped the Old Testament* London 1971

Spink, V.S. *French Thought from Gassendi to Voltaire* London 1960

Stevenson, J. ed *A New Eusebius* London 1957; corrected edn, London 1968

Surtz, E. ed *Utopia* (by More) intro and notes by E. Surtz, New Haven 1964

Sykes, S.W. and J.P. Clayton ed *Christ, Faith and History: Cambridge Studies in Christology* Cambridge 1972

Talmon, J. *Origins of Totalitarian Democracy* London 1952

Tarn, W.W. *Hellenistic Civilization* first pub 1927; 3rd rev edn with G.T. Griffith, London 1952

Taylor, K. ed 'Introduction' in *Henri de Saint-Simon (1760–1825), Selected Writings on Science, Industry and Social Organization* tr K. Taylor, London 1975

Thomas, D.W. *Documents from Old Testament Times* London 1958

Thrupp, S. ed *Millennial Dreams in Action* The Hague 1962

Tillich, P. 'Critique and Justification of Utopia' in F. Manuel ed *Utopias and Utopian Thought* Boston 1967, 296–309

Tonelli, G. 'The "Weakness of Reason" in the Age of Enlightenment' *Diderot Studies* XIV (1971) 217–42

Toon, P. ed *Puritans, the Millennium and the Future of Israel: Puritan Eschatology, 1601–1660* Cambridge 1970

Turgot, A.R.J.: R.L. Meek ed *Turgot on Progress, Sociology and Economics* tr and intro by R.L. Meek, Cambridge 1973

Tuveson, E.L. *Millennium and Utopia* Berkeley, Calif, 1949

– *Redeemer Nation* Chicago 1968

van Leeuwen, A.T. *Christianity in World History* New York 1961

van Unnik, W.C. 'Epistle to Rheginos "On the Resurrection," the Newly-Discovered Gnostic' *Journal of Ecclesiastical History* XV (1964) 141–67

Venturi, F. *Utopia and Reform in the Enlightenment* Cambridge 1971

Voegelin, E. *The World of the Polis* vol 2 of *Order in History* Baton Rouge, La, 1957

Vokes, F.E. 'Montanism and the Ministry' in F.M. Cross ed *Studia Patristica* IX pt 3, Berlin 1966, 306–15

– 'The Opposition to Montanism from Church and State in the Christian Empire' in F.M. Cross ed *Studia Patristica* IV pt 2, Berlin 1961, 518–26

von Rad, G. *Deuteronomy* London 1960

– *Genesis* London 1961, 1972

– *Old Testament Theology* 2 vol, tr D.G.M. Stalker, London 1962, 1965

– *Studies in Deuteronomy* London 1953

Vriezen, T.C. *Outline of Old Testament Theology* 2nd rev edn, Oxford 1970

Wade, I.O. *The Structure and Form of the French Enlightenment* 2 vol, Princeton 1977

Wakefield, W.W. and Evans, A.P. ed *Heresies of the High Middle Ages* New York 1969

Wedel, T.O. *The Medieval Attitude toward Astrology, Particularly in England* first pub New Haven 1920; rpt 1968

Weippert, M. *Settlement of the Israelite Tribes in Palestine* London 1971

Weiss, J. *Jesus' Proclamation of the Kingdom of God* first pub Göttingen 1892; London 1971

Werner, M. *Formation of Christian Dogma* London 1957

West, D.C. 'The Re-formed Church and the Friars Minor: The Moderate Joachite Position of Fra Salimbene' *Archivum Franciscanum Historicum* LXIV (1971) 273–84

Westermann, C. *Creation* London 1974

Wheeler, H. ed *Beyond the Punitive Society* San Francisco 1973

Widengren, G. 'Iran and Israel in Parthian Times with Special Regard to the Ethiopic Book of Enoch' in B.A. Pearson ed *Religious Syncretism in Antiquity* Missoula, Mont, 1975, 85–129

Wilson, R.M. *Gnosis and the New Testament* Oxford 1968

Yates, F. *Giordano Bruno and the Hermetic Tradition* London 1964

– *The Rosicrucian Enlightenment* London 1972

Yolton, J.W. *Locke and the Compass of Human Understanding* Cambridge 1970

Zahrnt, H. *The Question of God: Protestant Theology in the Twentieth Century* London 1969

Index